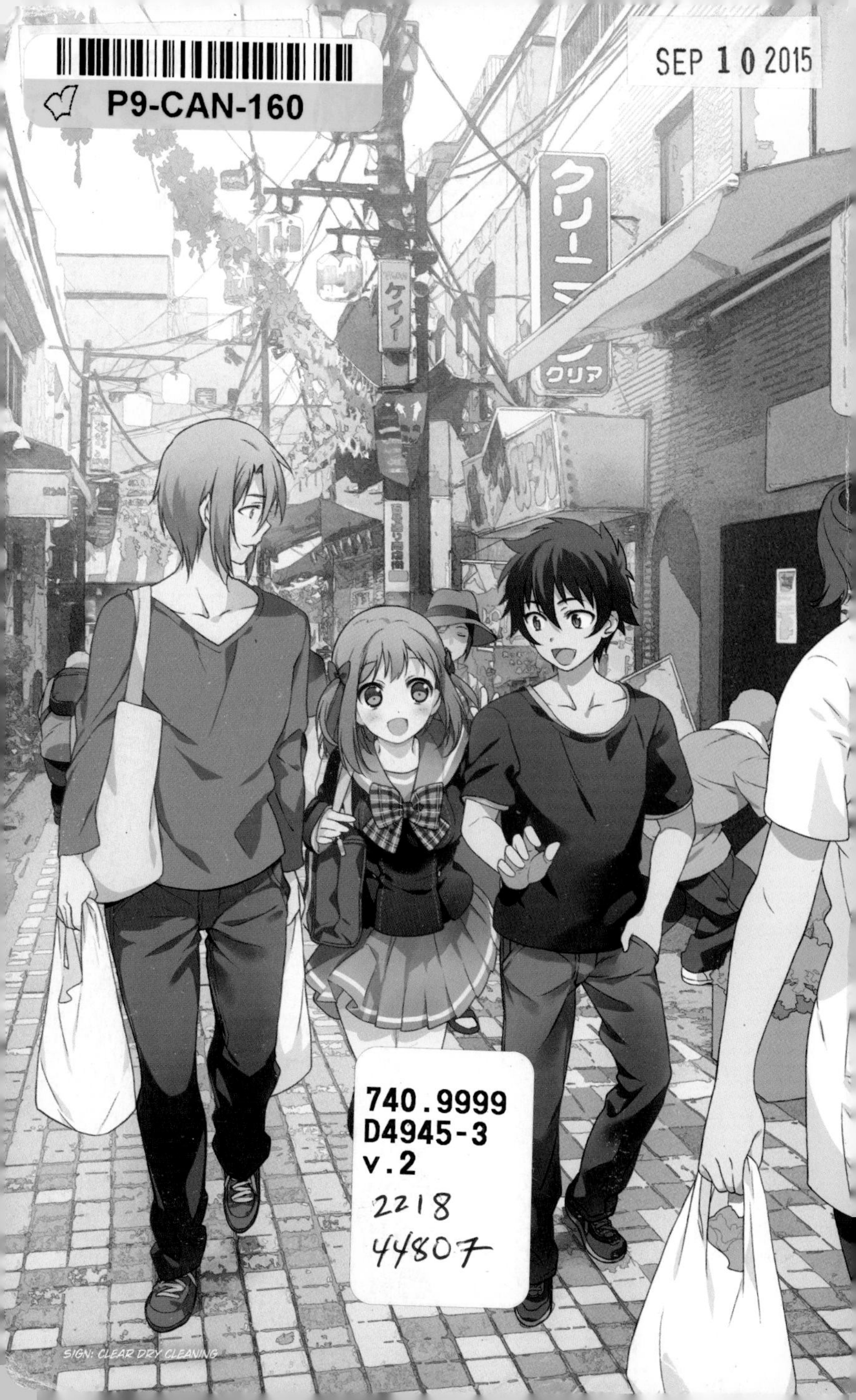
ケイノー
クリア
SIGN: CLEAR DRY CLEANING

The Devil Is a Part-Timer! 2

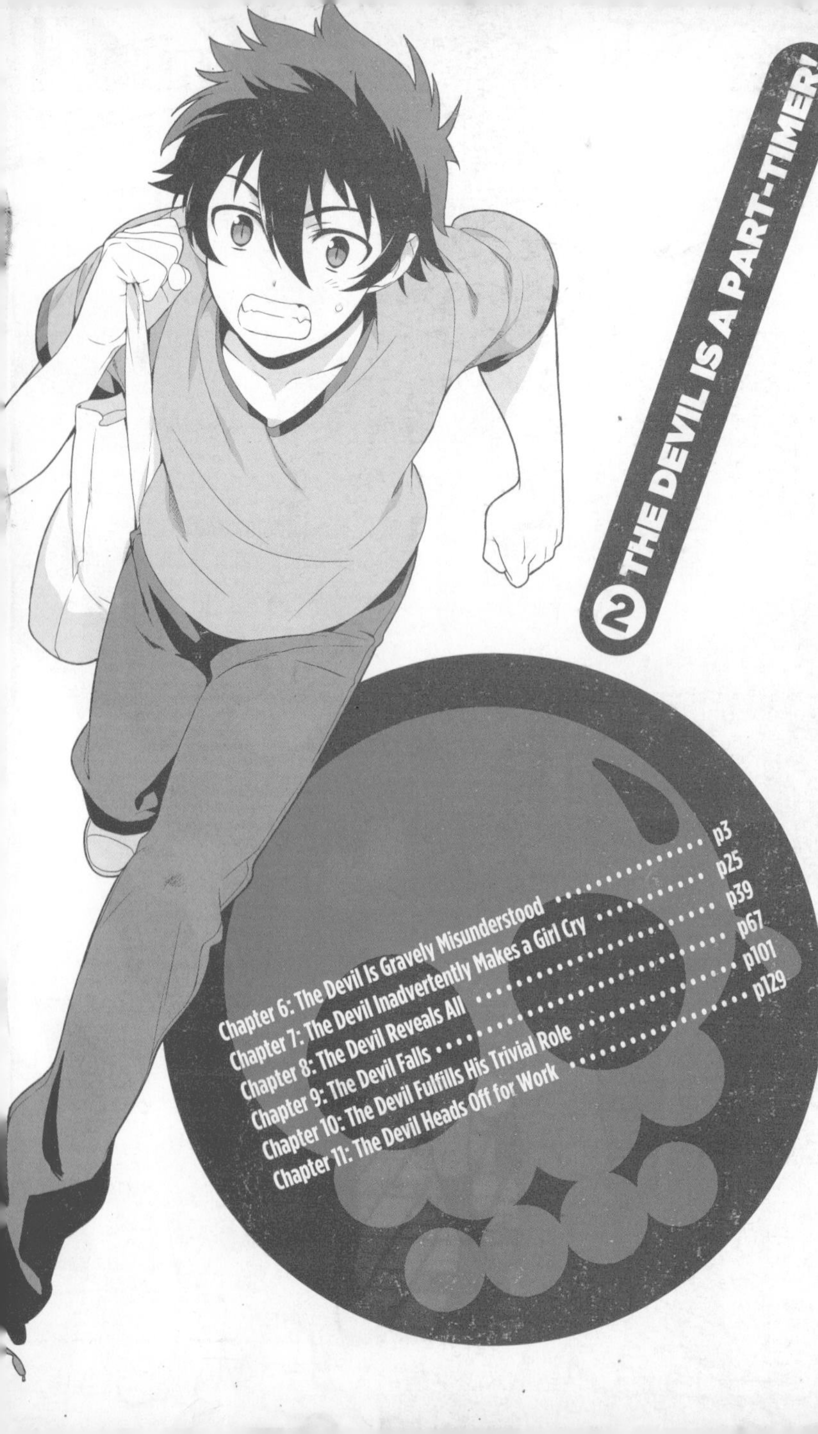

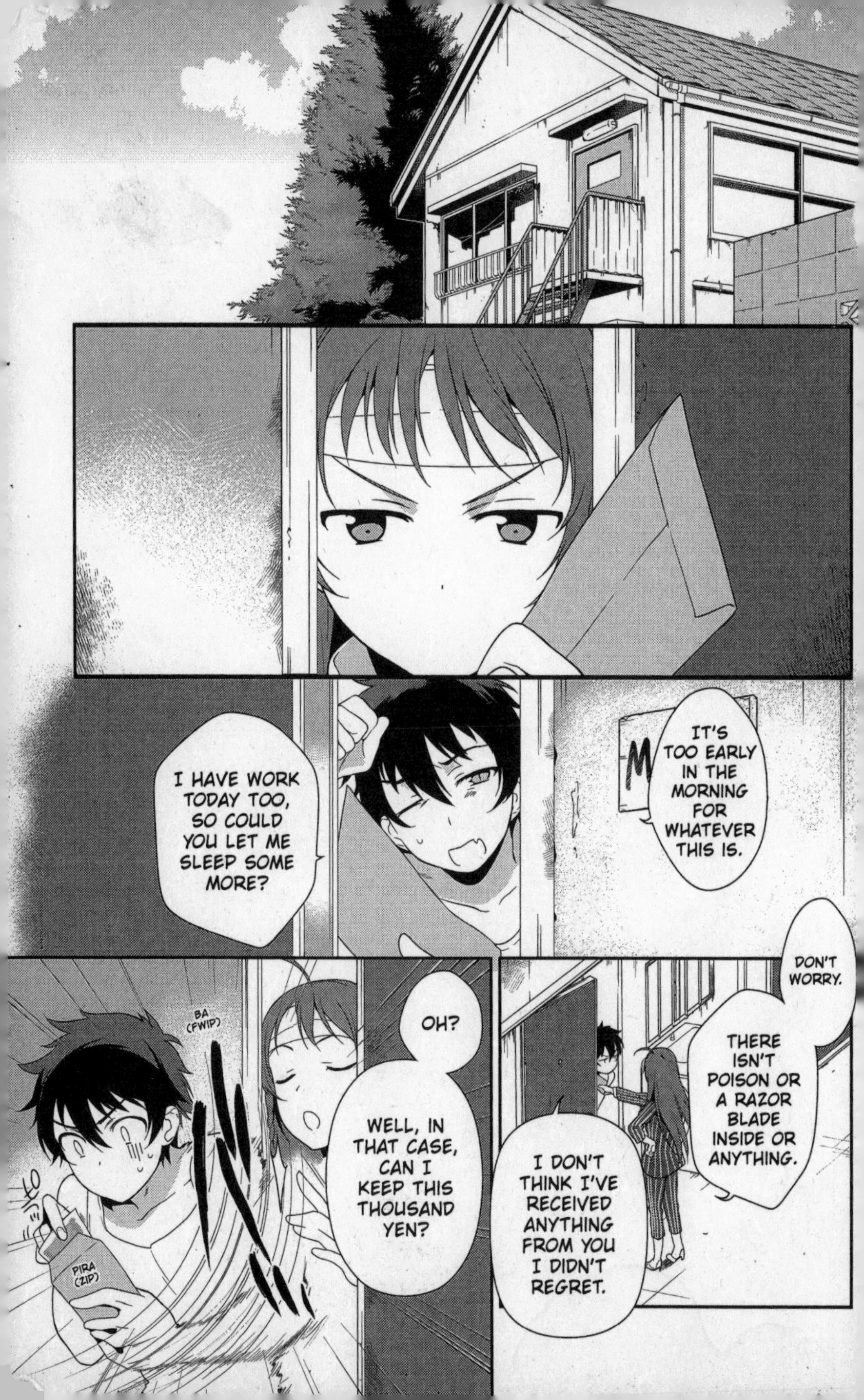
IT'S TOO EARLY IN THE MORNING FOR WHATEVER THIS IS.
I HAVE WORK TODAY TOO, SO COULD YOU LET ME SLEEP SOME MORE?
DON'T WORRY.
THERE ISN'T POISON OR A RAZOR BLADE INSIDE OR ANYTHING.
I DON'T THINK I'VE RECEIVED ANYTHING FROM YOU I DIDN'T REGRET.
OH?
WELL, IN THAT CASE, CAN I KEEP THIS THOUSAND YEN?
BA (FWIP)
PIRA (ZIP)

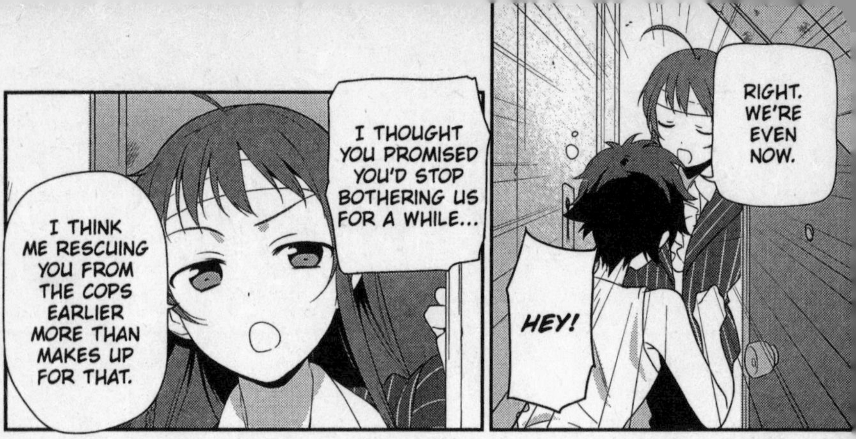
RIGHT. WE'RE EVEN NOW.
HEY!
I THOUGHT YOU PROMISED YOU'D STOP BOTHERING US FOR A WHILE...
I THINK ME RESCUING YOU FROM THE COPS EARLIER MORE THAN MAKES UP FOR THAT.

CHAPTER 6: THE DEVIL IS GRAVELY MISUNDERSTOOD

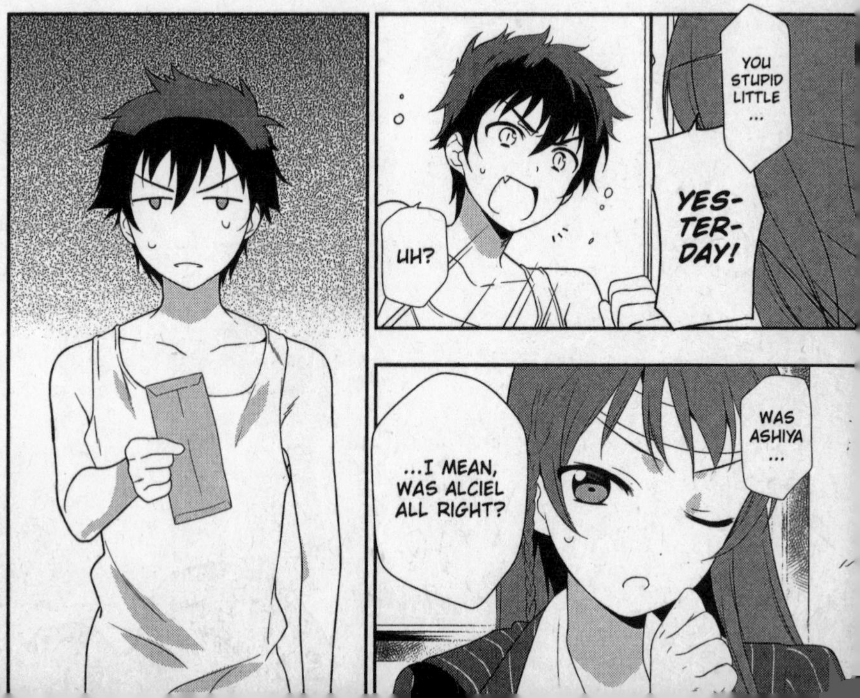
YOU STUPID LITTLE ...
YES-TER-DAY!
UH?
WAS ASHIYA ...
...I MEAN, WAS ALCIEL ALL RIGHT?

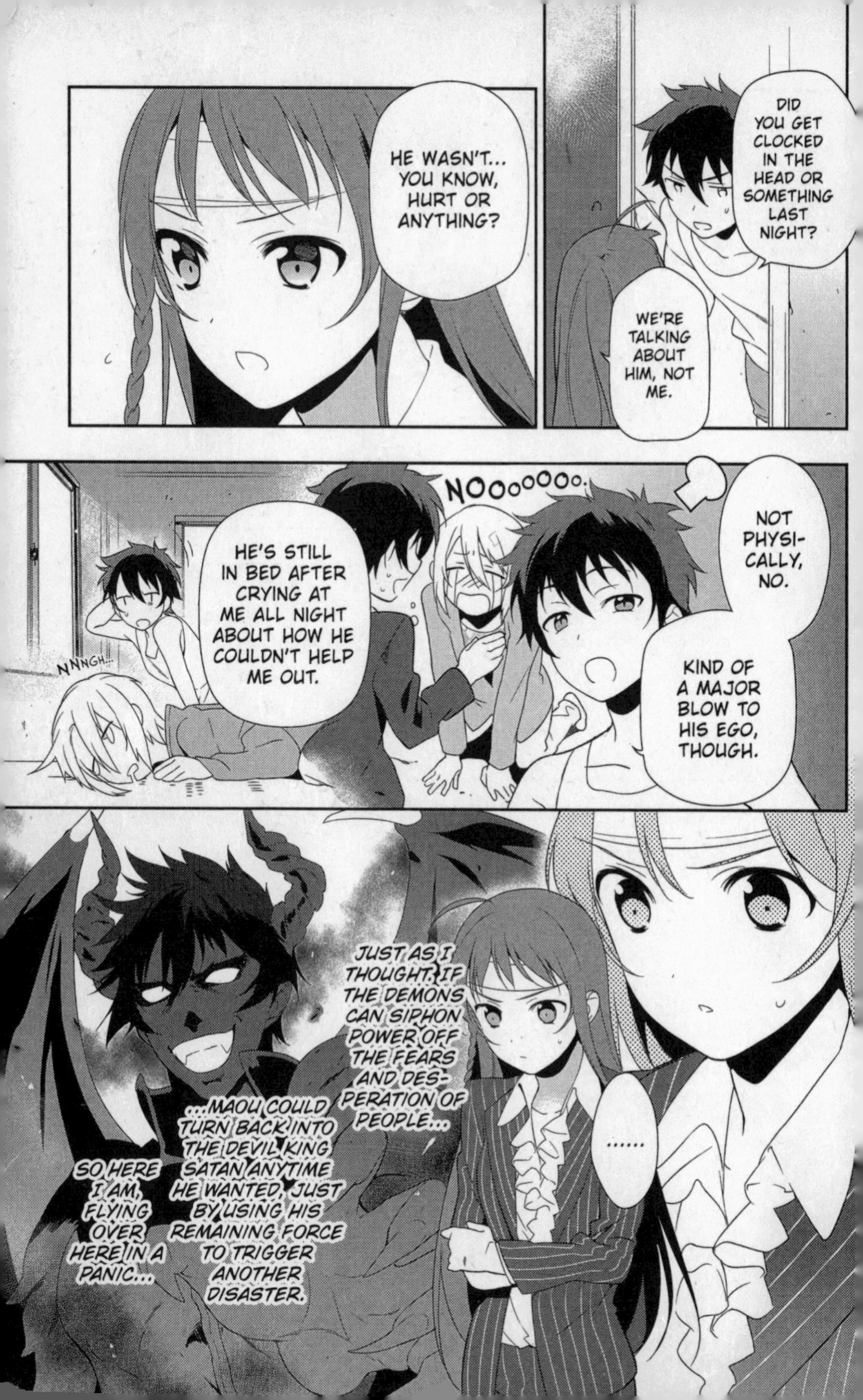
DID YOU GET CLOCKED IN THE HEAD OR SOMETHING LAST NIGHT?
WE'RE TALKING ABOUT HIM, NOT ME.
HE WASN'T... YOU KNOW, HURT OR ANYTHING?
NOT PHYSICALLY, NO.
KIND OF A MAJOR BLOW TO HIS EGO, THOUGH.
NOOooooo.
HE'S STILL IN BED AFTER CRYING AT ME ALL NIGHT ABOUT HOW HE COULDN'T HELP ME OUT.
NNNGH...
......
JUST AS I THOUGHT. IF THE DEMONS CAN SIPHON POWER OFF THE FEARS AND DESPERATION OF PEOPLE...
...MAOU COULD TURN BACK INTO THE DEVIL KING SATAN ANYTIME HE WANTED, JUST BY USING HIS REMAINING FORCE TO TRIGGER ANOTHER DISASTER.
SO HERE I AM, FLYING OVER HERE IN A PANIC...

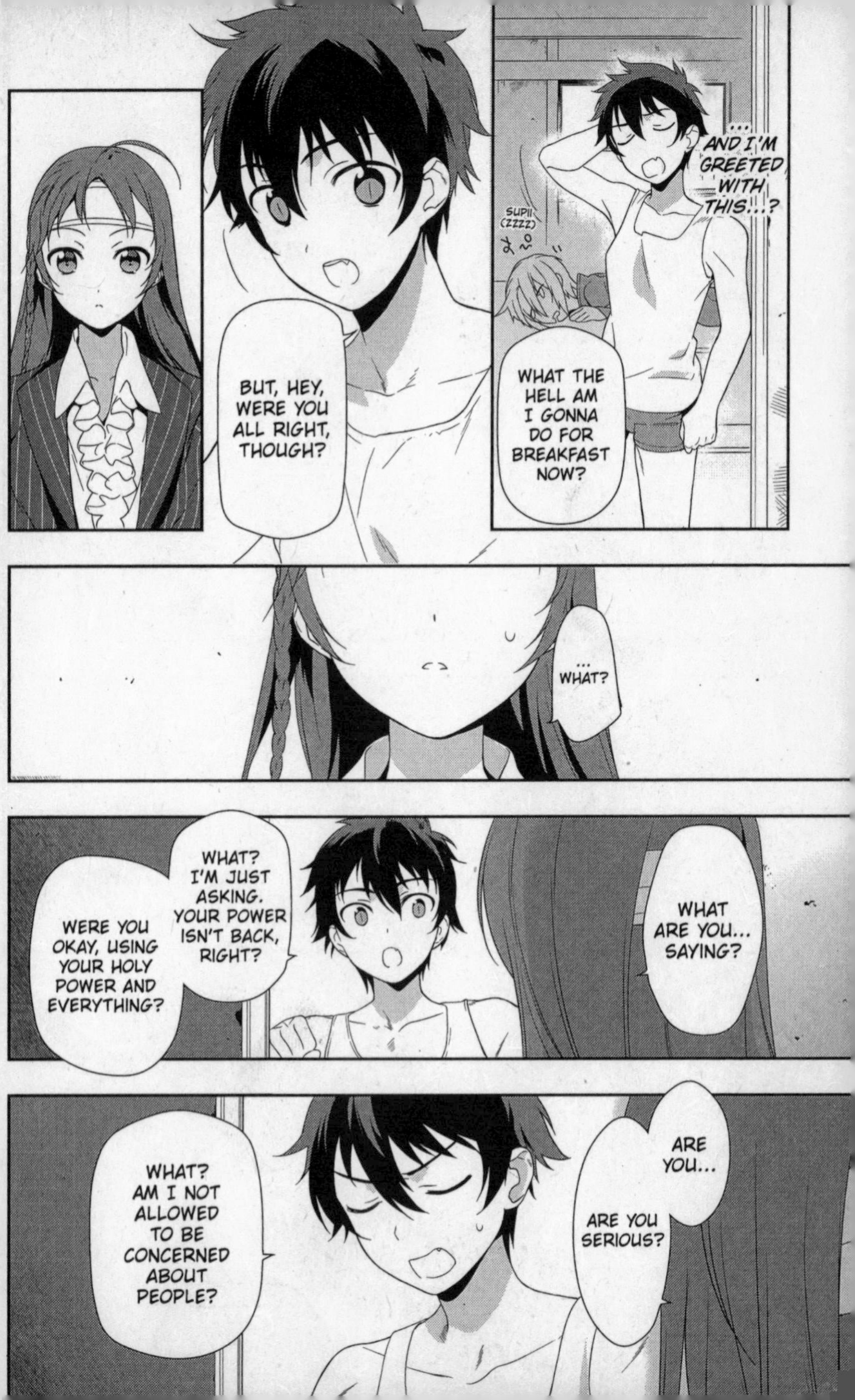
...AND I'M GREETED WITH THIS...?
SUPII (ZZZZ)
WHAT THE HELL AM I GONNA DO FOR BREAKFAST NOW?
BUT, HEY, WERE YOU ALL RIGHT, THOUGH?
...WHAT?
WHAT ARE YOU... SAYING?
WHAT? I'M JUST ASKING. YOUR POWER ISN'T BACK, RIGHT?
WERE YOU OKAY, USING YOUR HOLY POWER AND EVERYTHING?
ARE YOU...
ARE YOU SERIOUS?
WHAT? AM I NOT ALLOWED TO BE CONCERNED ABOUT PEOPLE?

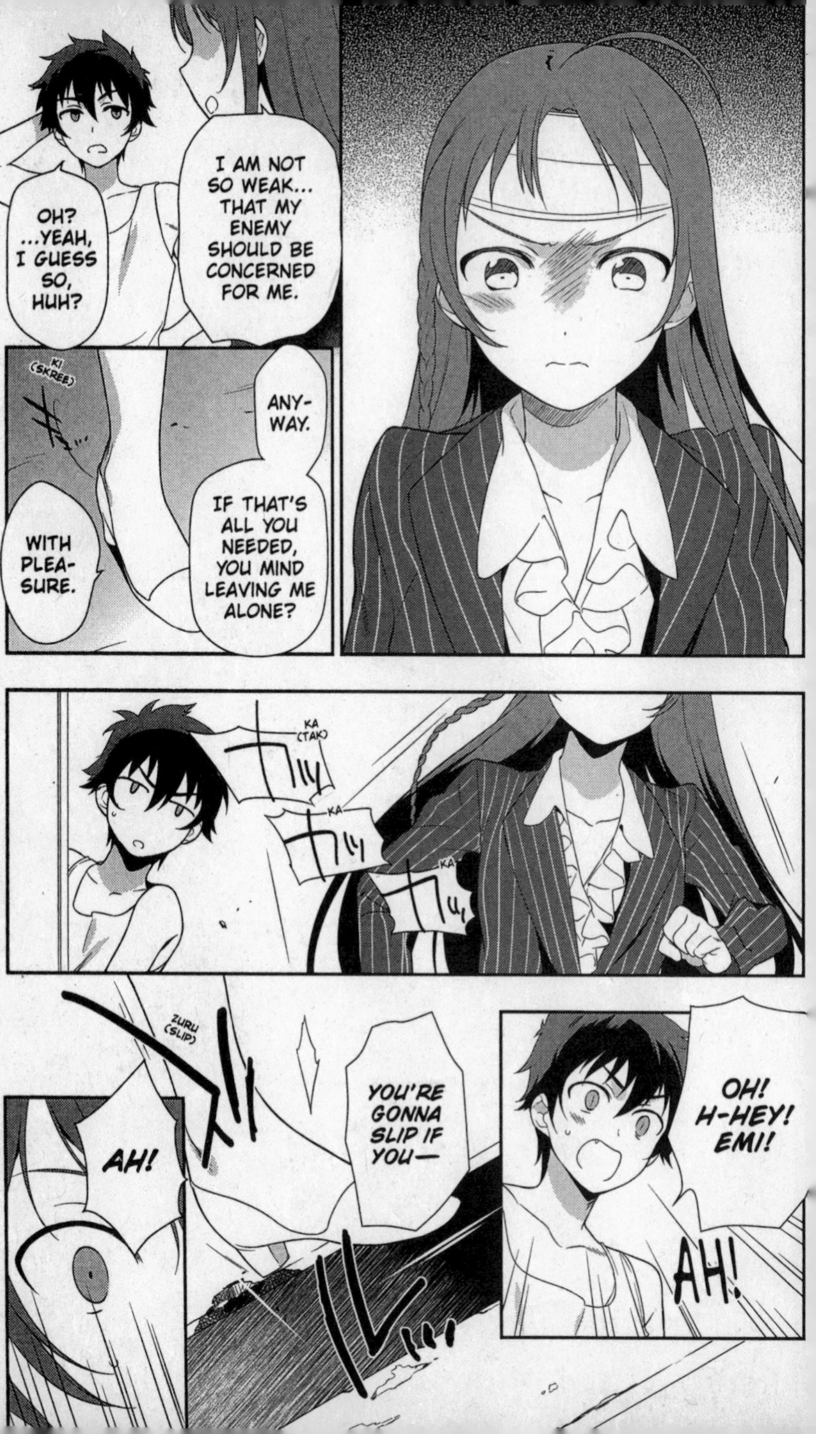

I AM NOT SO WEAK... THAT MY ENEMY SHOULD BE CONCERNED FOR ME.
OH? ...YEAH, I GUESS SO, HUH?
ANY-WAY.
IF THAT'S ALL YOU NEEDED, YOU MIND LEAVING ME ALONE?
KI (SKREE)
WITH PLEA-SURE.
KA (TAK)
KA
KA
OH! H-HEY! EMI!
AH!
YOU'RE GONNA SLIP IF YOU—
ZURU (SLIP)
AH!

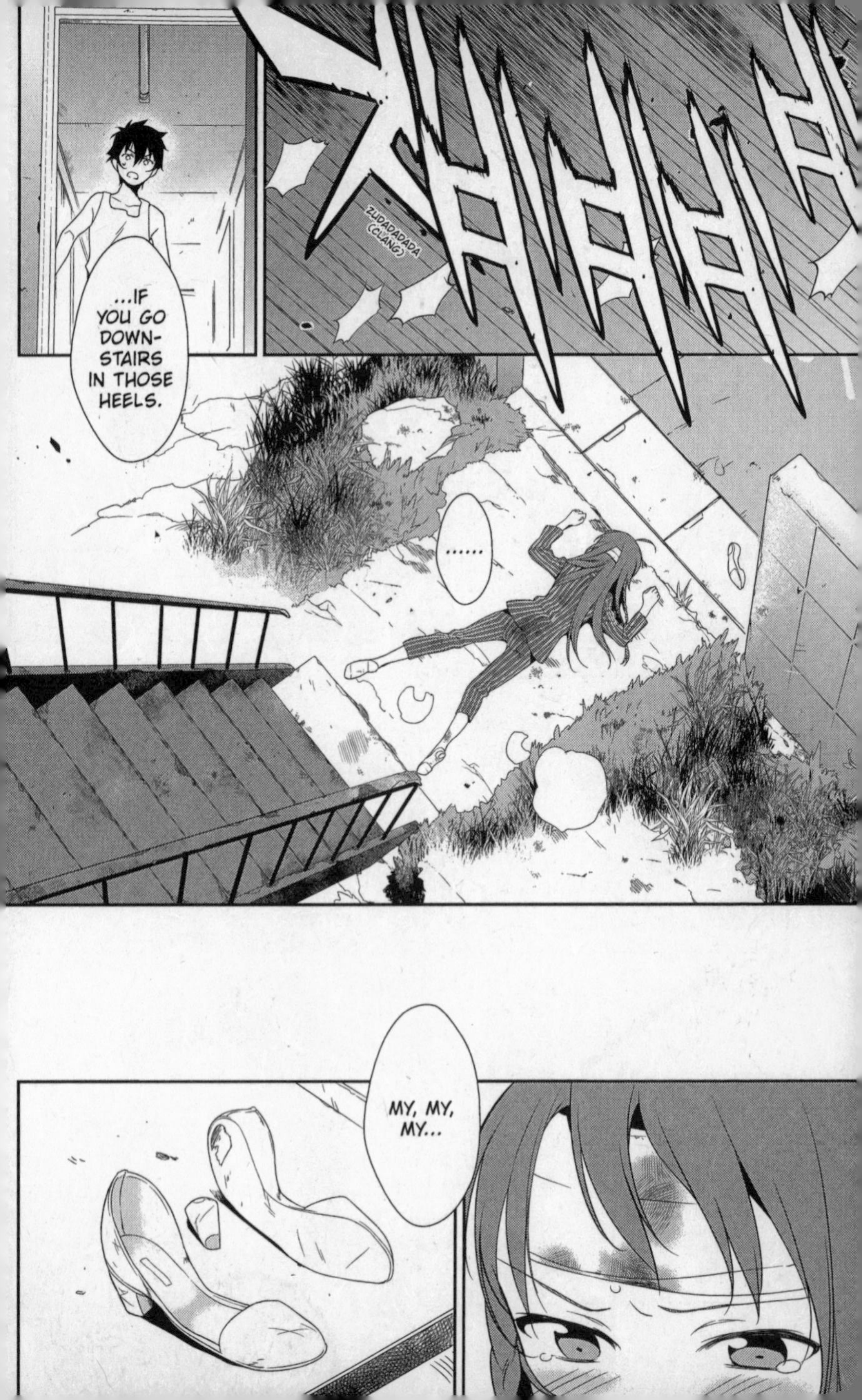
ZUDADADADA (CLANG)
...IF YOU GO DOWN-STAIRS IN THOSE HEELS.
......
MY, MY, MY...

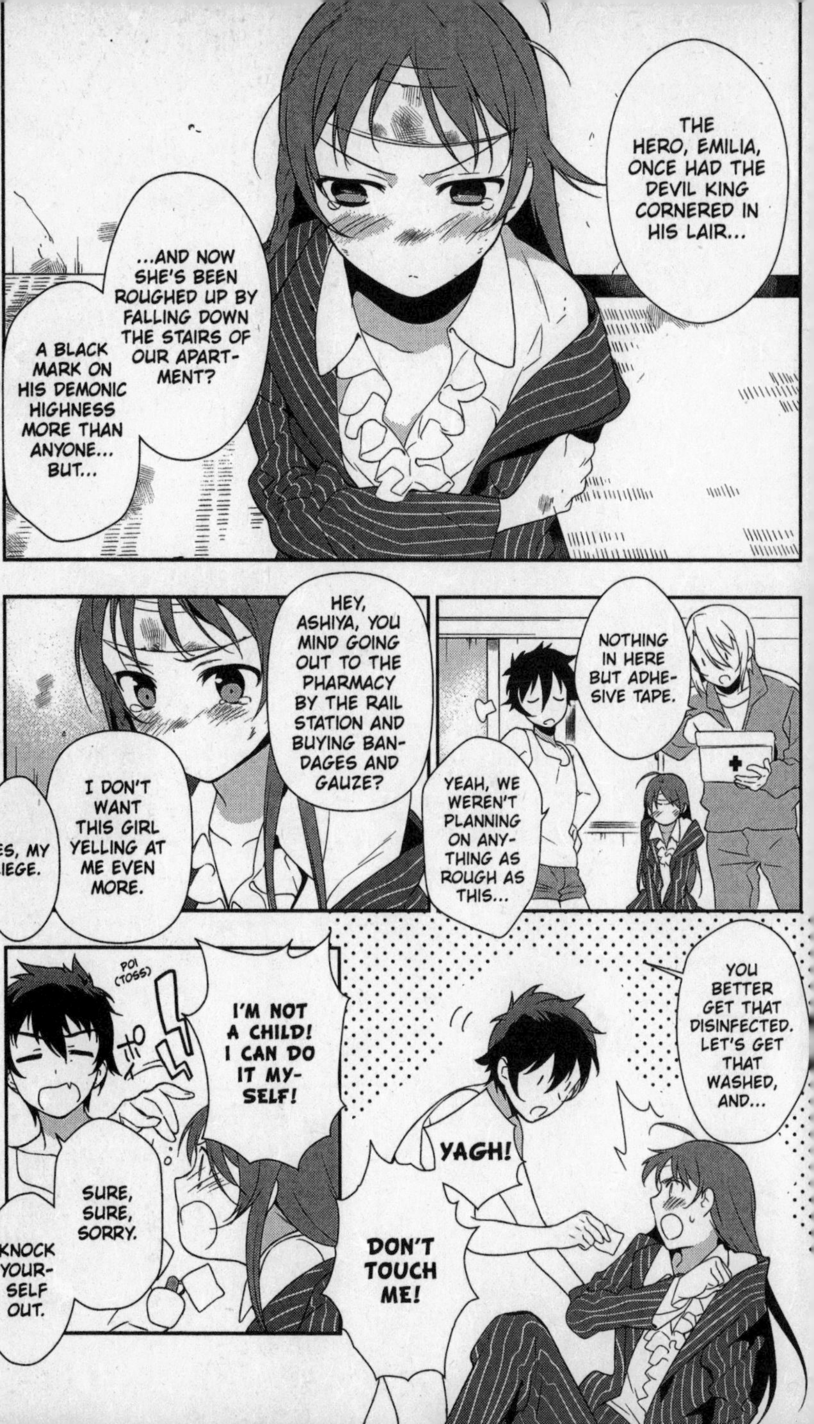
THE HERO, EMILIA, ONCE HAD THE DEVIL KING CORNERED IN HIS LAIR...
...AND NOW SHE'S BEEN ROUGHED UP BY FALLING DOWN THE STAIRS OF OUR APARTMENT?
A BLACK MARK ON HIS DEMONIC HIGHNESS MORE THAN ANYONE... BUT...
NOTHING IN HERE BUT ADHESIVE TAPE.
YEAH, WE WEREN'T PLANNING ON ANYTHING AS ROUGH AS THIS...
HEY, ASHIYA, YOU MIND GOING OUT TO THE PHARMACY BY THE RAIL STATION AND BUYING BANDAGES AND GAUZE?
I DON'T WANT THIS GIRL YELLING AT ME EVEN MORE.
YES, MY LIEGE.
YOU BETTER GET THAT DISINFECTED. LET'S GET THAT WASHED, AND...
YAGH!
DON'T TOUCH ME!
I'M NOT A CHILD! I CAN DO IT MYSELF!
POI (TOSS)
SURE, SURE, SORRY.
KNOCK YOURSELF OUT.

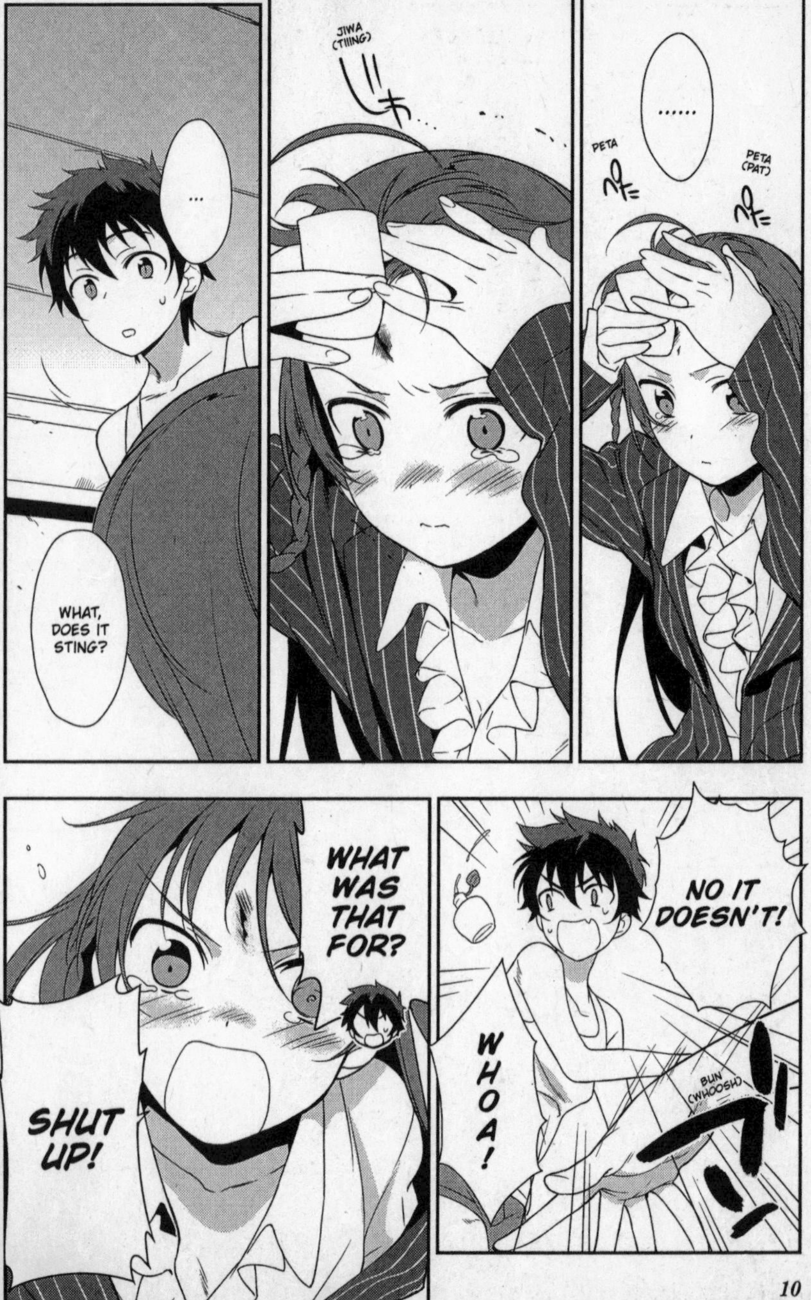
PETA
PETA (PAT)
......
JIWA (TIIING)
...
WHAT, DOES IT STING?
NO IT DOESN'T!
WHOA!
BUN (WHOOSH)
WHAT WAS THAT FOR?
SHUT UP!

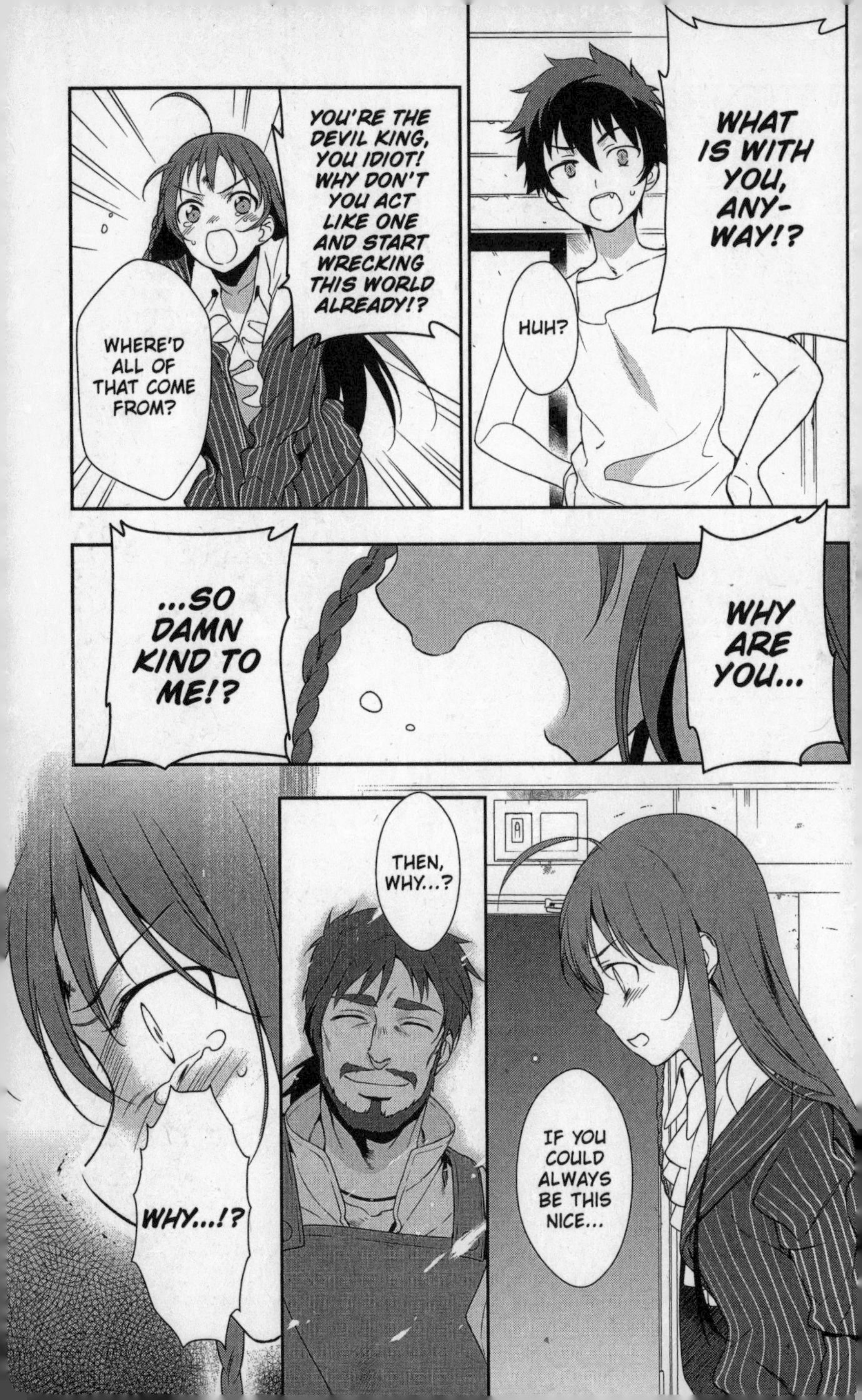
WHAT IS WITH YOU, ANY-WAY!?
HUH?
YOU'RE THE DEVIL KING, YOU IDIOT! WHY DON'T YOU ACT LIKE ONE AND START WRECKING THIS WORLD ALREADY!?
WHERE'D ALL OF THAT COME FROM?
WHY ARE YOU...
...SO DAMN KIND TO ME!?
IF YOU COULD ALWAYS BE THIS NICE...
THEN, WHY...?
WHY...!?

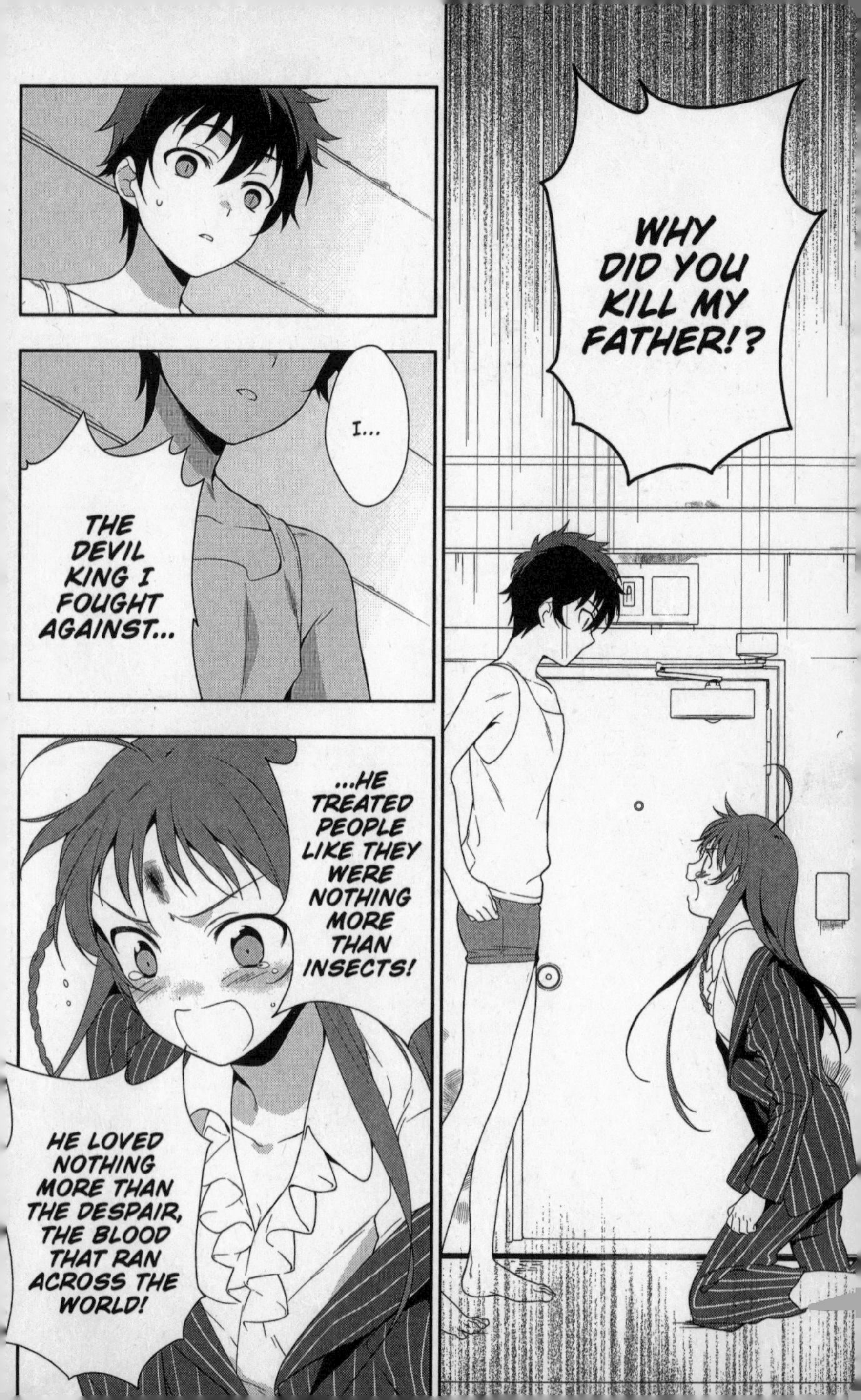
WHY DID YOU KILL MY FATHER!?
I...
THE DEVIL KING I FOUGHT AGAINST...
...HE TREATED PEOPLE LIKE THEY WERE NOTHING MORE THAN INSECTS!
HE LOVED NOTHING MORE THAN THE DESPAIR, THE BLOOD THAT RAN ACROSS THE WORLD!

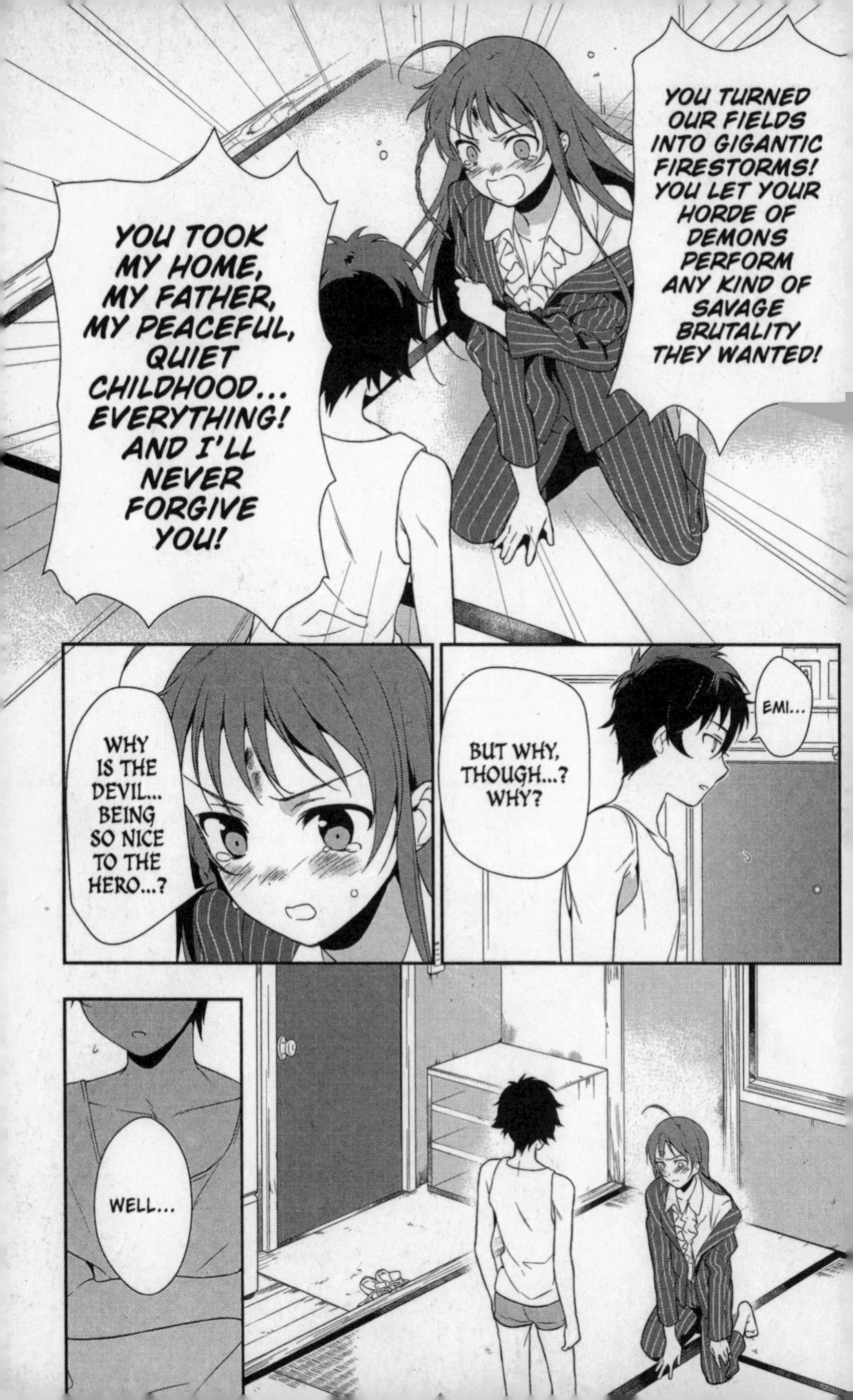
YOU TURNED OUR FIELDS INTO GIGANTIC FIRESTORMS! YOU LET YOUR HORDE OF DEMONS PERFORM ANY KIND OF SAVAGE BRUTALITY THEY WANTED!
YOU TOOK MY HOME, MY FATHER, MY PEACEFUL, QUIET CHILDHOOD... EVERYTHING! AND I'LL NEVER FORGIVE YOU!
EMI...
BUT WHY, THOUGH...? WHY?
WHY IS THE DEVIL... BEING SO NICE TO THE HERO...?
WELL...

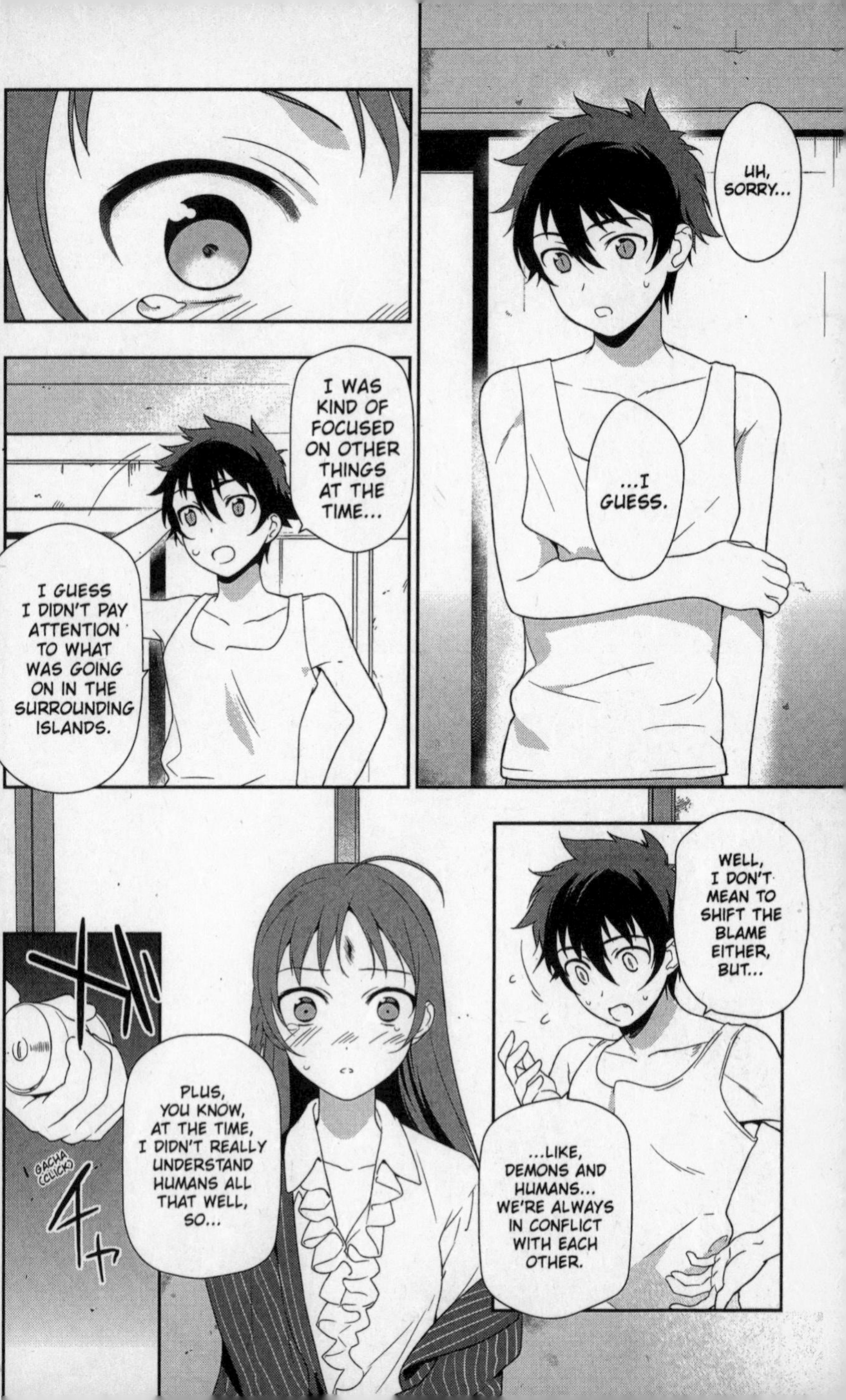
UH, SORRY...
...I GUESS.
I WAS KIND OF FOCUSED ON OTHER THINGS AT THE TIME...
I GUESS I DIDN'T PAY ATTENTION TO WHAT WAS GOING ON IN THE SURROUNDING ISLANDS.
WELL, I DON'T MEAN TO SHIFT THE BLAME EITHER, BUT...
...LIKE, DEMONS AND HUMANS... WE'RE ALWAYS IN CONFLICT WITH EACH OTHER.
PLUS, YOU KNOW, AT THE TIME, I DIDN'T REALLY UNDERSTAND HUMANS ALL THAT WELL, SO...
GACHA (CLICK)

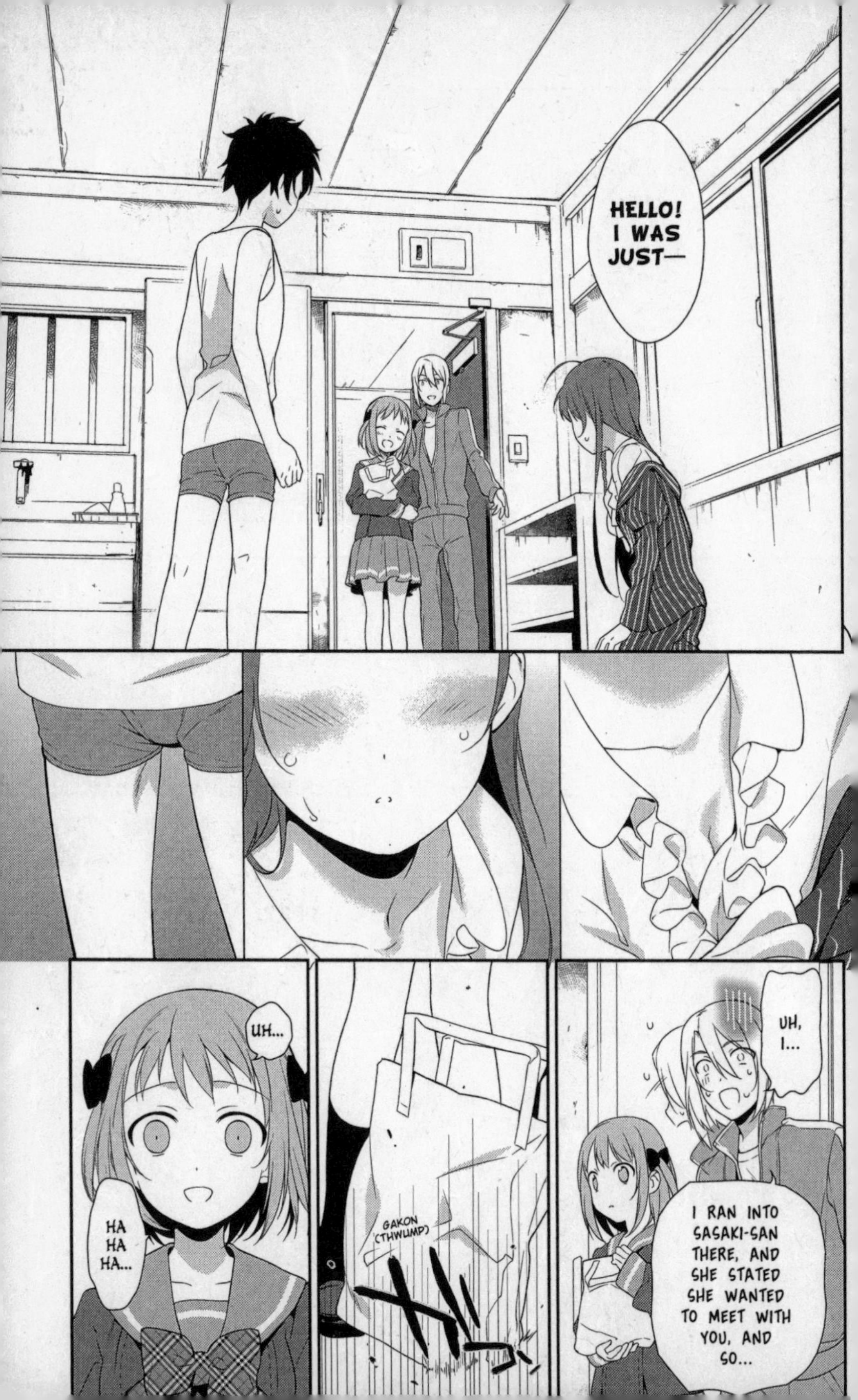
HELLO! I WAS JUST—
UH, I...
I RAN INTO SASAKI-SAN THERE, AND SHE STATED SHE WANTED TO MEET WITH YOU, AND SO...
GAKON (THWUMP)
UH...
HA HA HA...

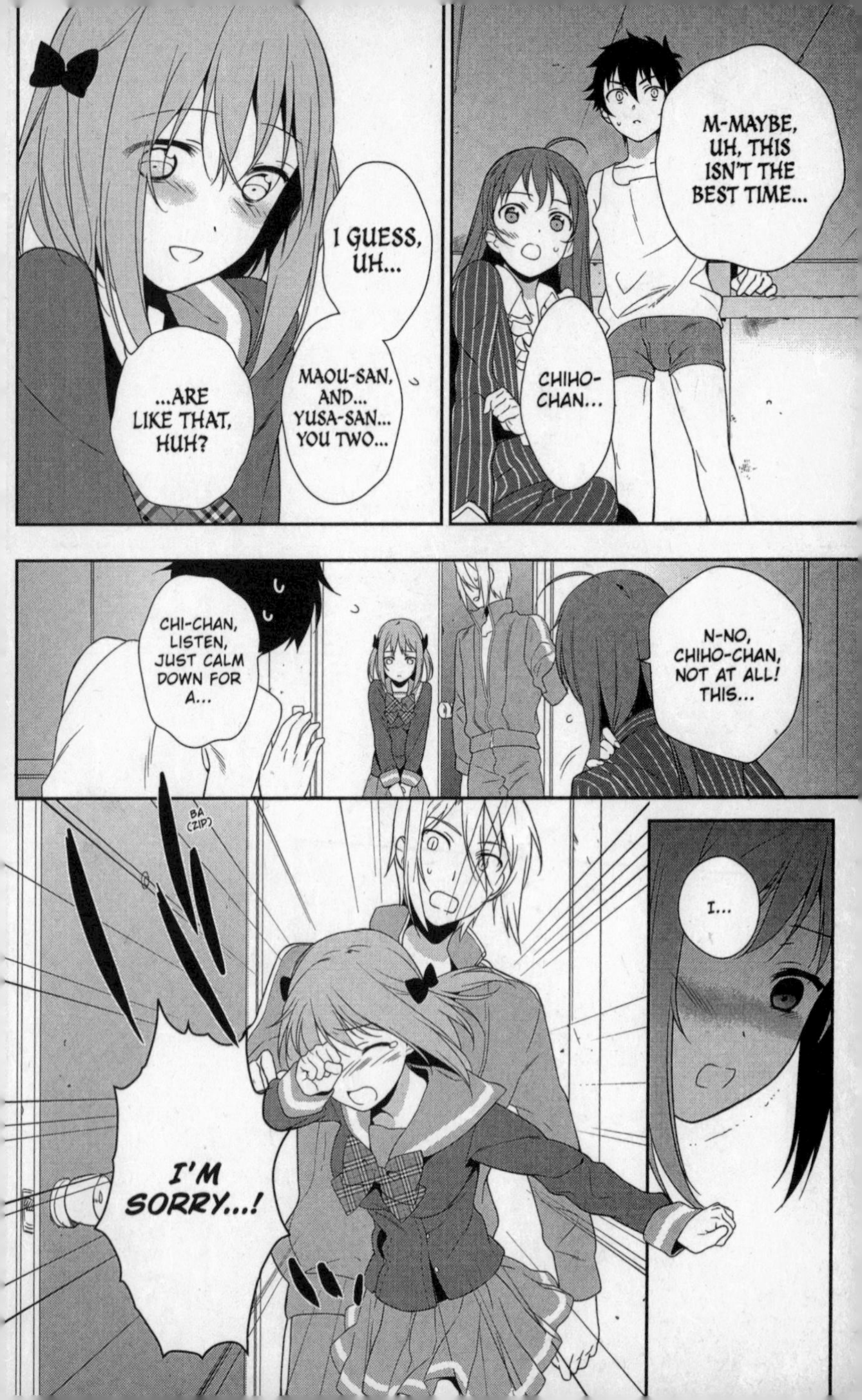
M-MAYBE, UH, THIS ISN'T THE BEST TIME...
CHIHO-CHAN...
I GUESS, UH...
MAOU-SAN, AND... YUSA-SAN... YOU TWO...
...ARE LIKE THAT, HUH?
N-NO, CHIHO-CHAN, NOT AT ALL! THIS...
CHI-CHAN, LISTEN, JUST CALM DOWN FOR A...
I...
BA (ZIP)
I'M SORRY...!

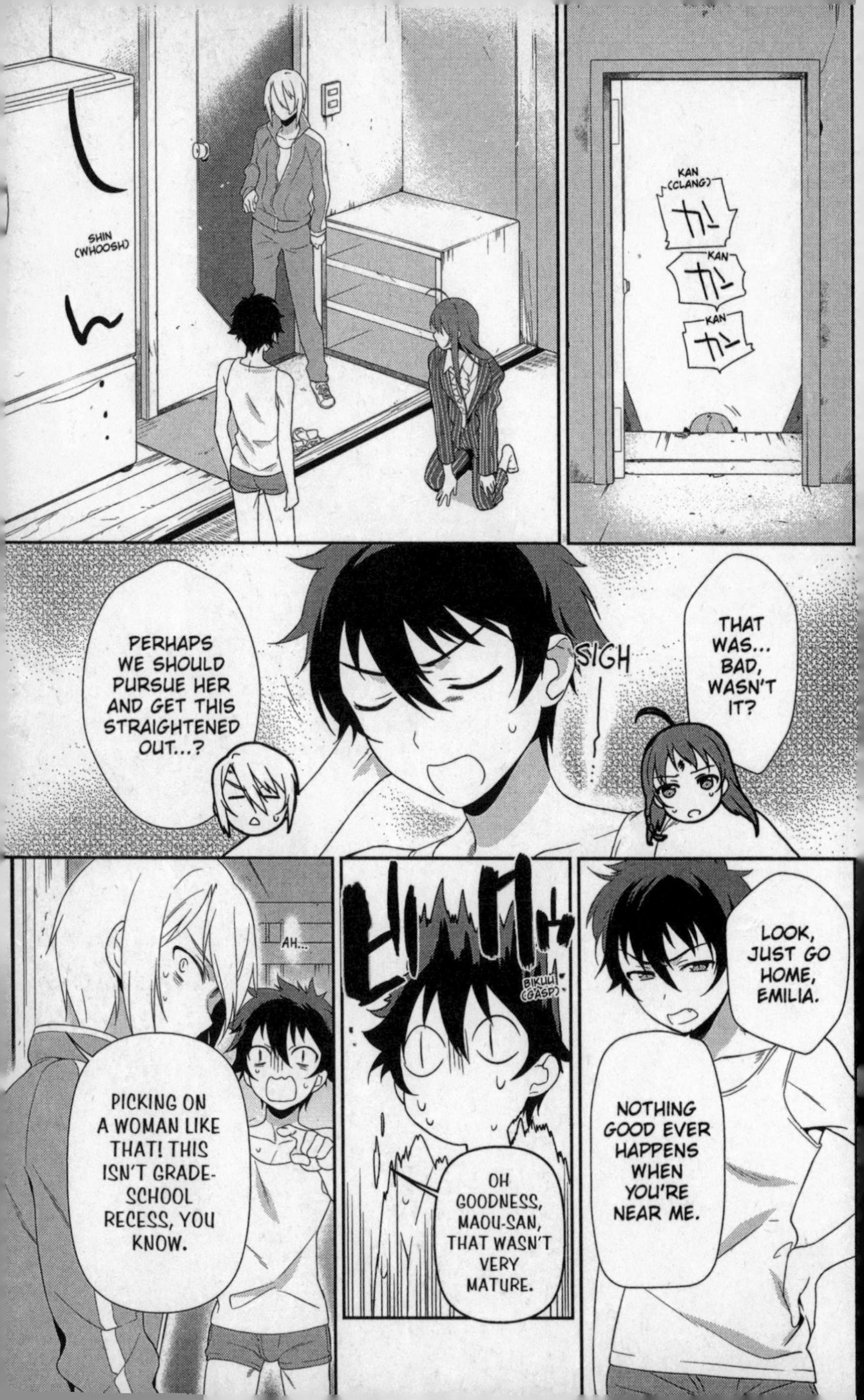

KAN (CLANG)
KAN
KAN
SHIN (WHOOSH)
THAT WAS... BAD, WASN'T IT?
SIGH
PERHAPS WE SHOULD PURSUE HER AND GET THIS STRAIGHTENED OUT...?
LOOK, JUST GO HOME, EMILIA.
NOTHING GOOD EVER HAPPENS WHEN YOU'RE NEAR ME.
BIKUU! (GASP)
OH GOODNESS, MAOU-SAN, THAT WASN'T VERY MATURE.
AH...
PICKING ON A WOMAN LIKE THAT! THIS ISN'T GRADE-SCHOOL RECESS, YOU KNOW.

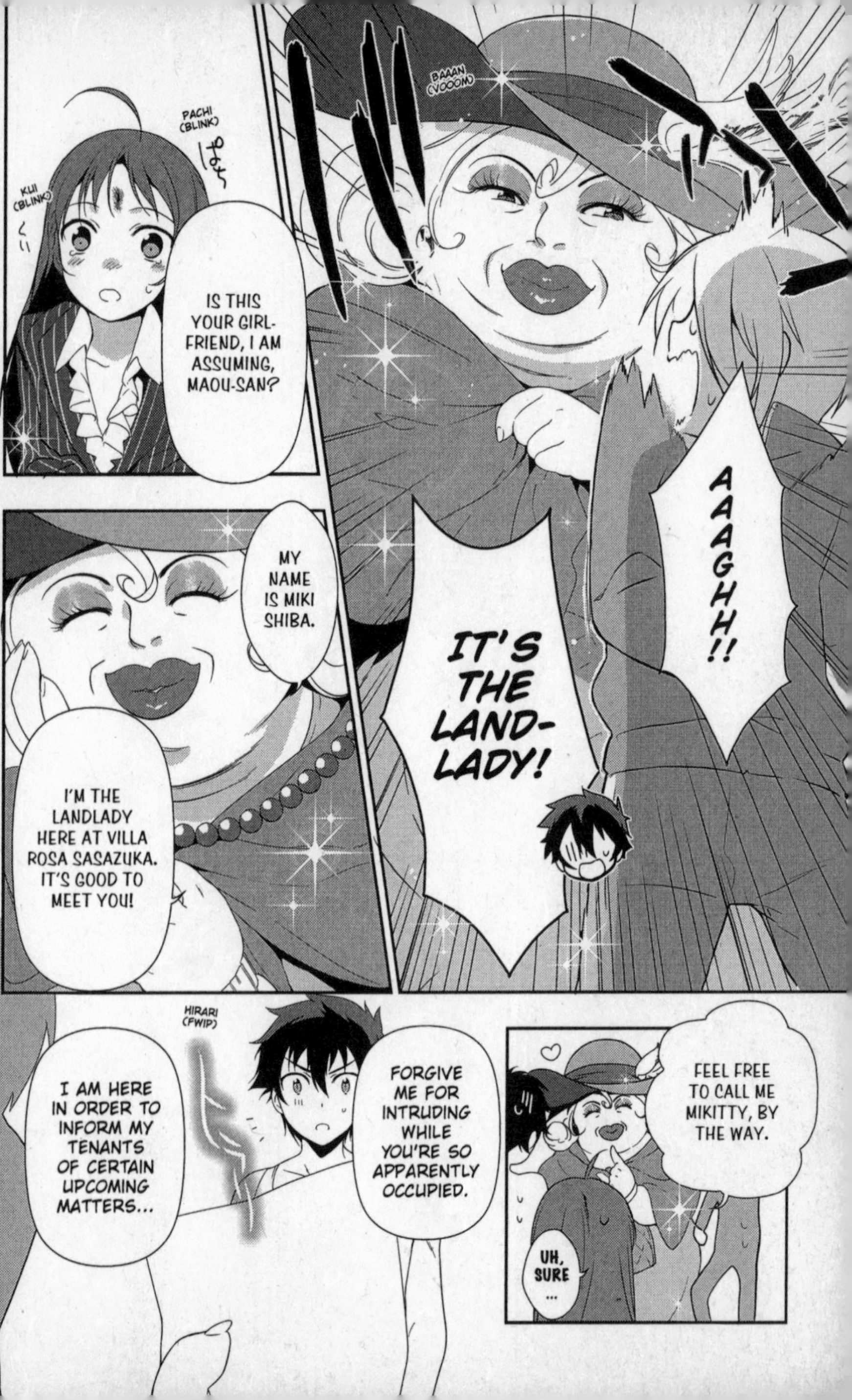
BAAAN (VOOOM)
AAAGHH!!
IT'S THE LAND-LADY!
PACHI (BLINK)
KUI (BLINK)
IS THIS YOUR GIRL-FRIEND, I AM ASSUMING, MAOU-SAN?
MY NAME IS MIKI SHIBA.
I'M THE LANDLADY HERE AT VILLA ROSA SASAZUKA. IT'S GOOD TO MEET YOU!
FEEL FREE TO CALL ME MIKITTY, BY THE WAY.
UH, SURE...
HIRARI (FWIP)
FORGIVE ME FOR INTRUDING WHILE YOU'RE SO APPARENTLY OCCUPIED.
I AM HERE IN ORDER TO INFORM MY TENANTS OF CERTAIN UPCOMING MATTERS...

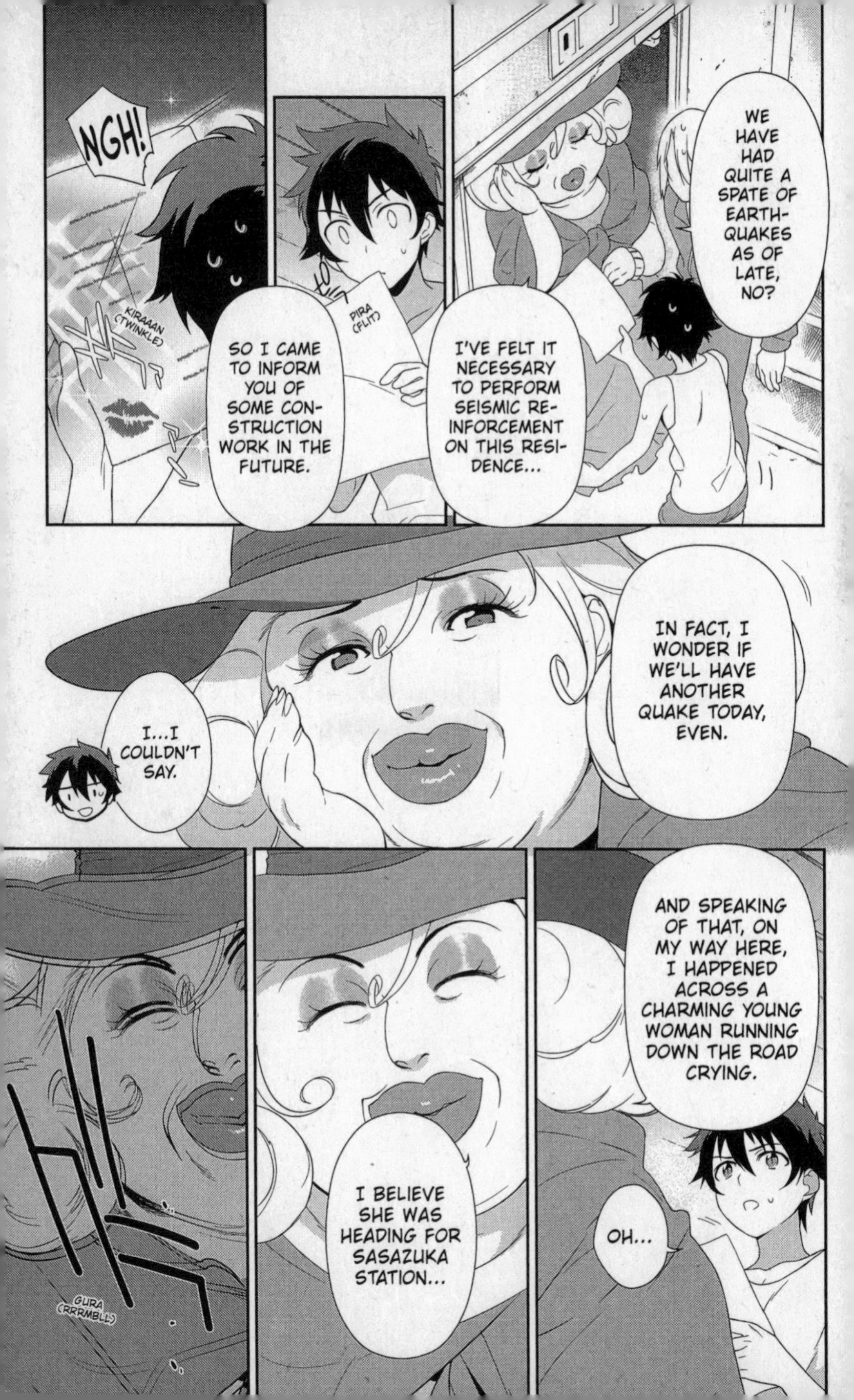
WE HAVE HAD QUITE A SPATE OF EARTHQUAKES AS OF LATE, NO?
I'VE FELT IT NECESSARY TO PERFORM SEISMIC REINFORCEMENT ON THIS RESIDENCE...
PIRA (FLIT)
SO I CAME TO INFORM YOU OF SOME CONSTRUCTION WORK IN THE FUTURE.
NGH!
KIRAAAN (TWINKLE)
IN FACT, I WONDER IF WE'LL HAVE ANOTHER QUAKE TODAY, EVEN.
I...I COULDN'T SAY.
AND SPEAKING OF THAT, ON MY WAY HERE, I HAPPENED ACROSS A CHARMING YOUNG WOMAN RUNNING DOWN THE ROAD CRYING.
OH...
I BELIEVE SHE WAS HEADING FOR SASAZUKA STATION...
GURA (RRRMBL!)

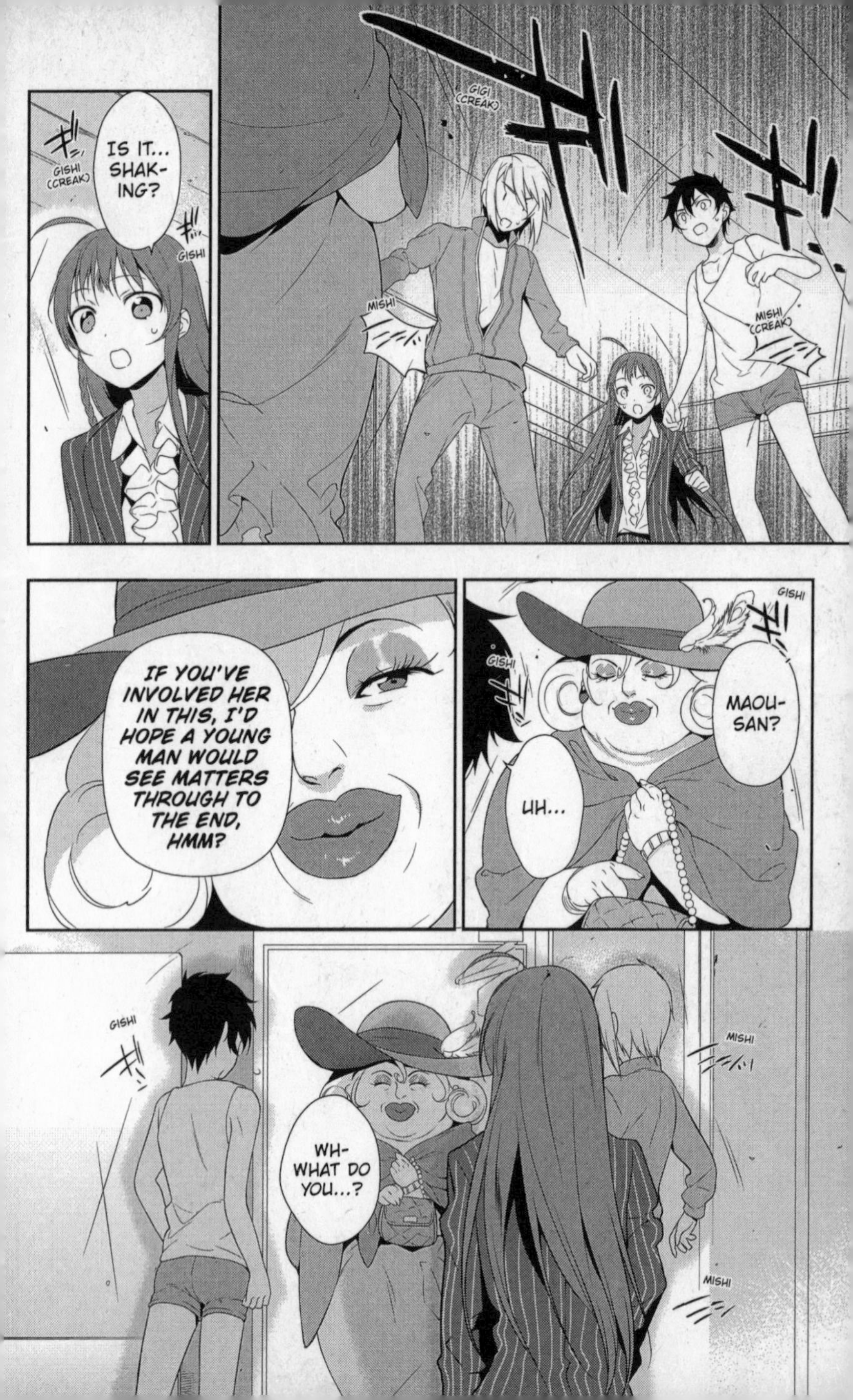
GIGI (CREAK)
MISHI
MISHI (CREAK)
GISHI (CREAK)
IS IT... SHAKING?
GISHI
GISHI
MAOU-SAN?
GISHI
UH...
IF YOU'VE INVOLVED HER IN THIS, I'D HOPE A YOUNG MAN WOULD SEE MATTERS THROUGH TO THE END, HMM?
MISHI
GISHI
WH-WHAT DO YOU...?
MISHI

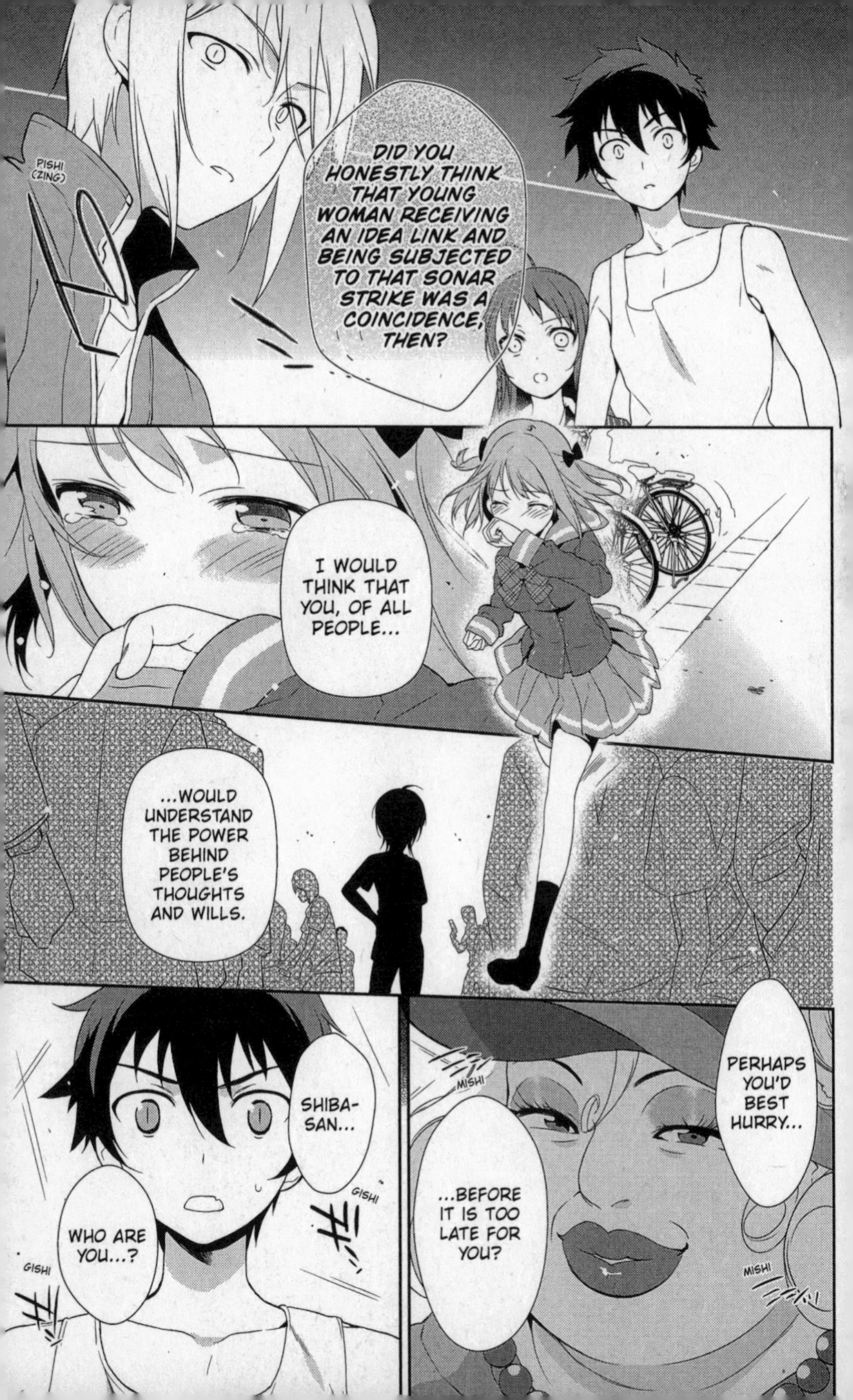
DID YOU HONESTLY THINK THAT YOUNG WOMAN RECEIVING AN IDEA LINK AND BEING SUBJECTED TO THAT SONAR STRIKE WAS A COINCIDENCE, THEN?
PISHI (ZING)
I WOULD THINK THAT YOU, OF ALL PEOPLE...
...WOULD UNDERSTAND THE POWER BEHIND PEOPLE'S THOUGHTS AND WILLS.
PERHAPS YOU'D BEST HURRY...
MISHI
...BEFORE IT IS TOO LATE FOR YOU?
MISHI
SHIBA-SAN...
GISHI
WHO ARE YOU...?
GISHI

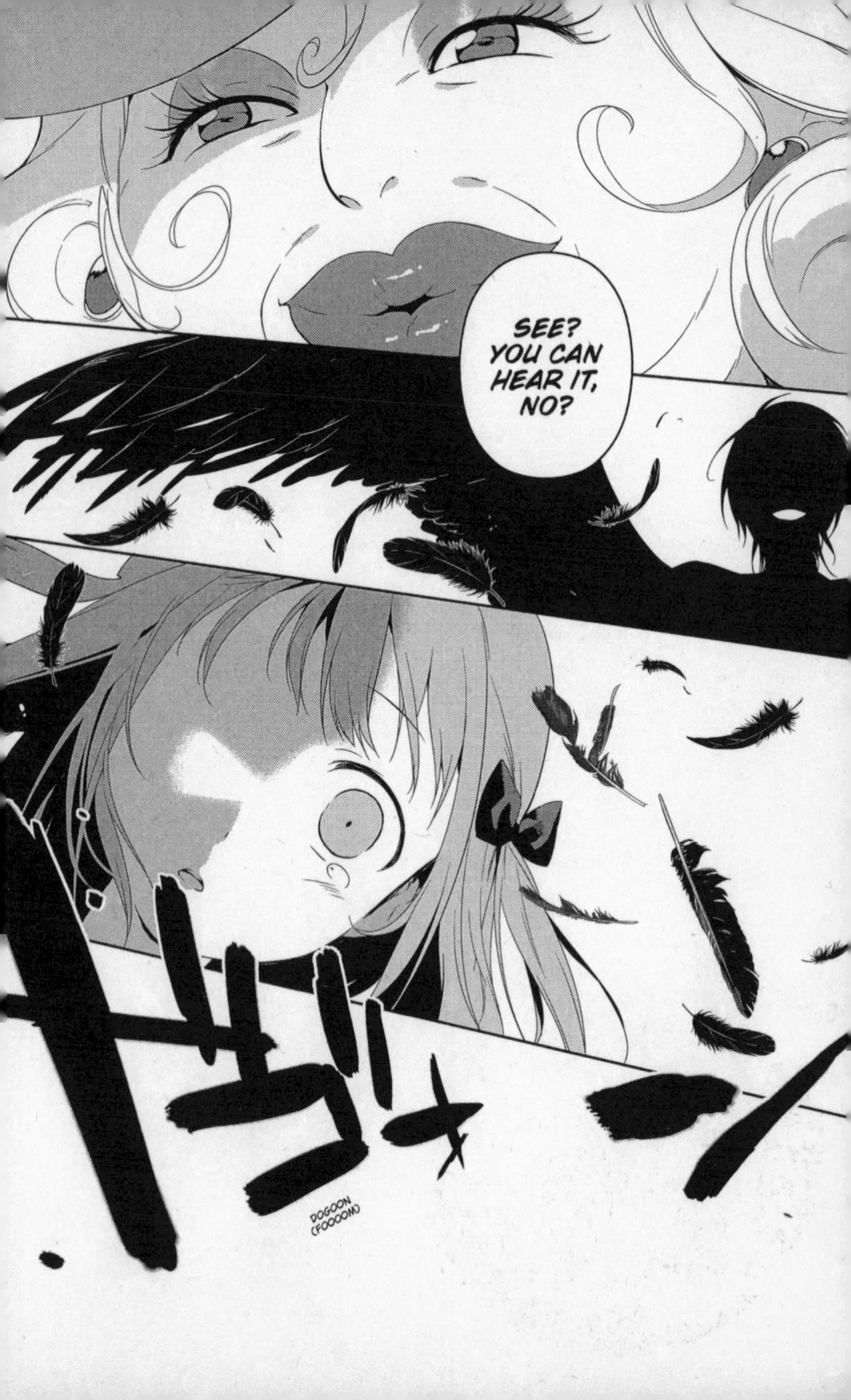
SEE? YOU CAN HEAR IT, NO?
DOGOON (FOOOOM)

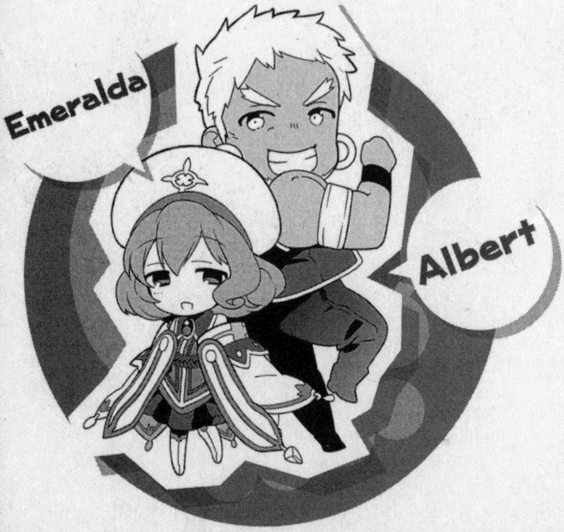Emeralda
Albert

THE DEVIL IS A PART-TIMER!

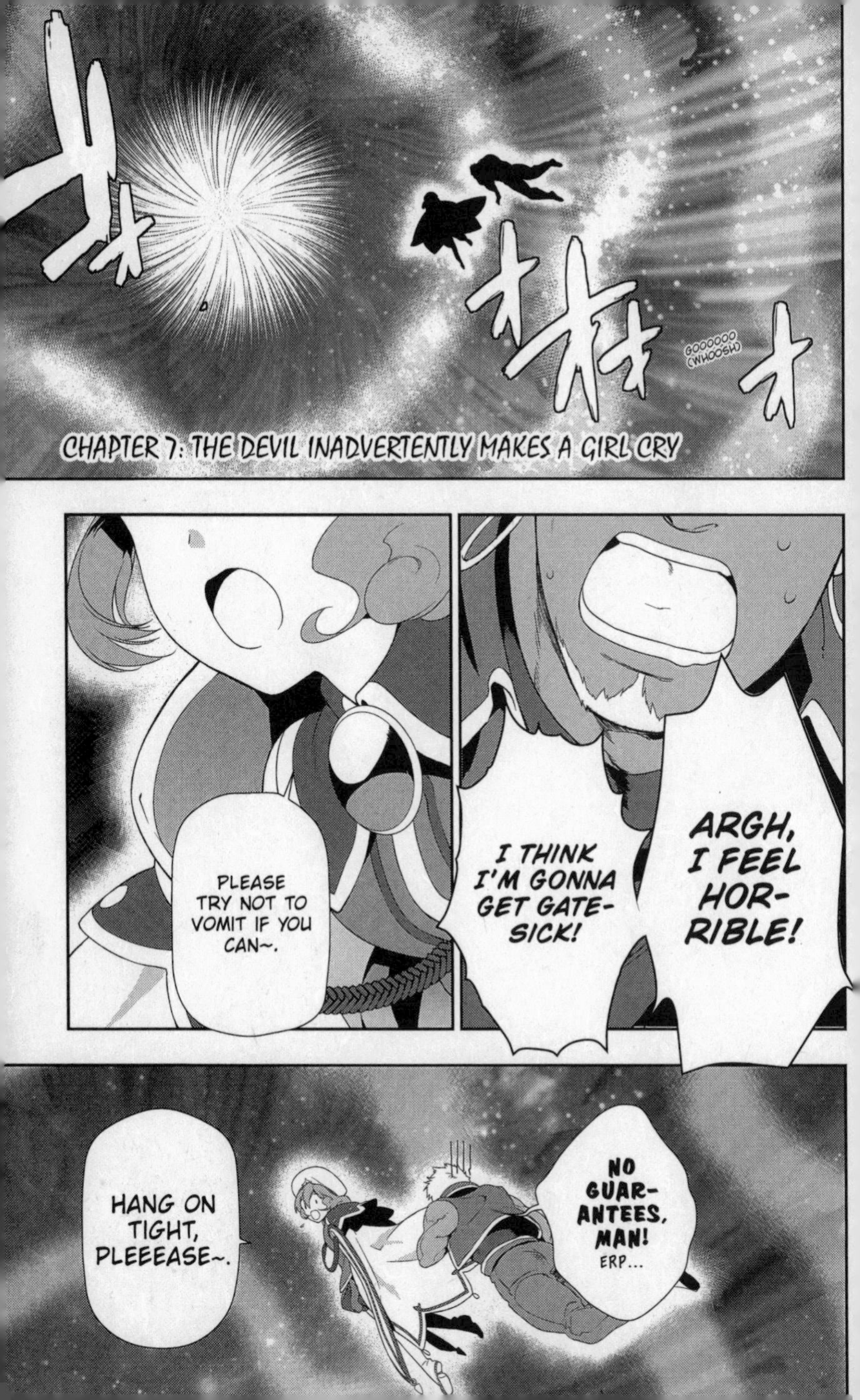
GOOOOOO (WHOOSH)
CHAPTER 7: THE DEVIL INADVERTENTLY MAKES A GIRL CRY
ARGH, I FEEL HOR-RIBLE!
I THINK I'M GONNA GET GATE-SICK!
PLEASE TRY NOT TO VOMIT IF YOU CAN~.
NO GUAR-ANTEES, MAN!
ERP...
HANG ON TIGHT, PLEEEASE~.

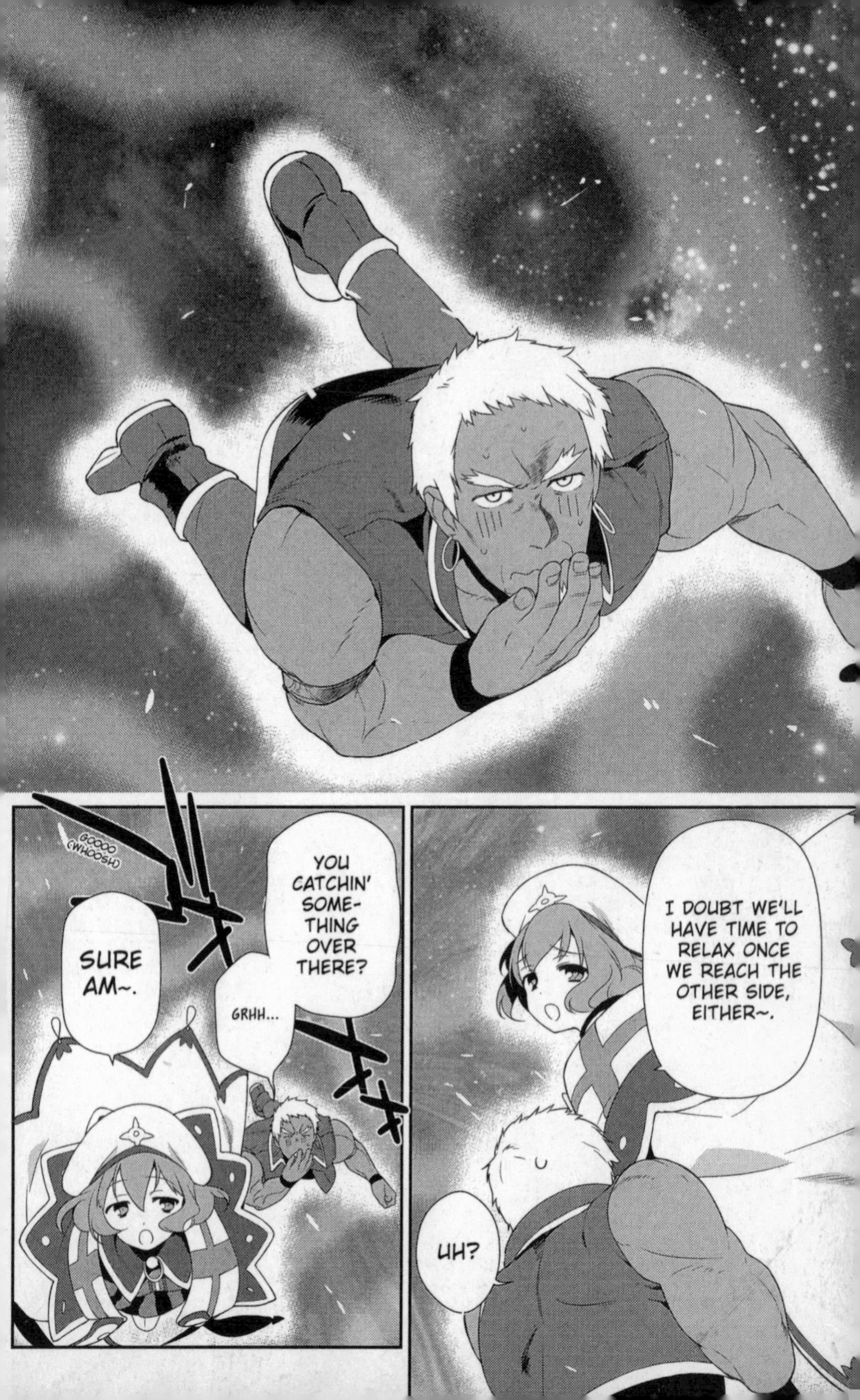
I DOUBT WE'LL HAVE TIME TO RELAX ONCE WE REACH THE OTHER SIDE, EITHER~.
UH?
YOU CATCHIN' SOMETHING OVER THERE?
GOOOO (WHOOSH)
SURE AM~.
GRHH...

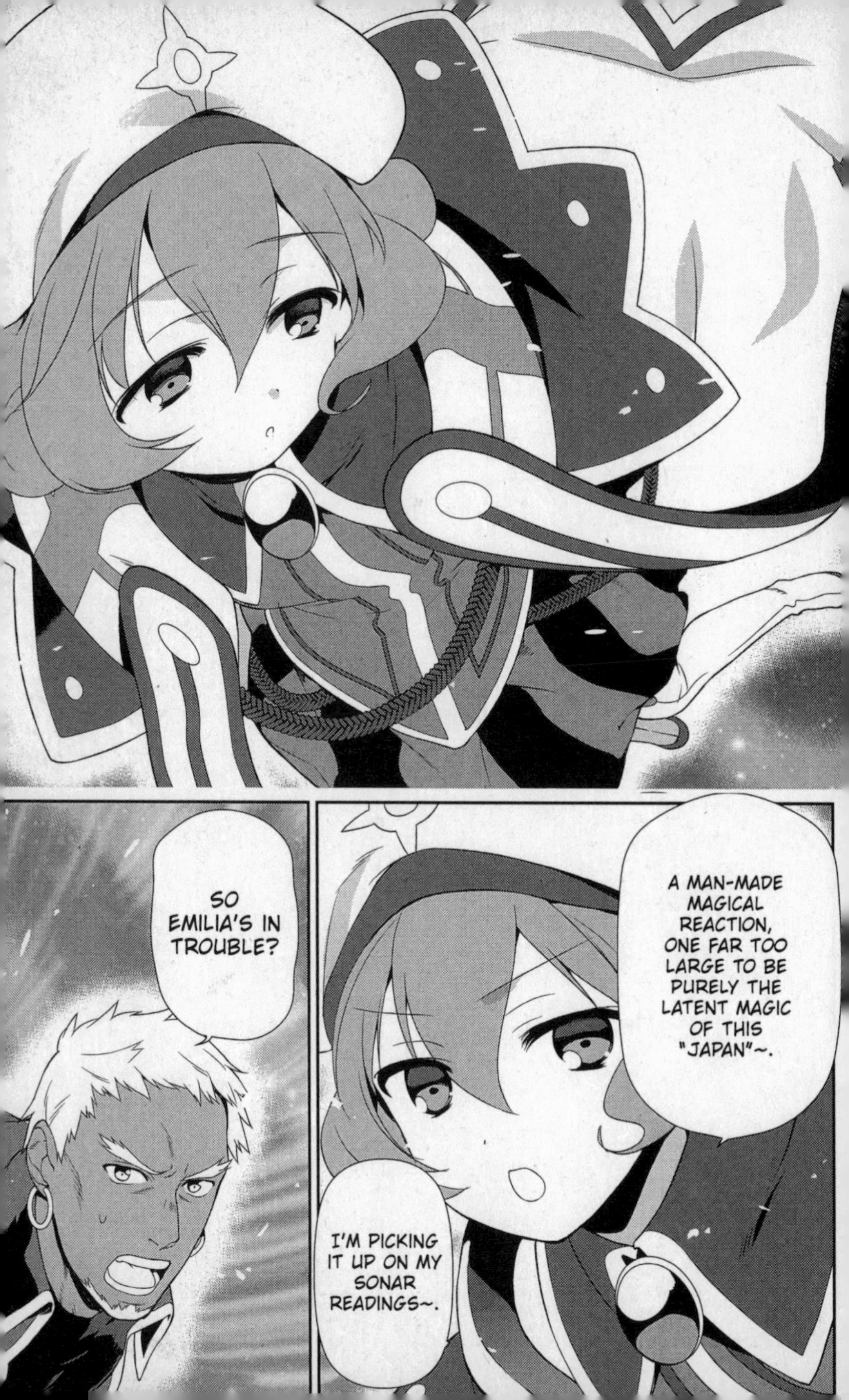
A MAN-MADE MAGICAL REACTION, ONE FAR TOO LARGE TO BE PURELY THE LATENT MAGIC OF THIS "JAPAN"~.
I'M PICKING IT UP ON MY SONAR READINGS~.
SO EMILIA'S IN TROUBLE?

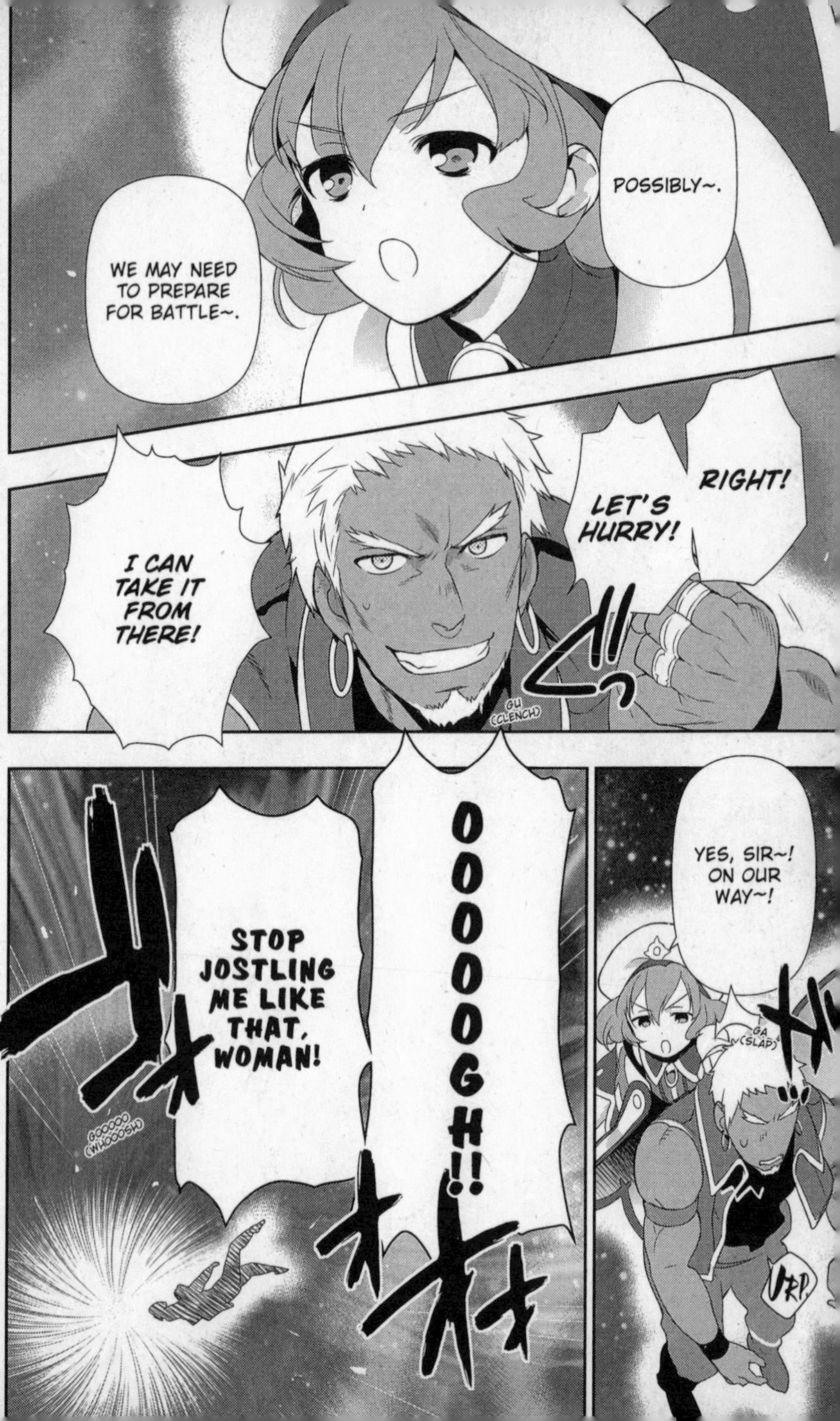
POSSIBLY~.
WE MAY NEED TO PREPARE FOR BATTLE~.
RIGHT!
LET'S HURRY!
I CAN TAKE IT FROM THERE!
GU (CLENCH)
YES, SIR~! ON OUR WAY~!
GA (SLAP)
URP.
OOOOOOOGH!!
STOP JOSTLING ME LIKE THAT, WOMAN!
GOOOOO (WHOOOSH)

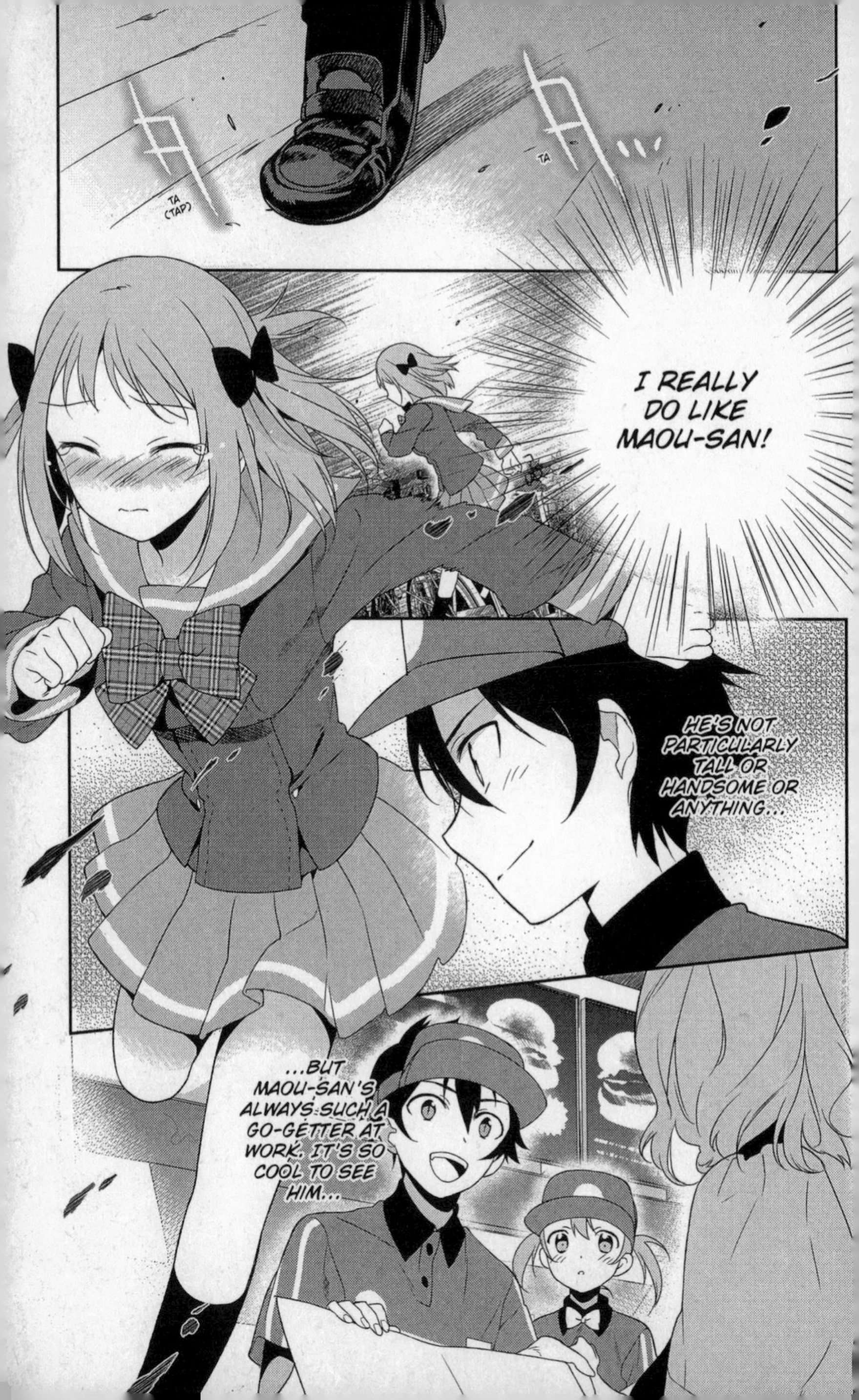
TA
TA (TAP)
I REALLY DO LIKE MAOU-SAN!
HE'S NOT PARTICULARLY TALL OR HANDSOME OR ANYTHING...
...BUT MAOU-SAN'S ALWAYS SUCH A GO-GETTER AT WORK. IT'S SO COOL TO SEE HIM...

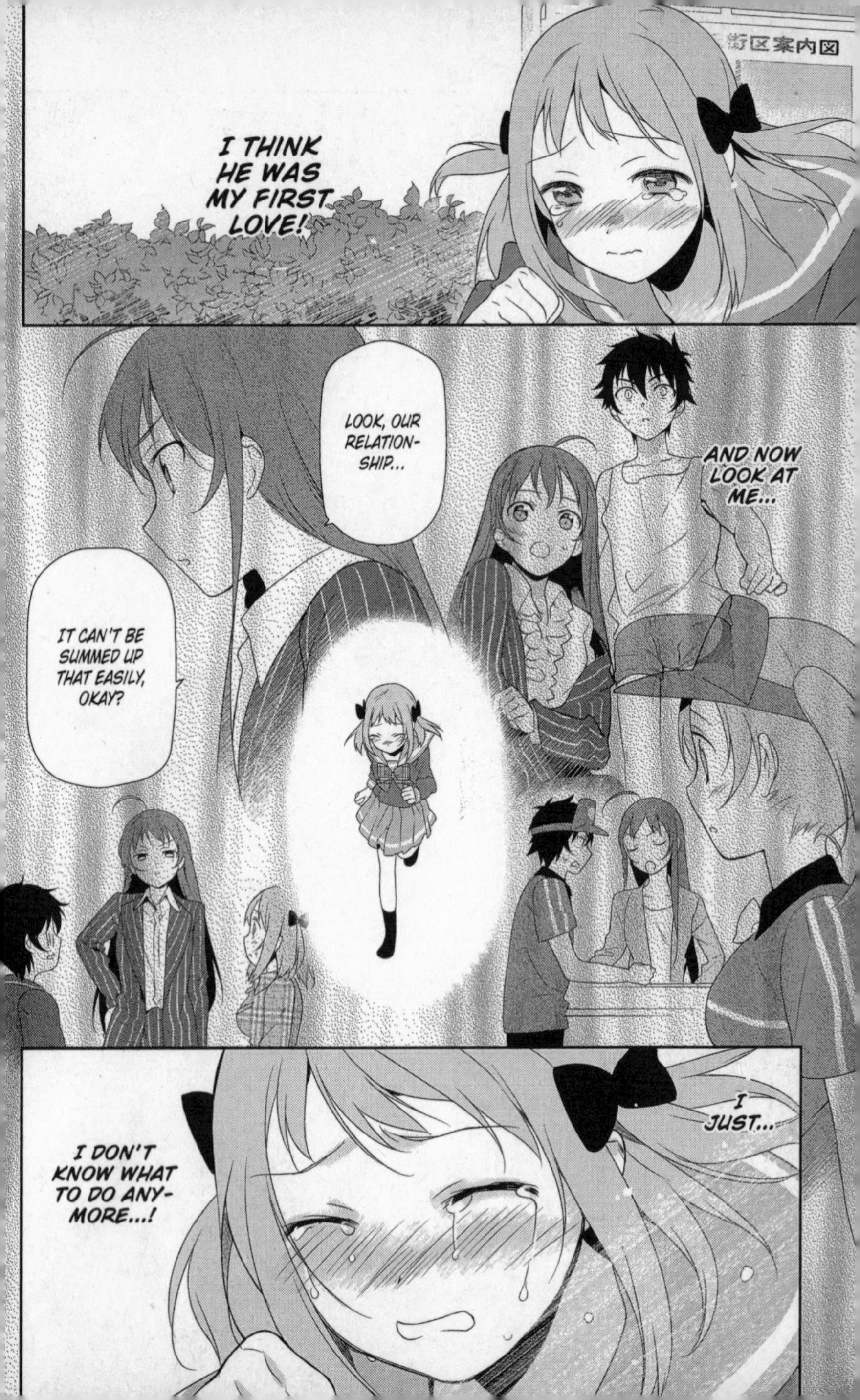
街区案内図
I THINK HE WAS MY FIRST LOVE!
AND NOW LOOK AT ME...
LOOK, OUR RELATION-SHIP...
IT CAN'T BE SUMMED UP THAT EASILY, OKAY?
I JUST...
I DON'T KNOW WHAT TO DO ANY-MORE...!

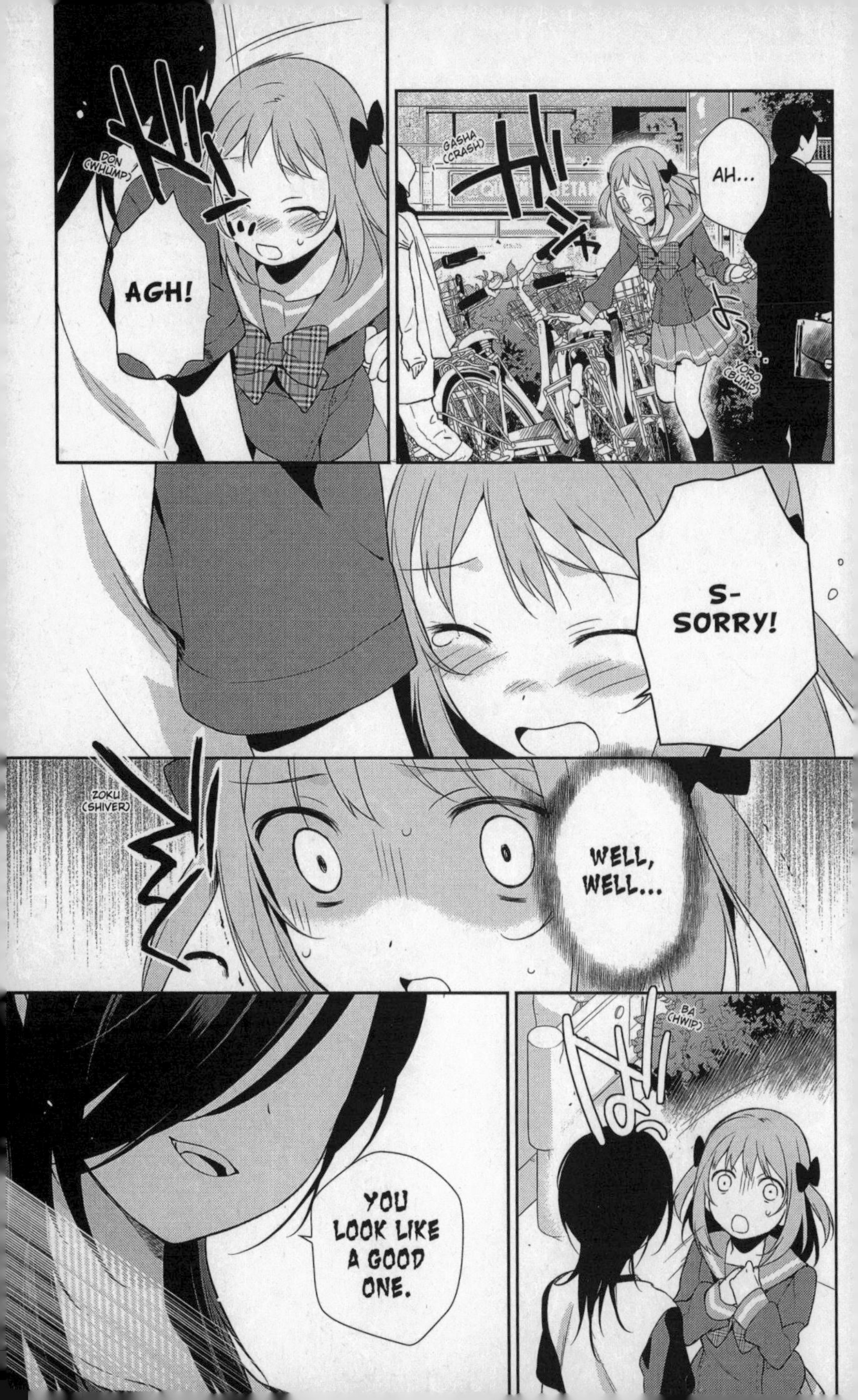
GASHA (CRASH)
AH...
YORO (BUMP)
DON (WHUMP)
AGH!
S-SORRY!
WELL, WELL...
ZOKU (SHIVER)
BA (HWIP)
YOU LOOK LIKE A GOOD ONE.

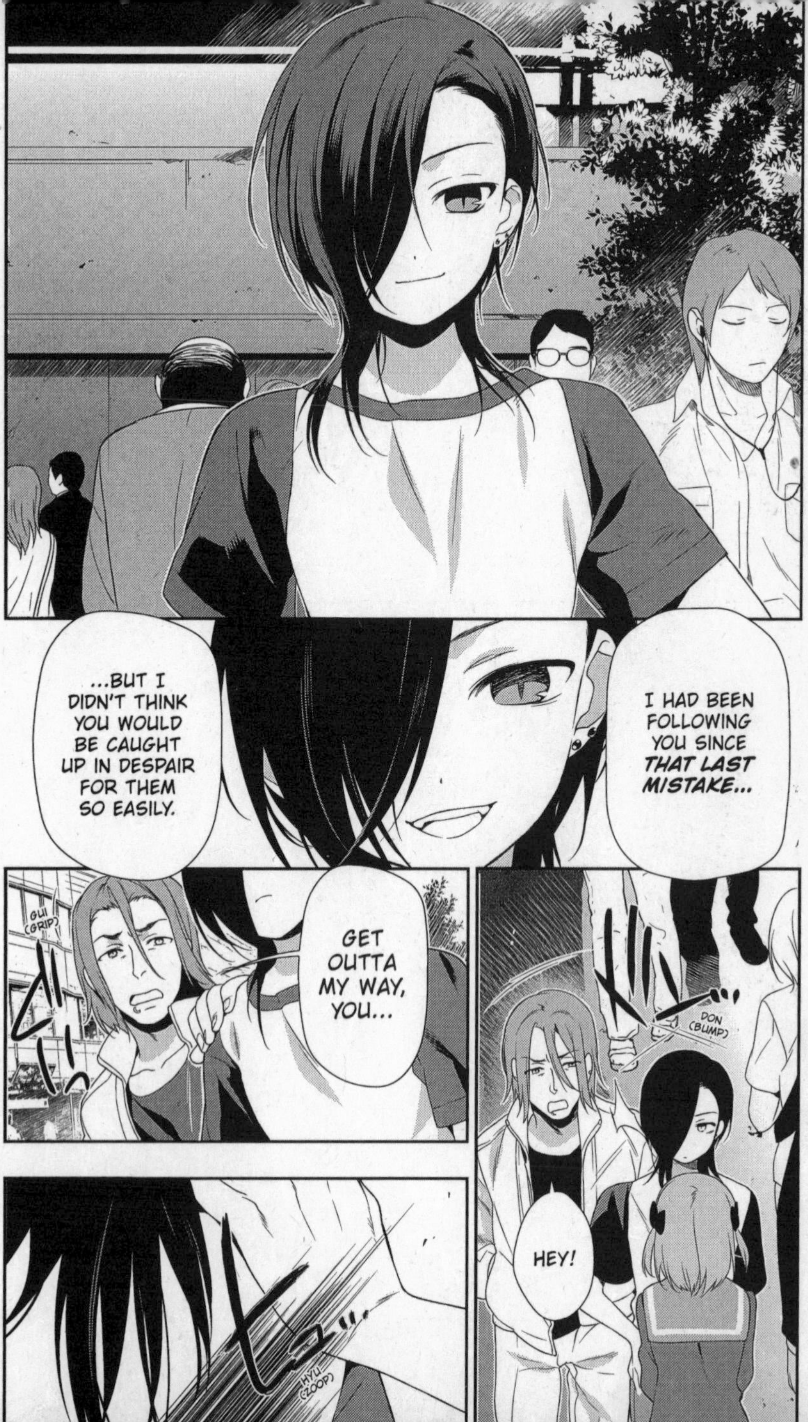
I HAD BEEN FOLLOWING YOU SINCE THAT LAST MISTAKE...
...BUT I DIDN'T THINK YOU WOULD BE CAUGHT UP IN DESPAIR FOR THEM SO EASILY.
DON (BUMP)
HEY!
GUI (GRIP)
GET OUTTA MY WAY, YOU...
HYU (ZOOP)

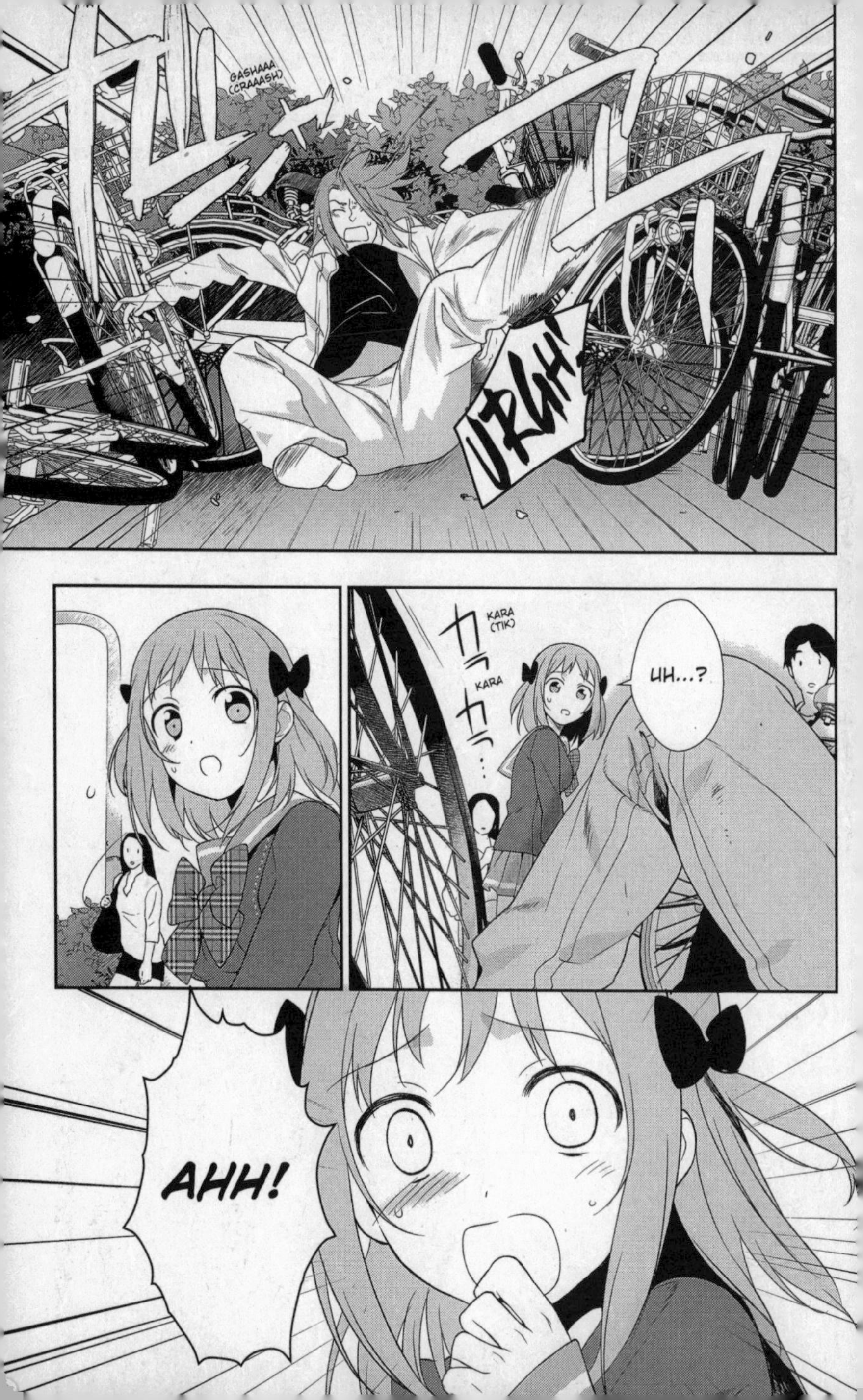
GASHAAA
(CRAAASH)
URGH!
KARA
(TIK)
KARA
UH...?
AHH!

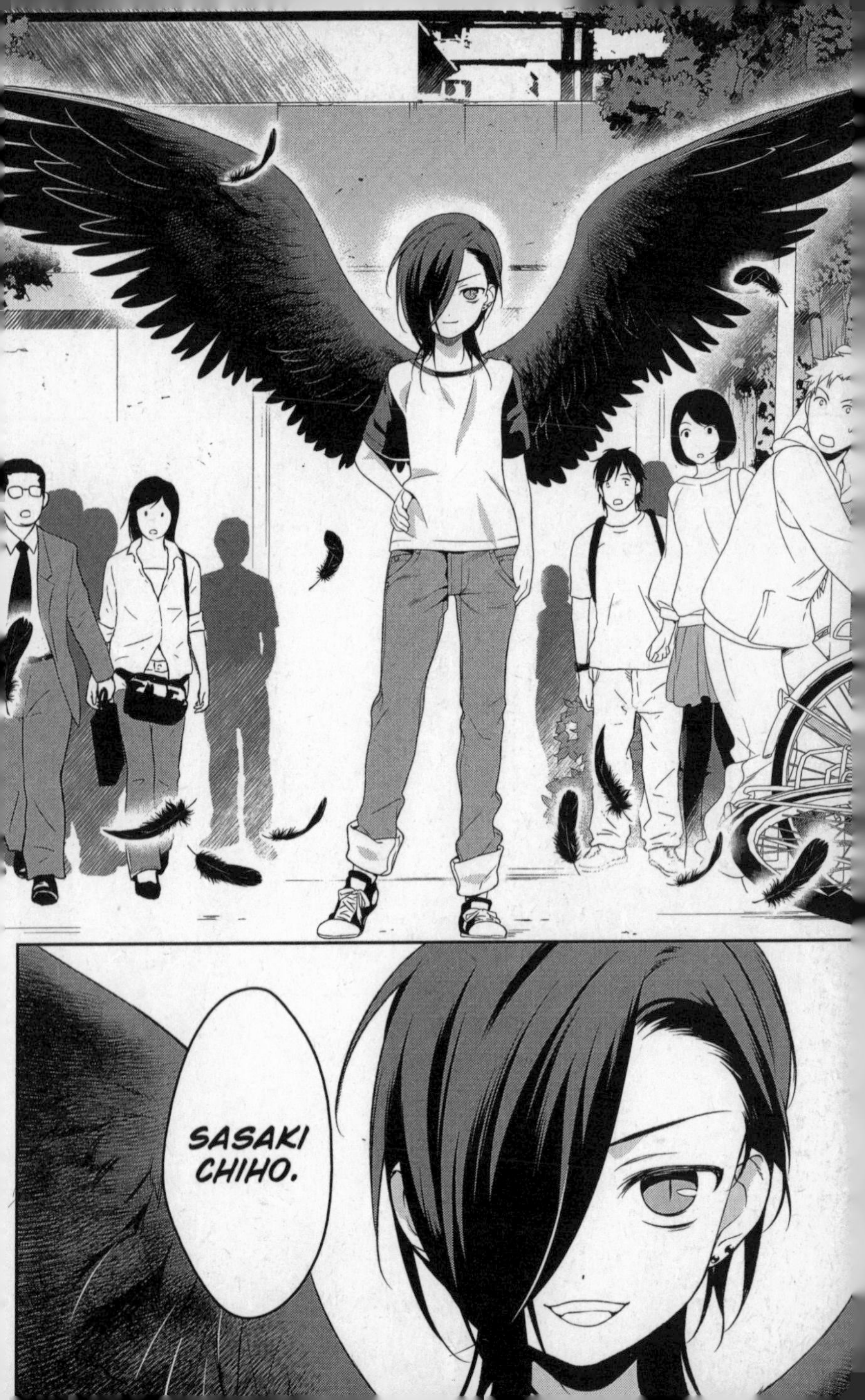
SASAKI CHIHO.

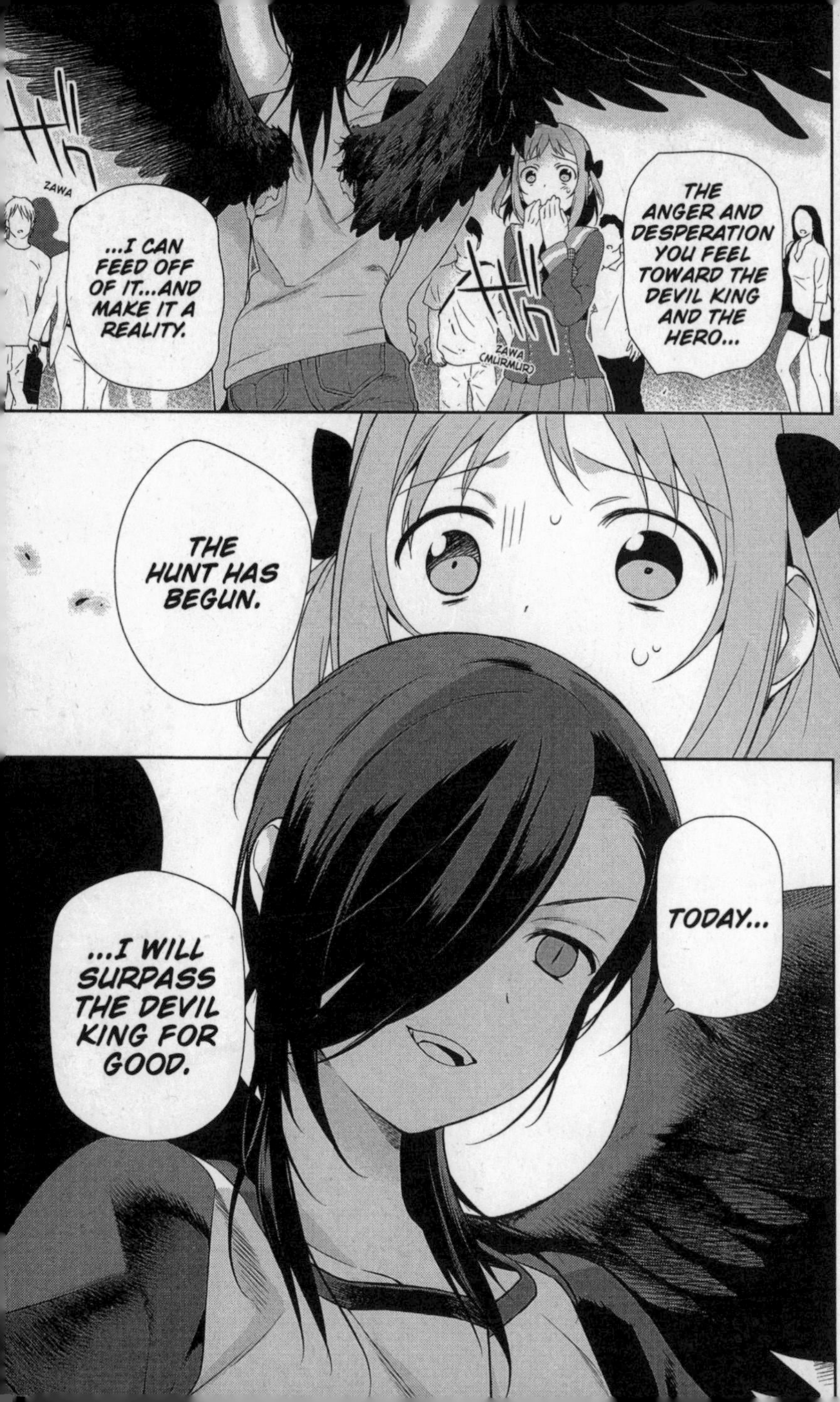
THE ANGER AND DESPERATION YOU FEEL TOWARD THE DEVIL KING AND THE HERO...
ZAWA (MURMUR)
...I CAN FEED OFF OF IT...AND MAKE IT A REALITY.
ZAWA
THE HUNT HAS BEGUN.
TODAY...
...I WILL SURPASS THE DEVIL KING FOR GOOD.

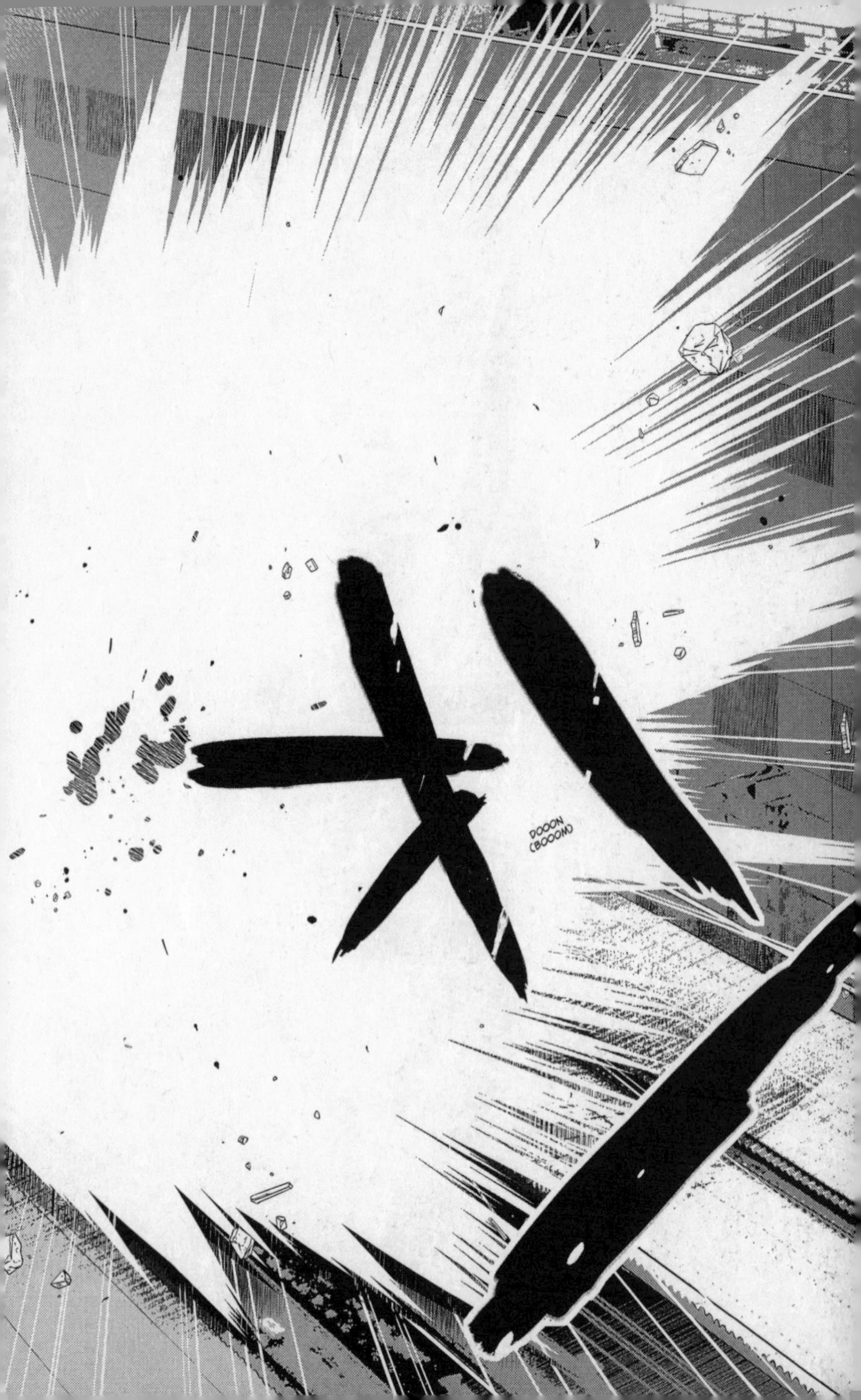
DOOON
(BOOOM)

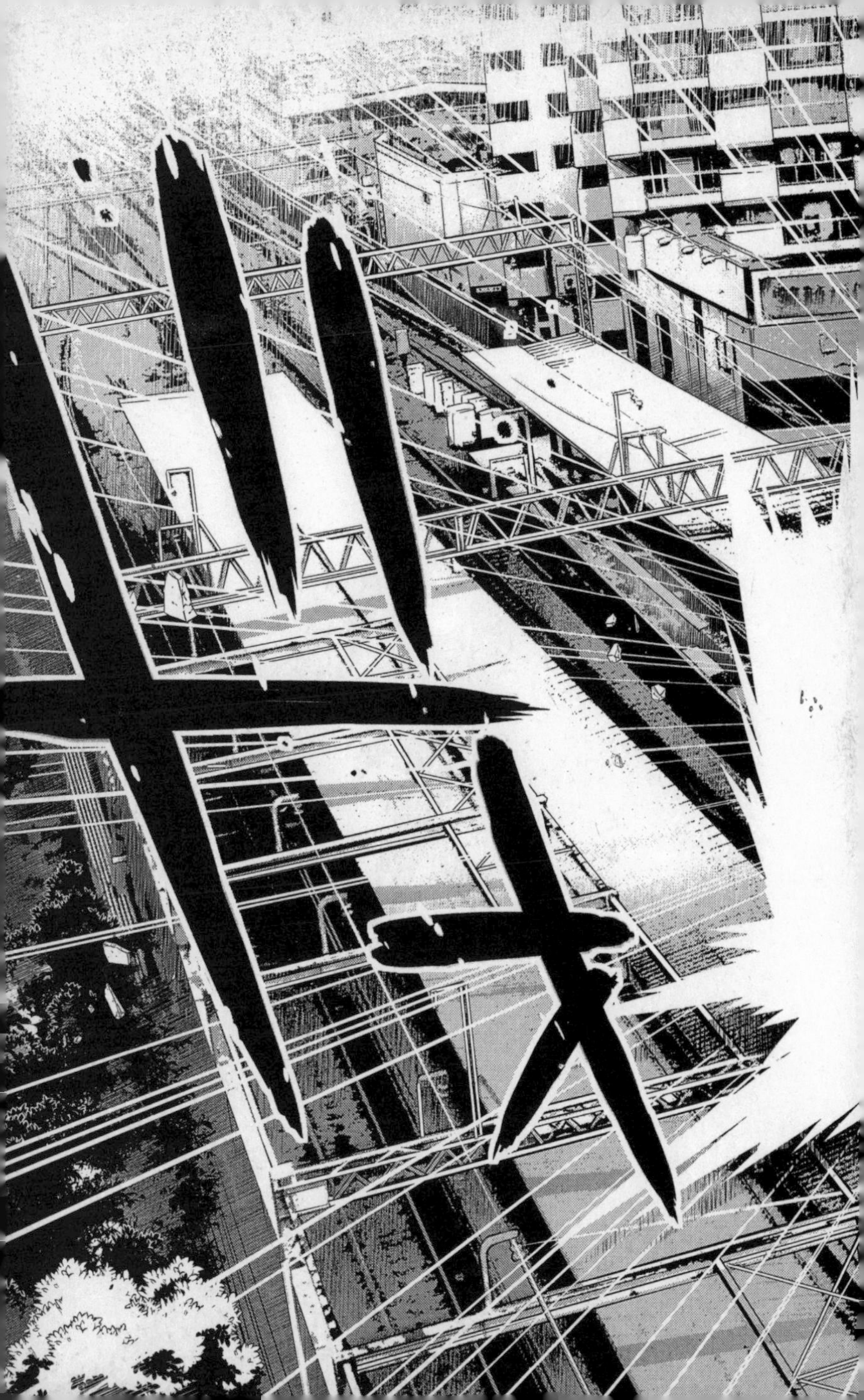

THE **DEVIL** IS A PART-TIMER!

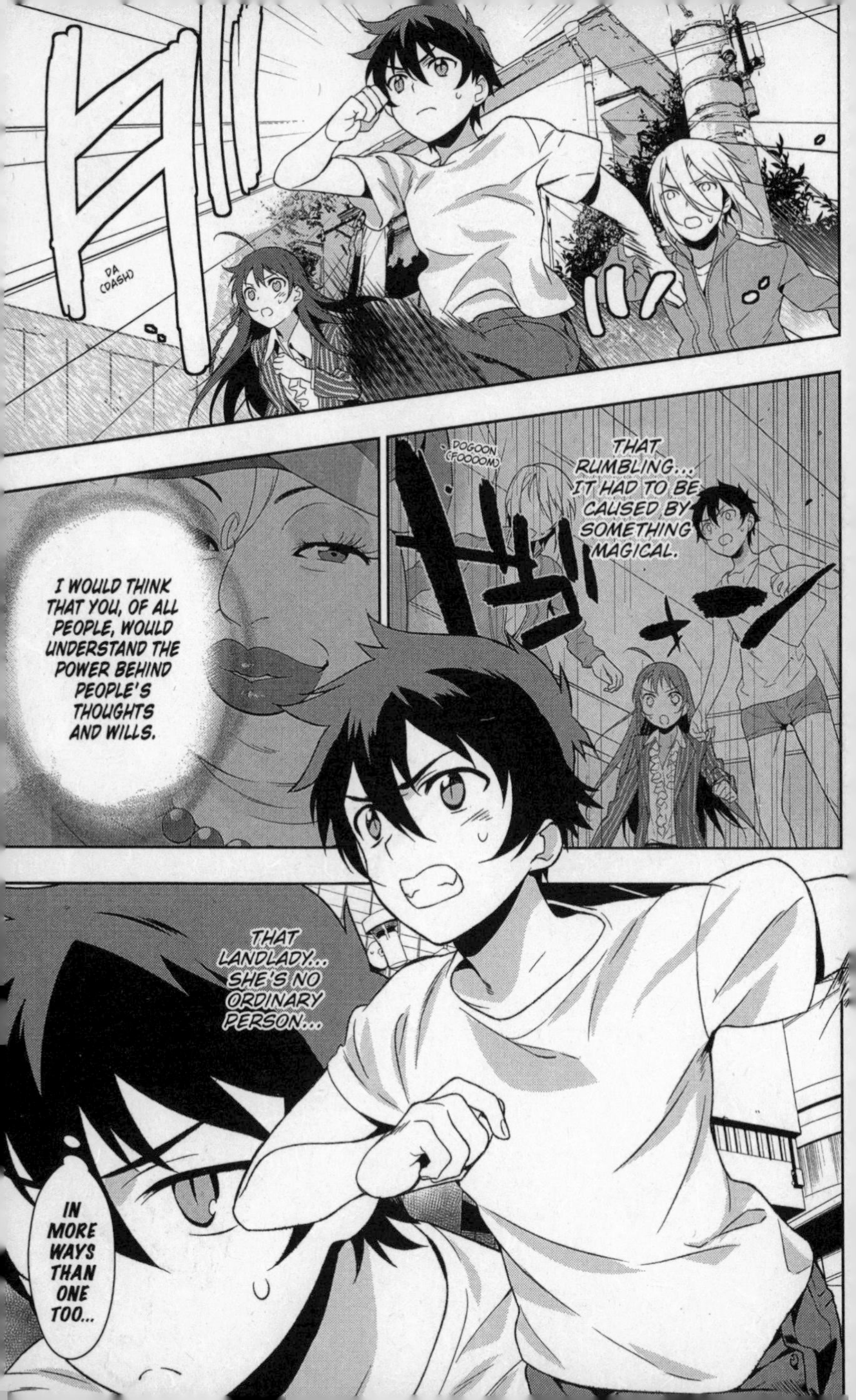
DA
(DASH)
DOGOON
(FOOOOM)
THAT RUMBLING... IT HAD TO BE CAUSED BY SOMETHING MAGICAL.
I WOULD THINK THAT YOU, OF ALL PEOPLE, WOULD UNDERSTAND THE POWER BEHIND PEOPLE'S THOUGHTS AND WILLS.
THAT LANDLADY... SHE'S NO ORDINARY PERSON...
IN MORE WAYS THAN ONE TOO...

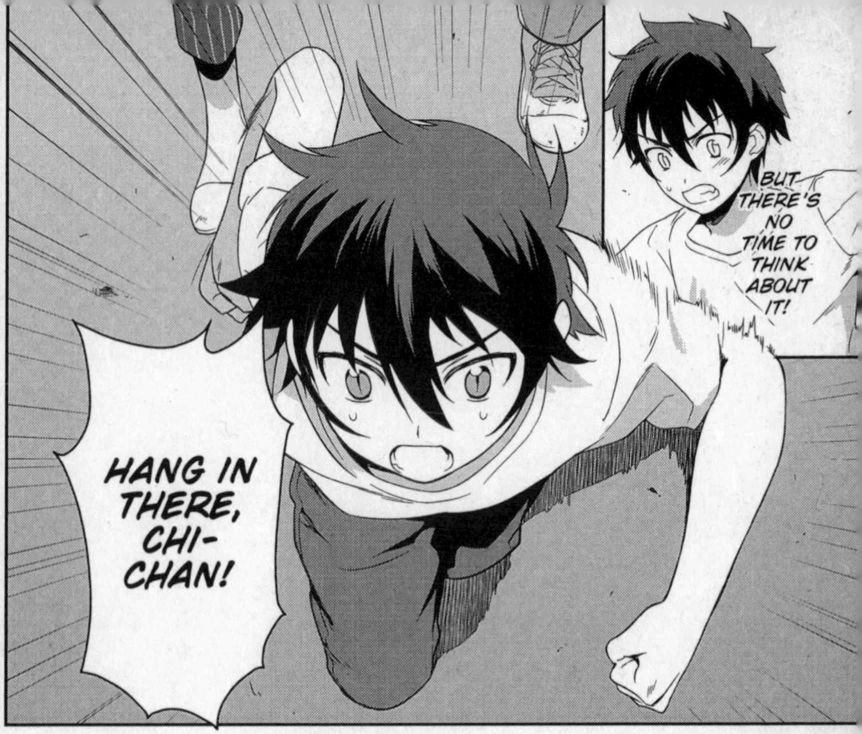
BUT THERE'S NO TIME TO THINK ABOUT IT!
HANG IN THERE, CHI-CHAN!

CHAPTER 8: THE DEVIL REVEALS ALL

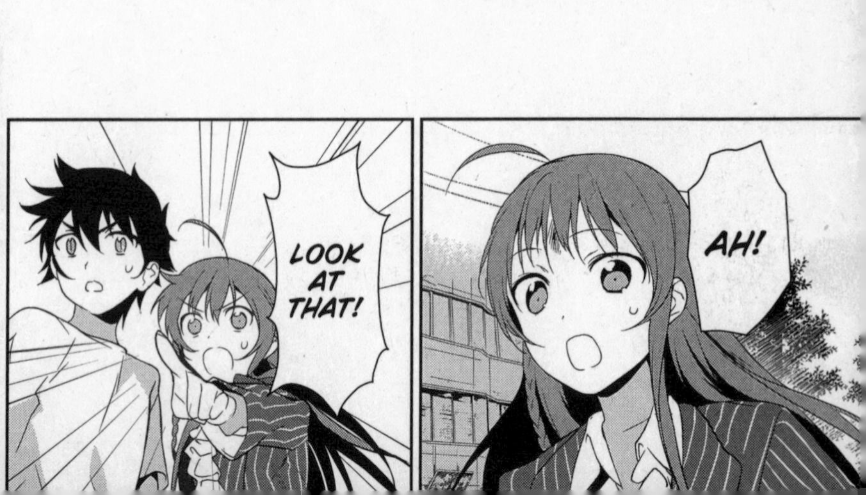
AH!
LOOK AT THAT!

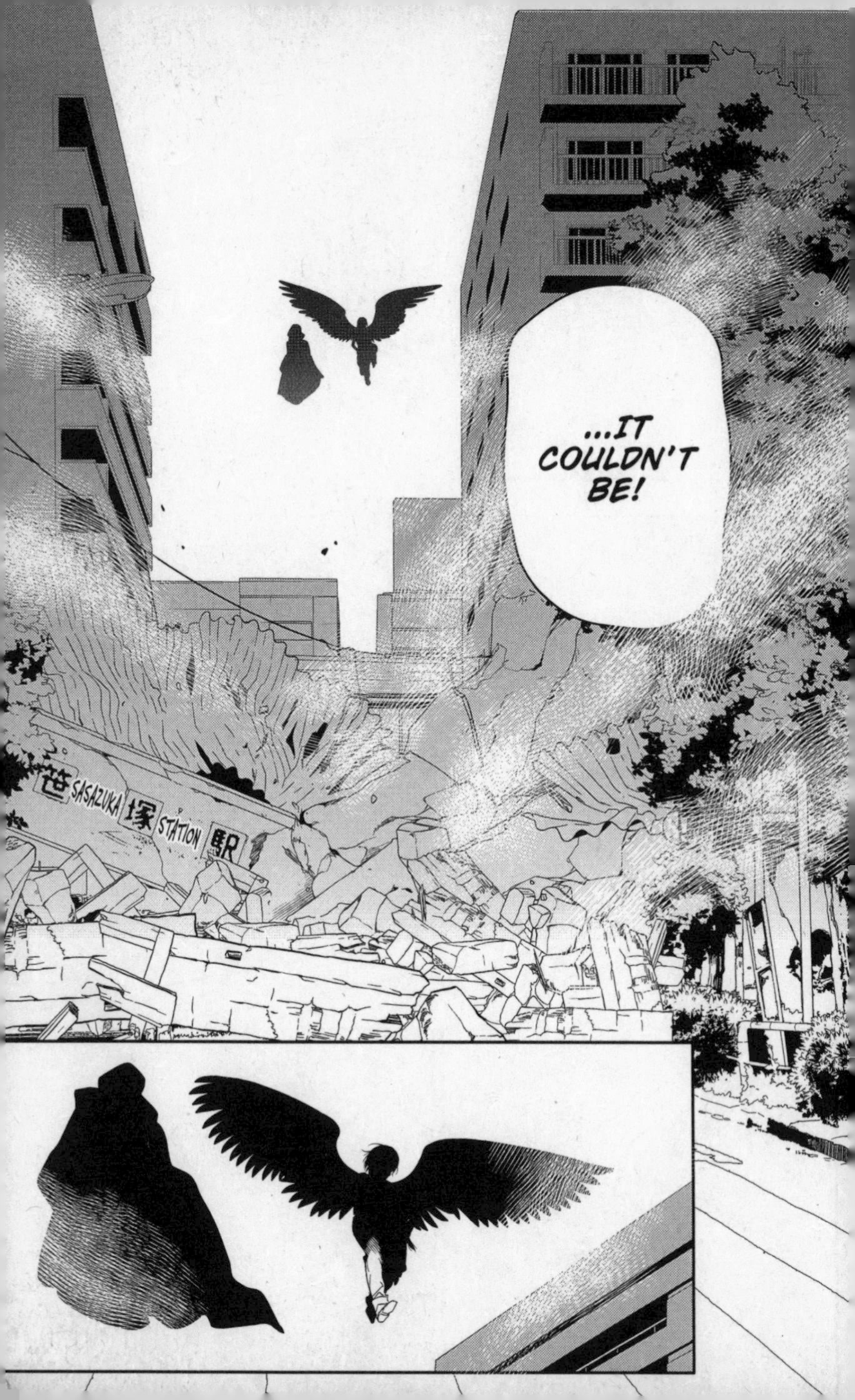
...IT COULDN'T BE!
笹 SASAZUKA 塚 STATION 駅

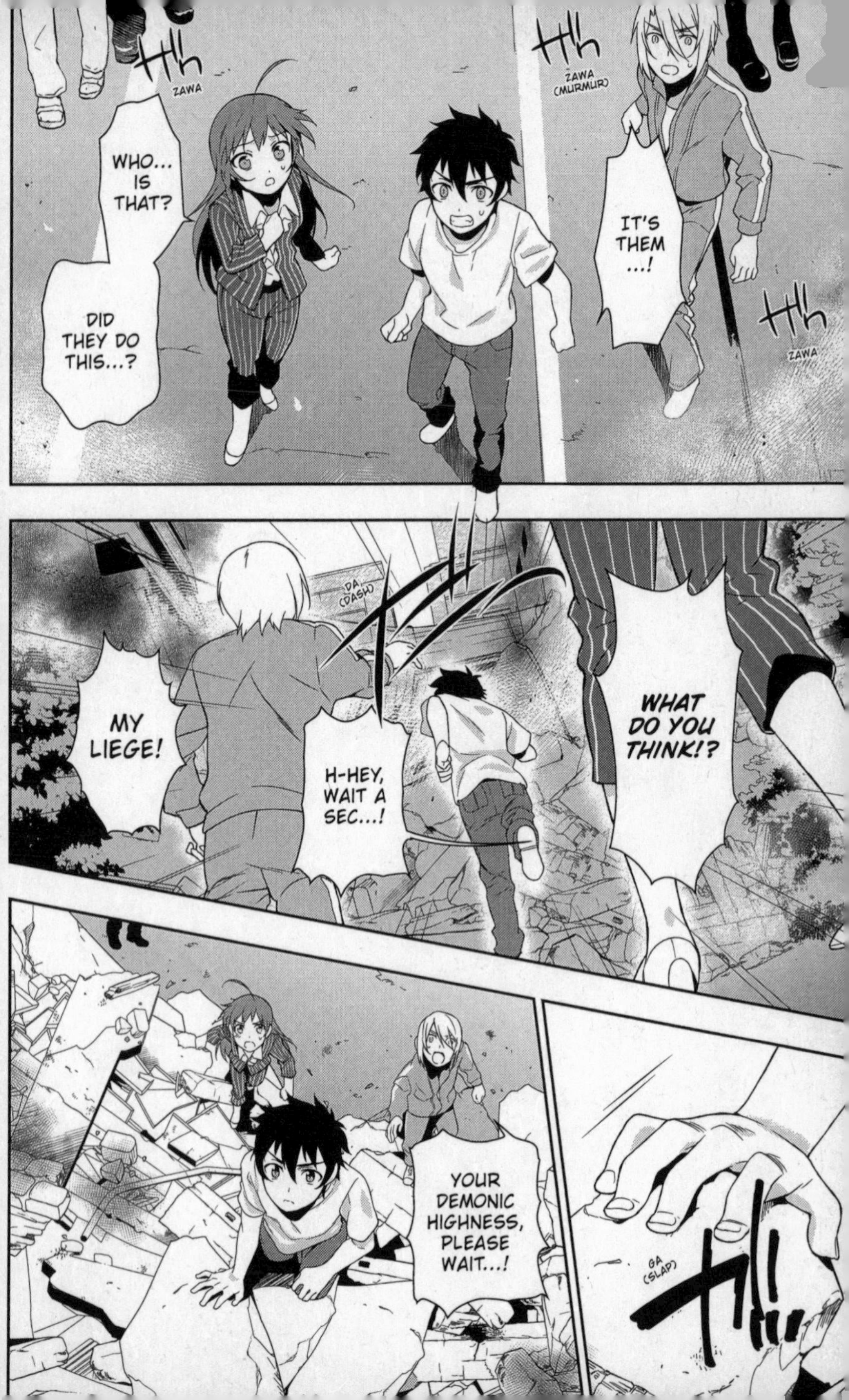
ZAWA (MURMUR)
IT'S THEM...!
ZAWA
ZAWA
WHO... IS THAT?
DID THEY DO THIS...?
WHAT DO YOU THINK!?
DA (DASH)
H-HEY, WAIT A SEC...!
MY LIEGE!
GA (SLAP)
YOUR DEMONIC HIGHNESS, PLEASE WAIT...!

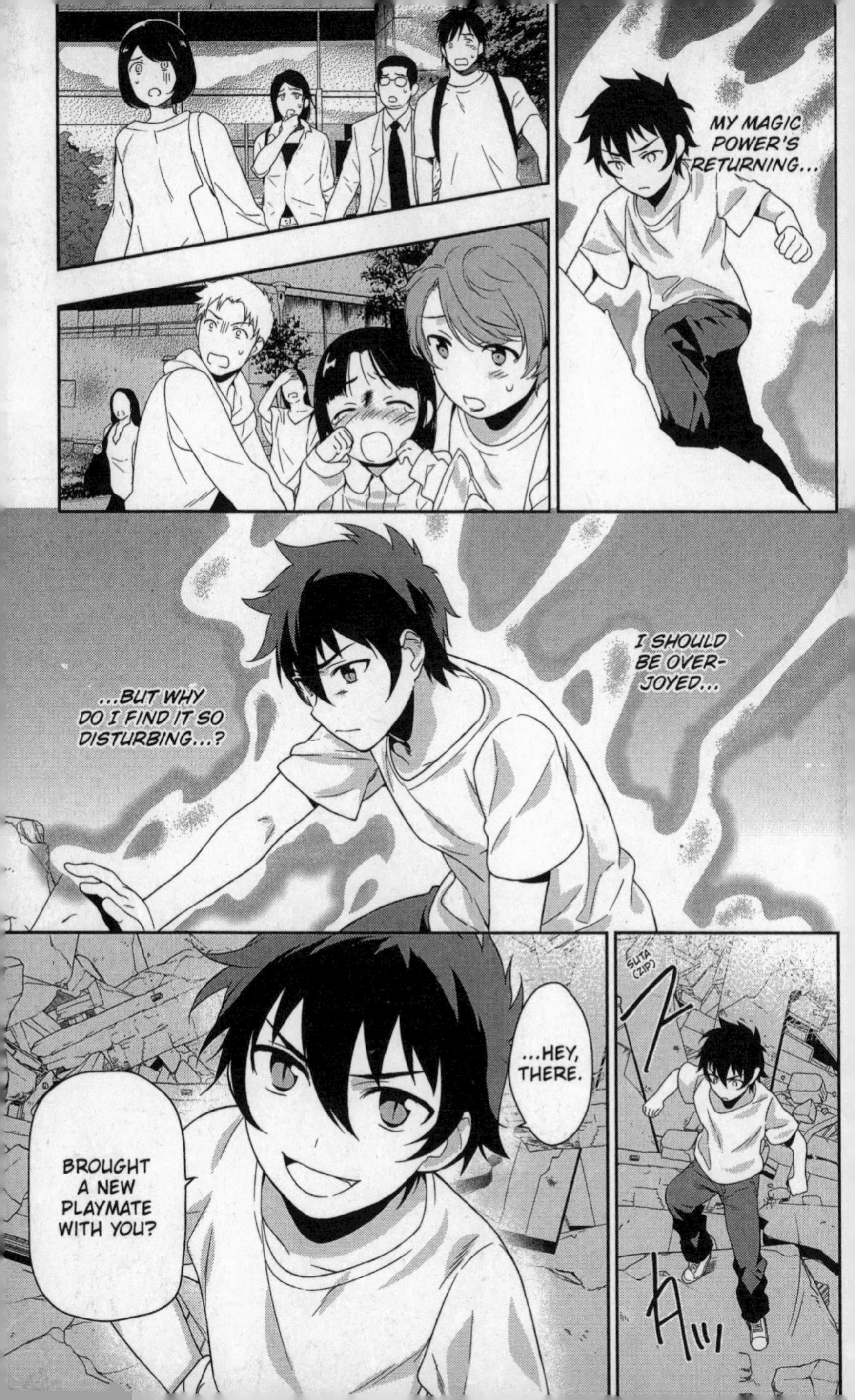
MY MAGIC POWER'S RETURNING...
I SHOULD BE OVER-JOYED...
...BUT WHY DO I FIND IT SO DISTURBING...?
SUTA (ZIP)
...HEY, THERE.
BROUGHT A NEW PLAYMATE WITH YOU?

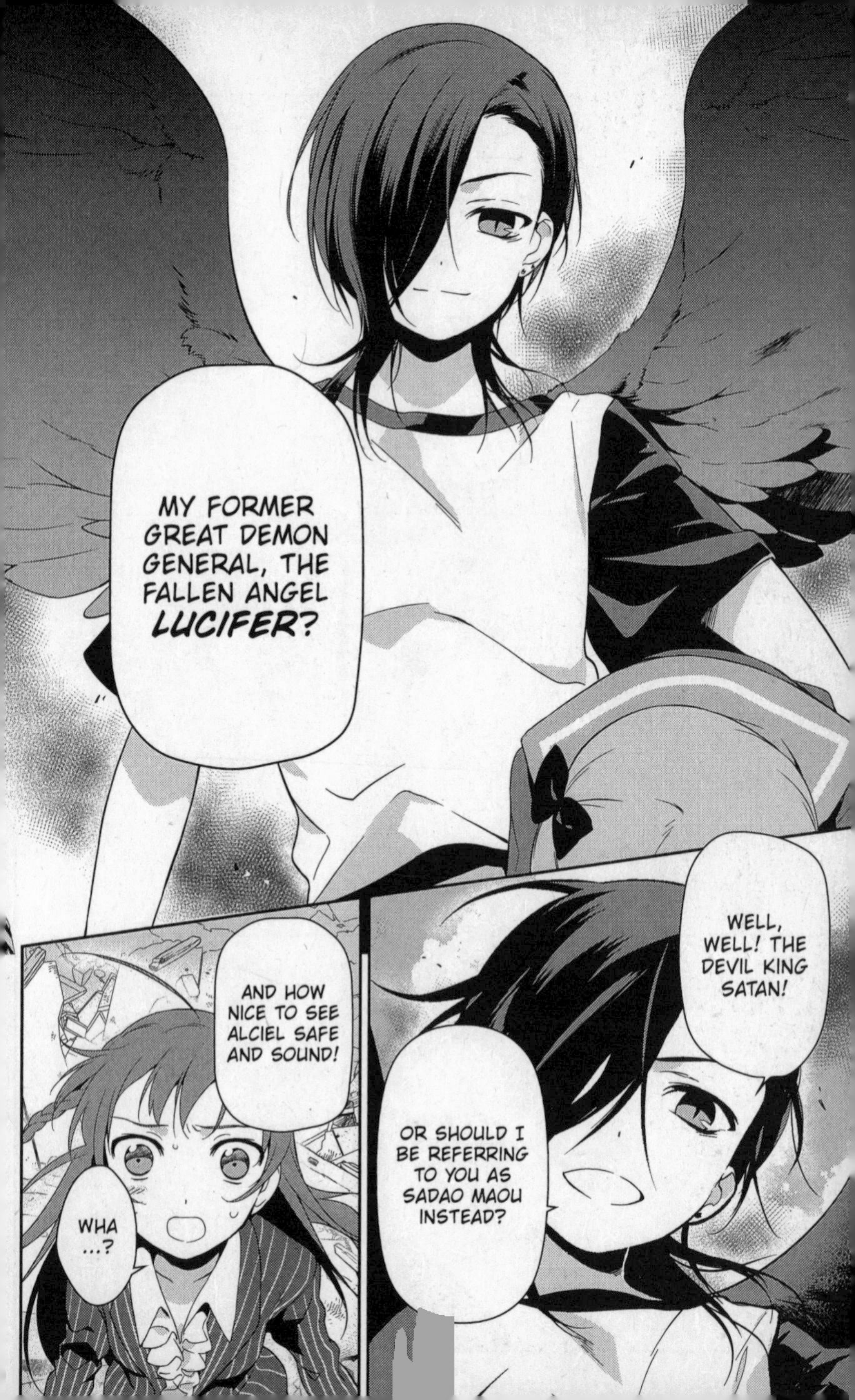
MY FORMER GREAT DEMON GENERAL, THE FALLEN ANGEL *LUCIFER*?
WELL, WELL! THE DEVIL KING SATAN!
OR SHOULD I BE REFERRING TO YOU AS SADAO MAOU INSTEAD?
AND HOW NICE TO SEE ALCIEL SAFE AND SOUND!
WHA ...?

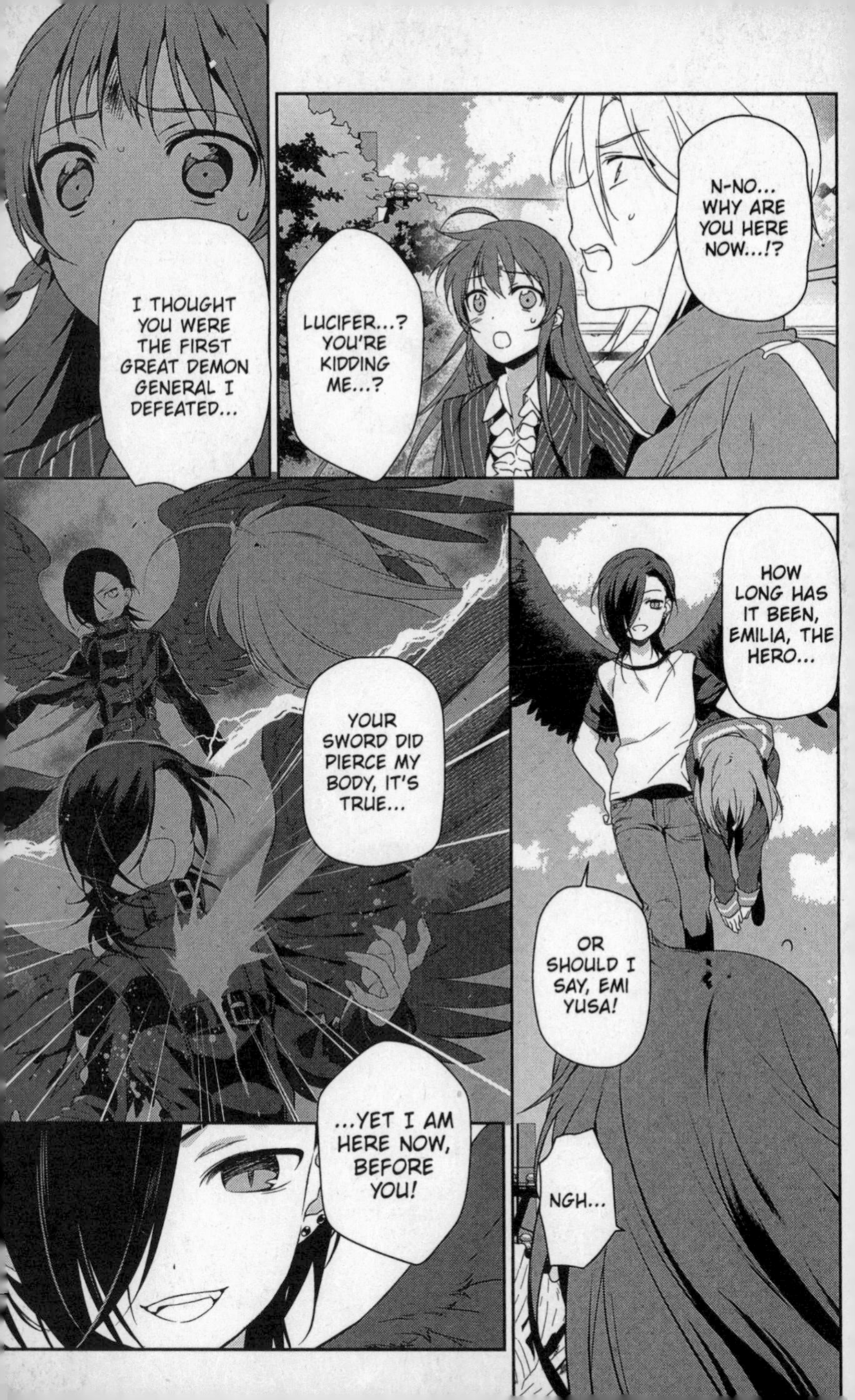

N-NO... WHY ARE YOU HERE NOW...!?
LUCIFER...? YOU'RE KIDDING ME...?
I THOUGHT YOU WERE THE FIRST GREAT DEMON GENERAL I DEFEATED...
HOW LONG HAS IT BEEN, EMILIA, THE HERO...
OR SHOULD I SAY, EMI YUSA!
YOUR SWORD DID PIERCE MY BODY, IT'S TRUE...
...YET I AM HERE NOW, BEFORE YOU!
NGH...

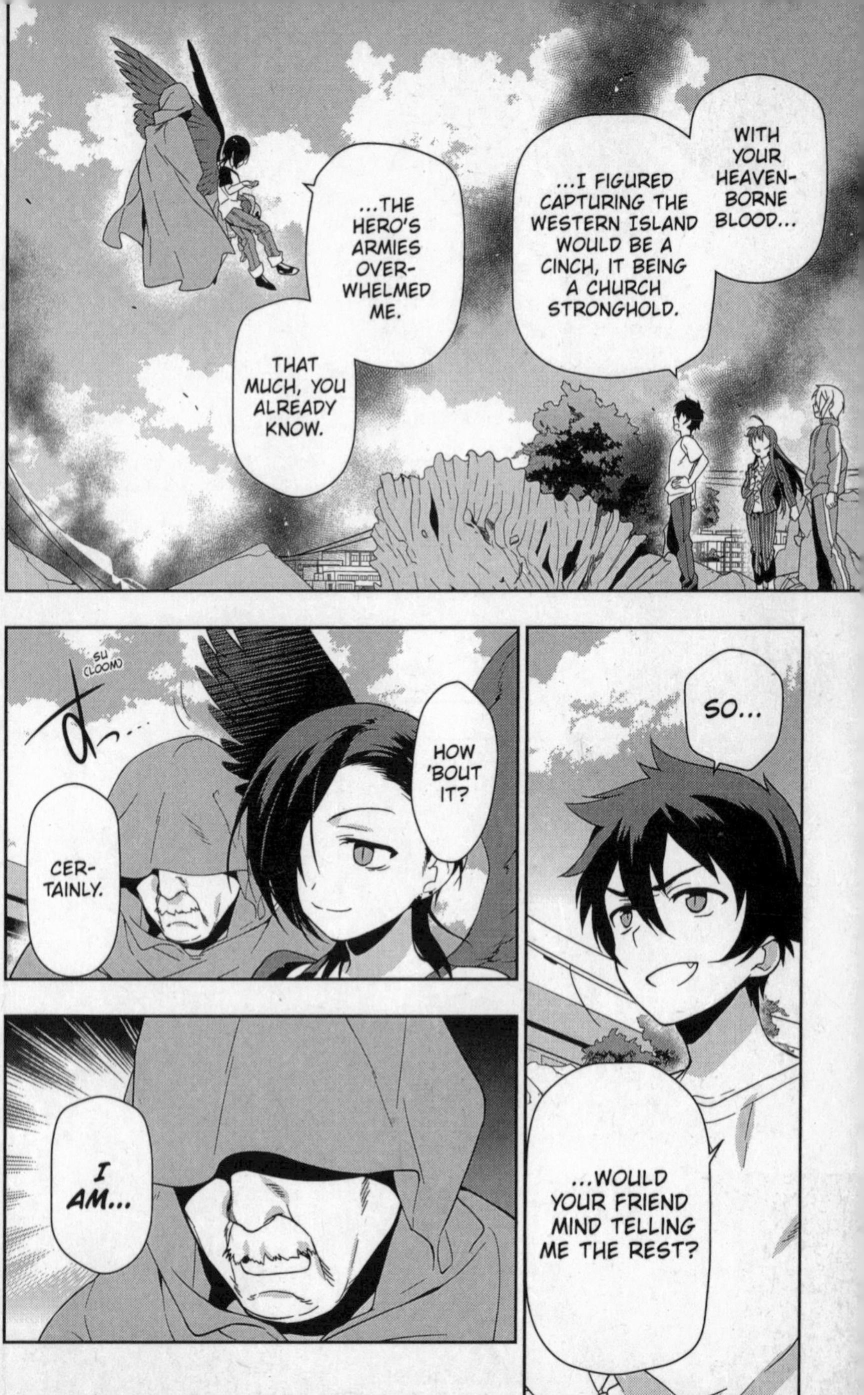
WITH YOUR HEAVEN-BORNE BLOOD...
...I FIGURED CAPTURING THE WESTERN ISLAND WOULD BE A CINCH, IT BEING A CHURCH STRONGHOLD.
...THE HERO'S ARMIES OVERWHELMED ME.
THAT MUCH, YOU ALREADY KNOW.
SO...
...WOULD YOUR FRIEND MIND TELLING ME THE REST?
HOW 'BOUT IT?
SU (LOOM)
CERTAINLY.
I AM...

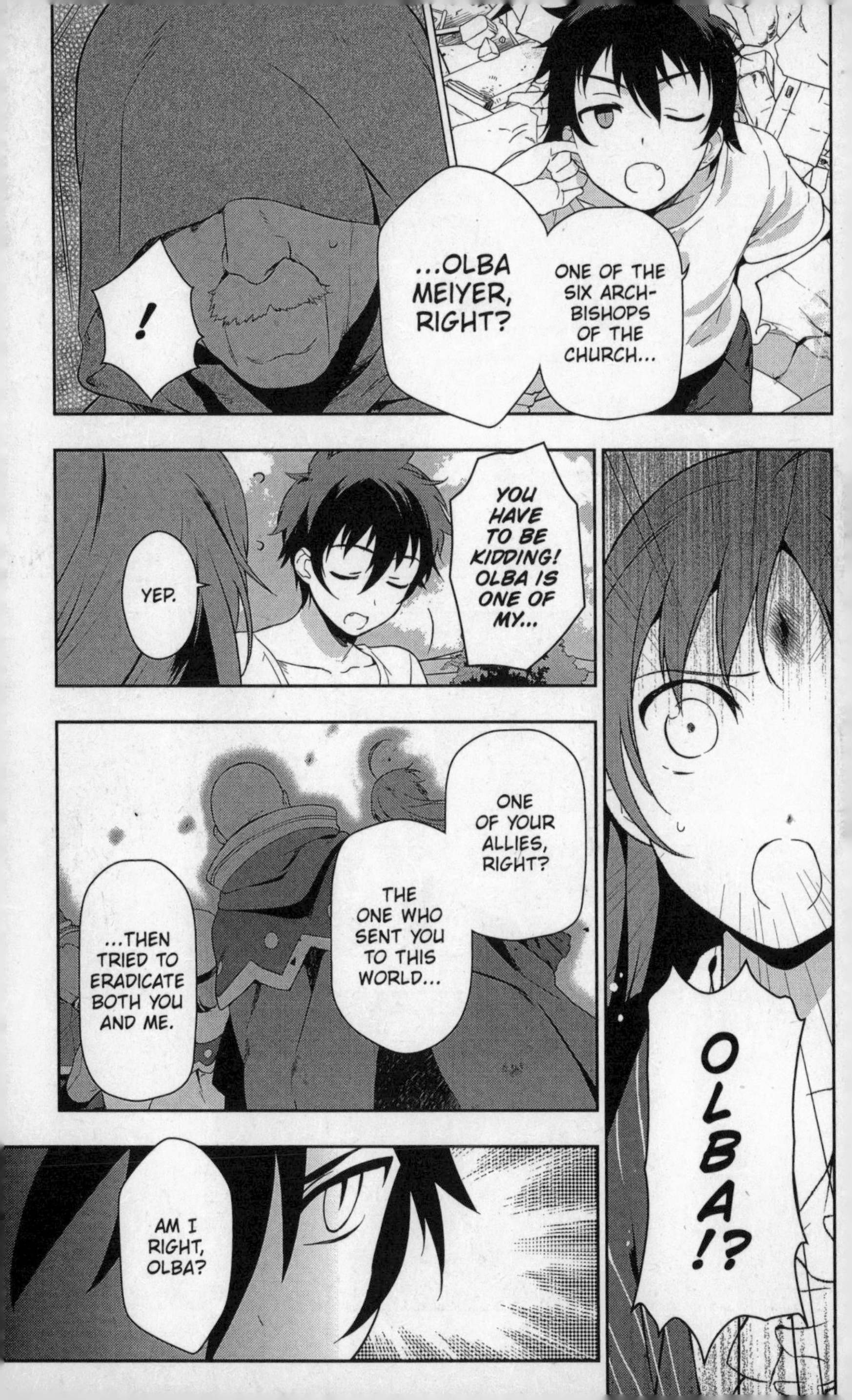
ONE OF THE SIX ARCH-BISHOPS OF THE CHURCH...
...OLBA MEIYER, RIGHT?
!
OLBA!?
YOU HAVE TO BE KIDDING! OLBA IS ONE OF MY...
YEP.
ONE OF YOUR ALLIES, RIGHT?
THE ONE WHO SENT YOU TO THIS WORLD...
...THEN TRIED TO ERADICATE BOTH YOU AND ME.
AM I RIGHT, OLBA?

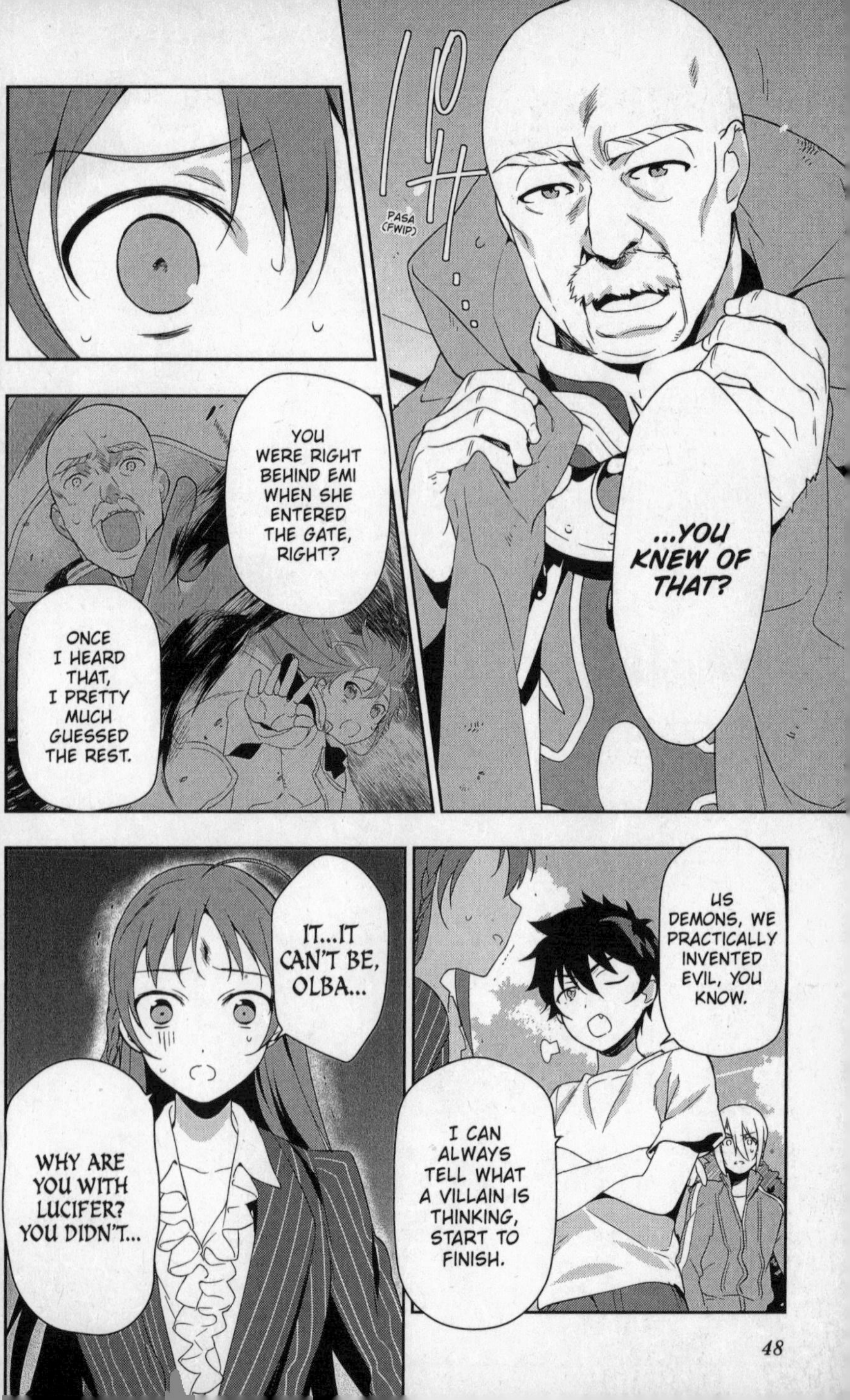
PASA (FWIP)
...YOU KNEW OF THAT?
YOU WERE RIGHT BEHIND EMI WHEN SHE ENTERED THE GATE, RIGHT?
ONCE I HEARD THAT, I PRETTY MUCH GUESSED THE REST.
US DEMONS, WE PRACTICALLY INVENTED EVIL, YOU KNOW.
I CAN ALWAYS TELL WHAT A VILLAIN IS THINKING, START TO FINISH.
IT...IT CAN'T BE, OLBA...
WHY ARE YOU WITH LUCIFER? YOU DIDN'T...

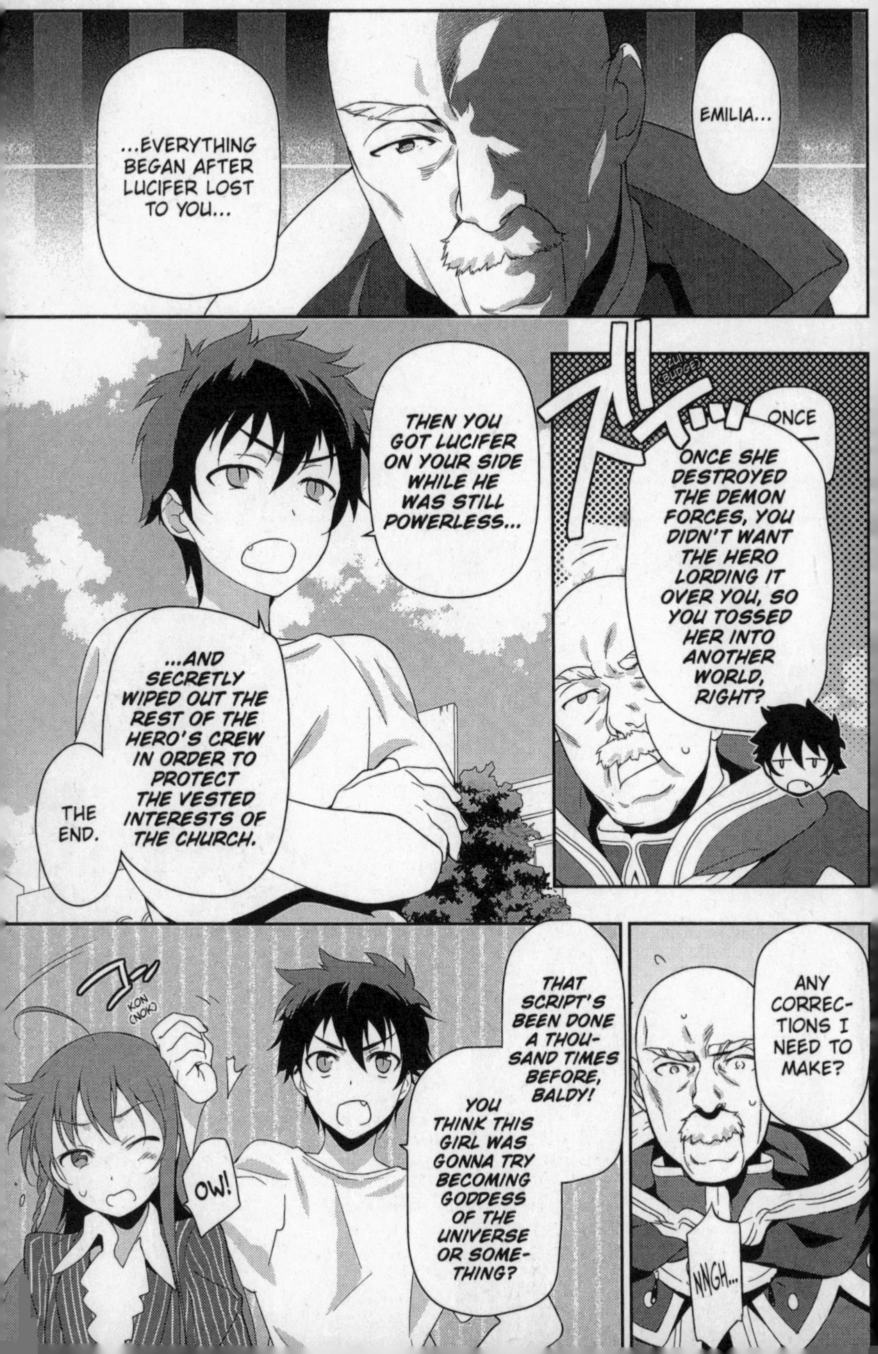
EMILIA...
...EVERYTHING BEGAN AFTER LUCIFER LOST TO YOU...
ZUI (BUDGE)
ONCE
ONCE SHE DESTROYED THE DEMON FORCES, YOU DIDN'T WANT THE HERO LORDING IT OVER YOU, SO YOU TOSSED HER INTO ANOTHER WORLD, RIGHT?
THEN YOU GOT LUCIFER ON YOUR SIDE WHILE HE WAS STILL POWERLESS...
...AND SECRETLY WIPED OUT THE REST OF THE HERO'S CREW IN ORDER TO PROTECT THE VESTED INTERESTS OF THE CHURCH.
THE END.
ANY CORREC-TIONS I NEED TO MAKE?
NNGH...
THAT SCRIPT'S BEEN DONE A THOU-SAND TIMES BEFORE, BALDY!
YOU THINK THIS GIRL WAS GONNA TRY BECOMING GODDESS OF THE UNIVERSE OR SOME-THING?
KON (NOK)
OW!

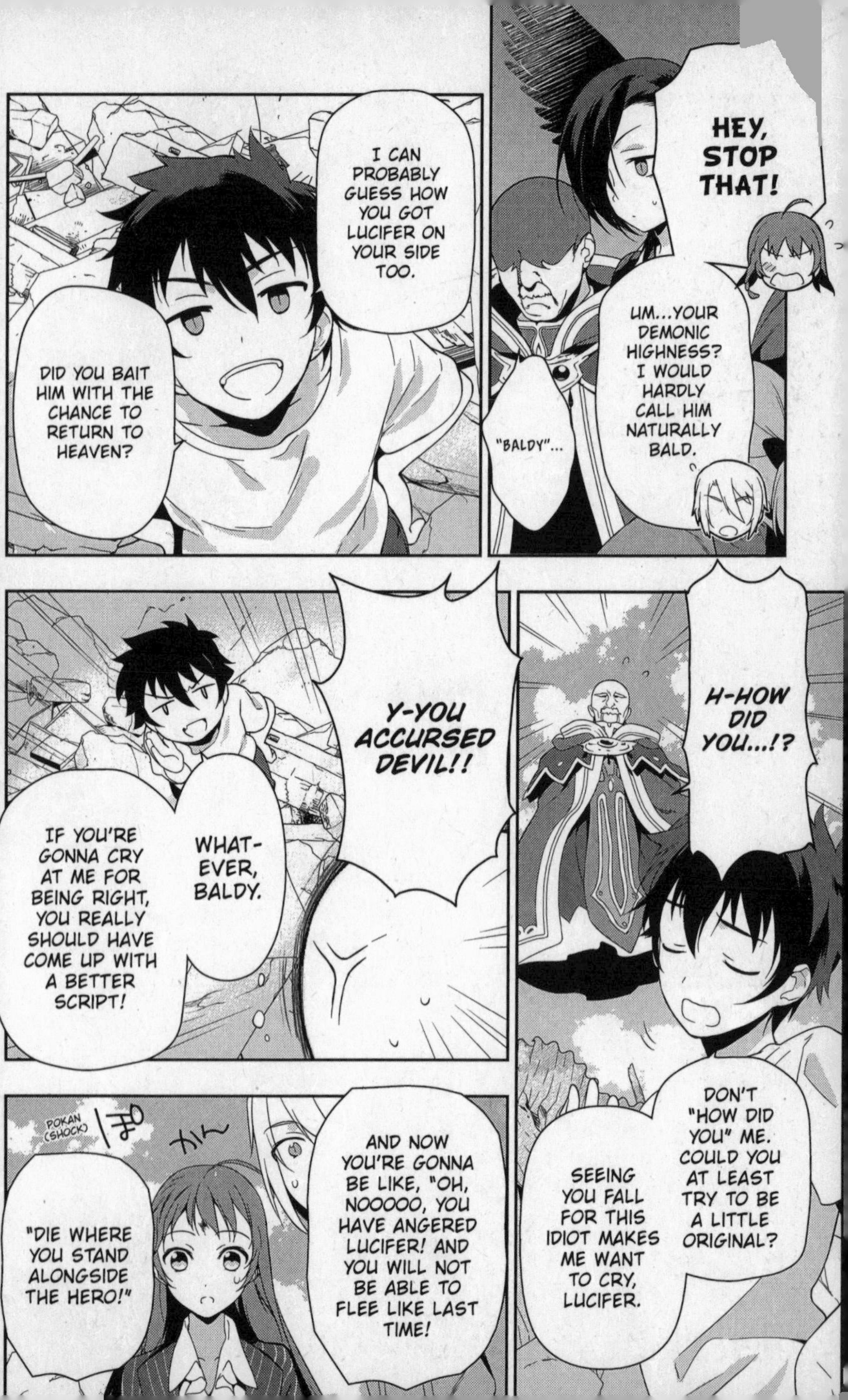
HEY, STOP THAT!
UM...YOUR DEMONIC HIGHNESS? I WOULD HARDLY CALL HIM NATURALLY BALD.
"BALDY"...
I CAN PROBABLY GUESS HOW YOU GOT LUCIFER ON YOUR SIDE TOO.
DID YOU BAIT HIM WITH THE CHANCE TO RETURN TO HEAVEN?
H-HOW DID YOU...!?
Y-YOU ACCURSED DEVIL!!
WHAT-EVER, BALDY.
IF YOU'RE GONNA CRY AT ME FOR BEING RIGHT, YOU REALLY SHOULD HAVE COME UP WITH A BETTER SCRIPT!
DON'T "HOW DID YOU" ME. COULD YOU AT LEAST TRY TO BE A LITTLE ORIGINAL?
SEEING YOU FALL FOR THIS IDIOT MAKES ME WANT TO CRY, LUCIFER.
AND NOW YOU'RE GONNA BE LIKE, "OH, NOOOOO, YOU HAVE ANGERED LUCIFER! AND YOU WILL NOT BE ABLE TO FLEE LIKE LAST TIME!
POKAN (SHOCK)
"DIE WHERE YOU STAND ALONGSIDE THE HERO!"

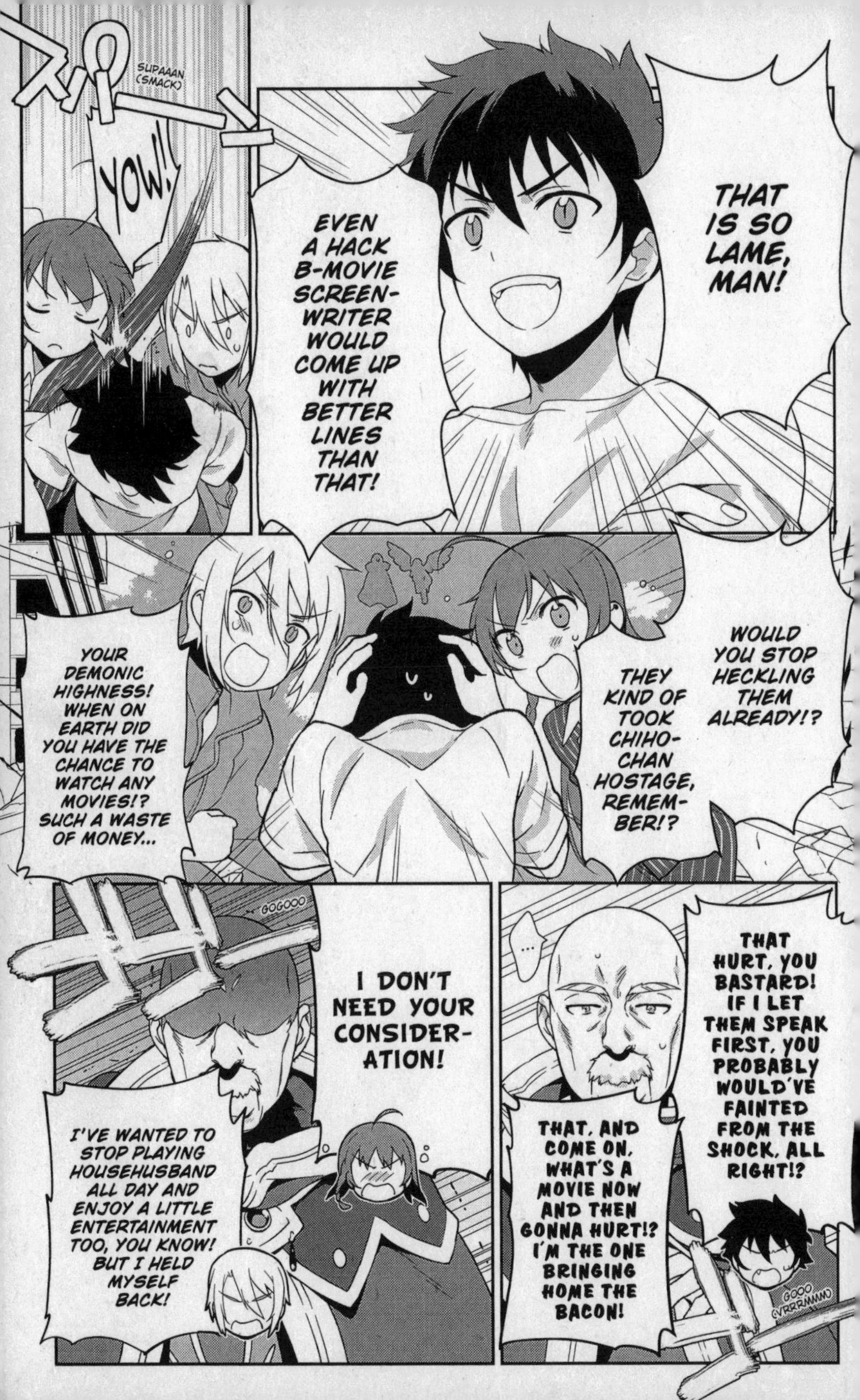
THAT IS SO LAME, MAN!
EVEN A HACK B-MOVIE SCREEN-WRITER WOULD COME UP WITH BETTER LINES THAN THAT!
SUPAAAN (SMACK)
YOW!!
WOULD YOU STOP HECKLING THEM ALREADY!?
THEY KIND OF TOOK CHIHO-CHAN HOSTAGE, REMEMBER!?
YOUR DEMONIC HIGHNESS! WHEN ON EARTH DID YOU HAVE THE CHANCE TO WATCH ANY MOVIES!? SUCH A WASTE OF MONEY...
...
THAT HURT, YOU BASTARD! IF I LET THEM SPEAK FIRST, YOU PROBABLY WOULD'VE FAINTED FROM THE SHOCK, ALL RIGHT!?
THAT, AND COME ON, WHAT'S A MOVIE NOW AND THEN GONNA HURT!? I'M THE ONE BRINGING HOME THE BACON!
GOOO (VRRRMMM)
GOGOOO
I DON'T NEED YOUR CONSIDER-ATION!
I'VE WANTED TO STOP PLAYING HOUSEHUSBAND ALL DAY AND ENJOY A LITTLE ENTERTAINMENT TOO, YOU KNOW! BUT I HELD MYSELF BACK!

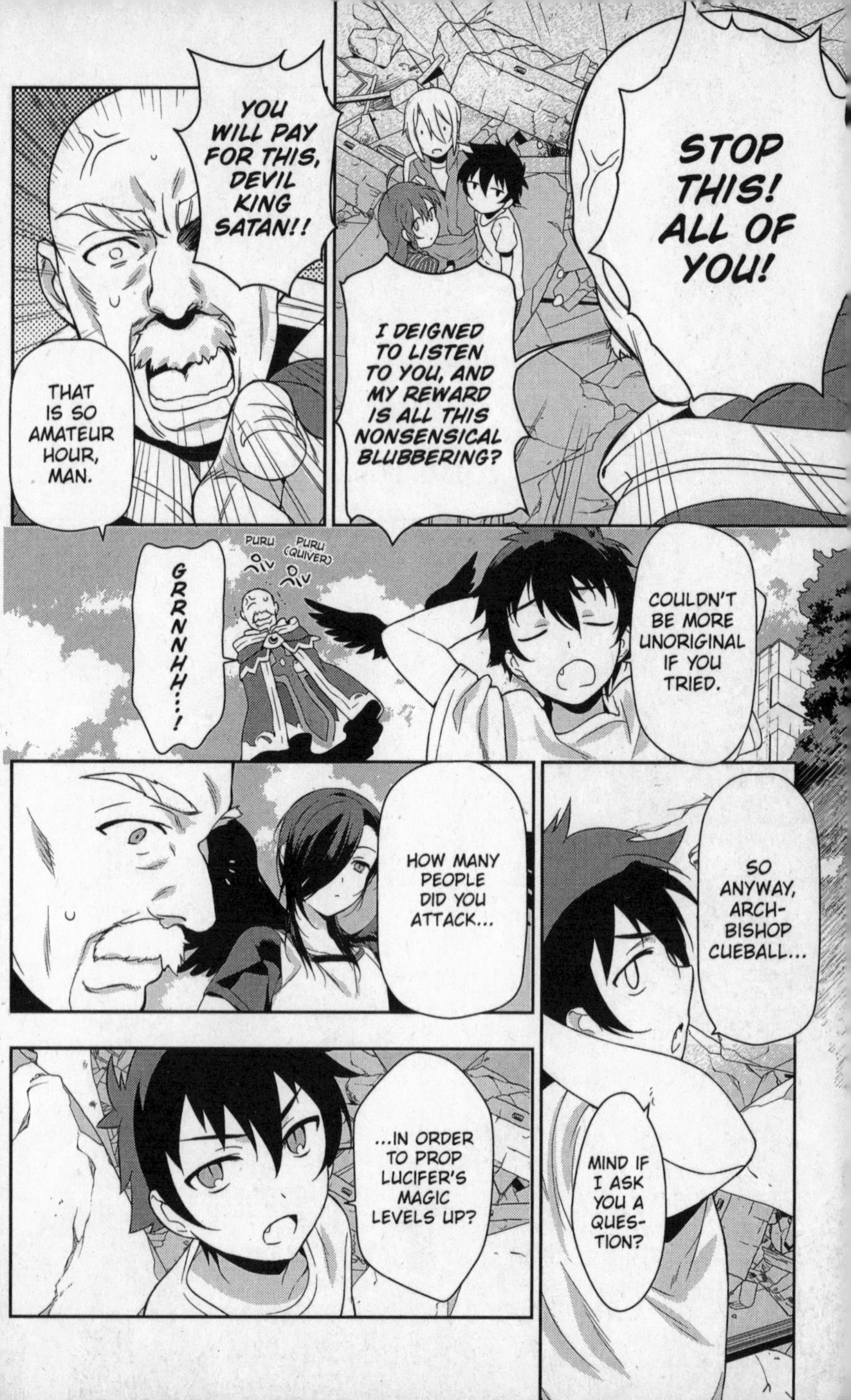

STOP THIS! ALL OF YOU!
I DEIGNED TO LISTEN TO YOU, AND MY REWARD IS ALL THIS NONSENSICAL BLUBBERING?
YOU WILL PAY FOR THIS, DEVIL KING SATAN!!
THAT IS SO AMATEUR HOUR, MAN.
COULDN'T BE MORE UNORIGINAL IF YOU TRIED.
PURU PURU (QUIVER)
GRRNNHH...!
SO ANYWAY, ARCH-BISHOP CUEBALL...
MIND IF I ASK YOU A QUES-TION?
HOW MANY PEOPLE DID YOU ATTACK...
...IN ORDER TO PROP LUCIFER'S MAGIC LEVELS UP?

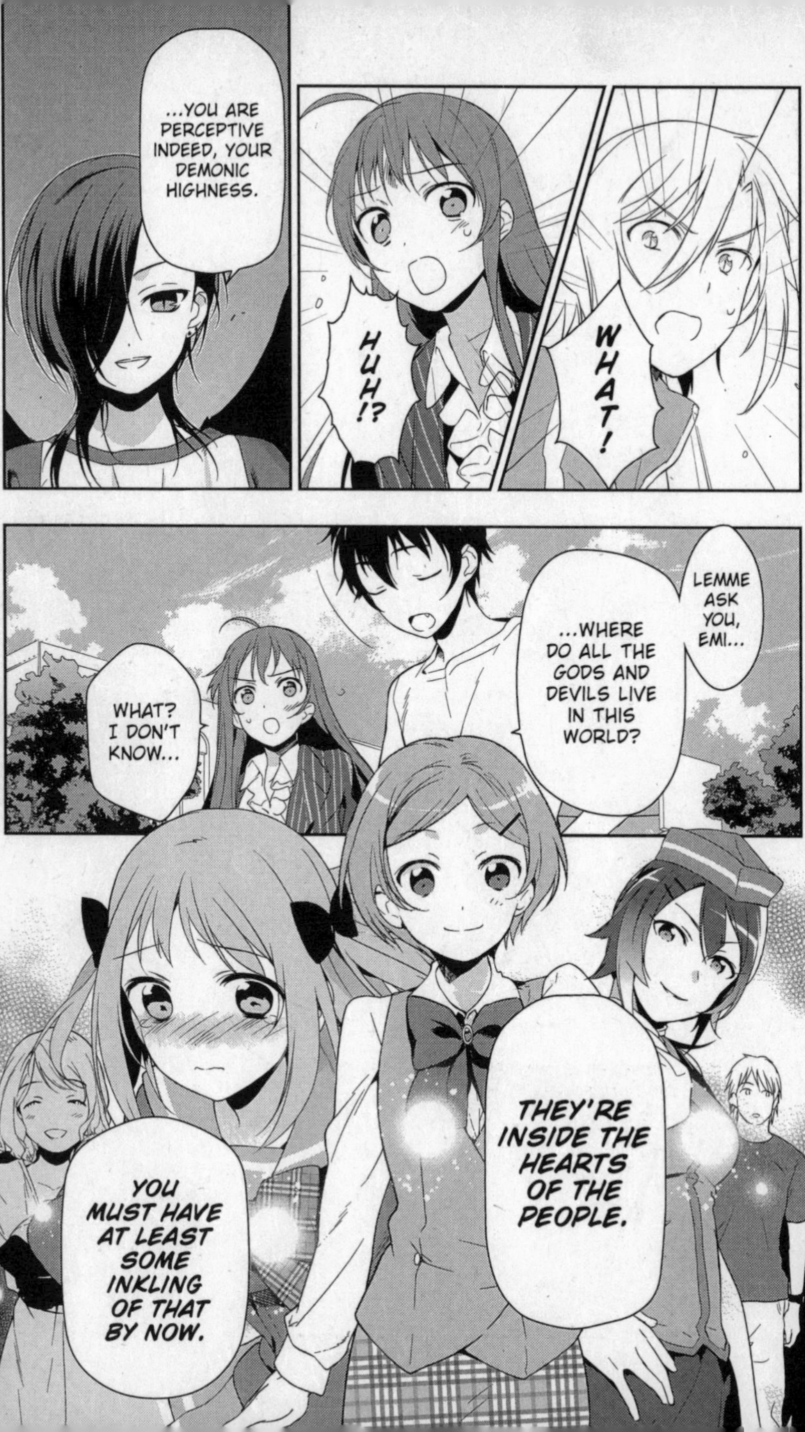
WHAT!
HUH!?
...YOU ARE PERCEPTIVE INDEED, YOUR DEMONIC HIGHNESS.
LEMME ASK YOU, EMI...
...WHERE DO ALL THE GODS AND DEVILS LIVE IN THIS WORLD?
WHAT? I DON'T KNOW...
THEY'RE INSIDE THE HEARTS OF THE PEOPLE.
YOU MUST HAVE AT LEAST SOME INKLING OF THAT BY NOW.

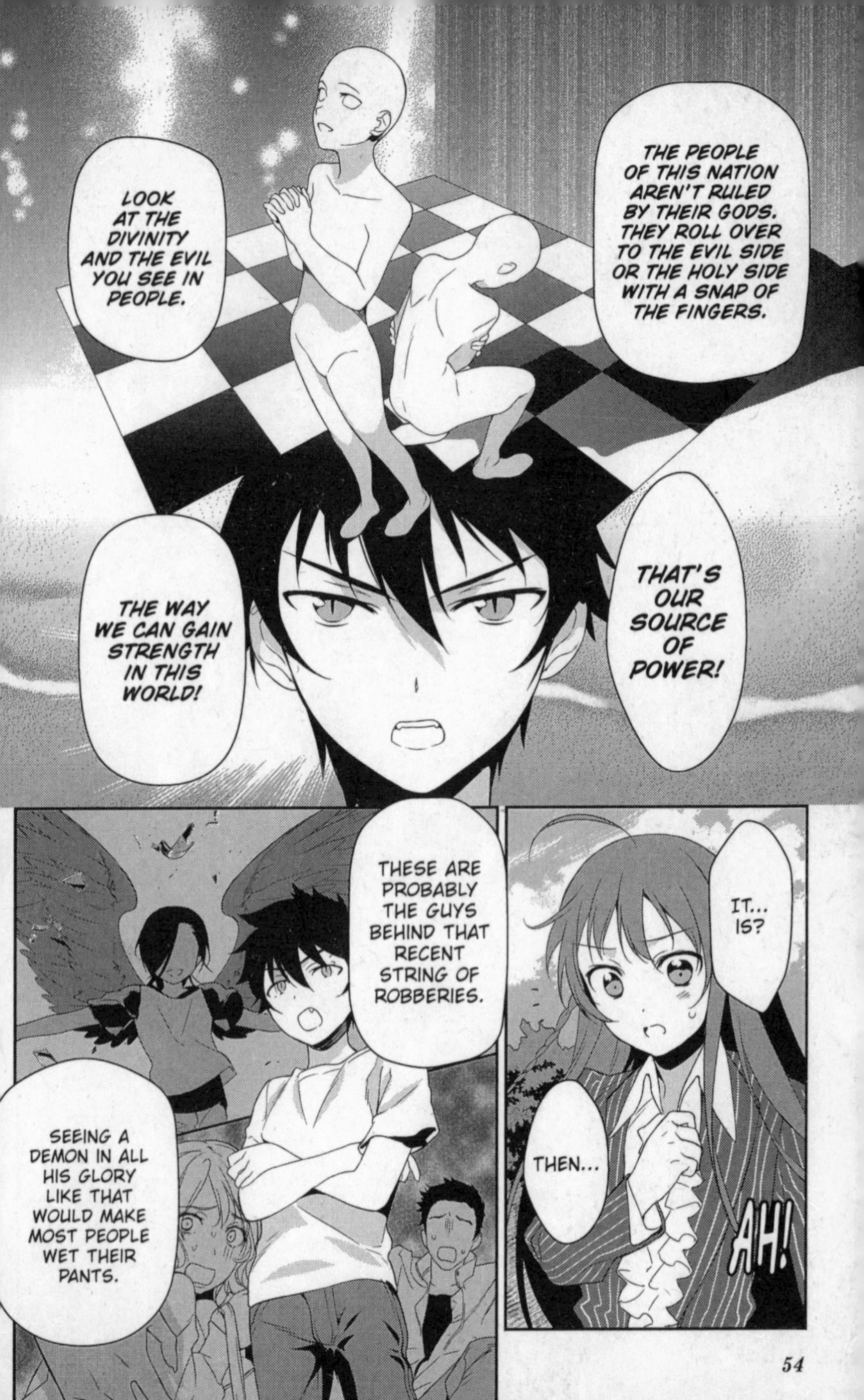
THE PEOPLE OF THIS NATION AREN'T RULED BY THEIR GODS. THEY ROLL OVER TO THE EVIL SIDE OR THE HOLY SIDE WITH A SNAP OF THE FINGERS.
LOOK AT THE DIVINITY AND THE EVIL YOU SEE IN PEOPLE.
THAT'S OUR SOURCE OF POWER!
THE WAY WE CAN GAIN STRENGTH IN THIS WORLD!
IT... IS?
THEN...
AH!
THESE ARE PROBABLY THE GUYS BEHIND THAT RECENT STRING OF ROBBERIES.
SEEING A DEMON IN ALL HIS GLORY LIKE THAT WOULD MAKE MOST PEOPLE WET THEIR PANTS.

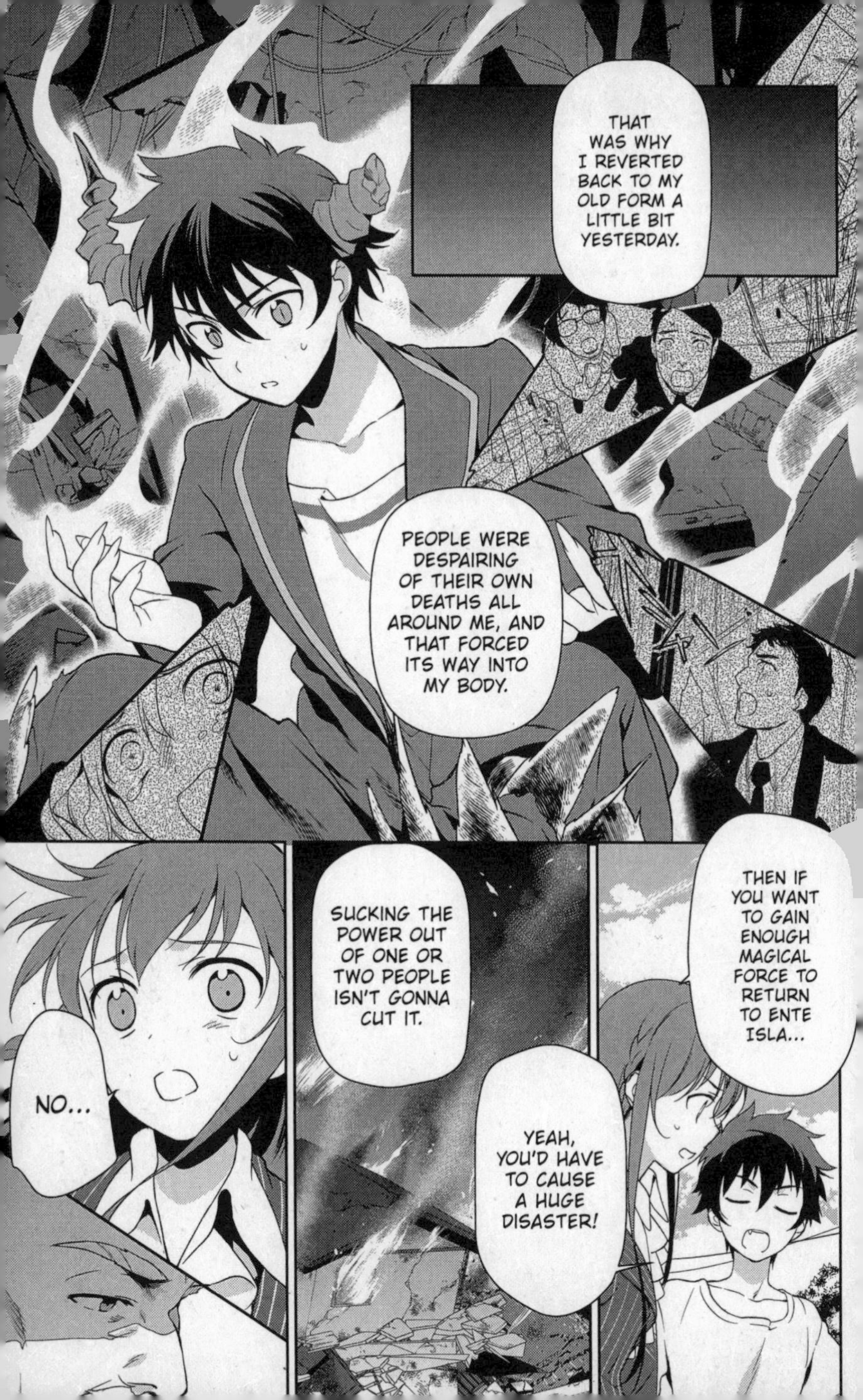
THAT WAS WHY I REVERTED BACK TO MY OLD FORM A LITTLE BIT YESTERDAY.
PEOPLE WERE DESPAIRING OF THEIR OWN DEATHS ALL AROUND ME, AND THAT FORCED ITS WAY INTO MY BODY.
THEN IF YOU WANT TO GAIN ENOUGH MAGICAL FORCE TO RETURN TO ENTE ISLA...
YEAH, YOU'D HAVE TO CAUSE A HUGE DISASTER!
SUCKING THE POWER OUT OF ONE OR TWO PEOPLE ISN'T GONNA CUT IT.
NO...

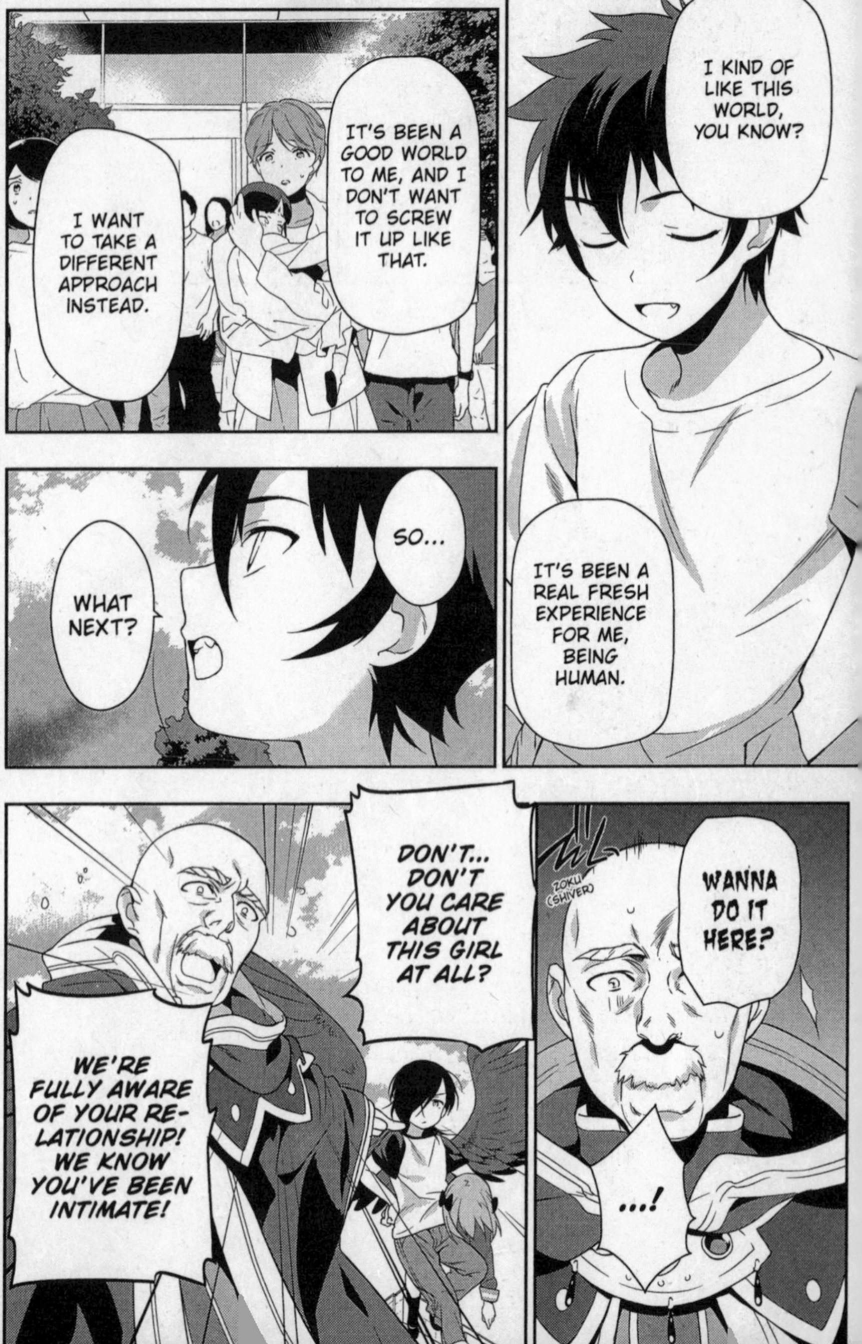
I KIND OF LIKE THIS WORLD, YOU KNOW?
IT'S BEEN A REAL FRESH EXPERIENCE FOR ME, BEING HUMAN.
IT'S BEEN A GOOD WORLD TO ME, AND I DON'T WANT TO SCREW IT UP LIKE THAT.
I WANT TO TAKE A DIFFERENT APPROACH INSTEAD.
SO...
WHAT NEXT?
ZOKU (SHIVER)
WANNA DO IT HERE?
...!
DON'T... DON'T YOU CARE ABOUT THIS GIRL AT ALL?
WE'RE FULLY AWARE OF YOUR RE-LATIONSHIP! WE KNOW YOU'VE BEEN INTIMATE!

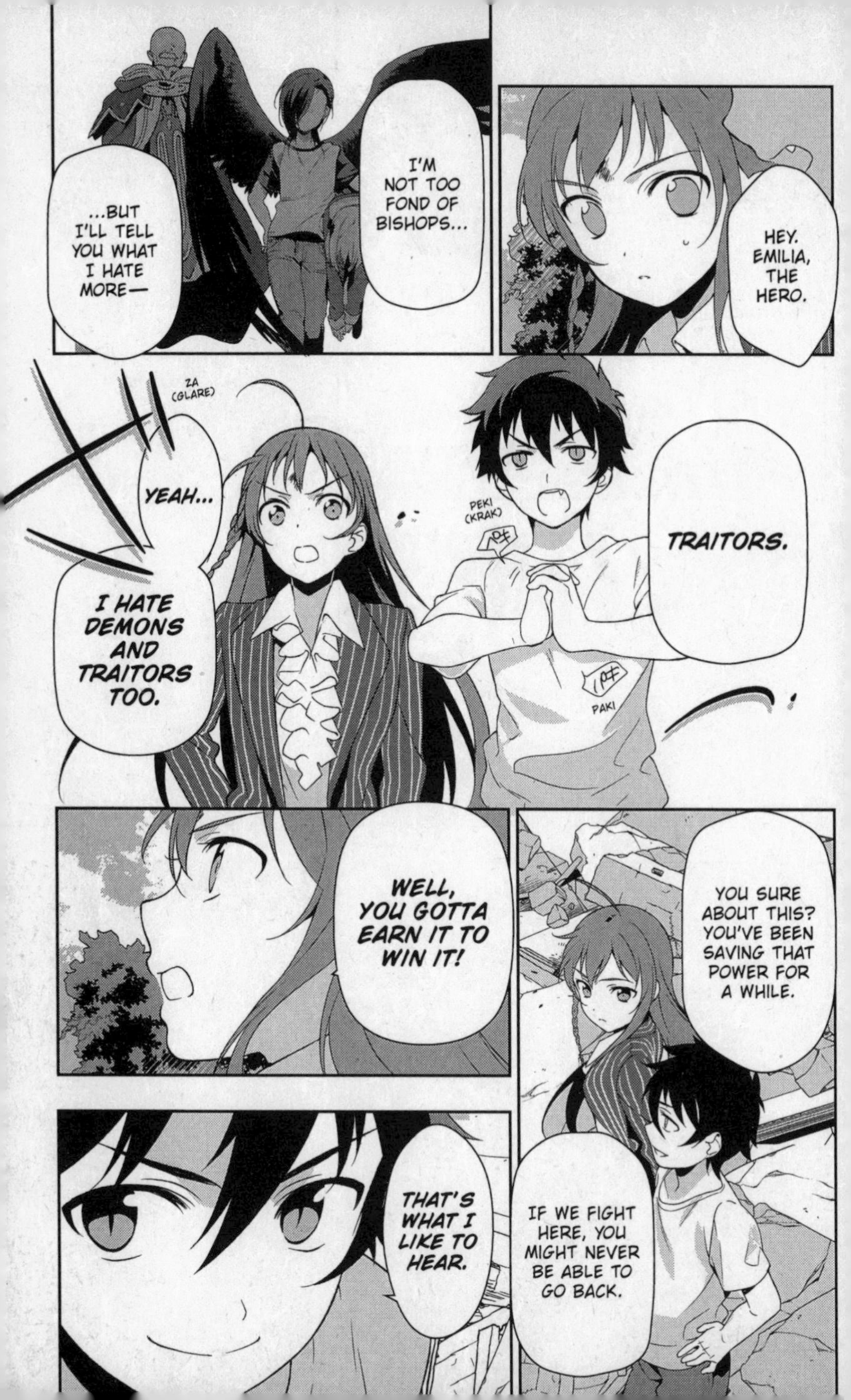
HEY. EMILIA, THE HERO.
I'M NOT TOO FOND OF BISHOPS...
...BUT I'LL TELL YOU WHAT I HATE MORE—
TRAITORS.
PEKI (KRAK)
PAKI
ZA (GLARE)
YEAH...
I HATE DEMONS AND TRAITORS TOO.
YOU SURE ABOUT THIS? YOU'VE BEEN SAVING THAT POWER FOR A WHILE.
IF WE FIGHT HERE, YOU MIGHT NEVER BE ABLE TO GO BACK.
WELL, YOU GOTTA EARN IT TO WIN IT!
THAT'S WHAT I LIKE TO HEAR.

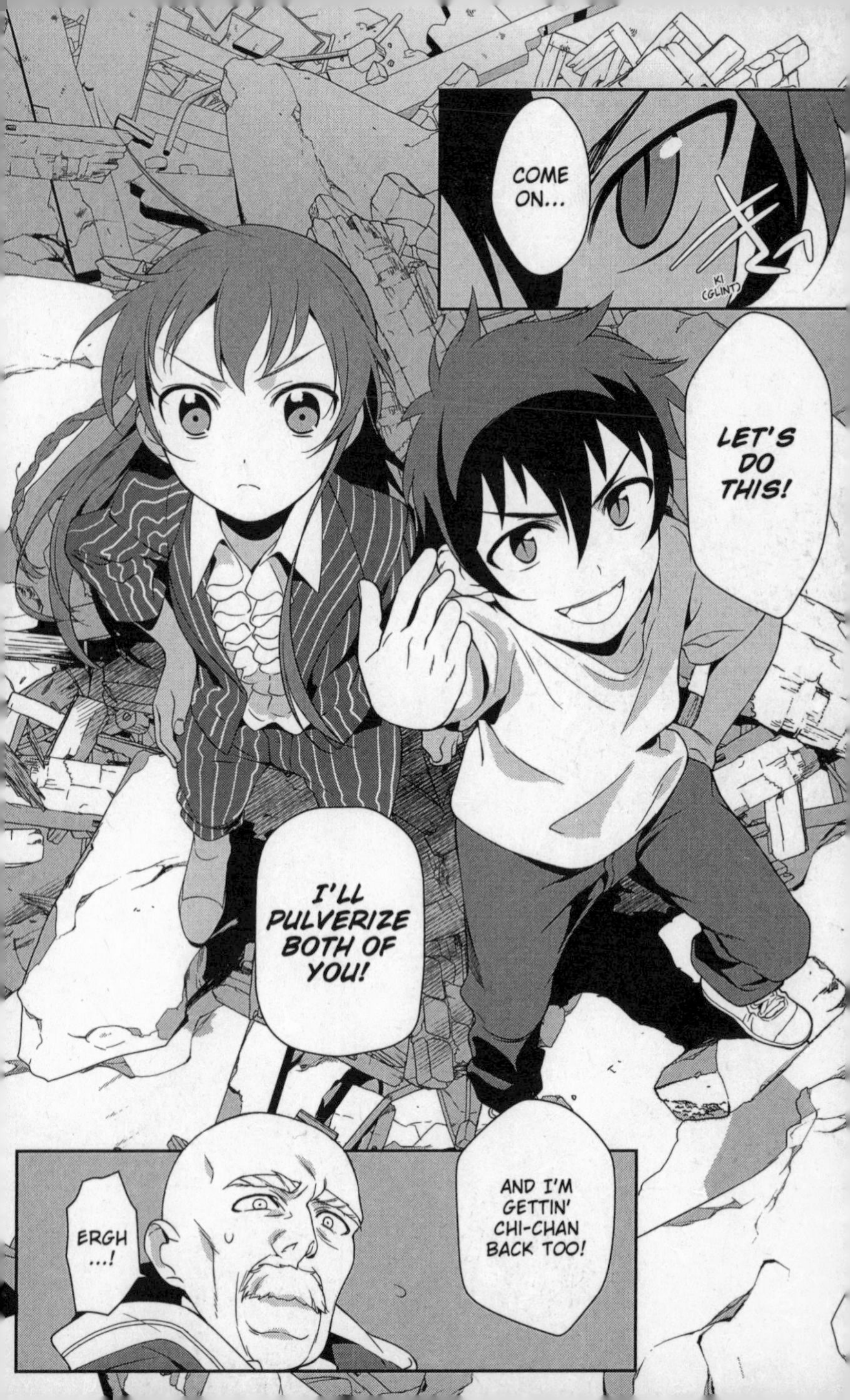
COME ON...
KI (GLINT)
LET'S DO THIS!
I'LL PULVERIZE BOTH OF YOU!
AND I'M GETTIN' CHI-CHAN BACK TOO!
ERGH ...!

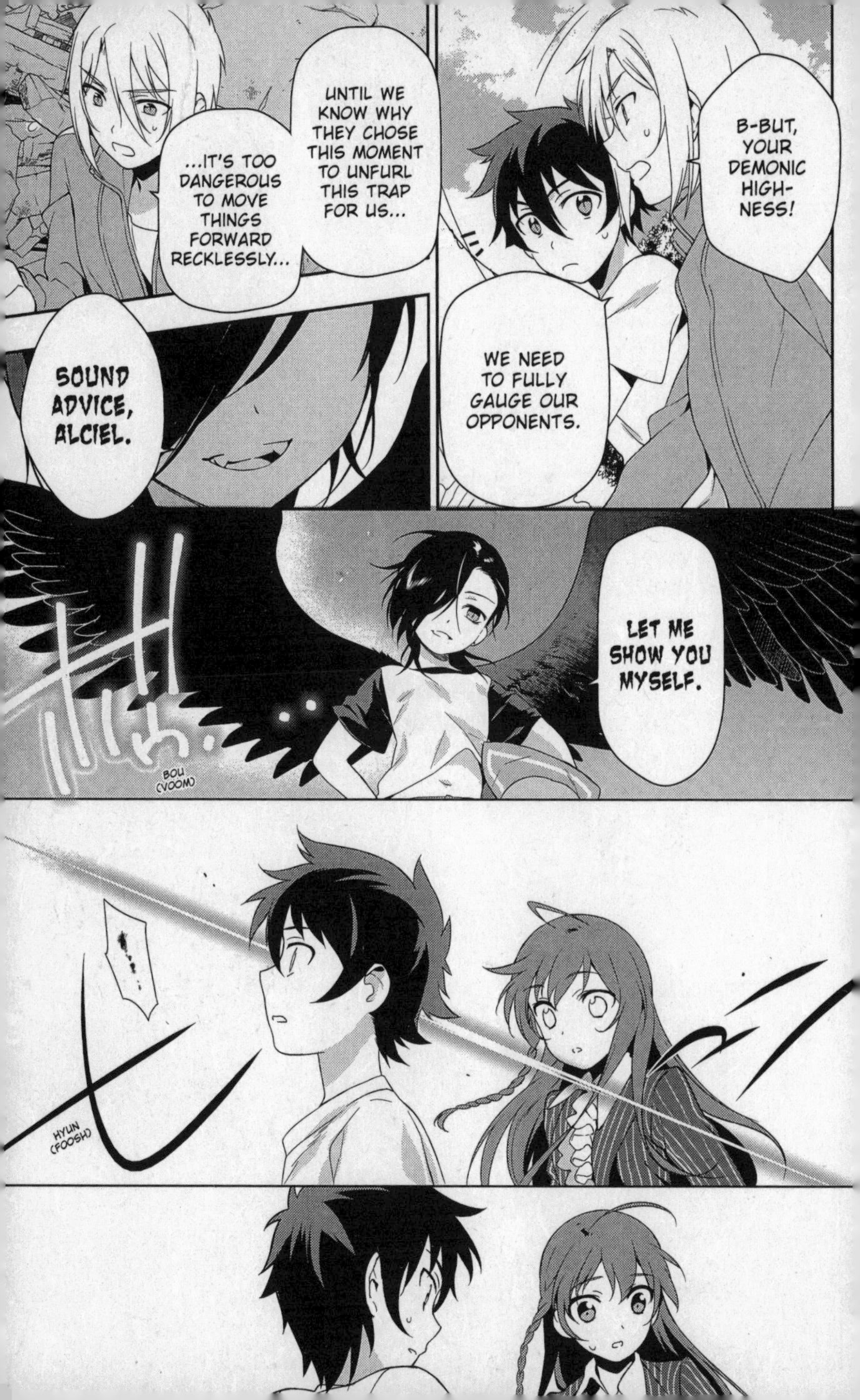
B-BUT, YOUR DEMONIC HIGHNESS!
WE NEED TO FULLY GAUGE OUR OPPONENTS.
UNTIL WE KNOW WHY THEY CHOSE THIS MOMENT TO UNFURL THIS TRAP FOR US...
...IT'S TOO DANGEROUS TO MOVE THINGS FORWARD RECKLESSLY...
SOUND ADVICE, ALCIEL.
LET ME SHOW YOU MYSELF.
BOU (VOOM)
HYUN (FOOSH)

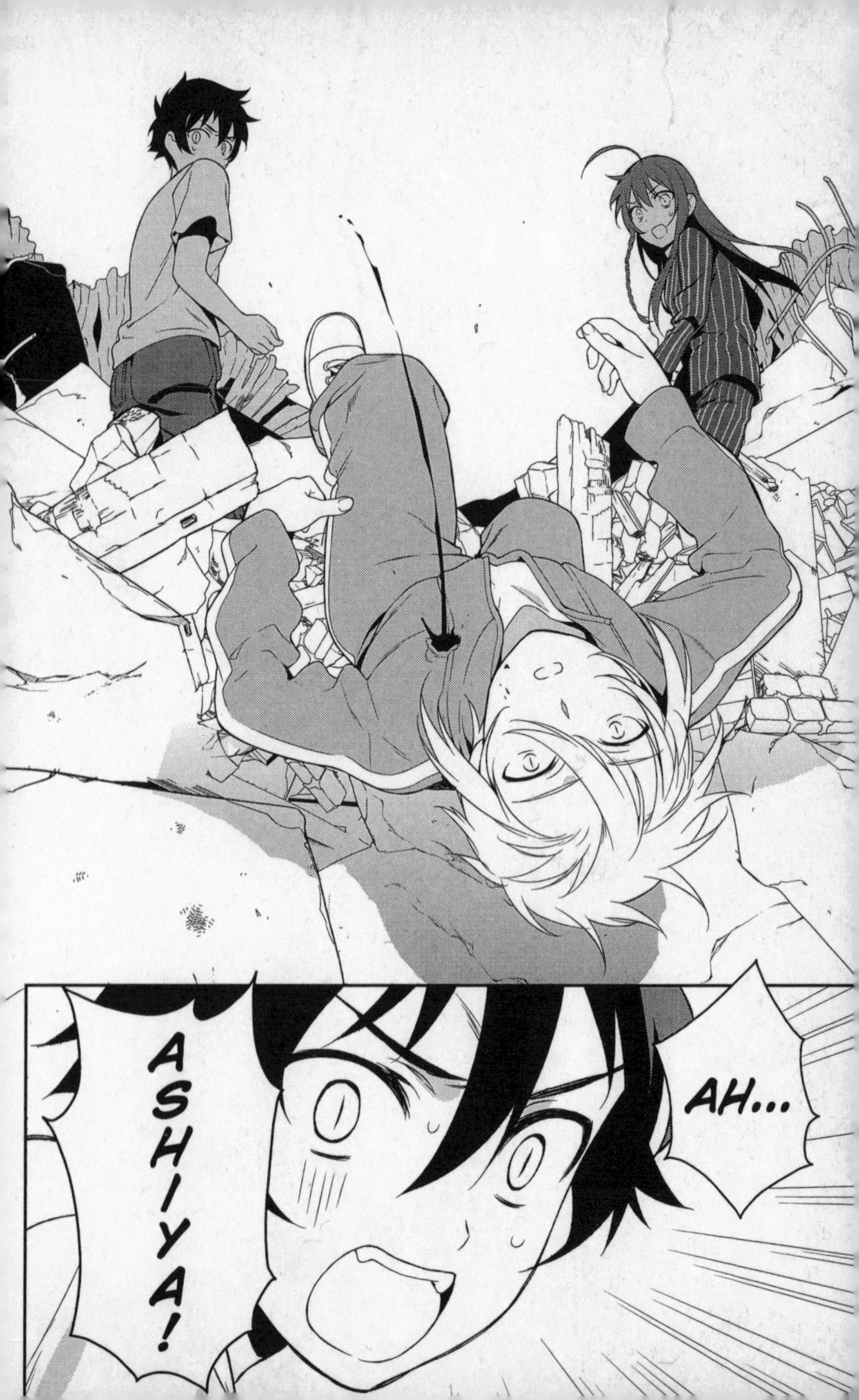
AH...
ASHIYA!

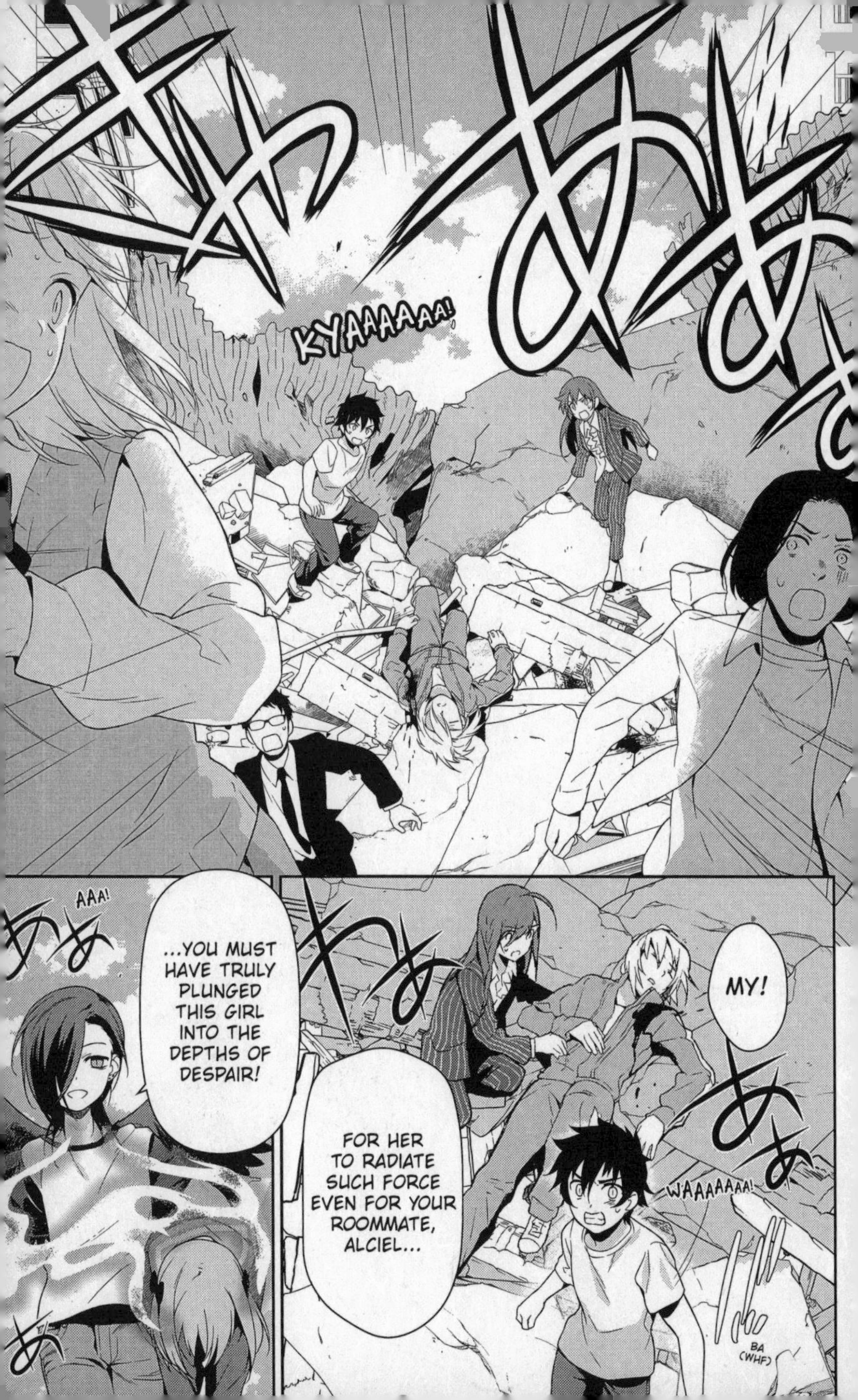
KYAAAAAAA!
MY!
WAAAAAAA!
FOR HER TO RADIATE SUCH FORCE EVEN FOR YOUR ROOMMATE, ALCIEL...
BA (WHF)
AAA!
...YOU MUST HAVE TRULY PLUNGED THIS GIRL INTO THE DEPTHS OF DESPAIR!

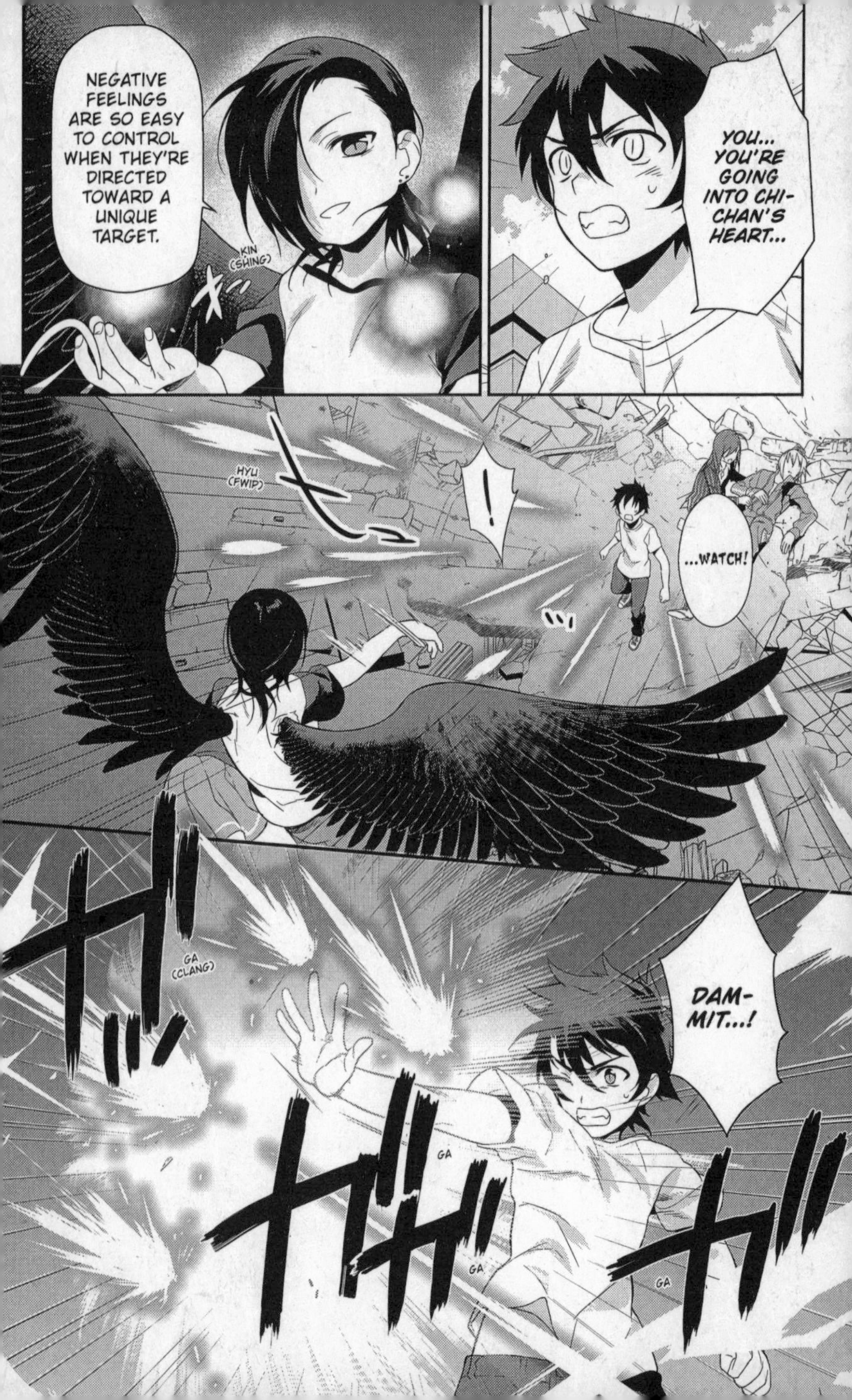
YOU... YOU'RE GOING INTO CHI-CHAN'S HEART...
NEGATIVE FEELINGS ARE SO EASY TO CONTROL WHEN THEY'RE DIRECTED TOWARD A UNIQUE TARGET.
KIN (SHING)
!
...WATCH!
HYU (FWIP)
DAM-MIT...!
GA (CLANG)
GA
GA
GA

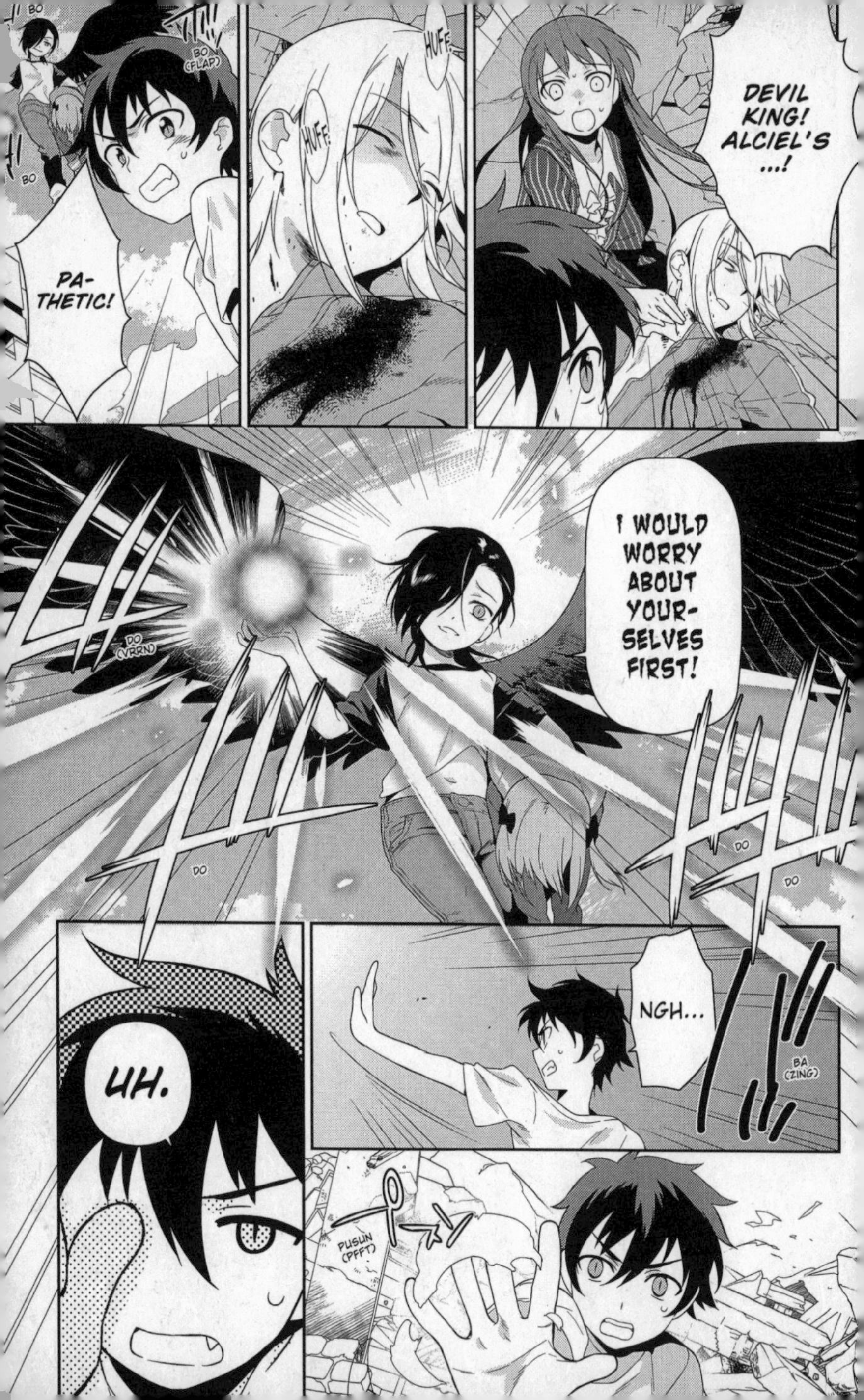
DEVIL KING! ALCIEL'S ...!
HUFF
HUFF
BO
BO (FLAP)
PA-THETIC!
BO
I WOULD WORRY ABOUT YOUR-SELVES FIRST!
DO (VRRN)
DO
DO
DO
NGH...
BA (ZING)
PUSUN (PFFT)
UH.

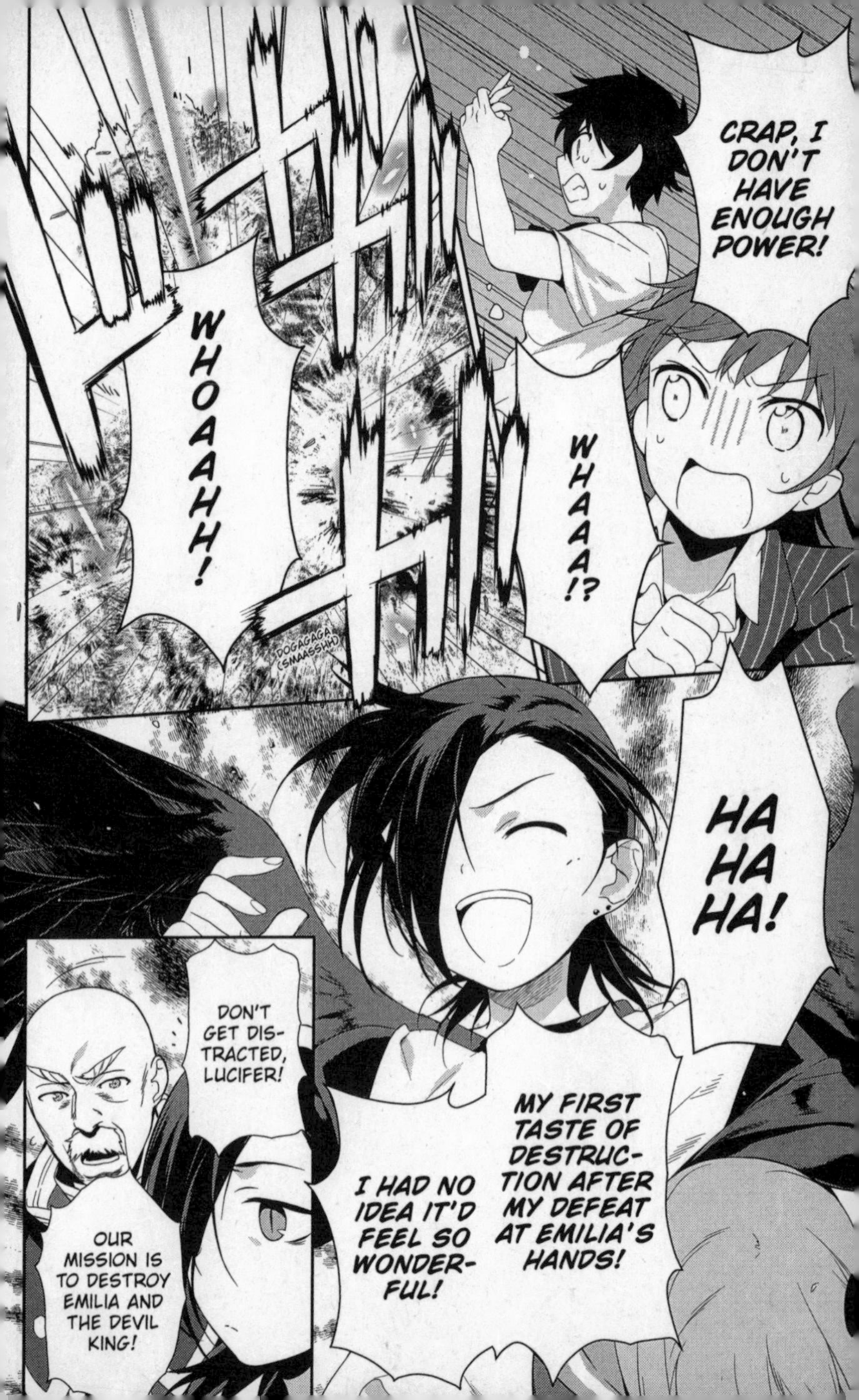
CRAP, I DON'T HAVE ENOUGH POWER!
WHAAAA!?
WHOAAAHH!
DOGAGAGA (SMAASSHH)
HA HA HA!
MY FIRST TASTE OF DESTRUCTION AFTER MY DEFEAT AT EMILIA'S HANDS!
I HAD NO IDEA IT'D FEEL SO WONDERFUL!
DON'T GET DISTRACTED, LUCIFER!
OUR MISSION IS TO DESTROY EMILIA AND THE DEVIL KING!

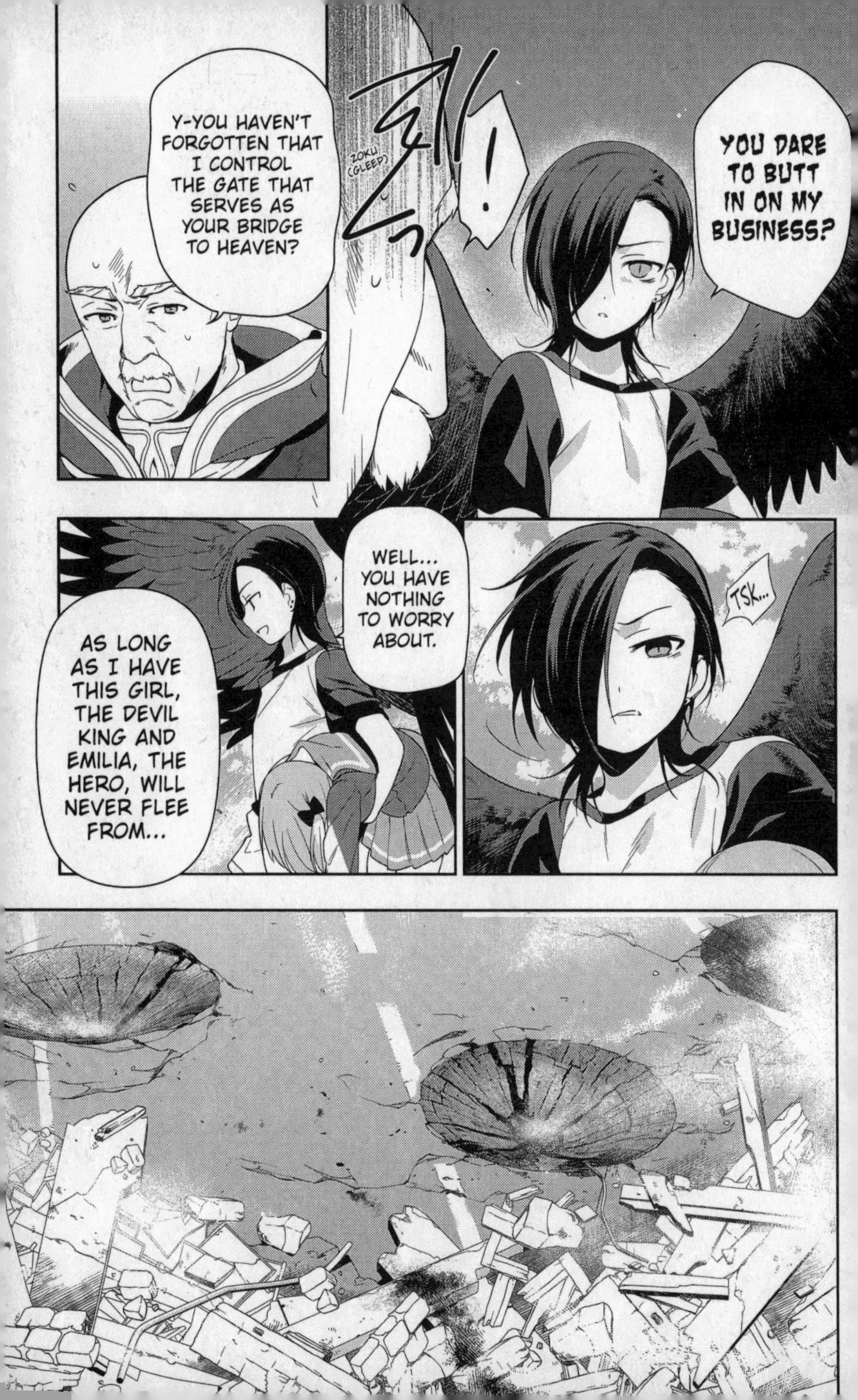
YOU DARE TO BUTT IN ON MY BUSINESS?
!
ZOKU (GLEEP)
Y-YOU HAVEN'T FORGOTTEN THAT I CONTROL THE GATE THAT SERVES AS YOUR BRIDGE TO HEAVEN?
TSK...
WELL... YOU HAVE NOTHING TO WORRY ABOUT.
AS LONG AS I HAVE THIS GIRL, THE DEVIL KING AND EMILIA, THE HERO, WILL NEVER FLEE FROM...

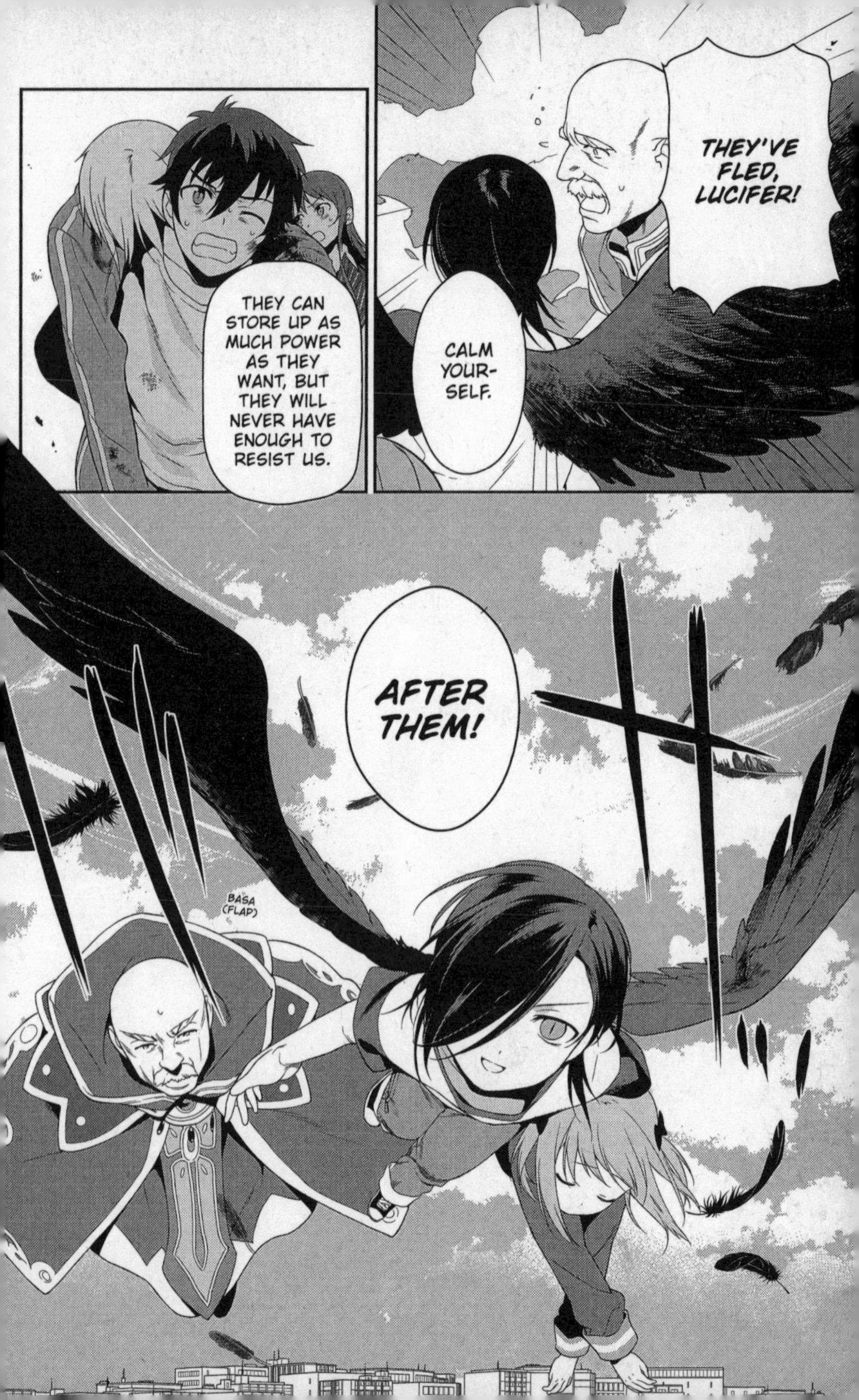
THEY'VE FLED, LUCIFER!
CALM YOURSELF.
THEY CAN STORE UP AS MUCH POWER AS THEY WANT, BUT THEY WILL NEVER HAVE ENOUGH TO RESIST US.
AFTER THEM!
BASA (FLAP)

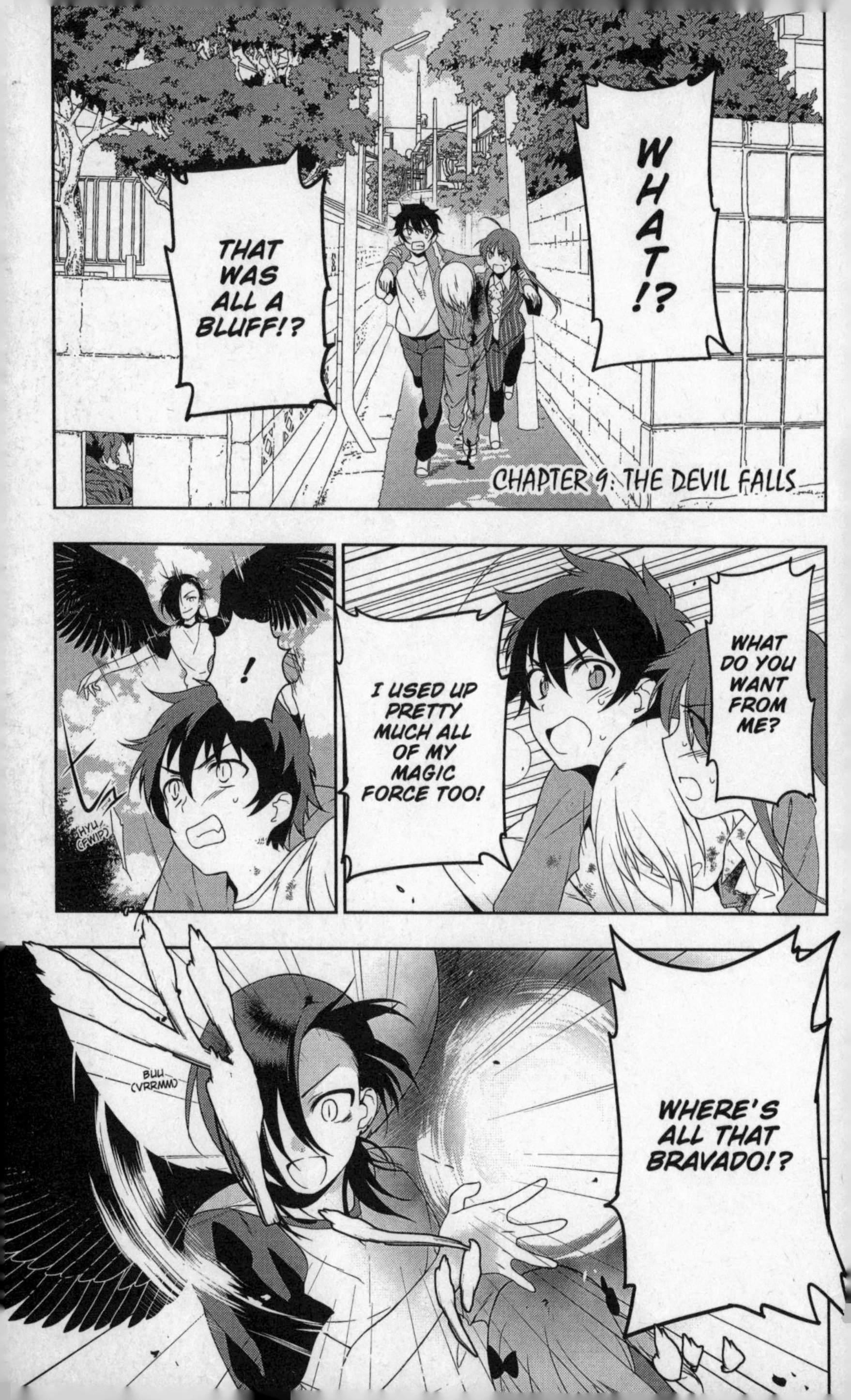
WHAT!?
THAT WAS ALL A BLUFF!?
CHAPTER 9: THE DEVIL FALLS
WHAT DO YOU WANT FROM ME?
I USED UP PRETTY MUCH ALL OF MY MAGIC FORCE TOO!
!
HYU (FWIP)
WHERE'S ALL THAT BRAVADO!?
BUU (VRRMM)

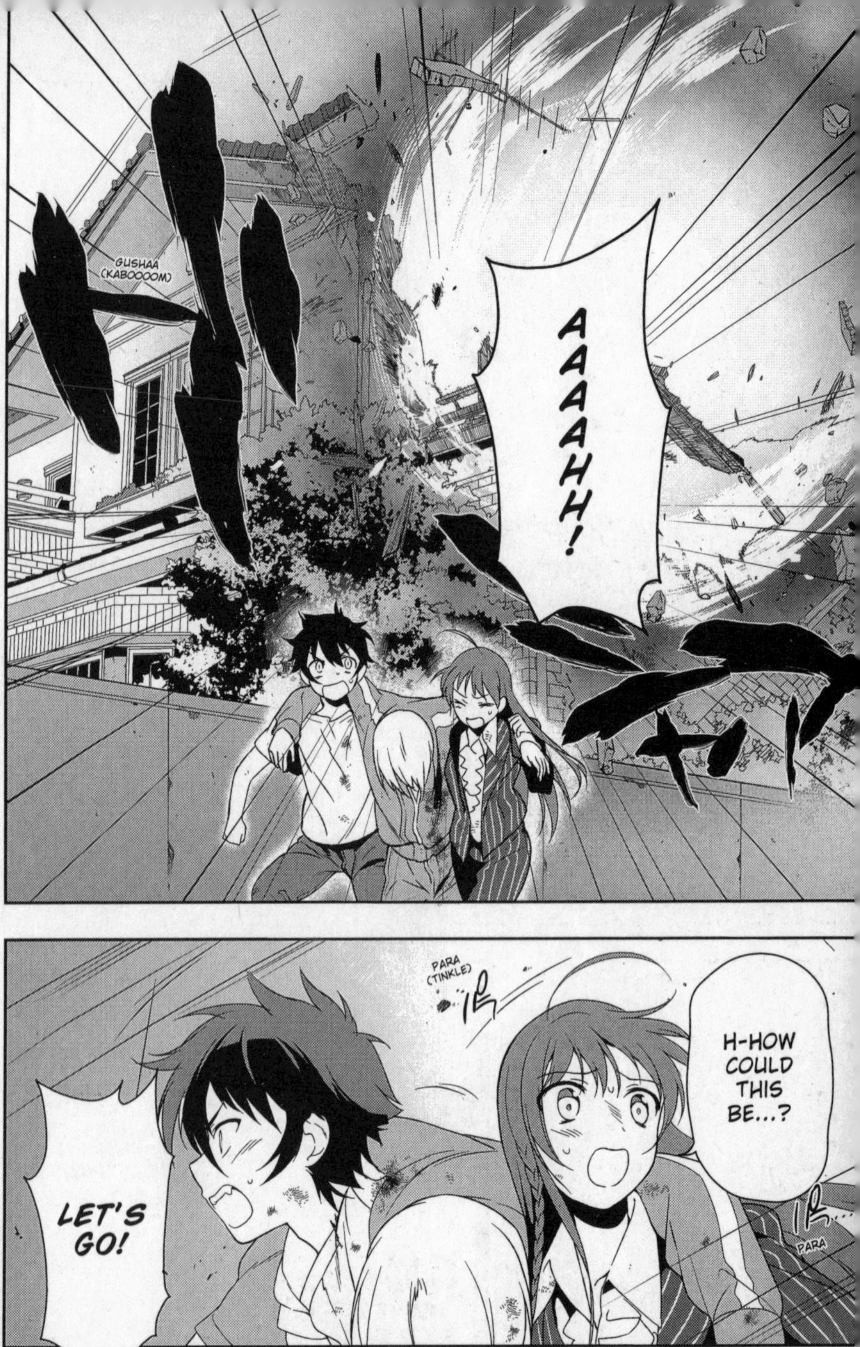
AAAAAHH!
GUSHAA (KABOOOOM)
H-HOW COULD THIS BE...?
PARA (TINKLE)
PARA
LET'S GO!

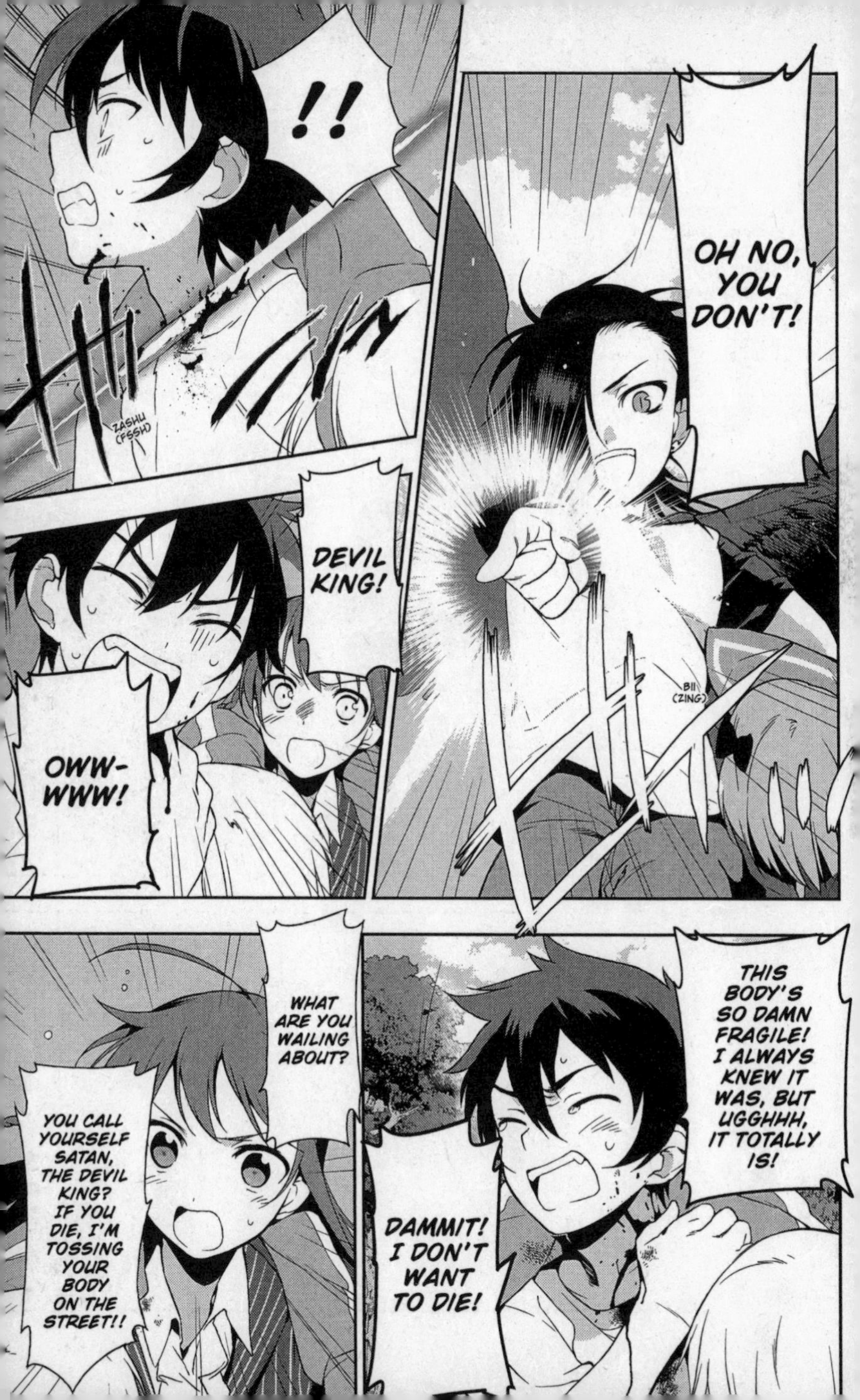

OH NO, YOU DON'T!
BII (ZING)
!!
ZASHU (FSSH)
DEVIL KING!
OWW-WWW!
THIS BODY'S SO DAMN FRAGILE! I ALWAYS KNEW IT WAS, BUT UGGHHH, IT TOTALLY IS!
DAMMIT! I DON'T WANT TO DIE!
WHAT ARE YOU WAILING ABOUT?
YOU CALL YOURSELF SATAN, THE DEVIL KING? IF YOU DIE, I'M TOSSING YOUR BODY ON THE STREET!!

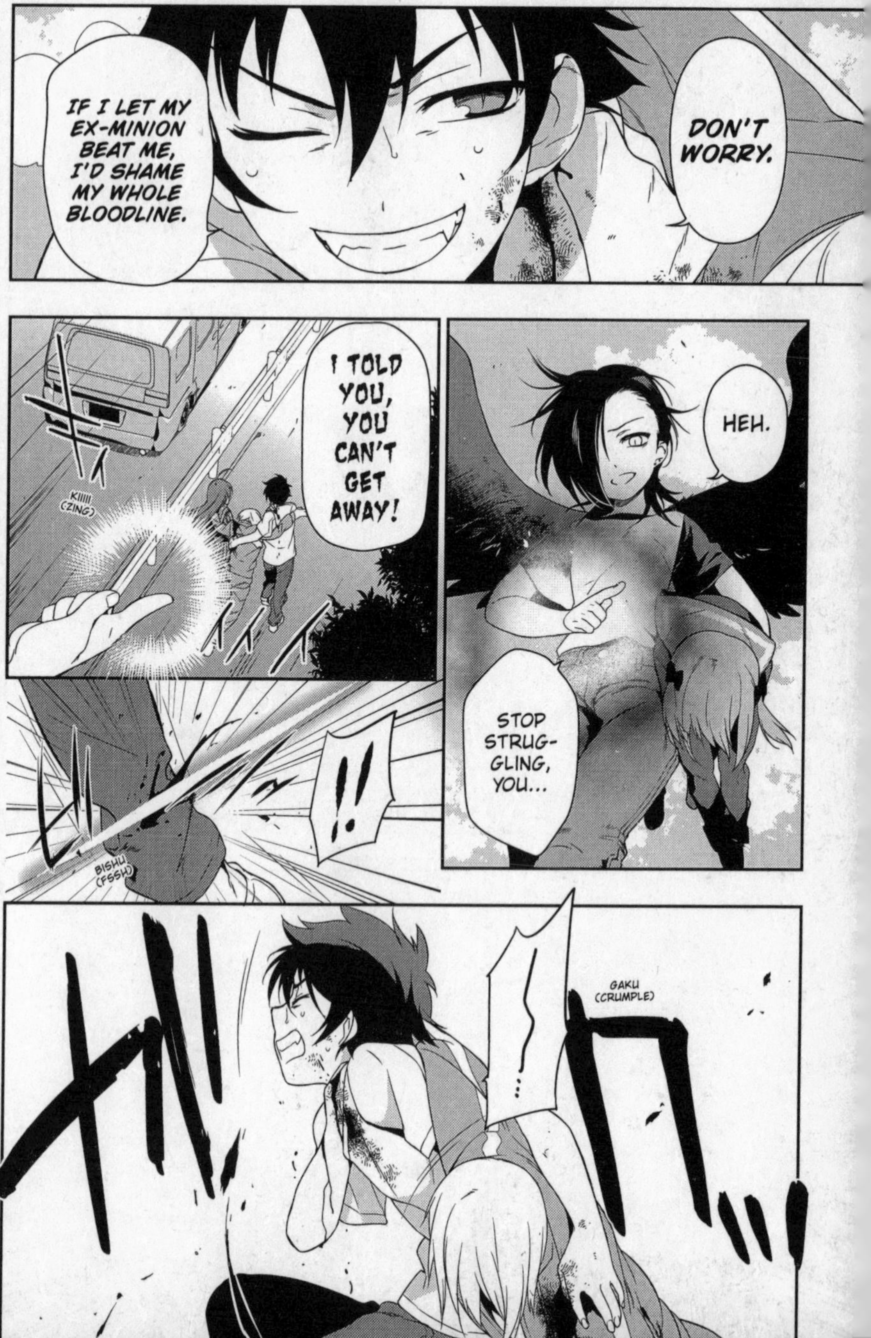
DON'T WORRY.
IF I LET MY EX-MINION BEAT ME, I'D SHAME MY WHOLE BLOODLINE.
HEH.
STOP STRUG-GLING, YOU...
I TOLD YOU, YOU CAN'T GET AWAY!
KIIIII (ZING)
!!
BISHU (FSSH)
!...
GAKU (CRUMPLE)

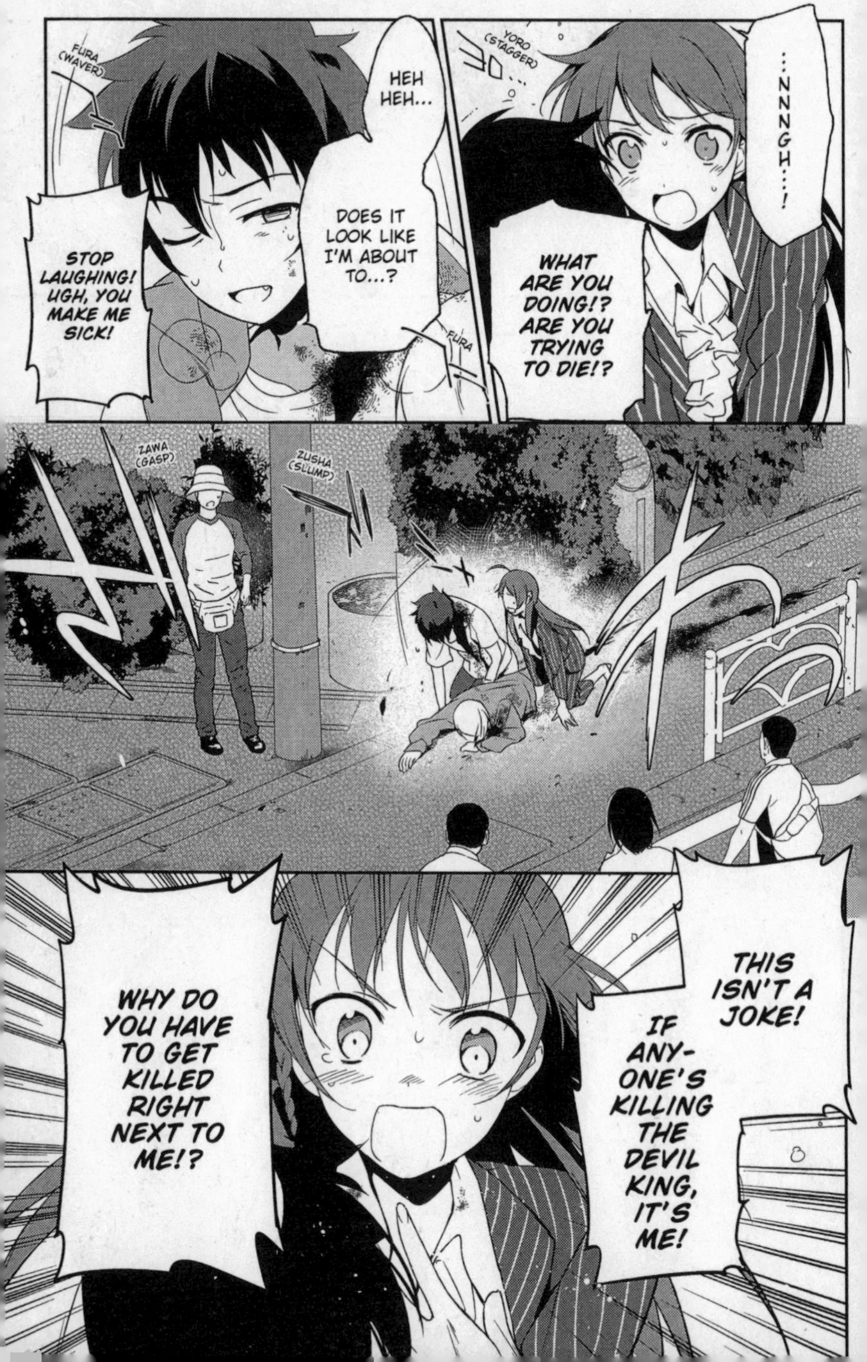
...NNNGH...!
YORO (STAGGER)
WHAT ARE YOU DOING!? ARE YOU TRYING TO DIE!?
HEH HEH...
FURA (WAVER)
DOES IT LOOK LIKE I'M ABOUT TO...?
FURA
STOP LAUGHING! UGH, YOU MAKE ME SICK!
ZUSHA (SLUMP)
ZAWA (GASP)
THIS ISN'T A JOKE!
IF ANY-ONE'S KILLING THE DEVIL KING, IT'S ME!
WHY DO YOU HAVE TO GET KILLED RIGHT NEXT TO ME!?

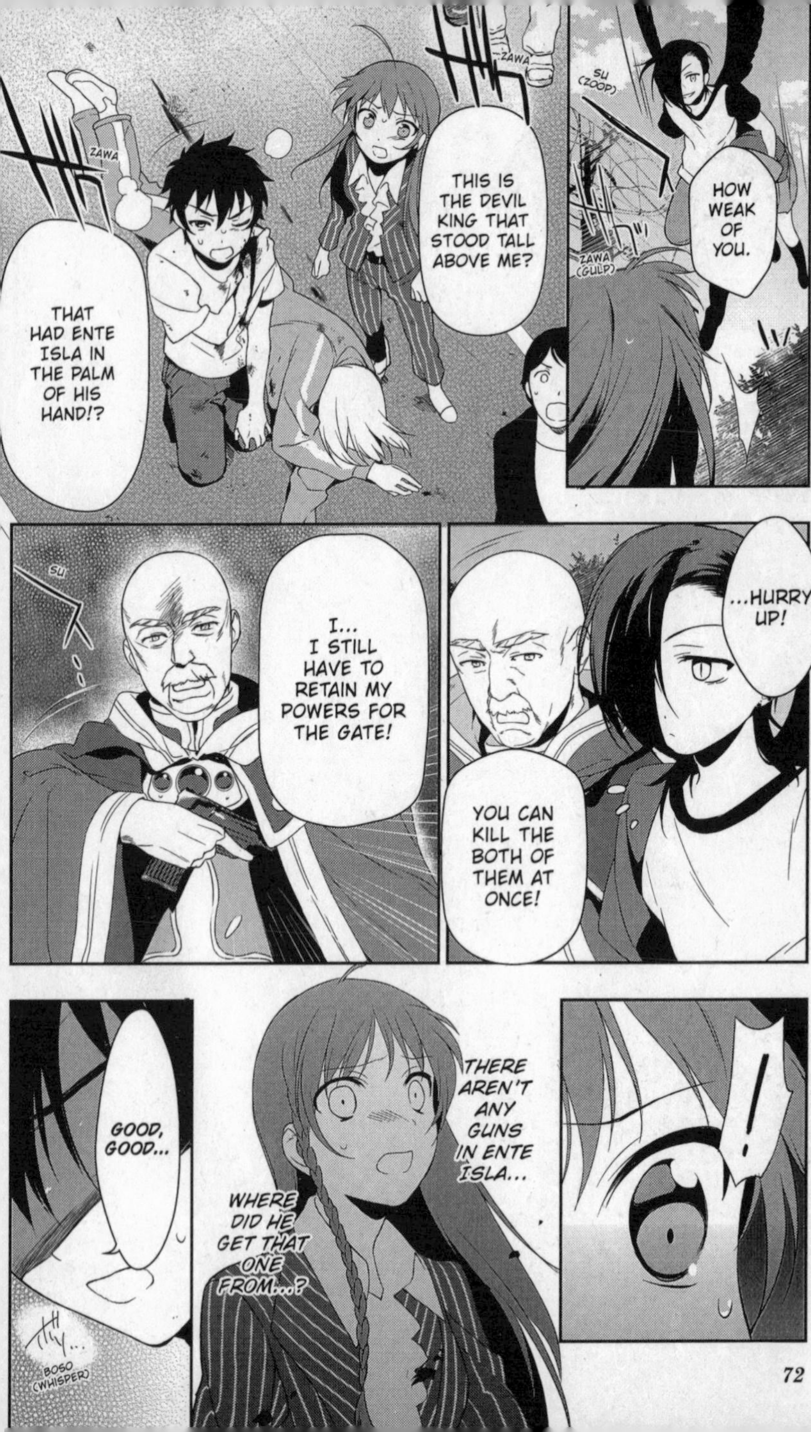
SU (ZOOP)
HOW WEAK OF YOU.
ZAWA (GULP)
ZAWA
THIS IS THE DEVIL KING THAT STOOD TALL ABOVE ME?
ZAWA
THAT HAD ENTE ISLA IN THE PALM OF HIS HAND!?
...HURRY UP!
YOU CAN KILL THE BOTH OF THEM AT ONCE!
SU
I... I STILL HAVE TO RETAIN MY POWERS FOR THE GATE!
!
THERE AREN'T ANY GUNS IN ENTE ISLA...
WHERE DID HE GET THAT ONE FROM...?
GOOD, GOOD...
BOSO (WHISPER)

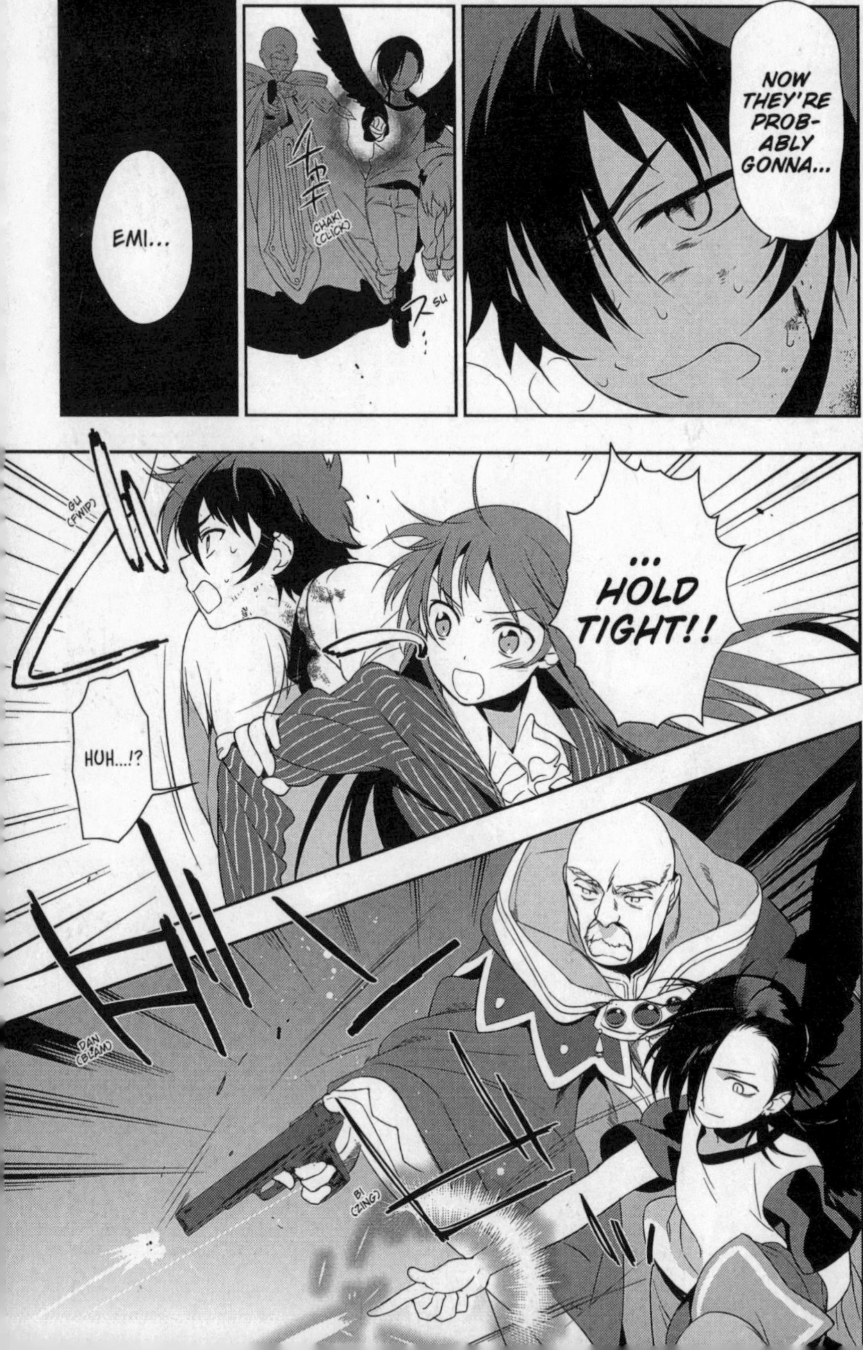
NOW THEY'RE PROB- ABLY GONNA...
CHAKI (CLICK)
SU
EMI...
... HOLD TIGHT!!
GU (FWIP)
HUH...!?
DAN (BLAM)
BI (ZING)

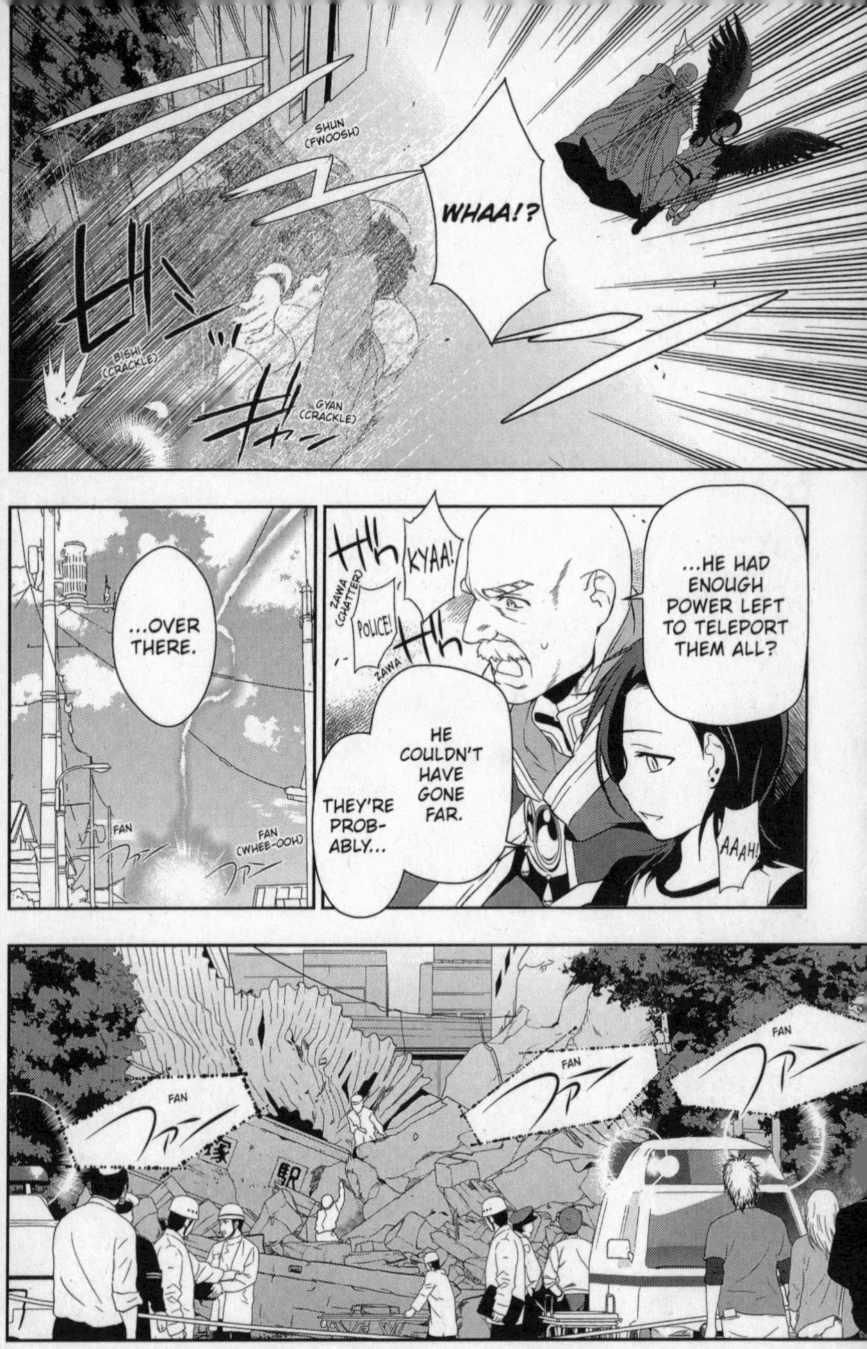
WHAA!?
SHUN (FWOOSH)
BISHI (CRACKLE)
GYAN (CRACKLE)
...HE HAD ENOUGH POWER LEFT TO TELEPORT THEM ALL?
KYAA!
ZAWA (CHATTER)
POLICE!
ZAWA
HE COULDN'T HAVE GONE FAR.
THEY'RE PROB-ABLY...
AAAH!
...OVER THERE.
FAN
FAN (WHEE-OOH)
FAN
FAN
FAN

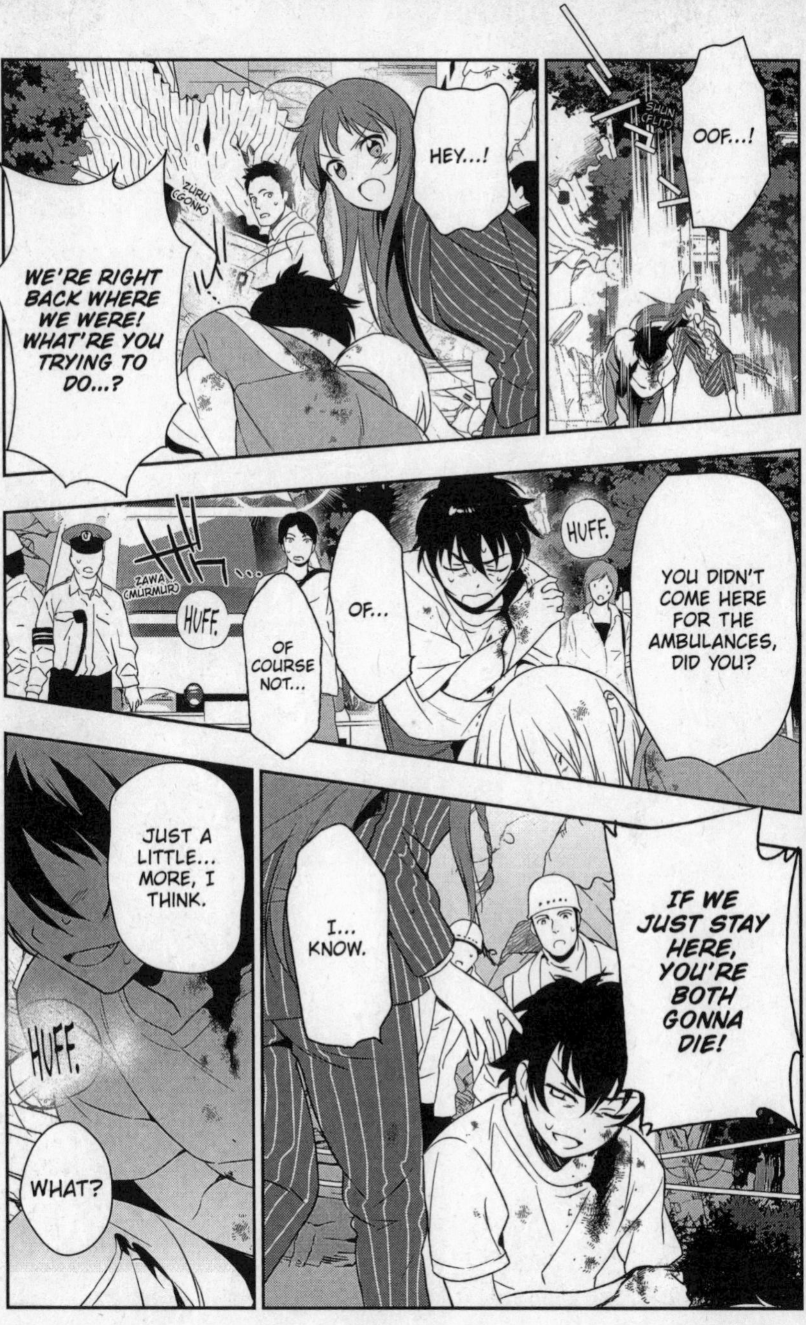
SHUN (FLIT)
OOF...!
HEY...!
ZURU (GONK)
WE'RE RIGHT BACK WHERE WE WERE! WHAT'RE YOU TRYING TO DO...?
YOU DIDN'T COME HERE FOR THE AMBULANCES, DID YOU?
HUFF.
OF...
OF COURSE NOT...
HUFF.
ZAWA (MURMUR)
IF WE JUST STAY HERE, YOU'RE BOTH GONNA DIE!
I... KNOW.
JUST A LITTLE... MORE, I THINK.
HUFF.
WHAT?

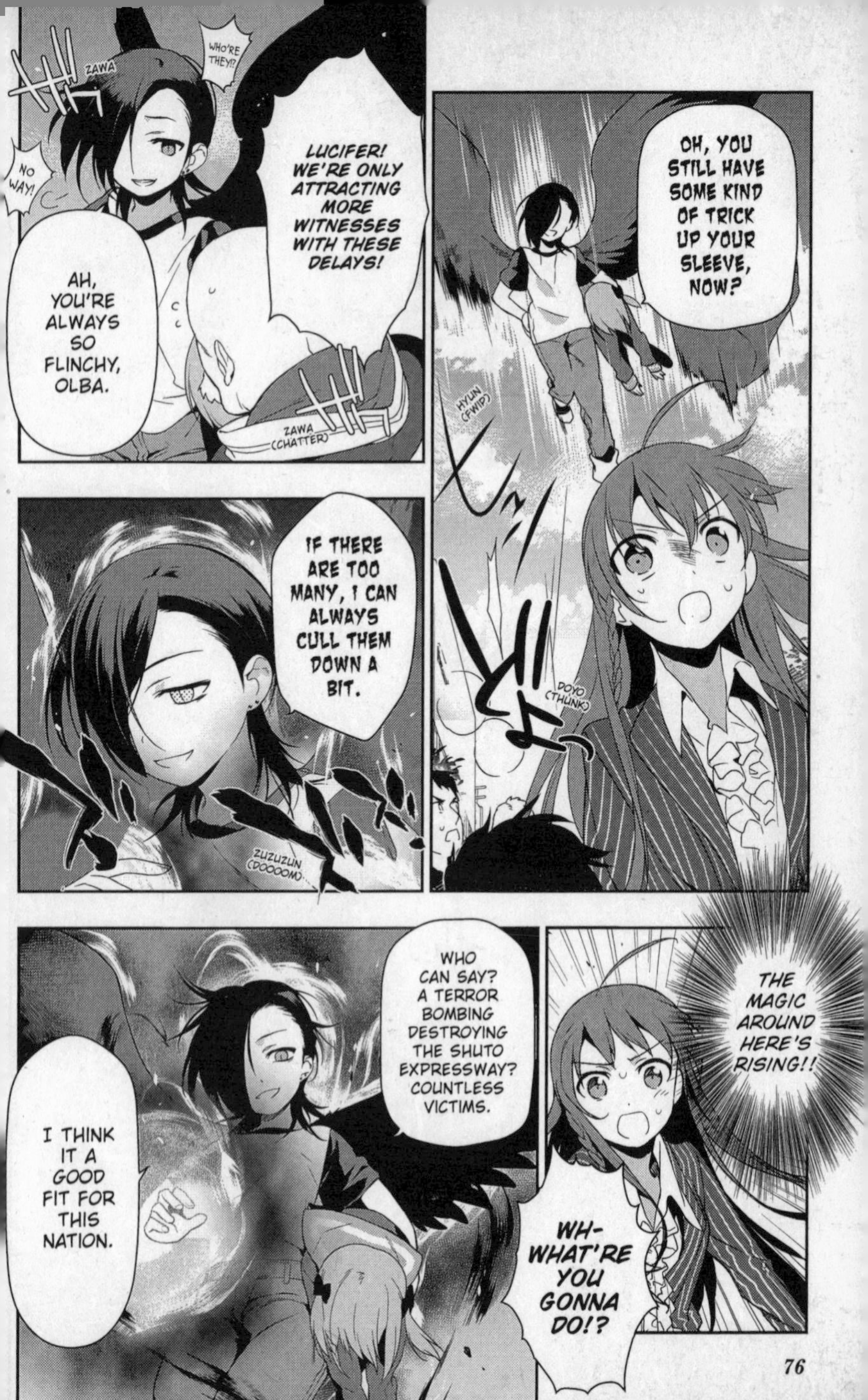
OH, YOU STILL HAVE SOME KIND OF TRICK UP YOUR SLEEVE, NOW?
HYUN (FWIP)
DOYO (THUNK)
WHO'RE THEY!?
ZAWA
LUCIFER! WE'RE ONLY ATTRACTING MORE WITNESSES WITH THESE DELAYS!
NO WAY!
AH, YOU'RE ALWAYS SO FLINCHY, OLBA.
ZAWA (CHATTER)
IF THERE ARE TOO MANY, I CAN ALWAYS CULL THEM DOWN A BIT.
ZUZUZUN (DOOOOM)
THE MAGIC AROUND HERE'S RISING!!
WH- WHAT'RE YOU GONNA DO!?
WHO CAN SAY? A TERROR BOMBING DESTROYING THE SHUTO EXPRESSWAY? COUNTLESS VICTIMS.
I THINK IT A GOOD FIT FOR THIS NATION.

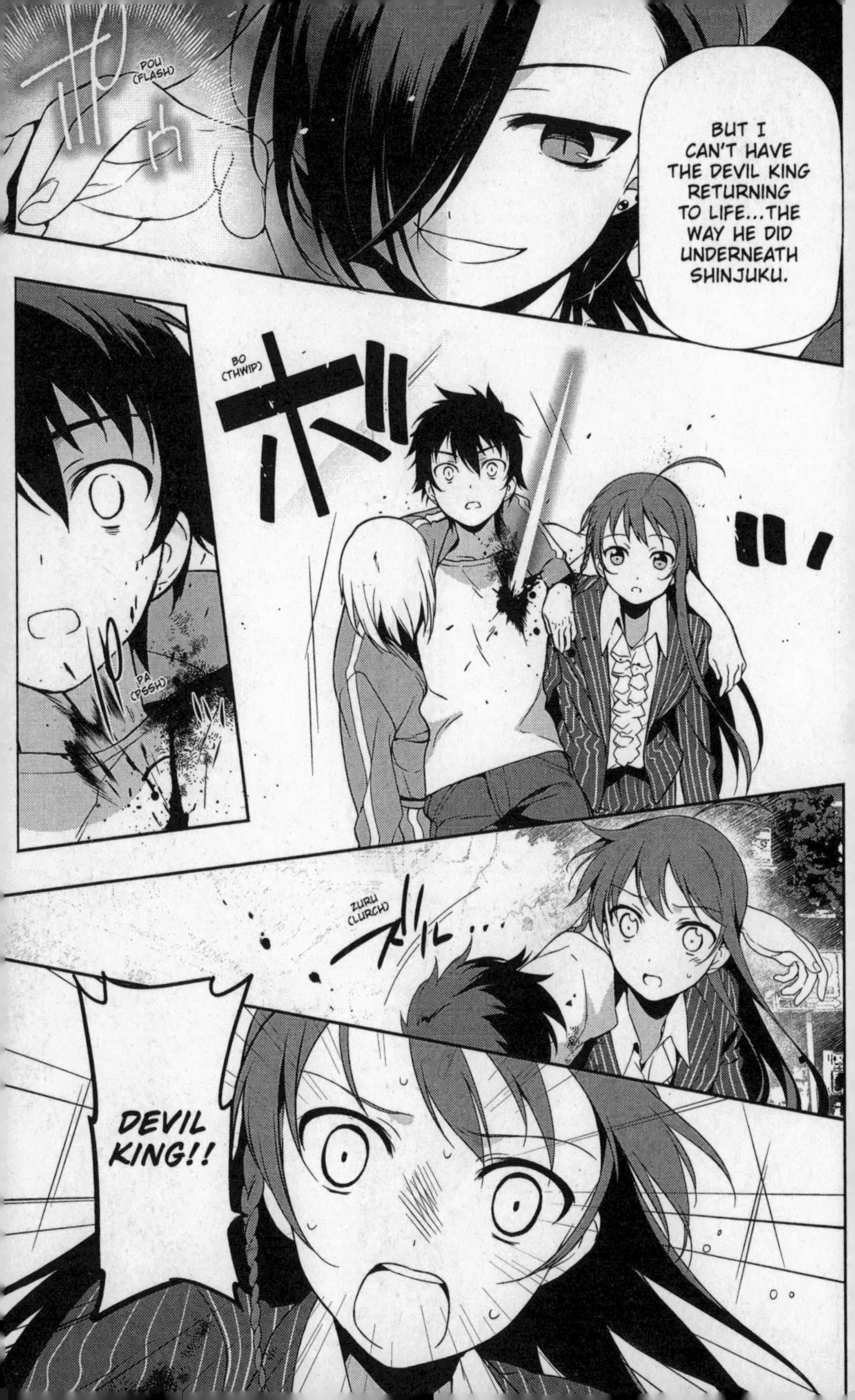
BUT I CAN'T HAVE THE DEVIL KING RETURNING TO LIFE...THE WAY HE DID UNDERNEATH SHINJUKU.
POU (FLASH)
BO (THWIP)
PA (PSSH)
ZURU (LURCH)
DEVIL KING!!

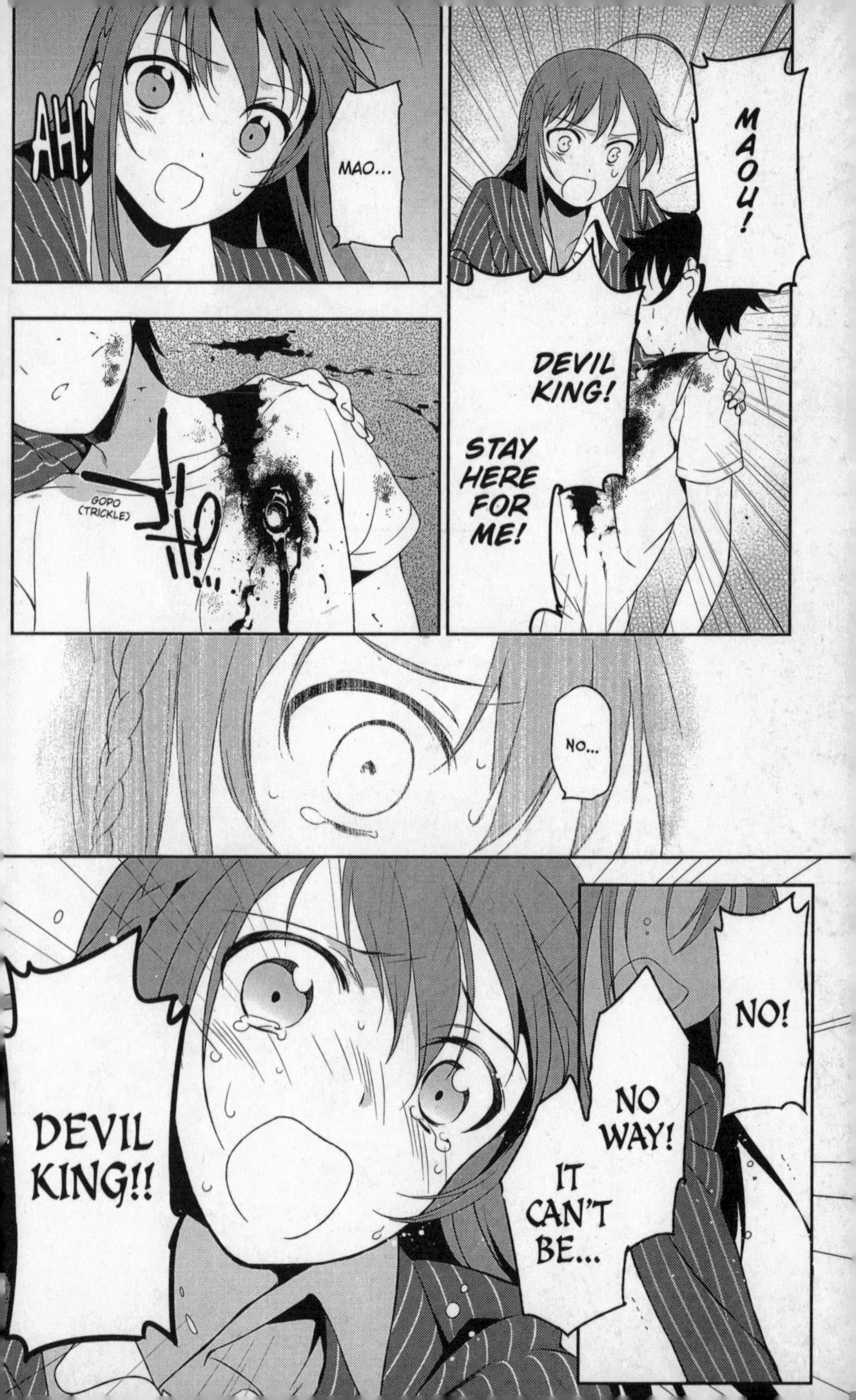
MAOU!
DEVIL KING!
STAY HERE FOR ME!
AH!
MAO...
GOPO (TRICKLE)
NO...
NO!
NO WAY!
IT CAN'T BE...
DEVIL KING!!

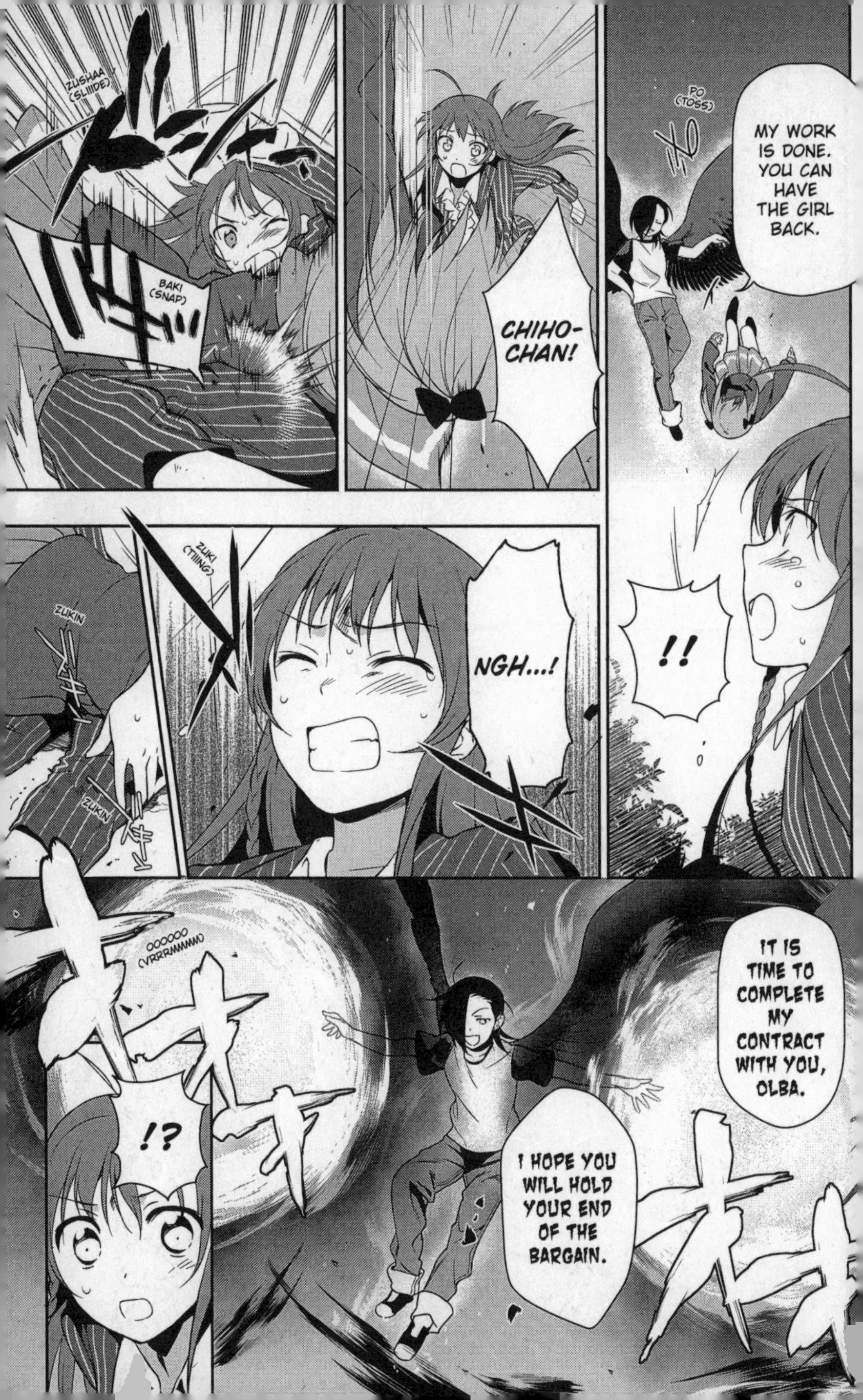
PO (TOSS)
MY WORK IS DONE. YOU CAN HAVE THE GIRL BACK.
CHIHO-CHAN!
ZUSHAA (SLIIIDE)
BAKI (SNAP)
!!
NGH...!
ZUKI (TIIING)
ZUKIN
ZUKIN
IT IS TIME TO COMPLETE MY CONTRACT WITH YOU, OLBA.
I HOPE YOU WILL HOLD YOUR END OF THE BARGAIN.
OOOOOO (VRRRMMMM)
!?

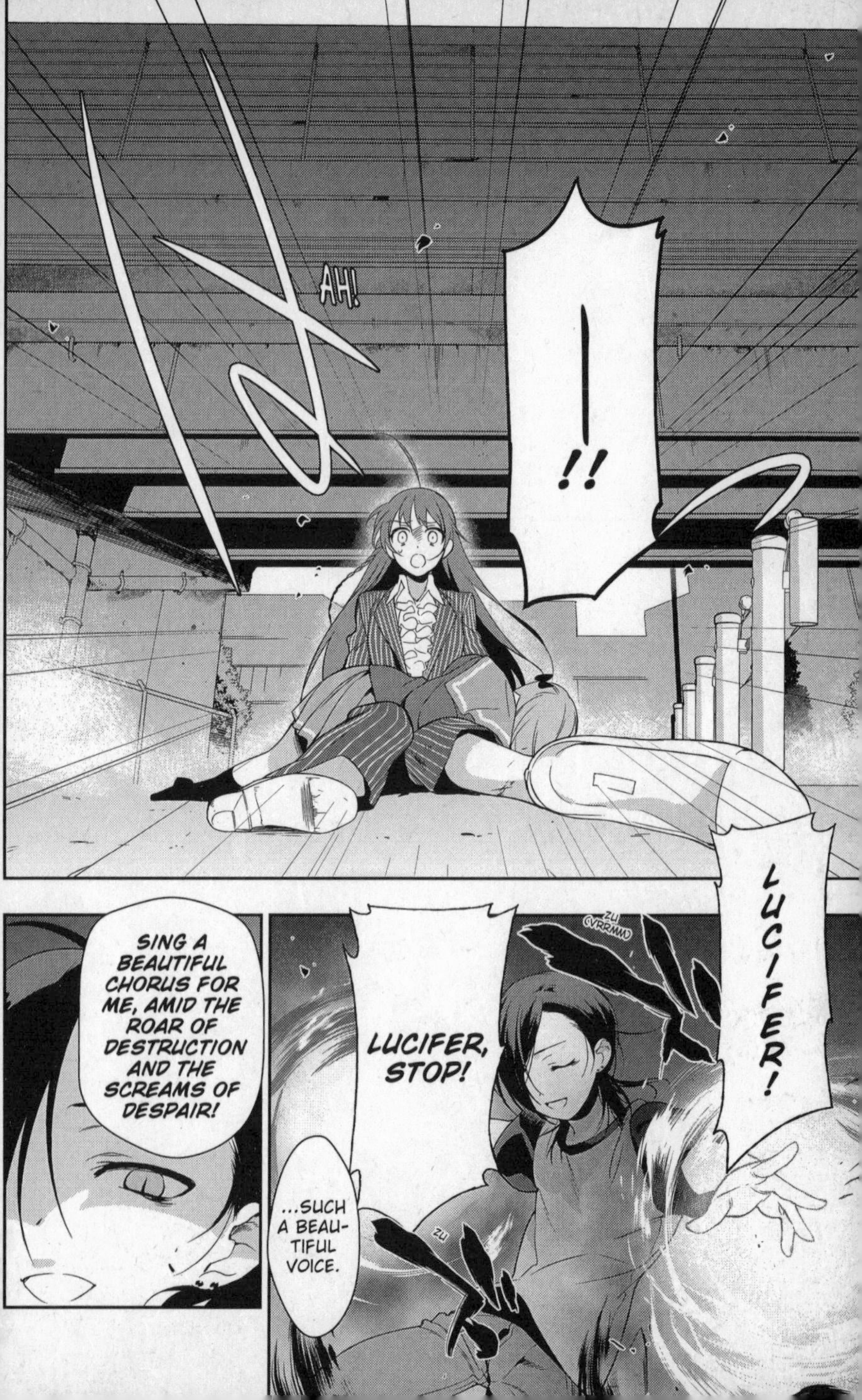
—!!
AH!
LUCIFER!
ZU (VRRMM)
LUCIFER, STOP!
ZU
...SUCH A BEAUTIFUL VOICE.
SING A BEAUTIFUL CHORUS FOR ME, AMID THE ROAR OF DESTRUCTION AND THE SCREAMS OF DESPAIR!

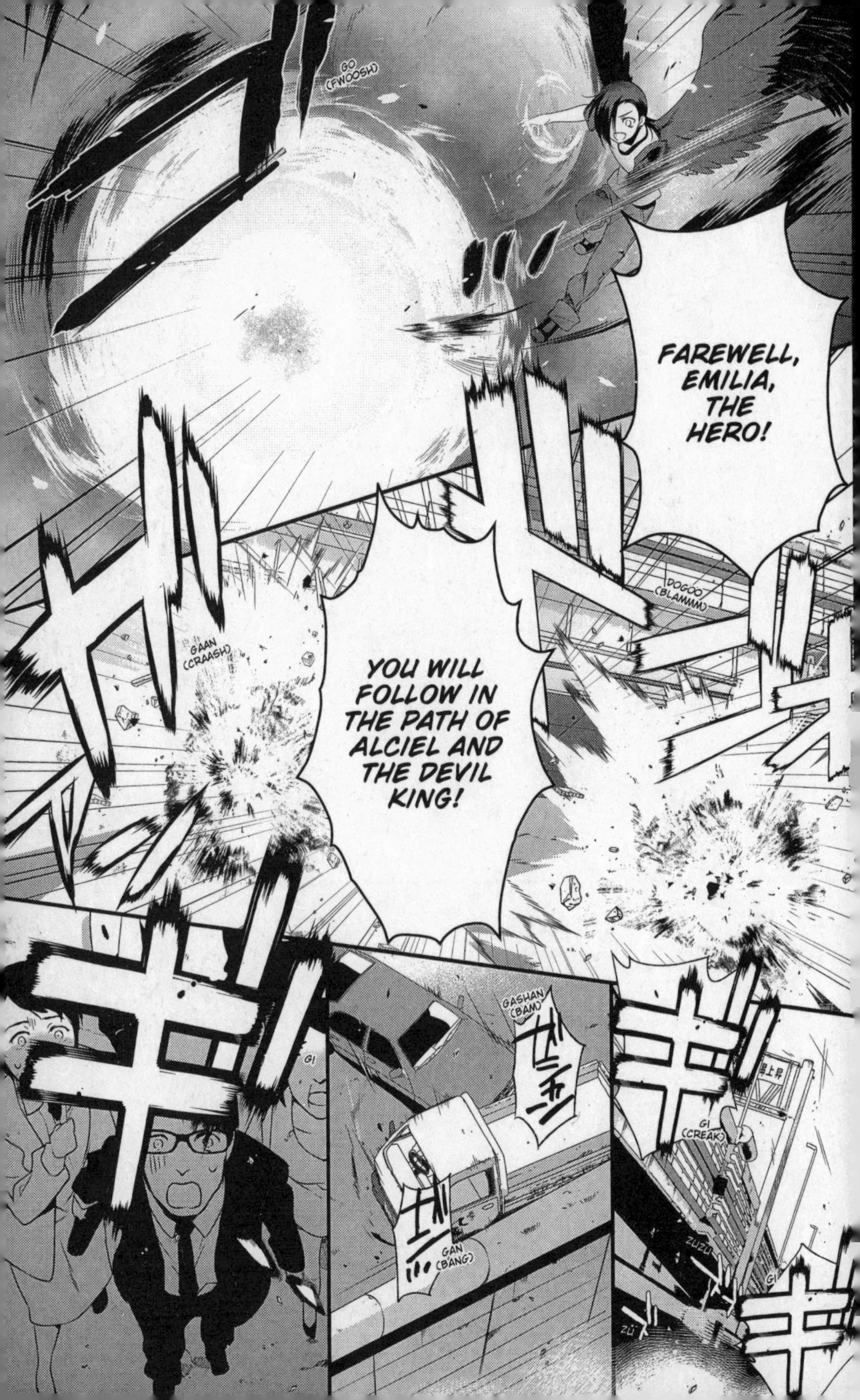
GO (FWOOSH)
FAREWELL, EMILIA, THE HERO!
YOU WILL FOLLOW IN THE PATH OF ALCIEL AND THE DEVIL KING!
DOGOO (BLAMMM)
GAAN (CRAASH)
GI (CREAK)
ZUZU
GI
ZU
GASHAN (BAM)
GAN (BANG)
GI

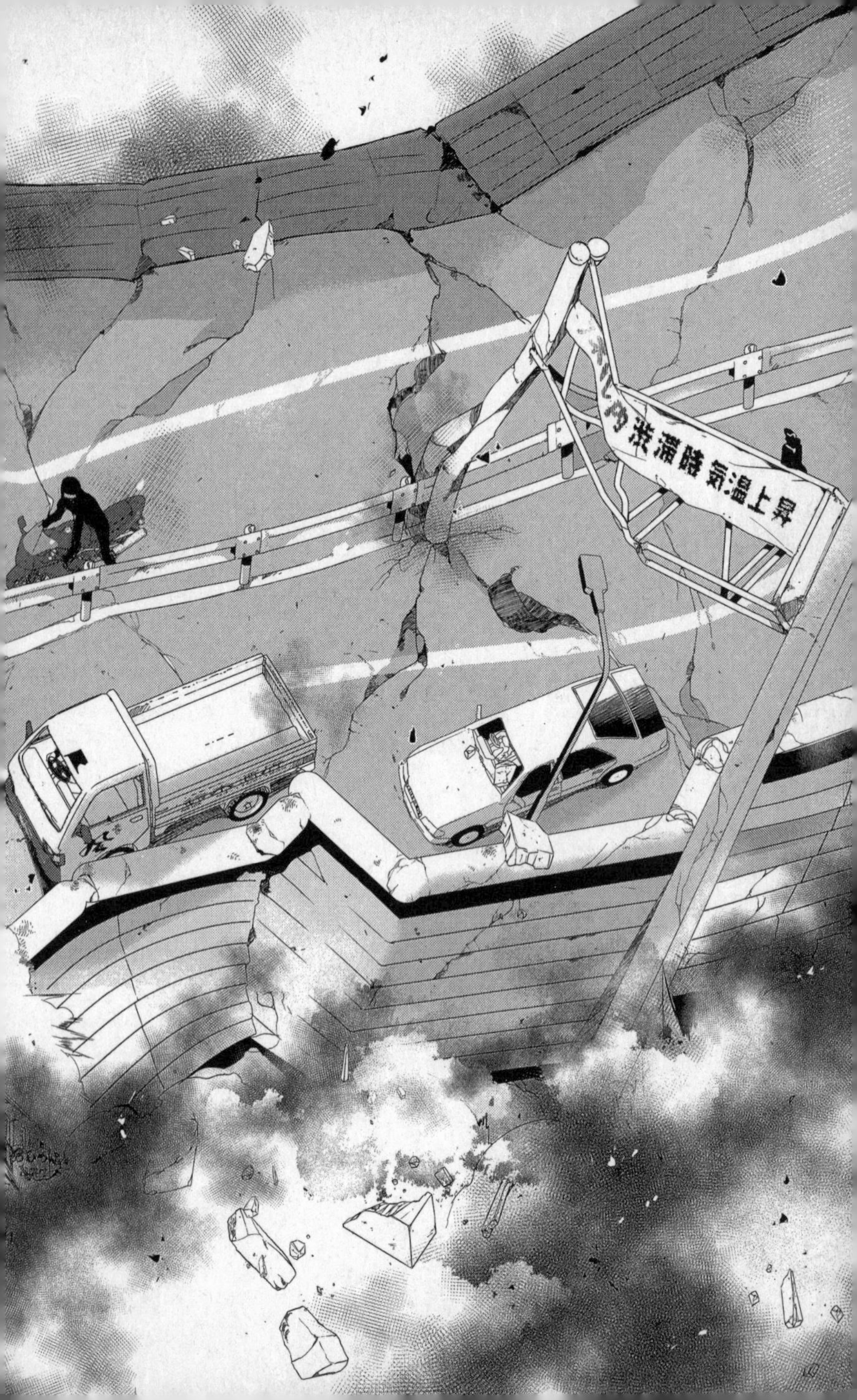
渋滞時 気温上昇

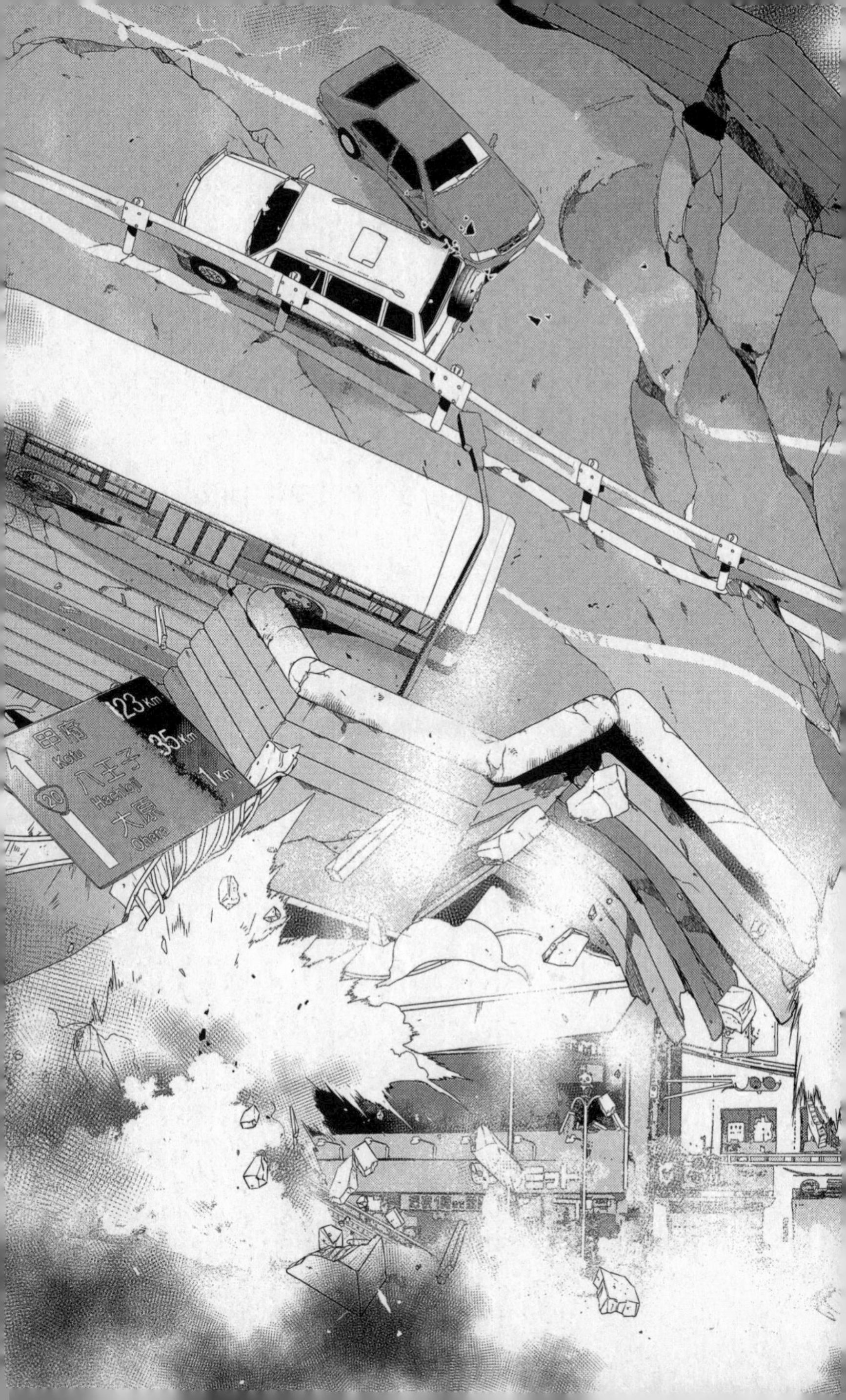
甲府 Kofu 123Km
八王子 Hachioji 35Km
大原 Ohara 1Km
20

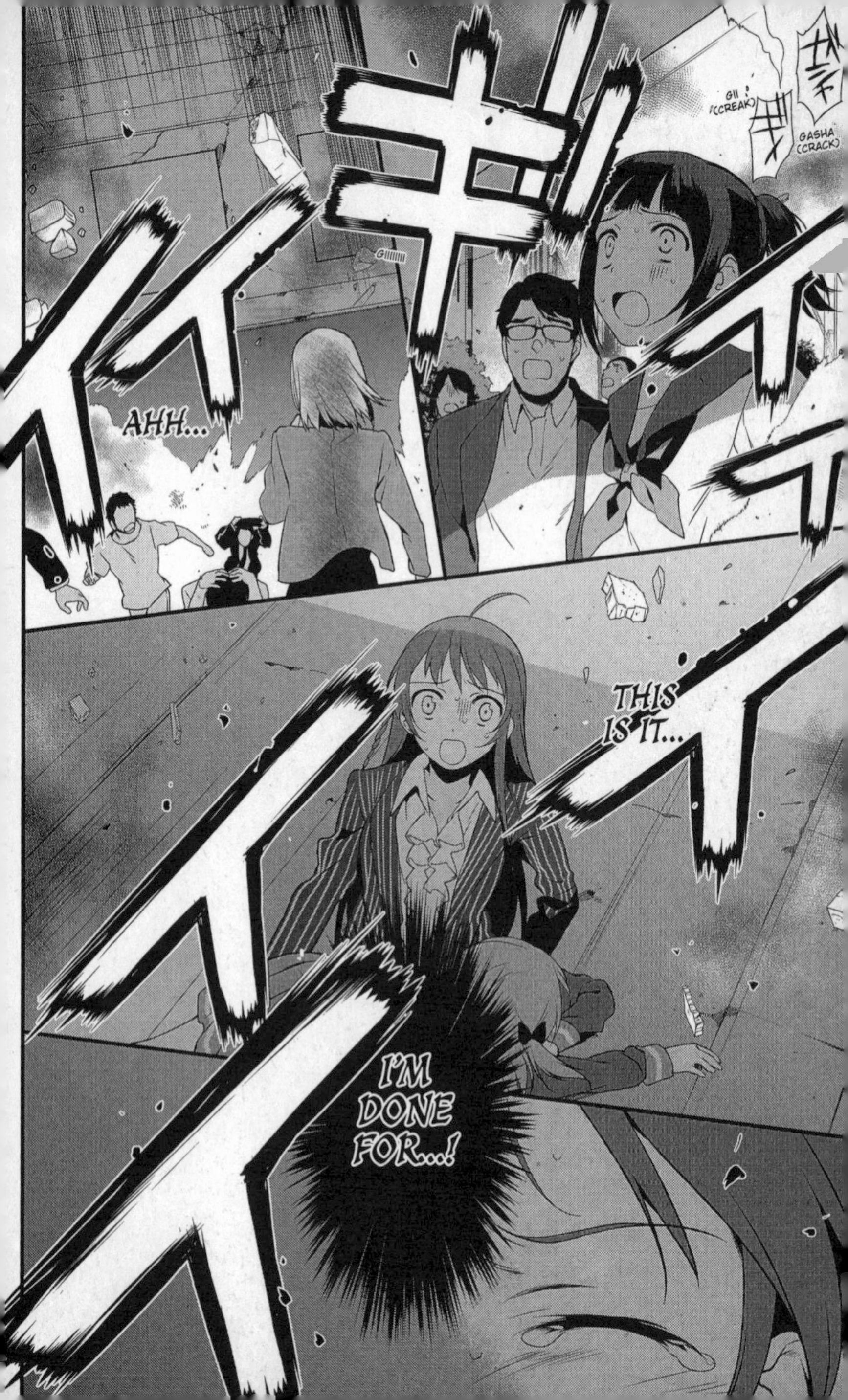
GASHA (CRACK)
GII (CREAK)
GIIIII
AHH...
THIS IS IT...
I'M DONE FOR...!

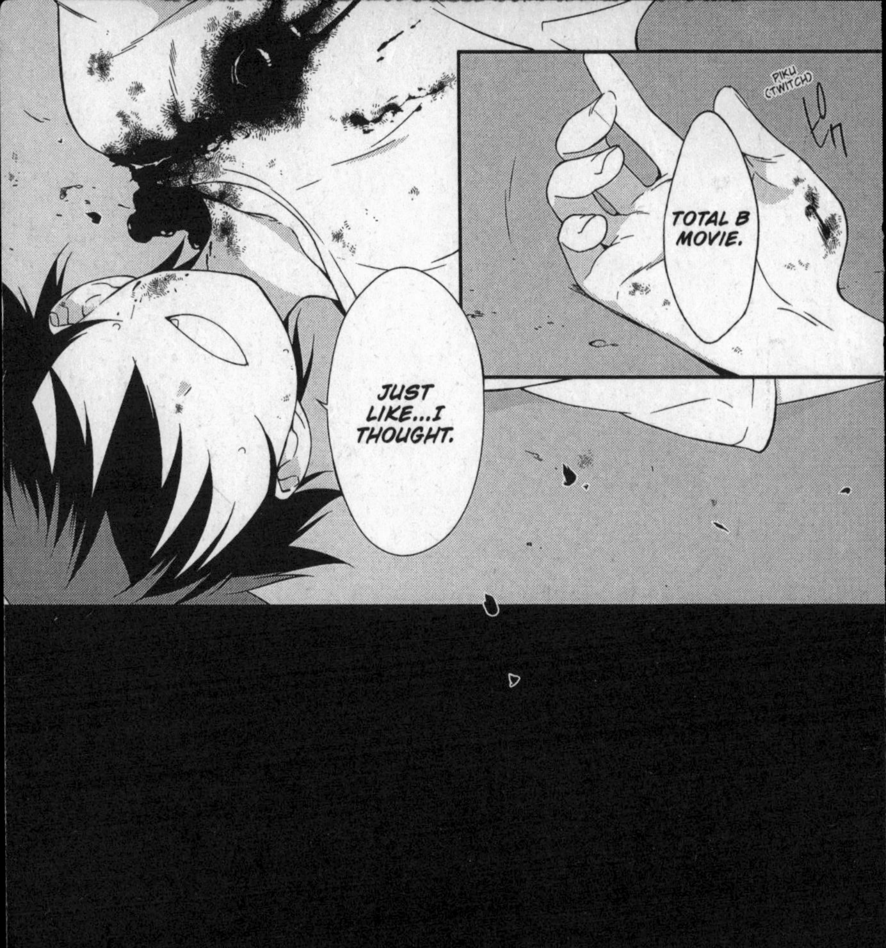
PIKU (TWITCH)
TOTAL B MOVIE.
JUST LIKE...I THOUGHT.

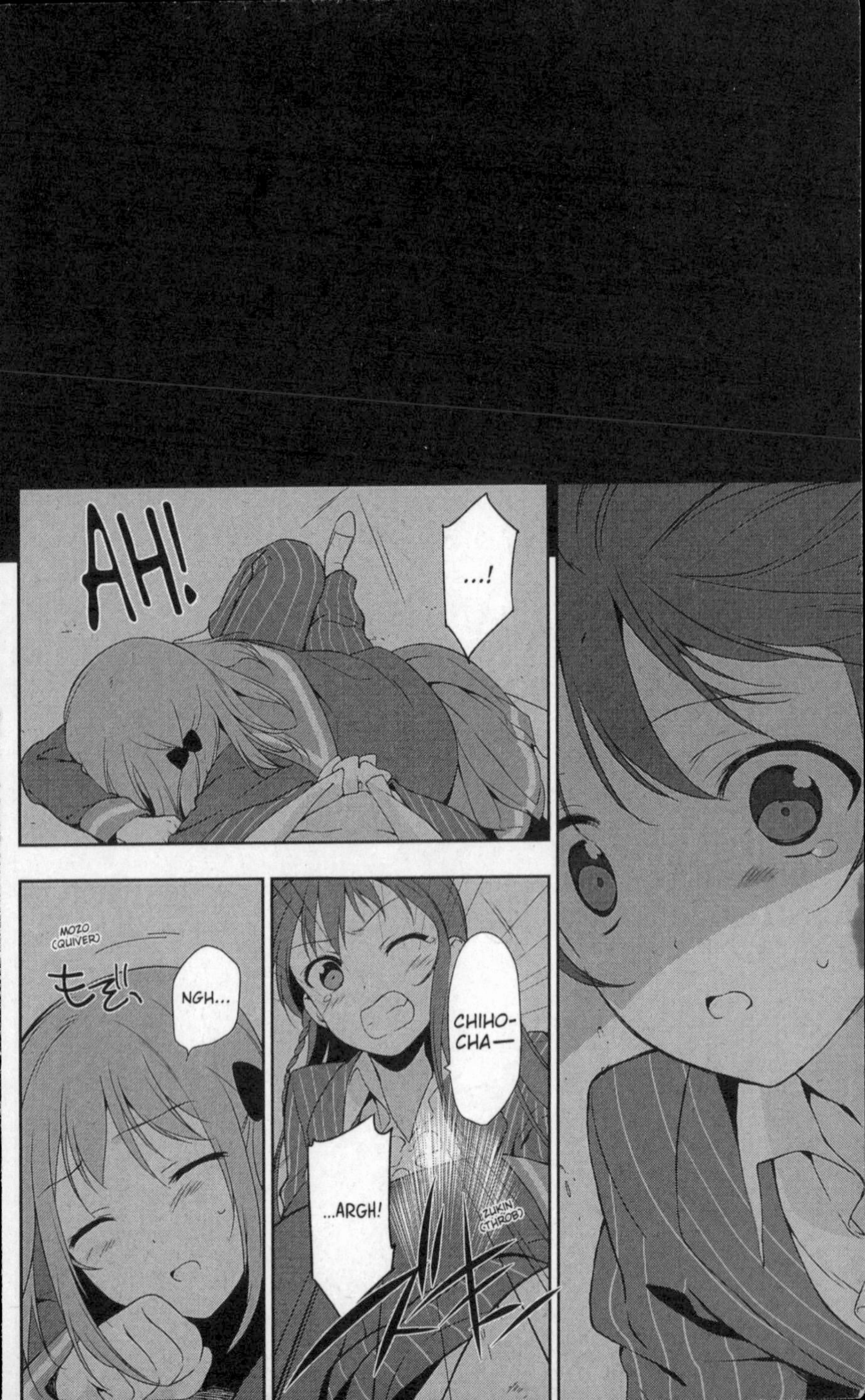
...!
AH!
CHIHO-
CHA—
...ARGH!
ZUKIN
(THROB)
NGH...
MOZO
(QUIVER)

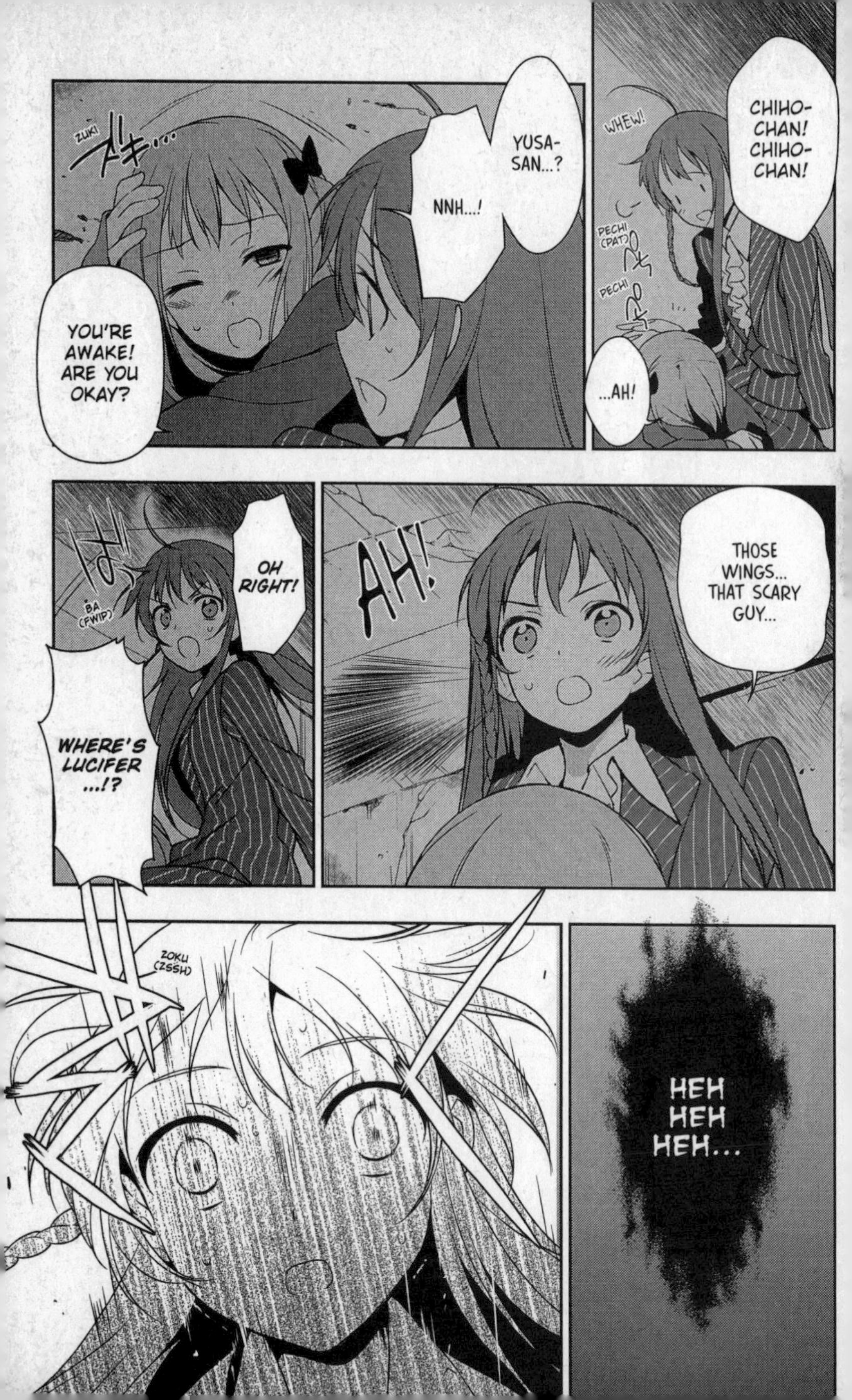
CHIHO-CHAN! CHIHO-CHAN!
WHEW!
PECHI (PAT)
PECHI
...AH!
YUSA-SAN...?
NNH...!
ZUKI
YOU'RE AWAKE! ARE YOU OKAY?
THOSE WINGS... THAT SCARY GUY...
AH!
OH RIGHT!
BA (FWIP)
WHERE'S LUCIFER ...!?
HEH HEH HEH...
ZOKU (ZSSH)

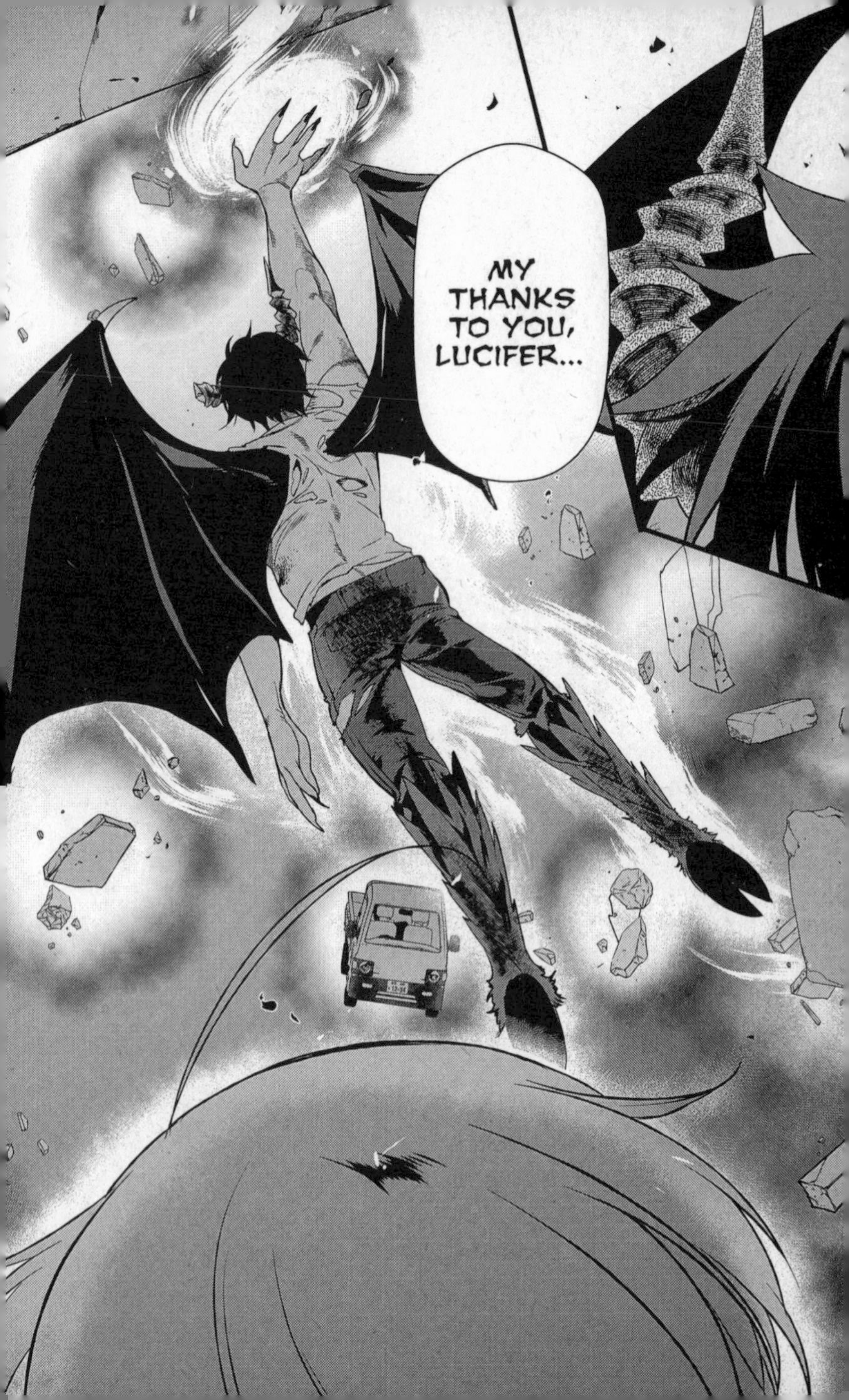
MY THANKS TO YOU, LUCIFER...

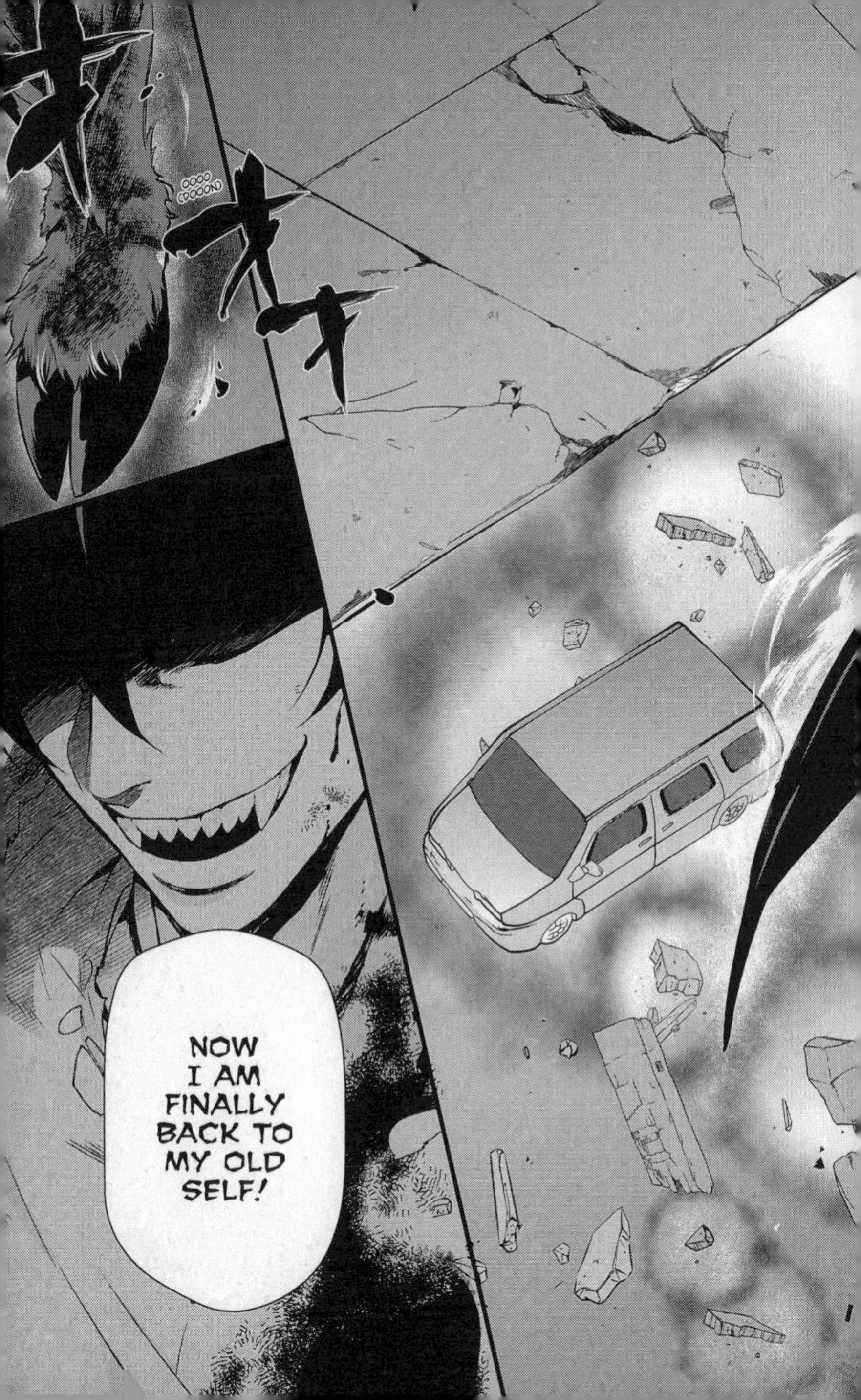
OOOO
(DOOON)
NOW I AM FINALLY BACK TO MY OLD SELF!

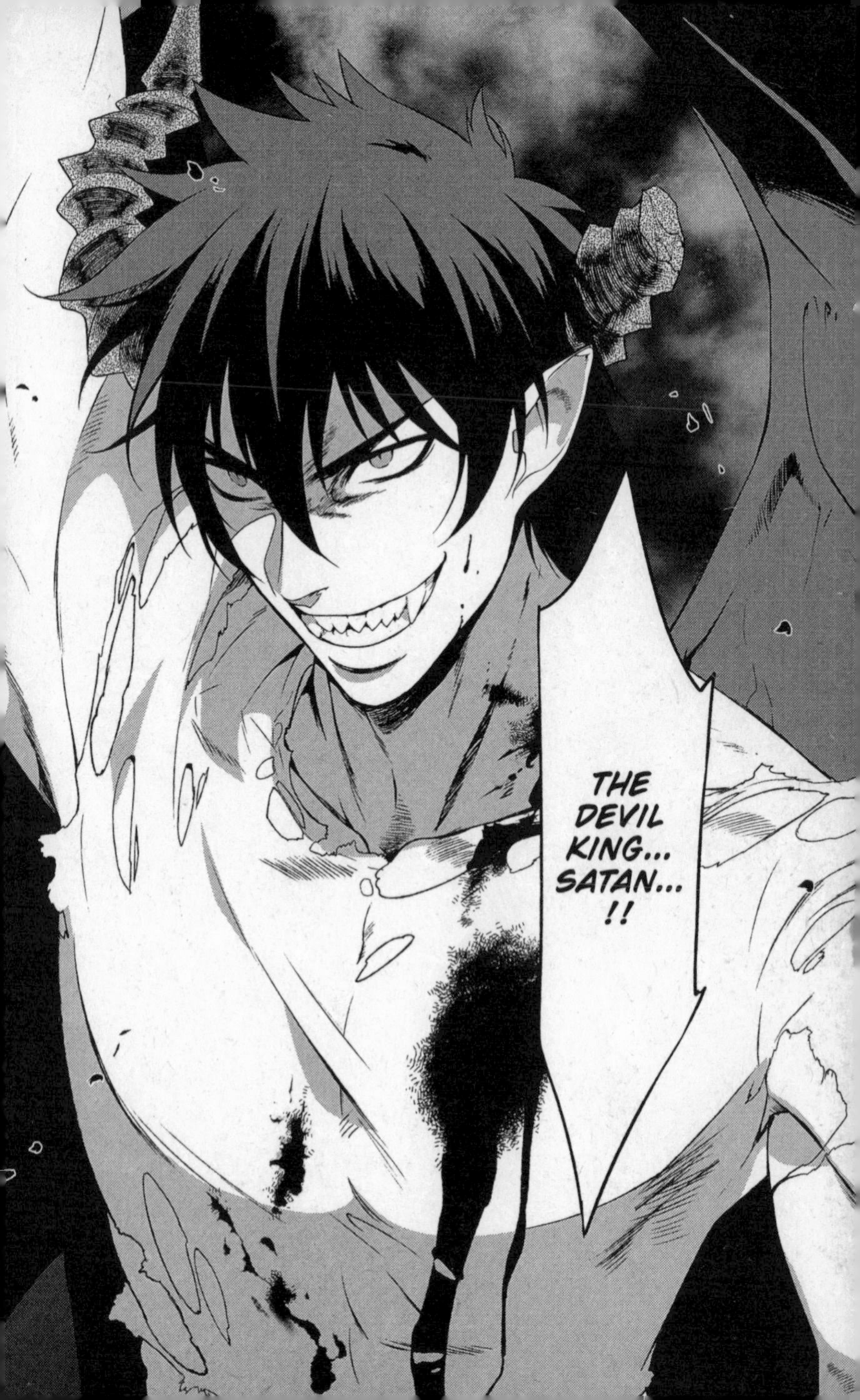
THE DEVIL KING... SATAN... !!

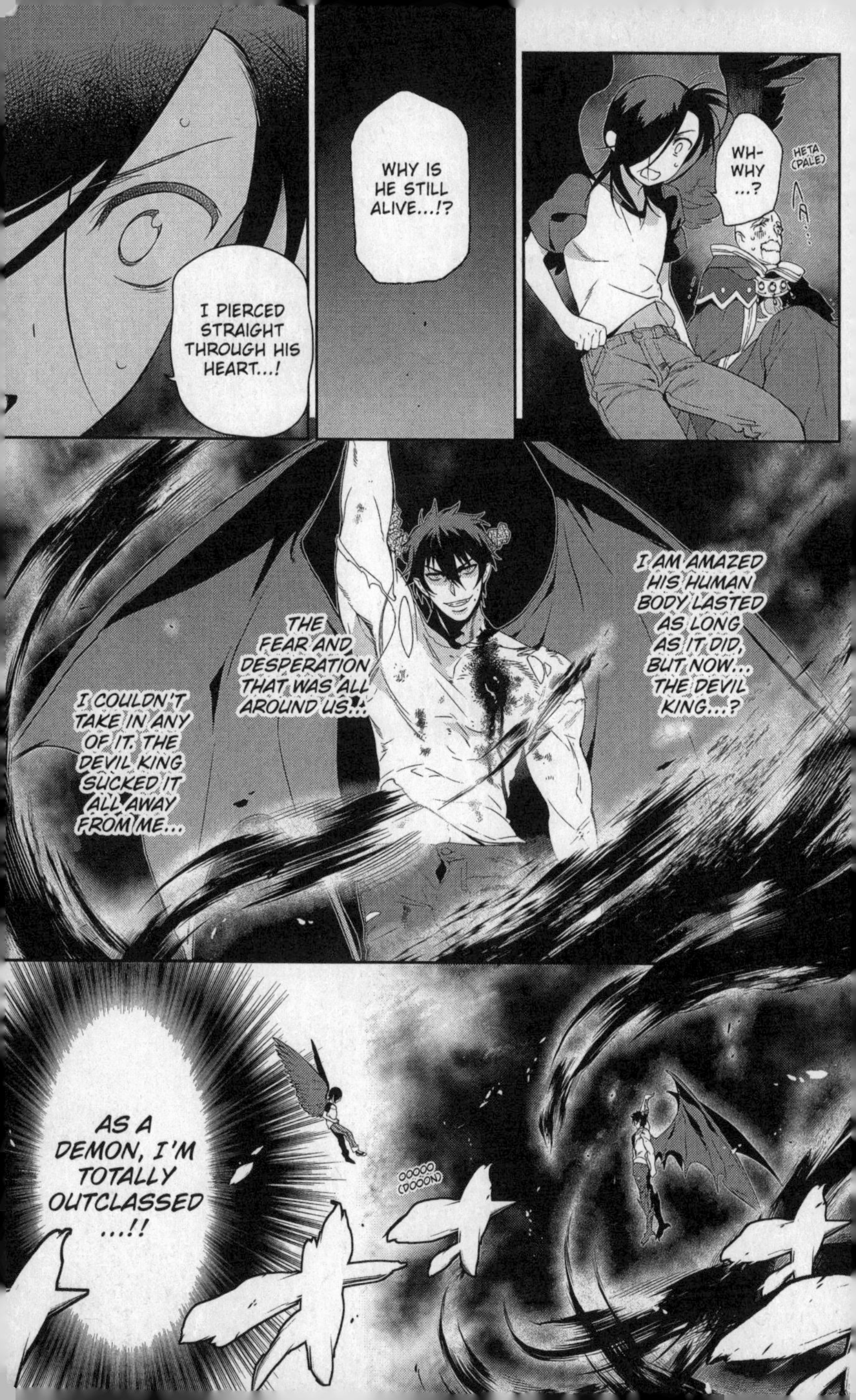
WH-
WHY
...?
HETA
(PALE)
WHY IS HE STILL ALIVE...!?
I PIERCED STRAIGHT THROUGH HIS HEART...!
I AM AMAZED HIS HUMAN BODY LASTED AS LONG AS IT DID, BUT NOW... THE DEVIL KING...?
THE FEAR AND DESPERATION THAT WAS ALL AROUND US...
I COULDN'T TAKE IN ANY OF IT. THE DEVIL KING SUCKED IT ALL AWAY FROM ME...
AS A DEMON, I'M TOTALLY OUTCLASSED...!!
OOOOO
(DOOON)

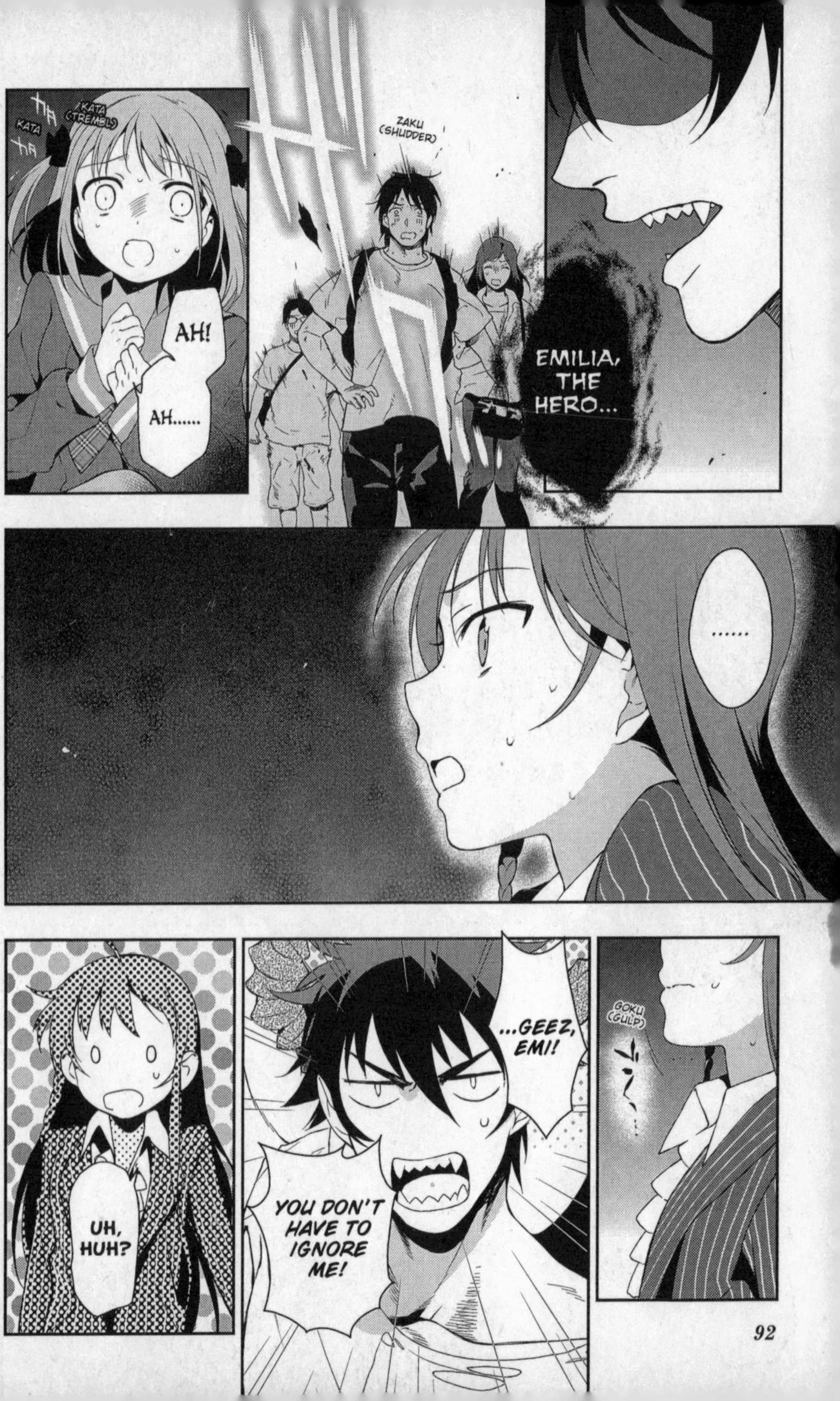
EMILIA, THE HERO...
ZAKU (SHUDDER)
KATA (TREMBL)
KATA
AH!
AH......
......
GOKU (GULP)
...GEEZ, EMI!
YOU DON'T HAVE TO IGNORE ME!
UH, HUH?

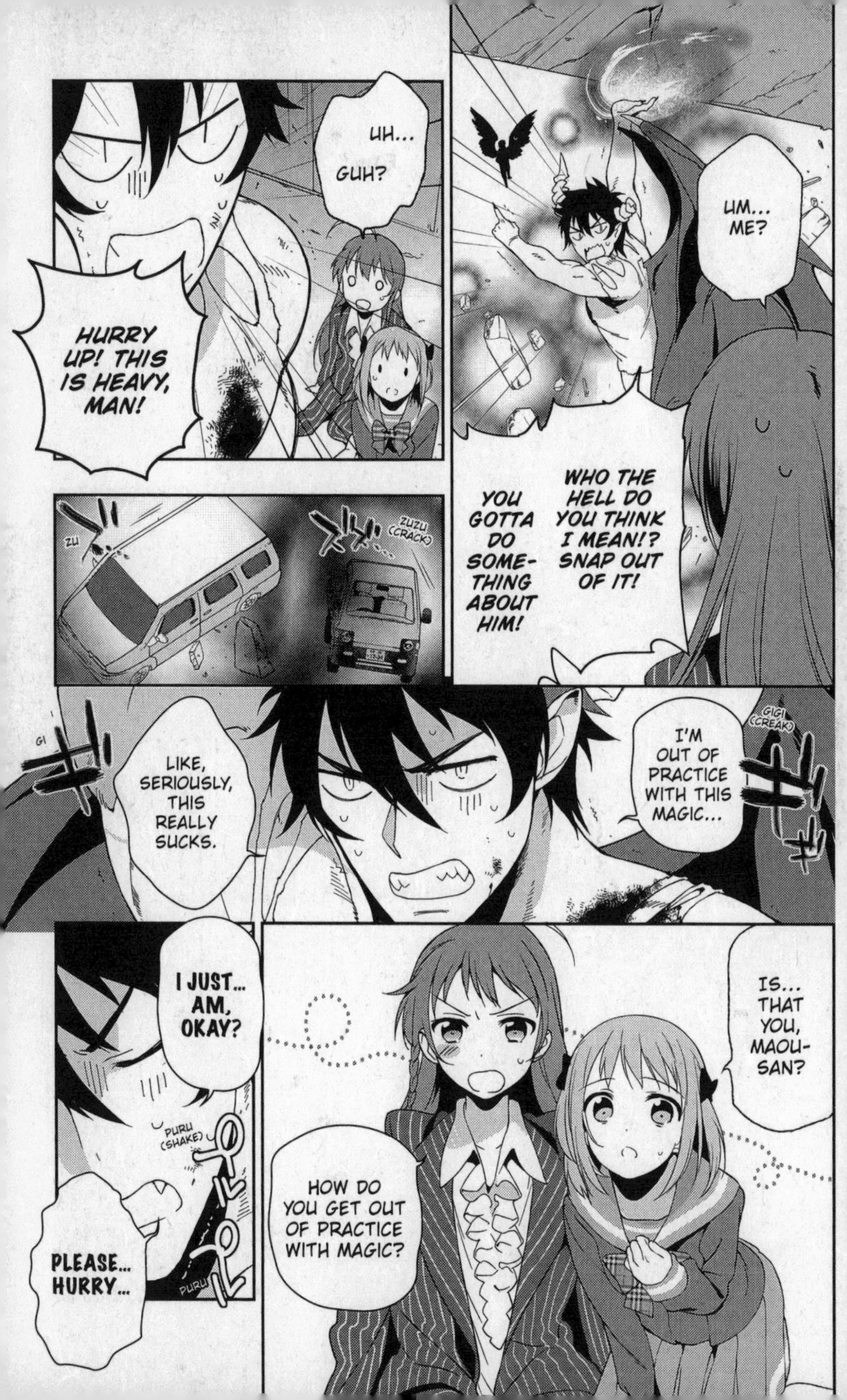
UM... ME?
WHO THE HELL DO YOU THINK I MEAN!? SNAP OUT OF IT!
YOU GOTTA DO SOME-THING ABOUT HIM!
UH... GUH?
HURRY UP! THIS IS HEAVY, MAN!
ZUZU (CRACK)
ZU
GIGI (CREAK)
I'M OUT OF PRACTICE WITH THIS MAGIC...
LIKE, SERIOUSLY, THIS REALLY SUCKS.
GI
IS... THAT YOU, MAOU-SAN?
HOW DO YOU GET OUT OF PRACTICE WITH MAGIC?
I JUST... AM, OKAY?
PURU (SHAKE)
PLEASE... HURRY...
PURU

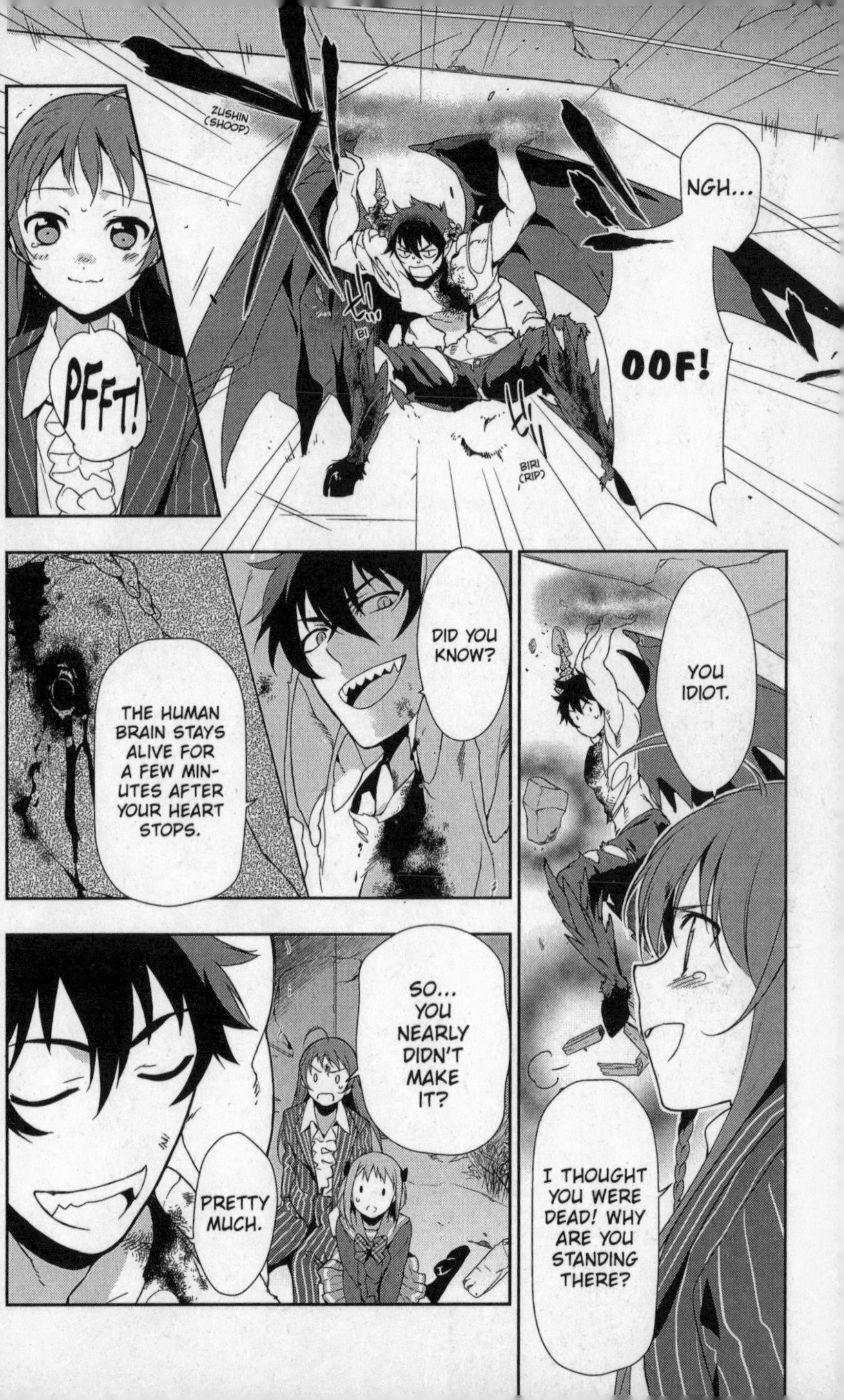
NGH...
OOF!
ZUSHIN (SHOOP)
BI
BIRI (RIP)
PFFT!
YOU IDIOT.
I THOUGHT YOU WERE DEAD! WHY ARE YOU STANDING THERE?
DID YOU KNOW?
THE HUMAN BRAIN STAYS ALIVE FOR A FEW MIN-UTES AFTER YOUR HEART STOPS.
SO... YOU NEARLY DIDN'T MAKE IT?
PRETTY MUCH.

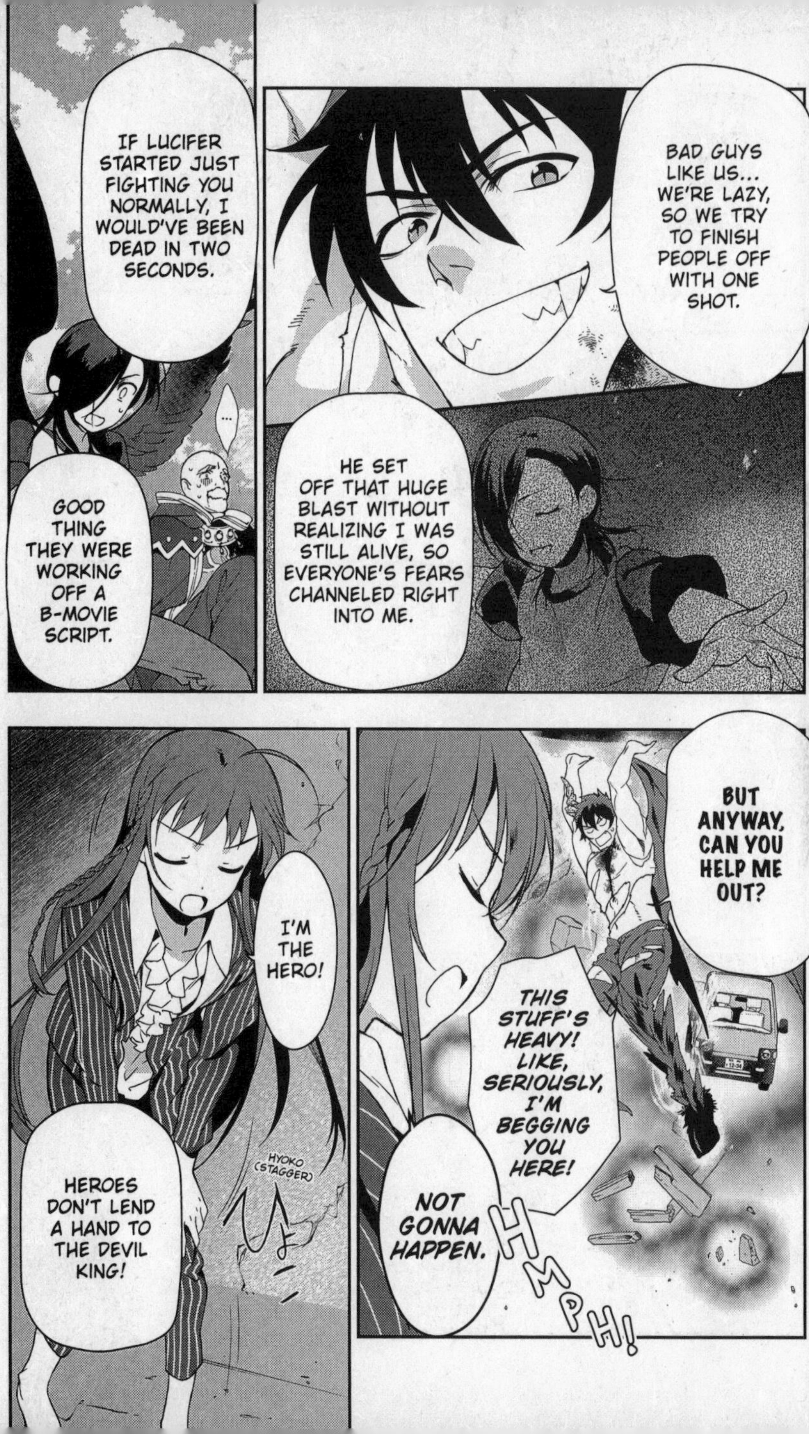
BAD GUYS LIKE US... WE'RE LAZY, SO WE TRY TO FINISH PEOPLE OFF WITH ONE SHOT.
HE SET OFF THAT HUGE BLAST WITHOUT REALIZING I WAS STILL ALIVE, SO EVERYONE'S FEARS CHANNELED RIGHT INTO ME.
IF LUCIFER STARTED JUST FIGHTING YOU NORMALLY, I WOULD'VE BEEN DEAD IN TWO SECONDS.
...
GOOD THING THEY WERE WORKING OFF A B-MOVIE SCRIPT.
BUT ANYWAY, CAN YOU HELP ME OUT?
THIS STUFF'S HEAVY! LIKE, SERIOUSLY, I'M BEGGING YOU HERE!
NOT GONNA HAPPEN.
HMPH!
I'M THE HERO!
HYOKO (STAGGER)
HEROES DON'T LEND A HAND TO THE DEVIL KING!

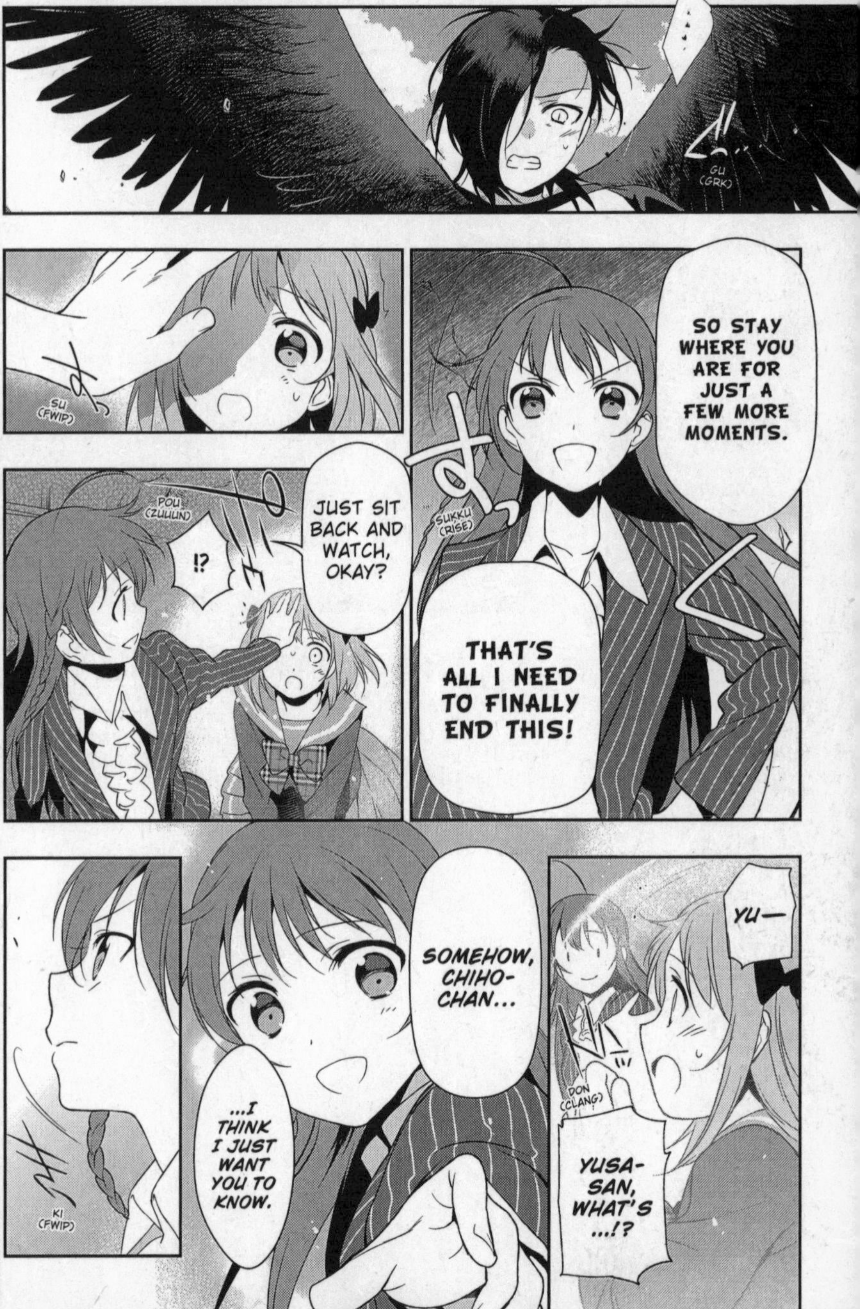
...
GU (GRK)
SO STAY WHERE YOU ARE FOR JUST A FEW MORE MOMENTS.
SUKKU (RISE)
THAT'S ALL I NEED TO FINALLY END THIS!
SU (FWIP)
JUST SIT BACK AND WATCH, OKAY?
!?
POU (ZUUUN)
YU—
DON (CLANG)
YUSA-SAN, WHAT'S ...!?
SOMEHOW, CHIHO-CHAN...
...I THINK I JUST WANT YOU TO KNOW.
KI (FWIP)

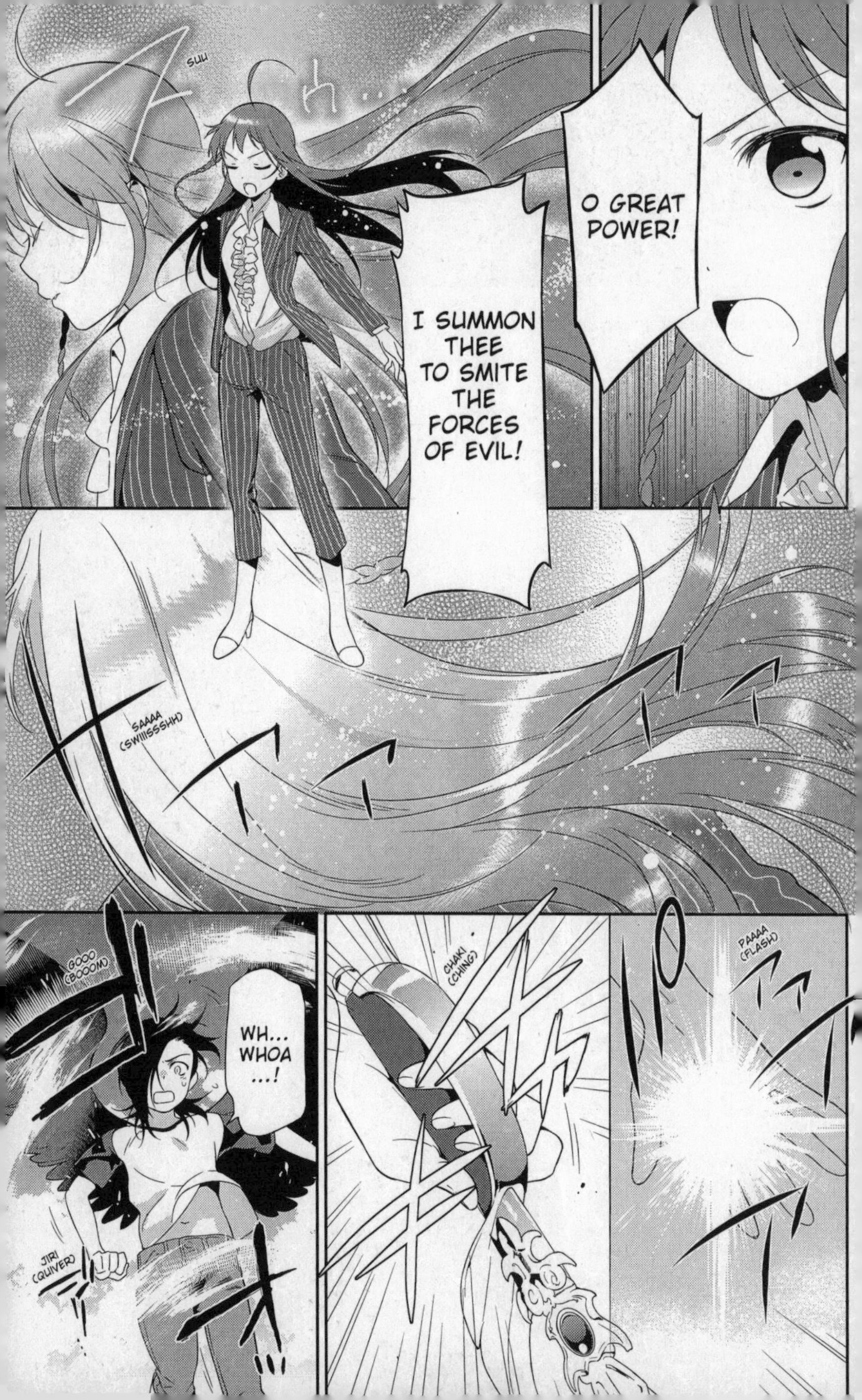

O GREAT POWER!
I SUMMON THEE TO SMITE THE FORCES OF EVIL!
SUU
SAAAA (SWIIISSSHH)
PAAAA (FLASH)
CHAKI (CHING)
GOOO (BOOOM)
WH... WHOA ...!
JIRI (QUIVER)

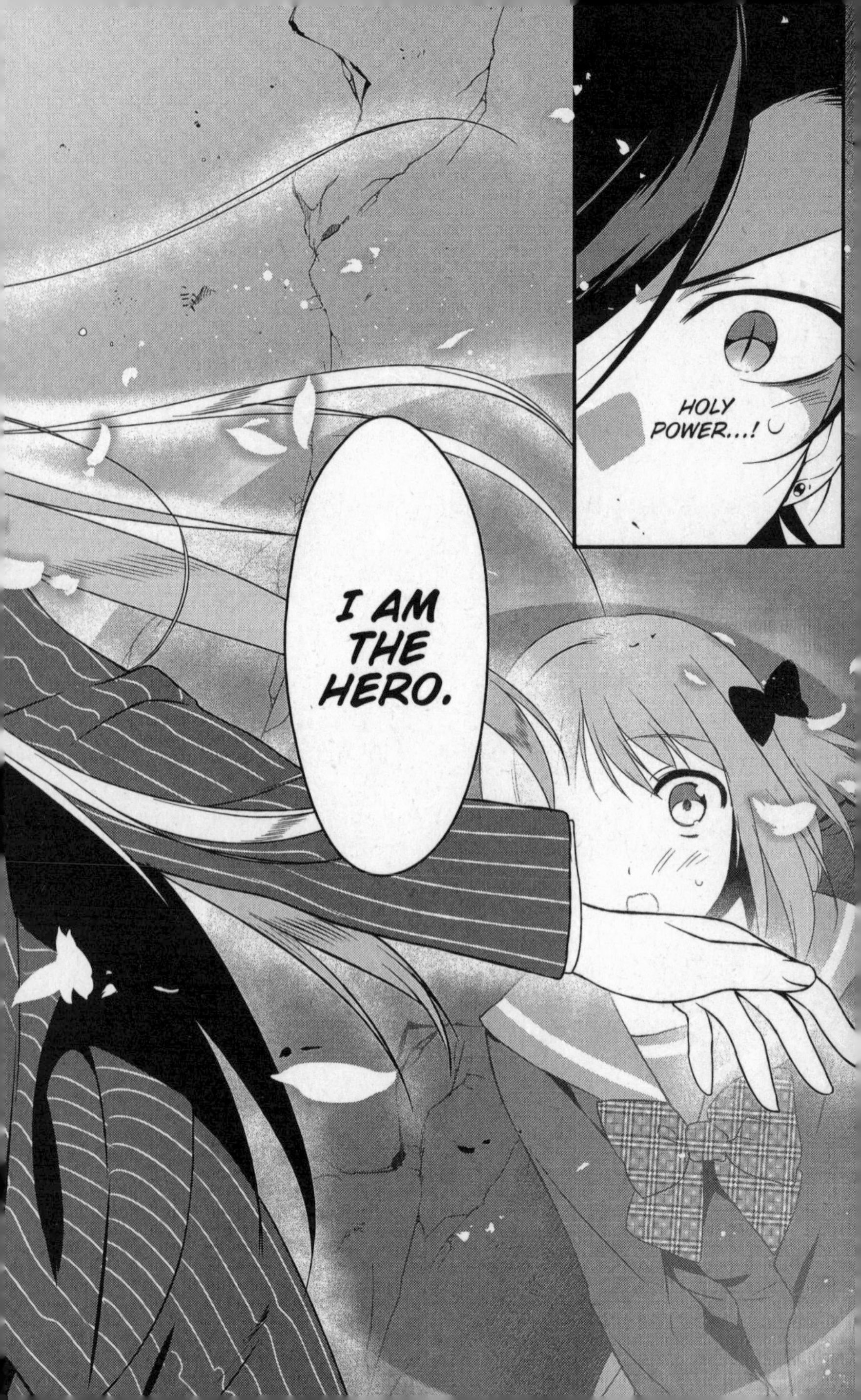
HOLY POWER...!
I AM THE HERO.

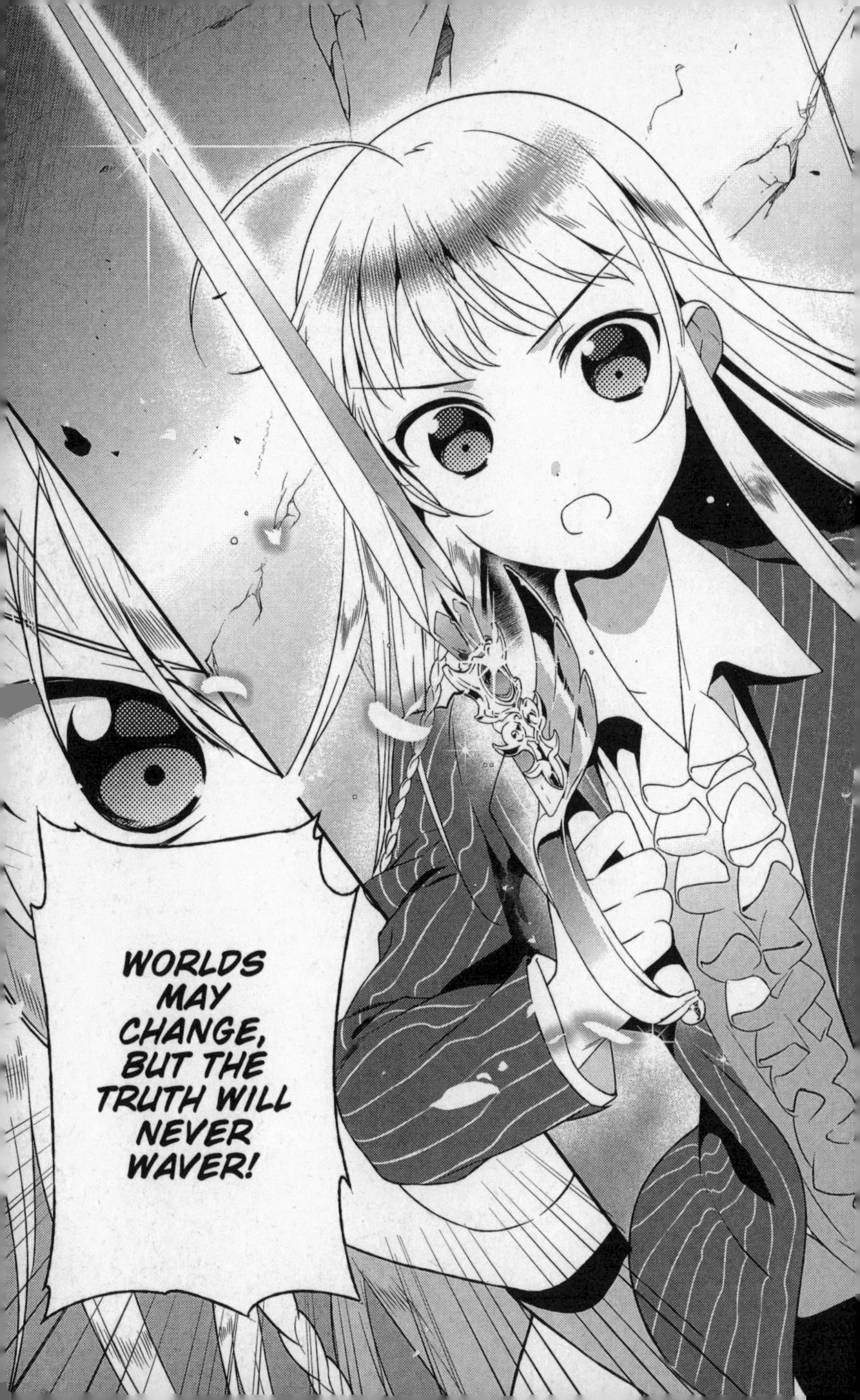
WORLDS MAY CHANGE, BUT THE TRUTH WILL NEVER WAVER!

THE DEVIL IS A PART-TIMER!

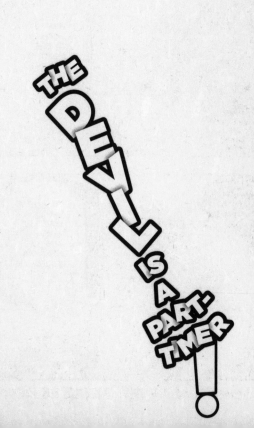

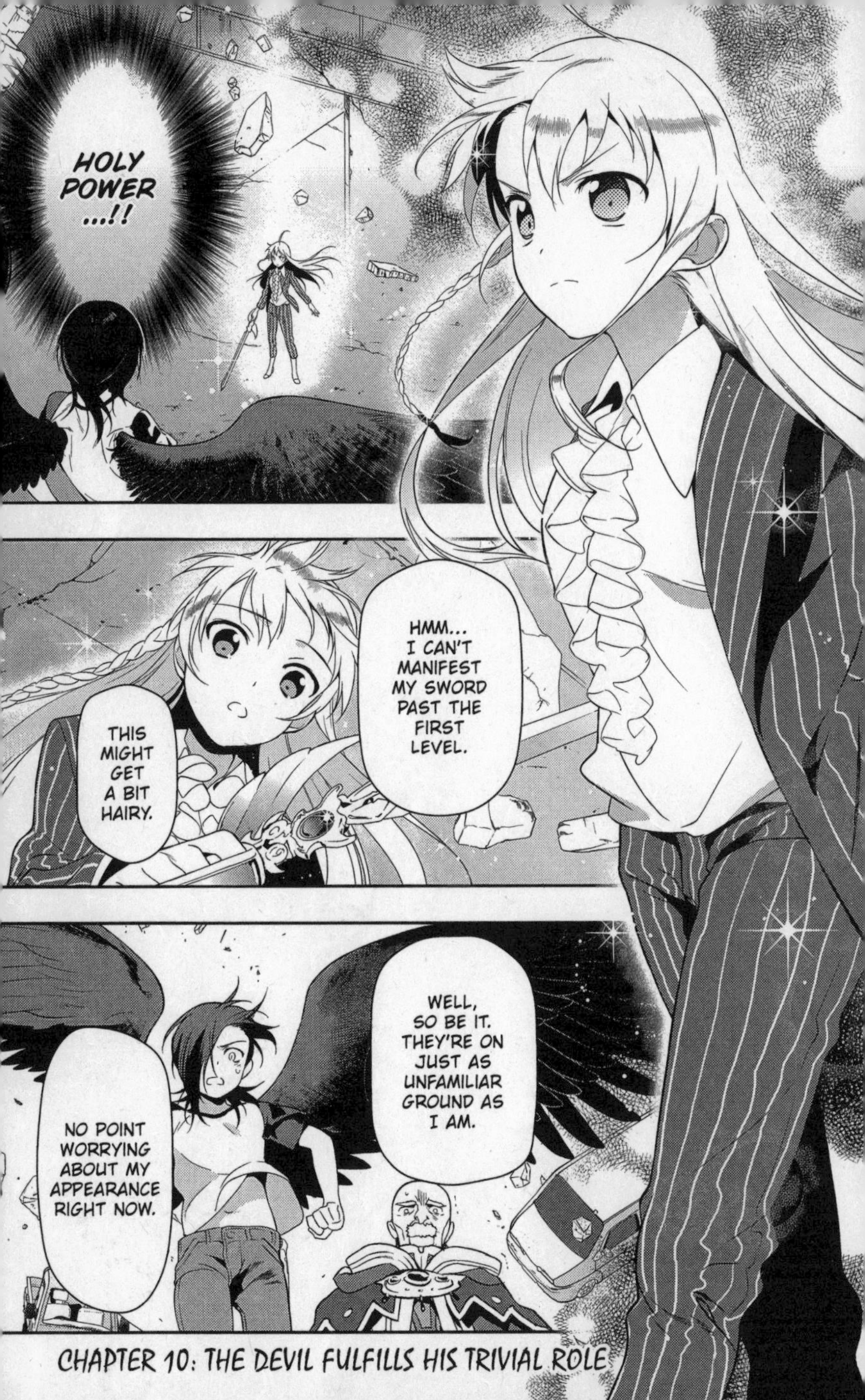
HOLY POWER ...!!
HMM... I CAN'T MANIFEST MY SWORD PAST THE FIRST LEVEL.
THIS MIGHT GET A BIT HAIRY.
WELL, SO BE IT. THEY'RE ON JUST AS UNFAMILIAR GROUND AS I AM.
NO POINT WORRYING ABOUT MY APPEARANCE RIGHT NOW.

CHAPTER 10: THE DEVIL FULFILLS HIS TRIVIAL ROLE

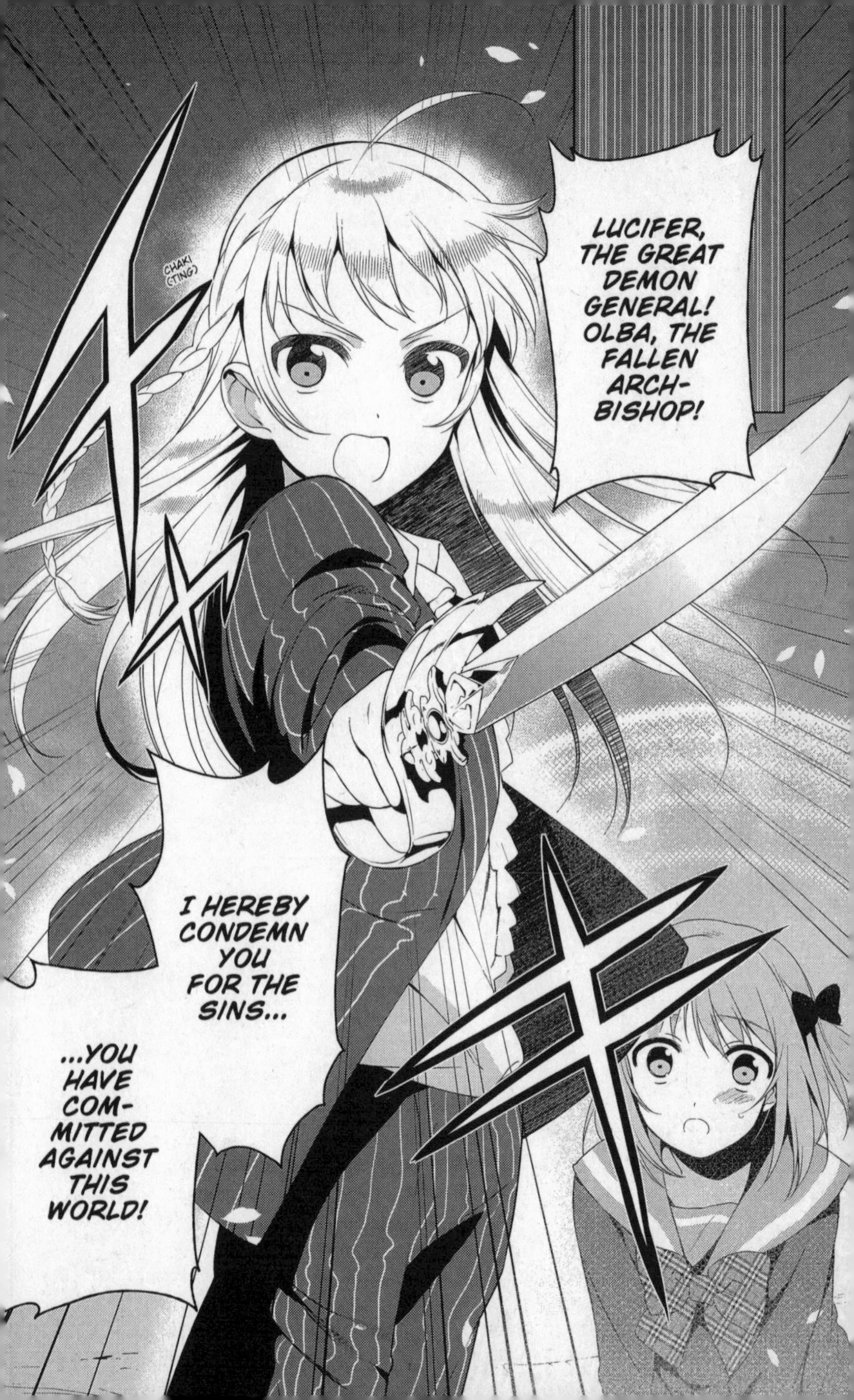
LUCIFER, THE GREAT DEMON GENERAL! OLBA, THE FALLEN ARCH-BISHOP!
CHAKI (TING)
I HEREBY CONDEMN YOU FOR THE SINS...
...YOU HAVE COM-MITTED AGAINST THIS WORLD!

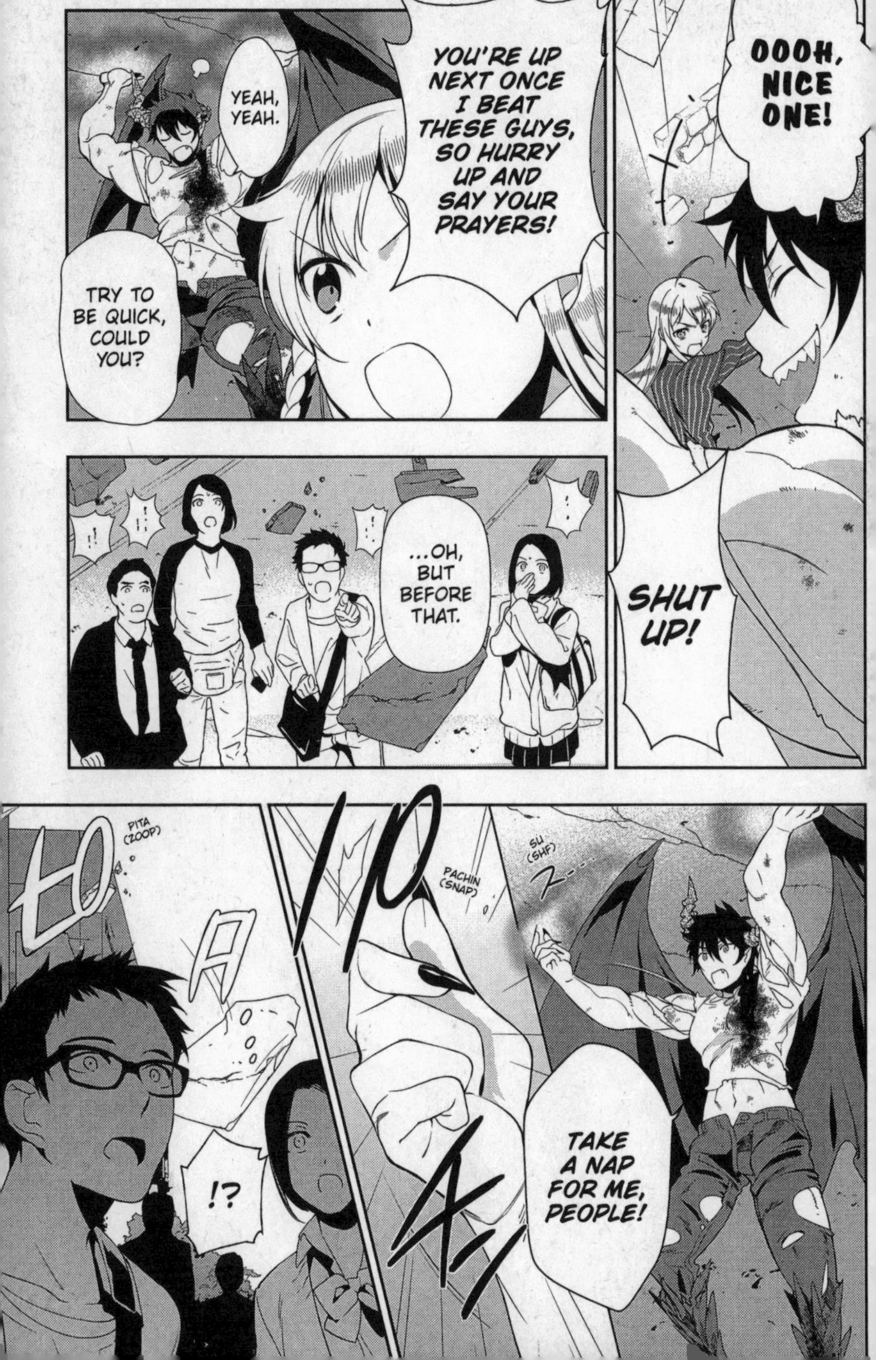
OOOH, NICE ONE!
SHUT UP!
YOU'RE UP NEXT ONCE I BEAT THESE GUYS, SO HURRY UP AND SAY YOUR PRAYERS!
YEAH, YEAH.
TRY TO BE QUICK, COULD YOU?
...OH, BUT BEFORE THAT.
SU (SHF)
TAKE A NAP FOR ME, PEOPLE!
PACHIN (SNAP)
PITA (ZOOP)
!?

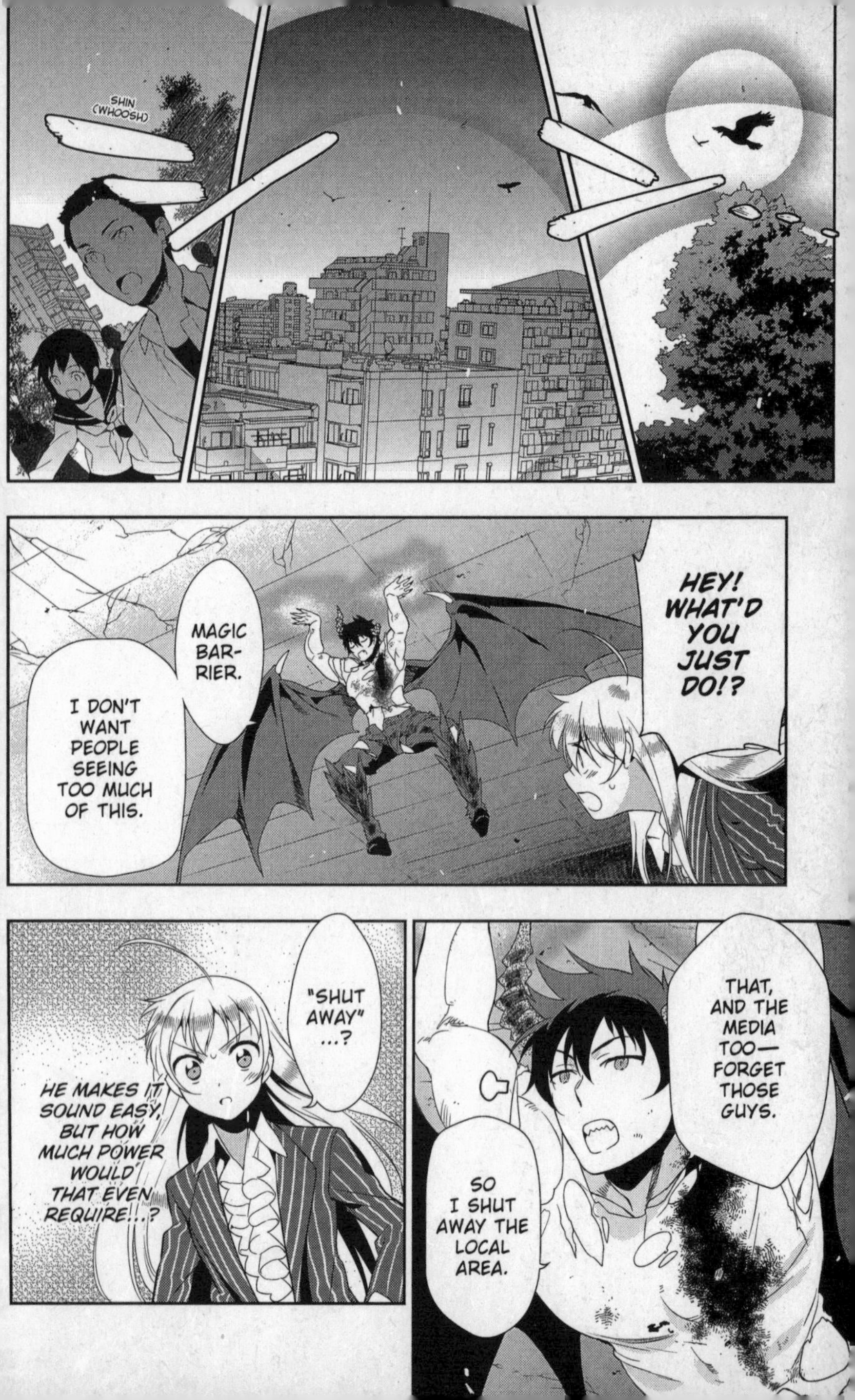
SHIN (WHOOSH)
HEY! WHAT'D YOU JUST DO!?
MAGIC BARRIER.
I DON'T WANT PEOPLE SEEING TOO MUCH OF THIS.
THAT, AND THE MEDIA TOO— FORGET THOSE GUYS.
SO I SHUT AWAY THE LOCAL AREA.
"SHUT AWAY" ...?
HE MAKES IT SOUND EASY, BUT HOW MUCH POWER WOULD THAT EVEN REQUIRE!..?

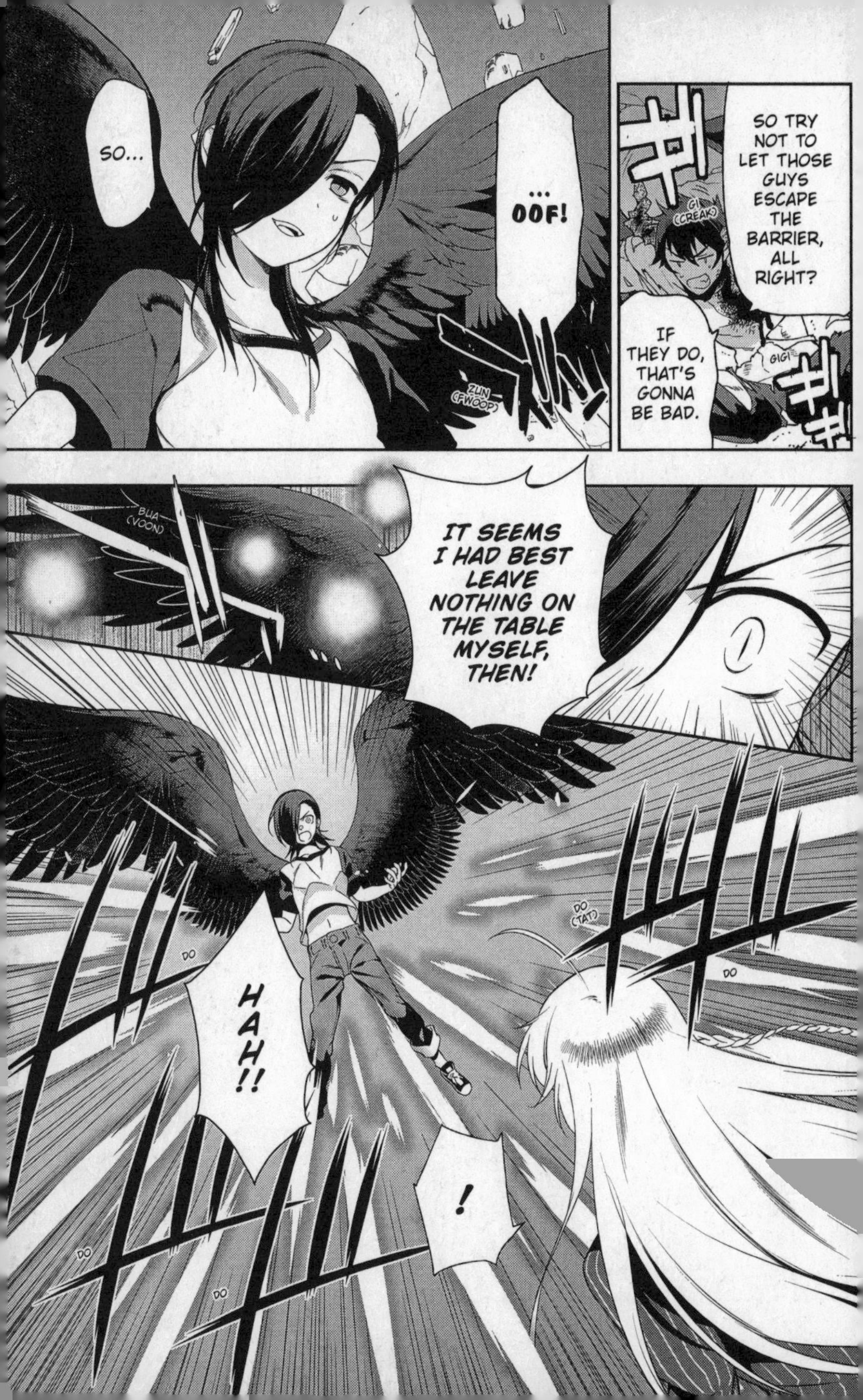
SO TRY NOT TO LET THOSE GUYS ESCAPE THE BARRIER, ALL RIGHT?
GI (CREAK)
IF THEY DO, THAT'S GONNA BE BAD.
GIGI
SO...
...OOF!
ZUN (FWOOP)
IT SEEMS I HAD BEST LEAVE NOTHING ON THE TABLE MYSELF, THEN!
BUA (VOON)
DO (TAT)
DO
DO
HAH!!
!
DO
DO

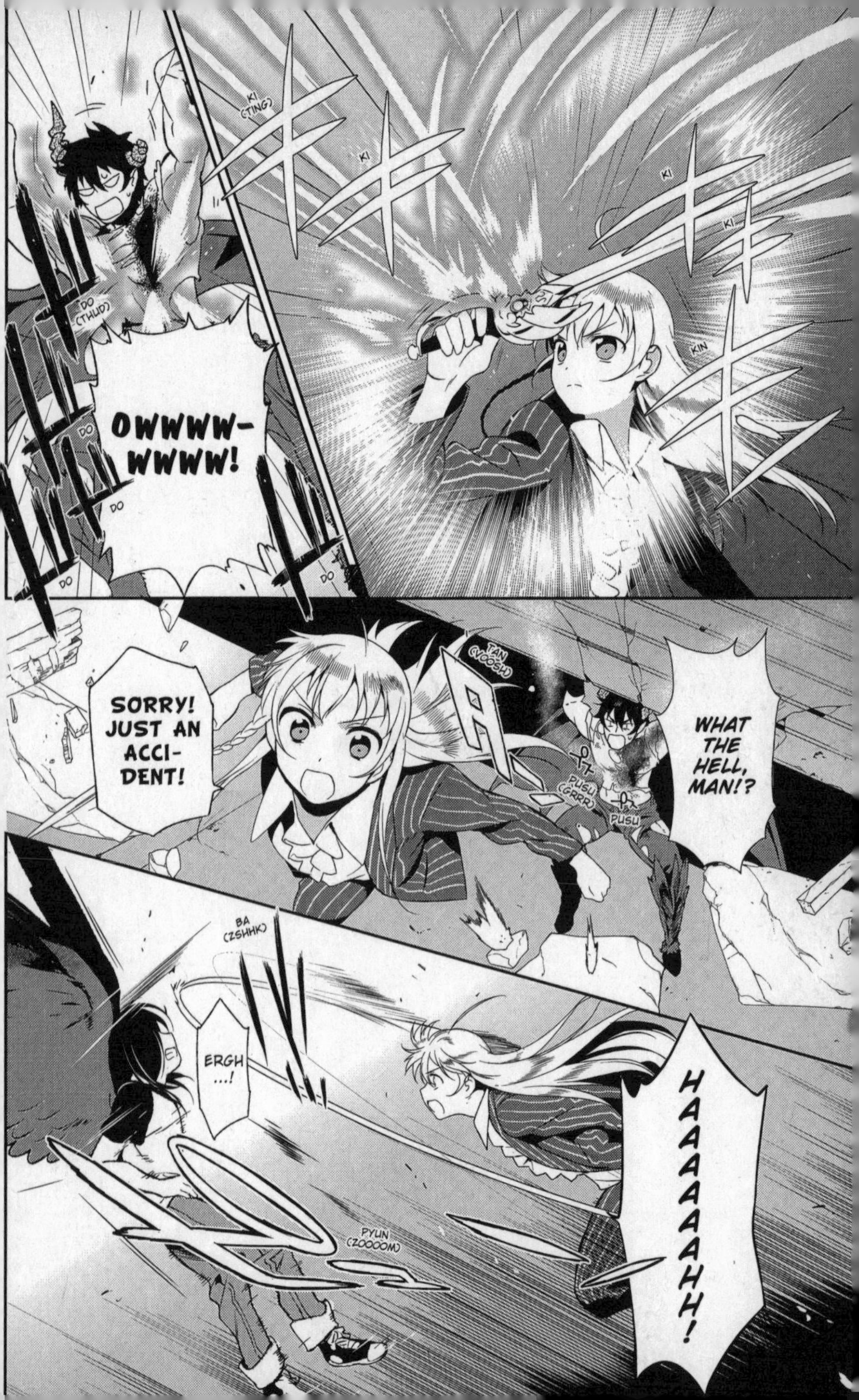
KI (TING)
KI
KI
KI
KIN
DO (THUD)
OWWWW-WWWW!
DO
DO
DO
DO
WHAT THE HELL, MAN!?
TAN (VOOSH)
PUSU (GRRR)
PUSU
SORRY! JUST AN ACCI-DENT!
HAAAAAAAH!
BA (ZSHHK)
ERGH ...!
PYUN (ZOOOOM)

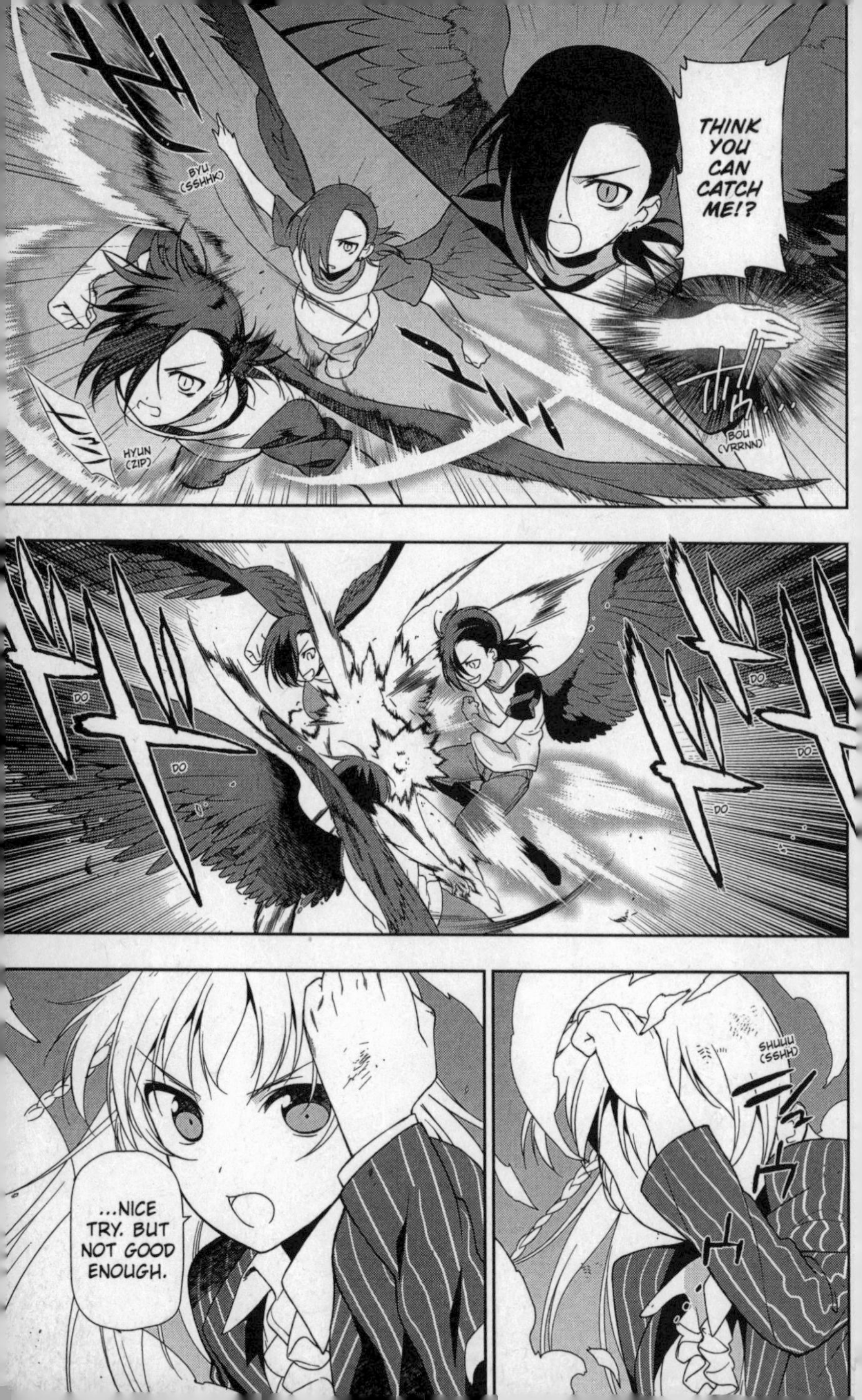
THINK YOU CAN CATCH ME!?
BOU (VRRNN)
BYU (SSHHK)
HYUN (ZIP)
DO
DO
DO
DO
DO
SHUUU (SSHH)
...NICE TRY. BUT NOT GOOD ENOUGH.

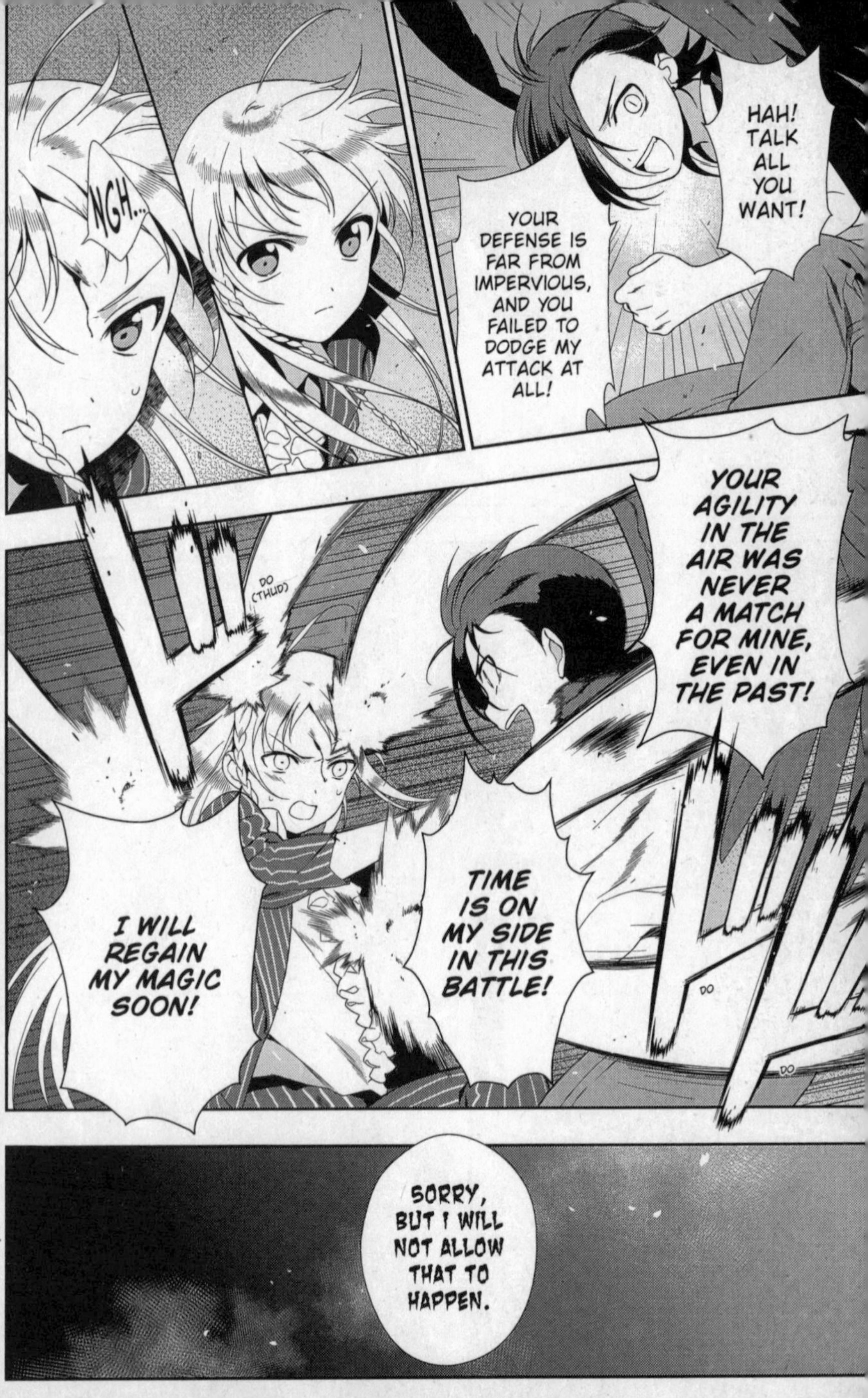
HAH! TALK ALL YOU WANT!
YOUR DEFENSE IS FAR FROM IMPERVIOUS, AND YOU FAILED TO DODGE MY ATTACK AT ALL!
NGH...
YOUR AGILITY IN THE AIR WAS NEVER A MATCH FOR MINE, EVEN IN THE PAST!
DO (THUD)
DO
DO
TIME IS ON MY SIDE IN THIS BATTLE!
I WILL REGAIN MY MAGIC SOON!
SORRY, BUT I WILL NOT ALLOW THAT TO HAPPEN.

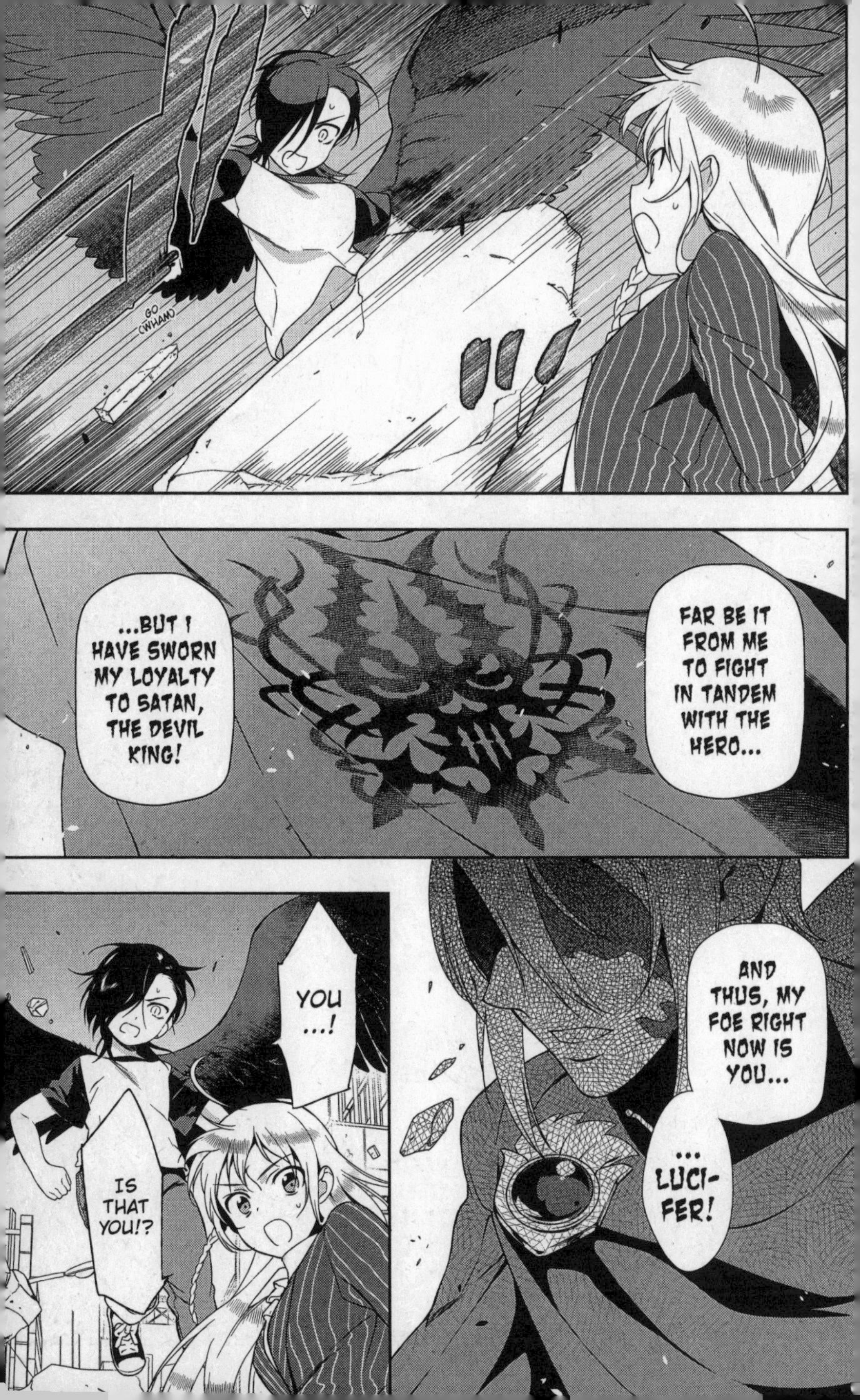
GO (WHAM)
FAR BE IT FROM ME TO FIGHT IN TANDEM WITH THE HERO...
...BUT I HAVE SWORN MY LOYALTY TO SATAN, THE DEVIL KING!
AND THUS, MY FOE RIGHT NOW IS YOU...
...LUCIFER!
YOU ...!
IS THAT YOU!?

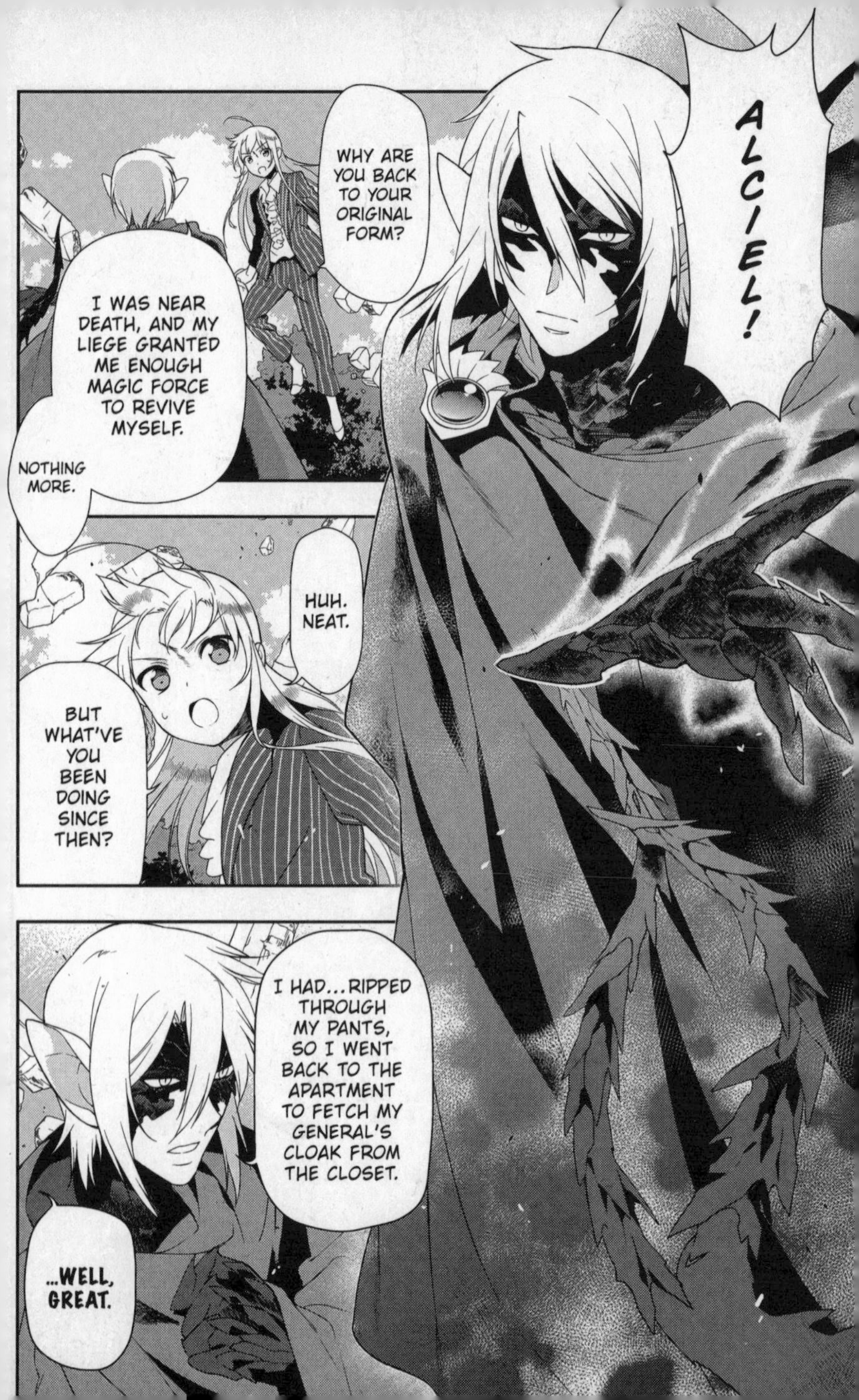
ALCIEL!
WHY ARE YOU BACK TO YOUR ORIGINAL FORM?
I WAS NEAR DEATH, AND MY LIEGE GRANTED ME ENOUGH MAGIC FORCE TO REVIVE MYSELF.
NOTHING MORE.
HUH. NEAT.
BUT WHAT'VE YOU BEEN DOING SINCE THEN?
I HAD...RIPPED THROUGH MY PANTS, SO I WENT BACK TO THE APARTMENT TO FETCH MY GENERAL'S CLOAK FROM THE CLOSET.
...WELL, GREAT.

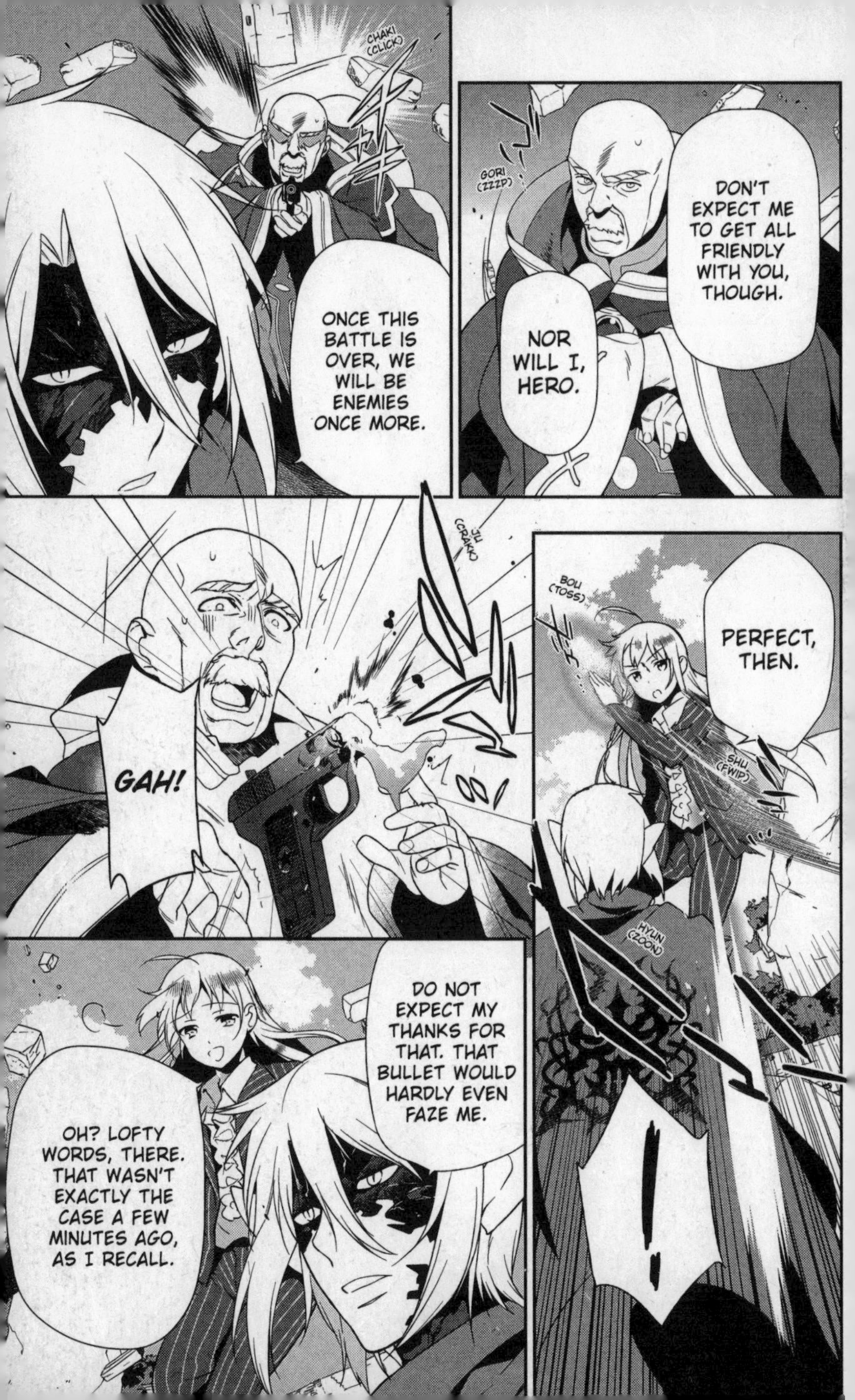

DON'T EXPECT ME TO GET ALL FRIENDLY WITH YOU, THOUGH.
GORI (ZZZP)
NOR WILL I, HERO.
CHAKI (CLICK)
ONCE THIS BATTLE IS OVER, WE WILL BE ENEMIES ONCE MORE.
PERFECT, THEN.
BOU (TOSS)
SHU (FWIP)
HYUN (ZOON)
!
JU (CRAKK)
GAH!
DO NOT EXPECT MY THANKS FOR THAT. THAT BULLET WOULD HARDLY EVEN FAZE ME.
OH? LOFTY WORDS, THERE. THAT WASN'T EXACTLY THE CASE A FEW MINUTES AGO, AS I RECALL.

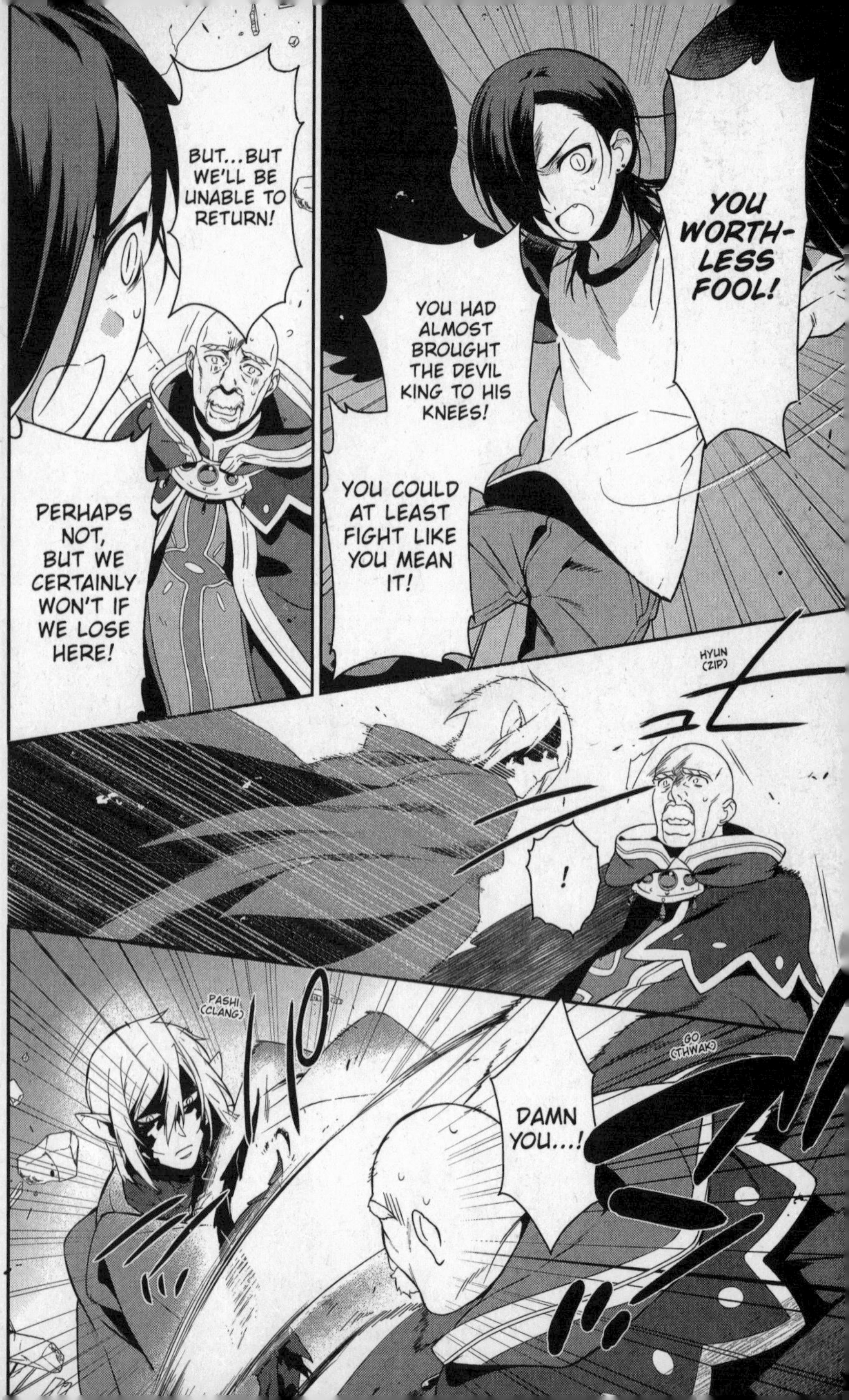
YOU WORTHLESS FOOL!
YOU HAD ALMOST BROUGHT THE DEVIL KING TO HIS KNEES!
YOU COULD AT LEAST FIGHT LIKE YOU MEAN IT!
BUT...BUT WE'LL BE UNABLE TO RETURN!
PERHAPS NOT, BUT WE CERTAINLY WON'T IF WE LOSE HERE!
HYUN (ZIP)
!
GO (THWAK)
DAMN YOU...!
PASHI (CLANG)

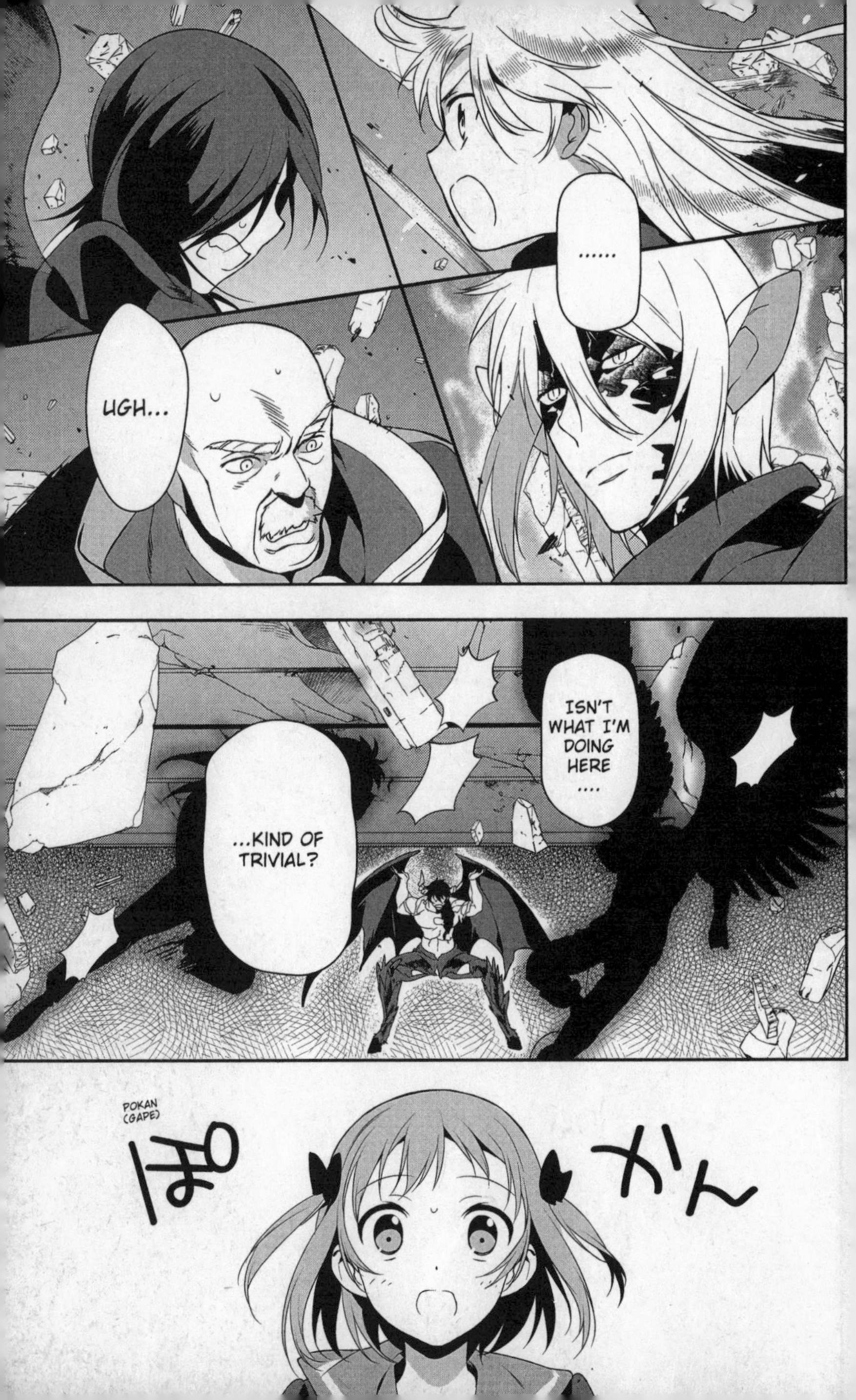
......
UGH...
ISN'T WHAT I'M DOING HERE ....
...KIND OF TRIVIAL?
POKAN (GAPE)
ぽかん

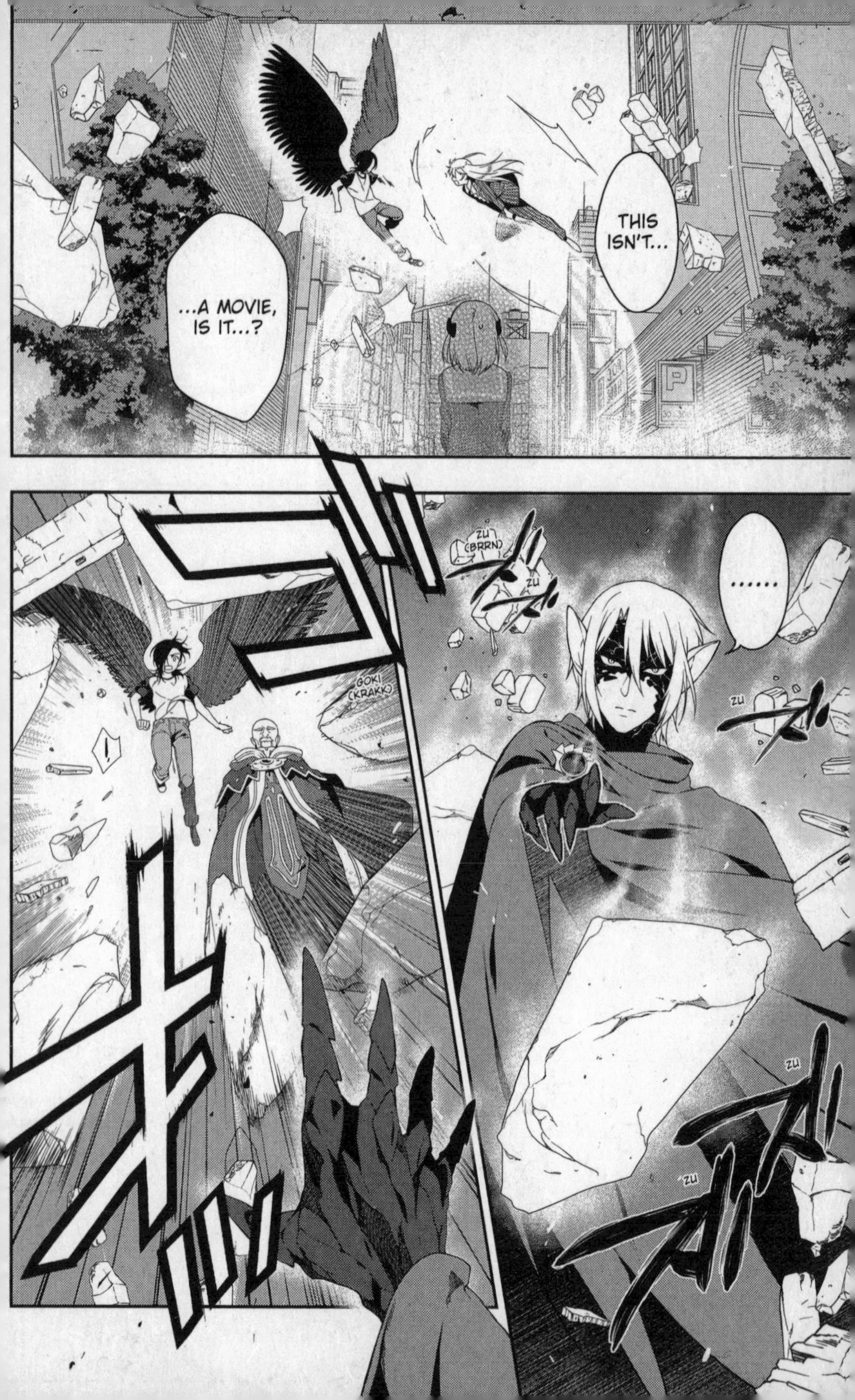
THIS ISN'T...
...A MOVIE, IS IT...?
......
ZU (BRRN)
ZU
ZU
GOKI (KRAKK)
!
ZU
ZU

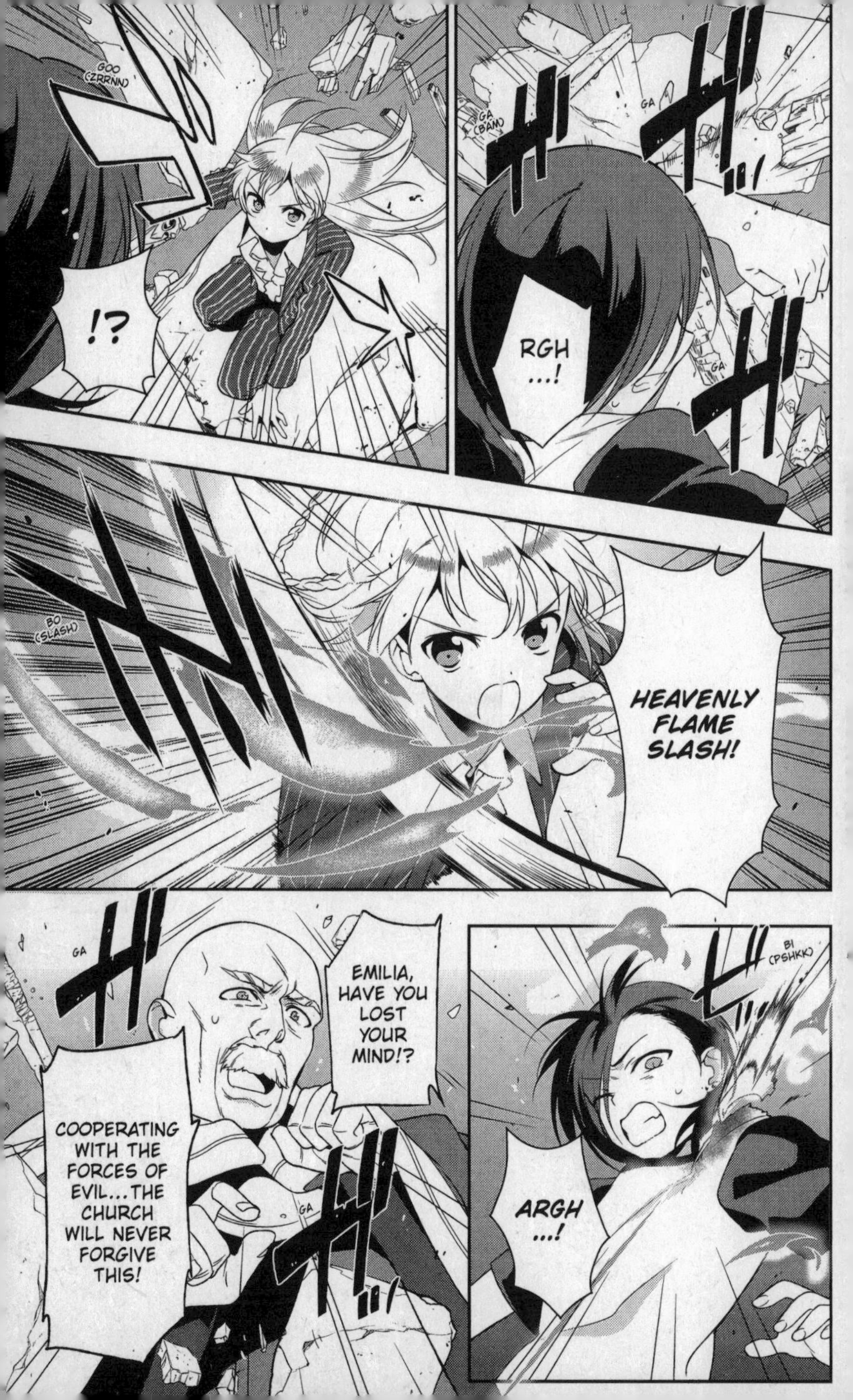
GA
GA (BAM)
GA
RGH ...!
GOO (ZRRNN)
!?
HEAVENLY FLAME SLASH!
BO (SLASH)
BI (PSHKK)
ARGH ...!
EMILIA, HAVE YOU LOST YOUR MIND!?
GA
COOPERATING WITH THE FORCES OF EVIL... THE CHURCH WILL NEVER FORGIVE THIS!
GA

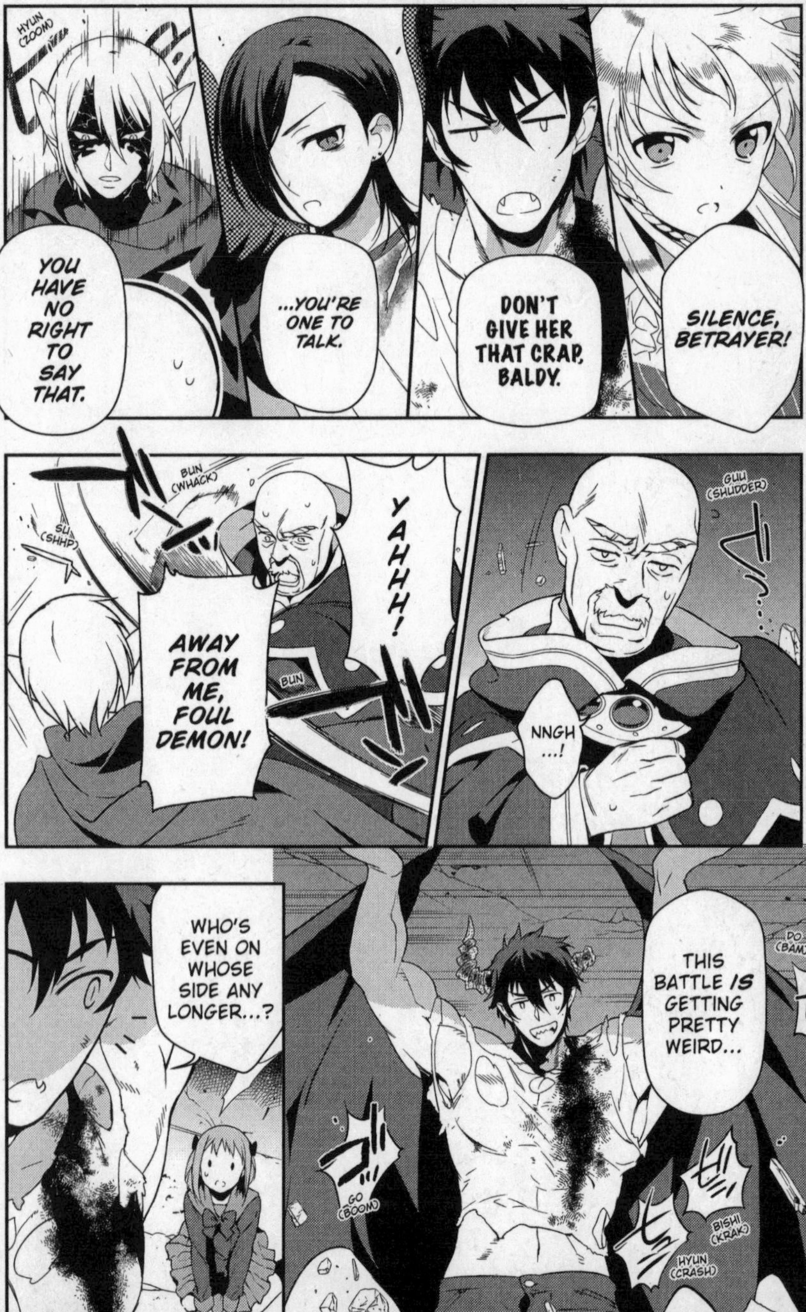
SILENCE, BETRAYER!
DON'T GIVE HER THAT CRAP, BALDY.
...YOU'RE ONE TO TALK.
YOU HAVE NO RIGHT TO SAY THAT.
HYUN (ZOOM)
GUU (SHUDDER)
NNGH ...!
YAHHH!
BUN (WHACK)
SU (SHHP)
AWAY FROM ME, FOUL DEMON!
BUN
DO (BAM)
THIS BATTLE IS GETTING PRETTY WEIRD...
GO (BOOM)
BISHI (KRAK)
HYUN (CRASH)
WHO'S EVEN ON WHOSE SIDE ANY LONGER...?

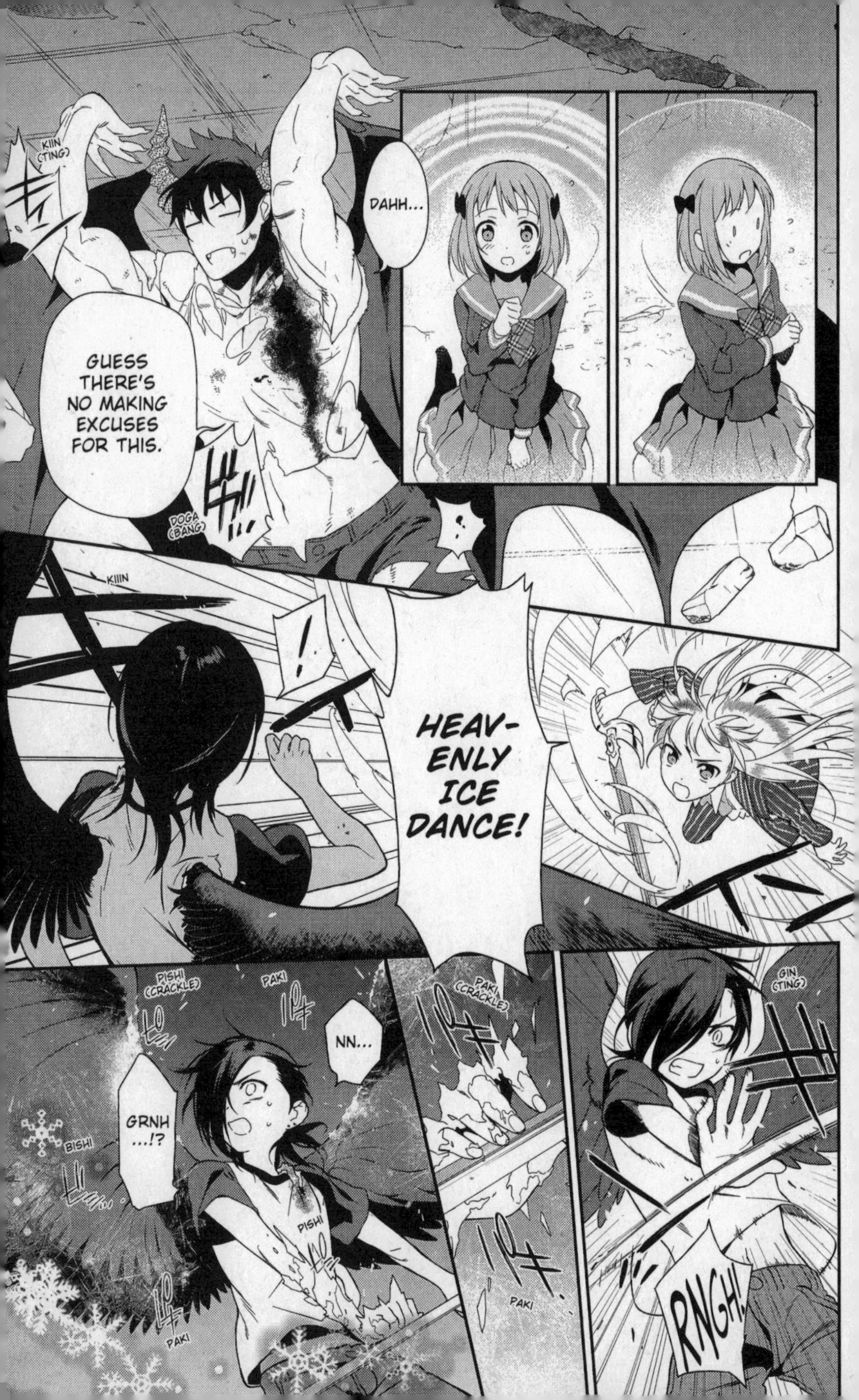

DAHH...
KIIN (TING)
GUESS THERE'S NO MAKING EXCUSES FOR THIS.
DOGA (BANG)
!
KIIN
!
HEAV-ENLY ICE DANCE!
GIN (TING)
RNGH!
PAKI (CRACKLE)
PAKI
PAKI
PISHI (CRACKLE)
NN...
GRNH ...!?
BISHI
PISHI
PAKI

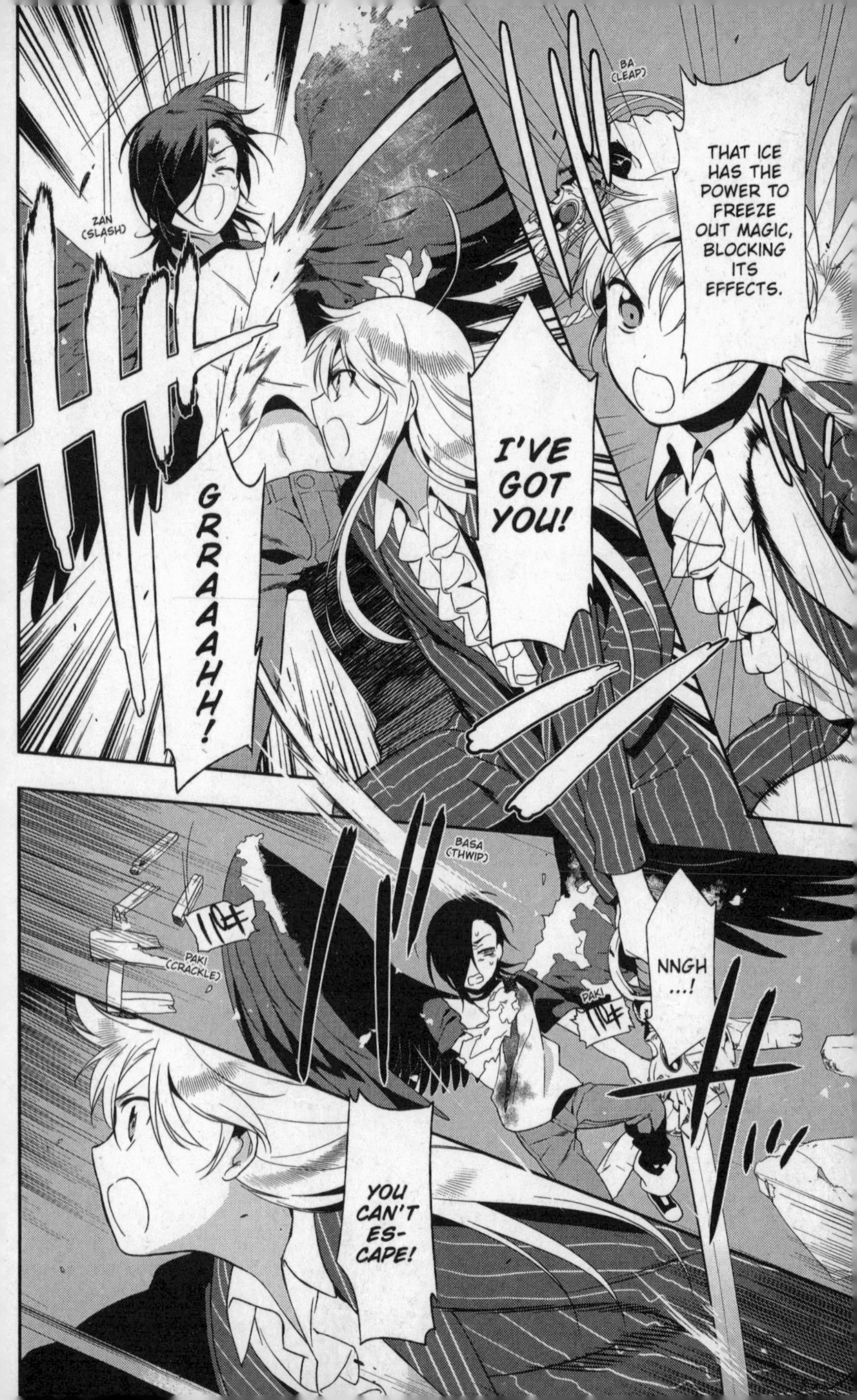
BA (LEAP)
THAT ICE HAS THE POWER TO FREEZE OUT MAGIC, BLOCKING ITS EFFECTS.
I'VE GOT YOU!
ZAN (SLASH)
GRRAAAAHH!
NNGH ...!
PAKI
BASA (THWIP)
PAKI (CRACKLE)
YOU CAN'T ES-CAPE!

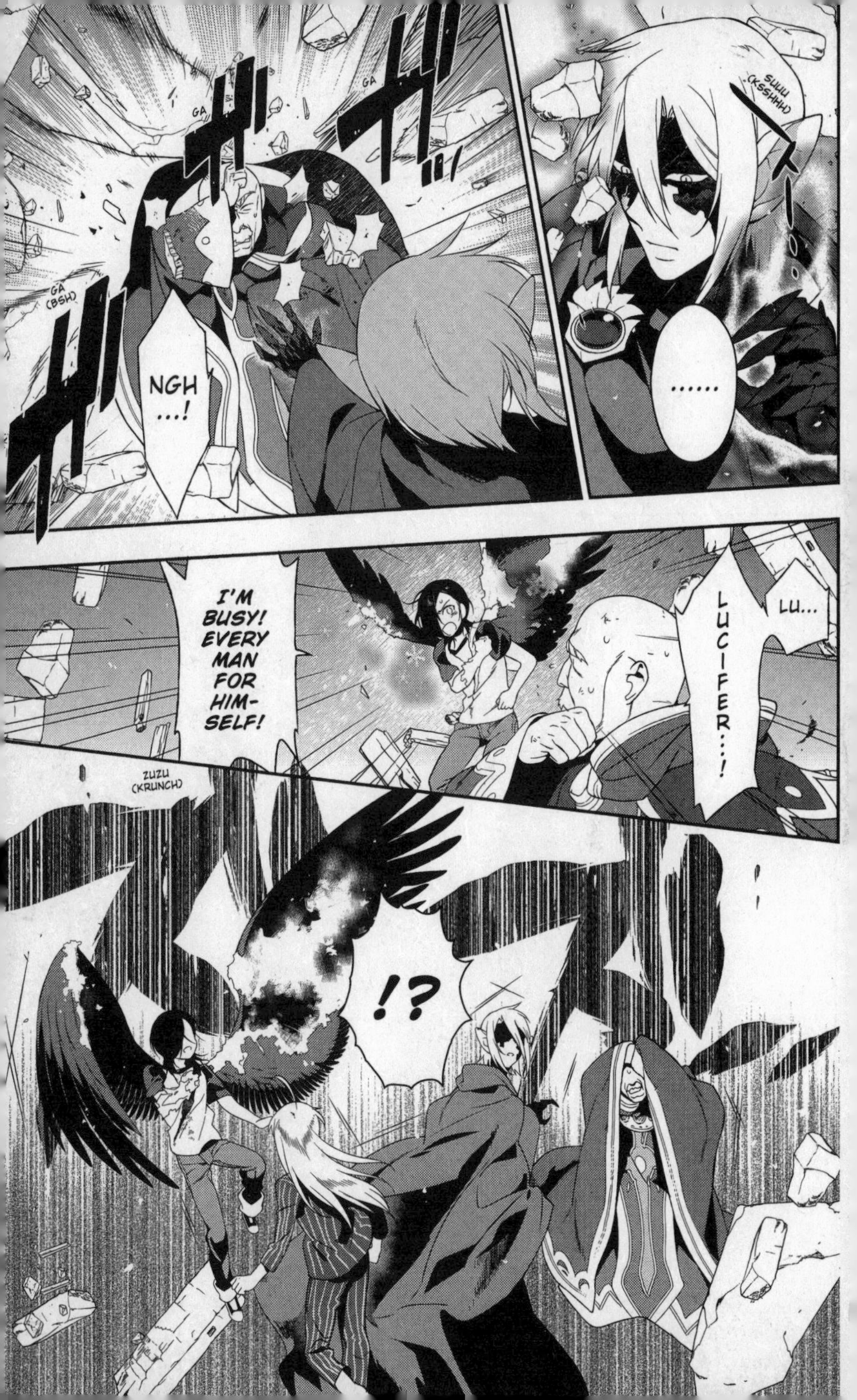
SUUU (KSSHHH)
......
GA
GA
GA (BSH)
NGH ...!
LU...
LUCIFER...!
I'M BUSY! EVERY MAN FOR HIM-SELF!
ZUZU (KRUNCH)
!?

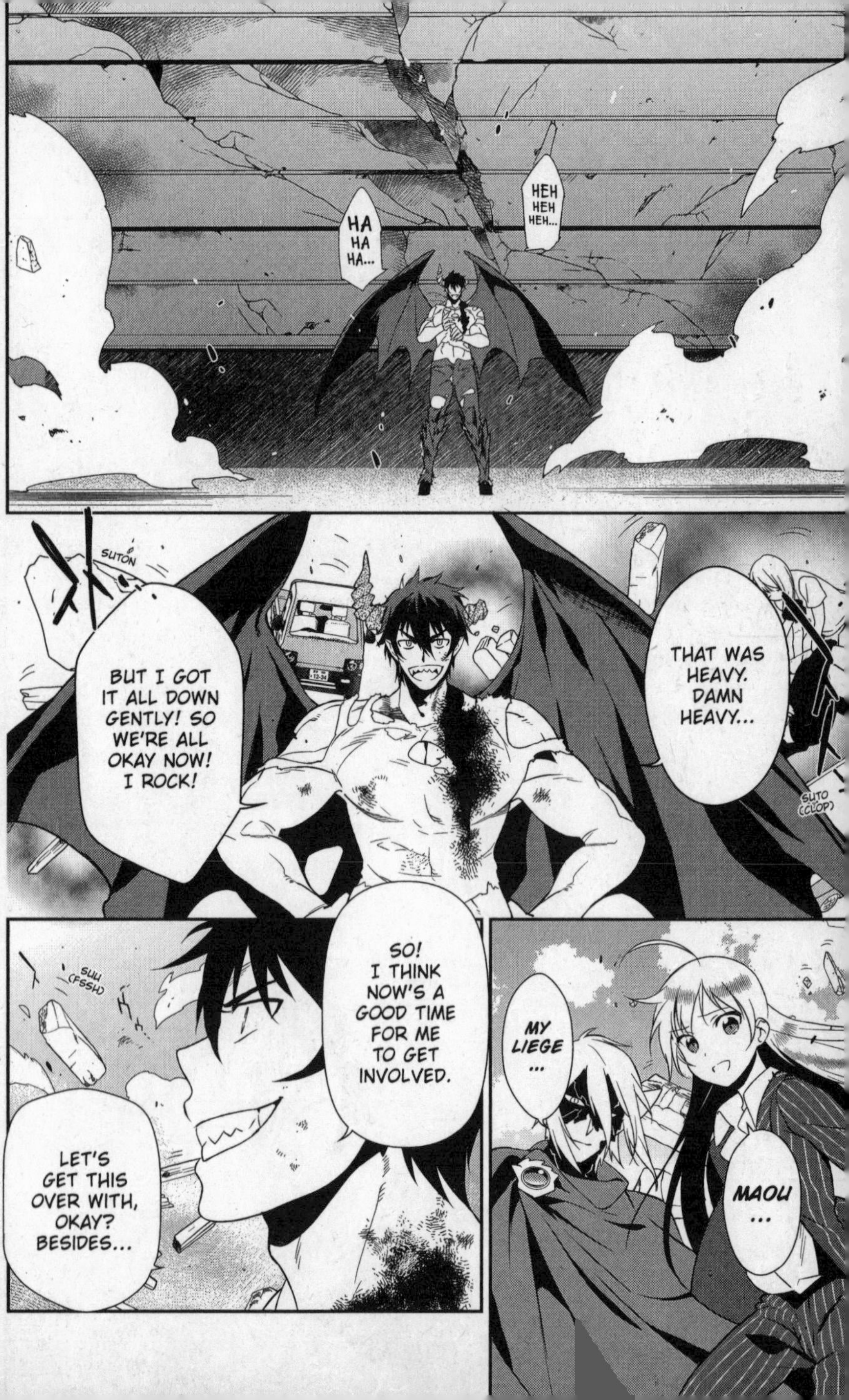
HEH HEH HEH...
HA HA HA...
THAT WAS HEAVY. DAMN HEAVY...
SUTO (CLOP)
SUTON
BUT I GOT IT ALL DOWN GENTLY! SO WE'RE ALL OKAY NOW! I ROCK!
MY LIEGE ...
MAOU ...
SO! I THINK NOW'S A GOOD TIME FOR ME TO GET INVOLVED.
SUU (FSSH)
LET'S GET THIS OVER WITH, OKAY? BESIDES...

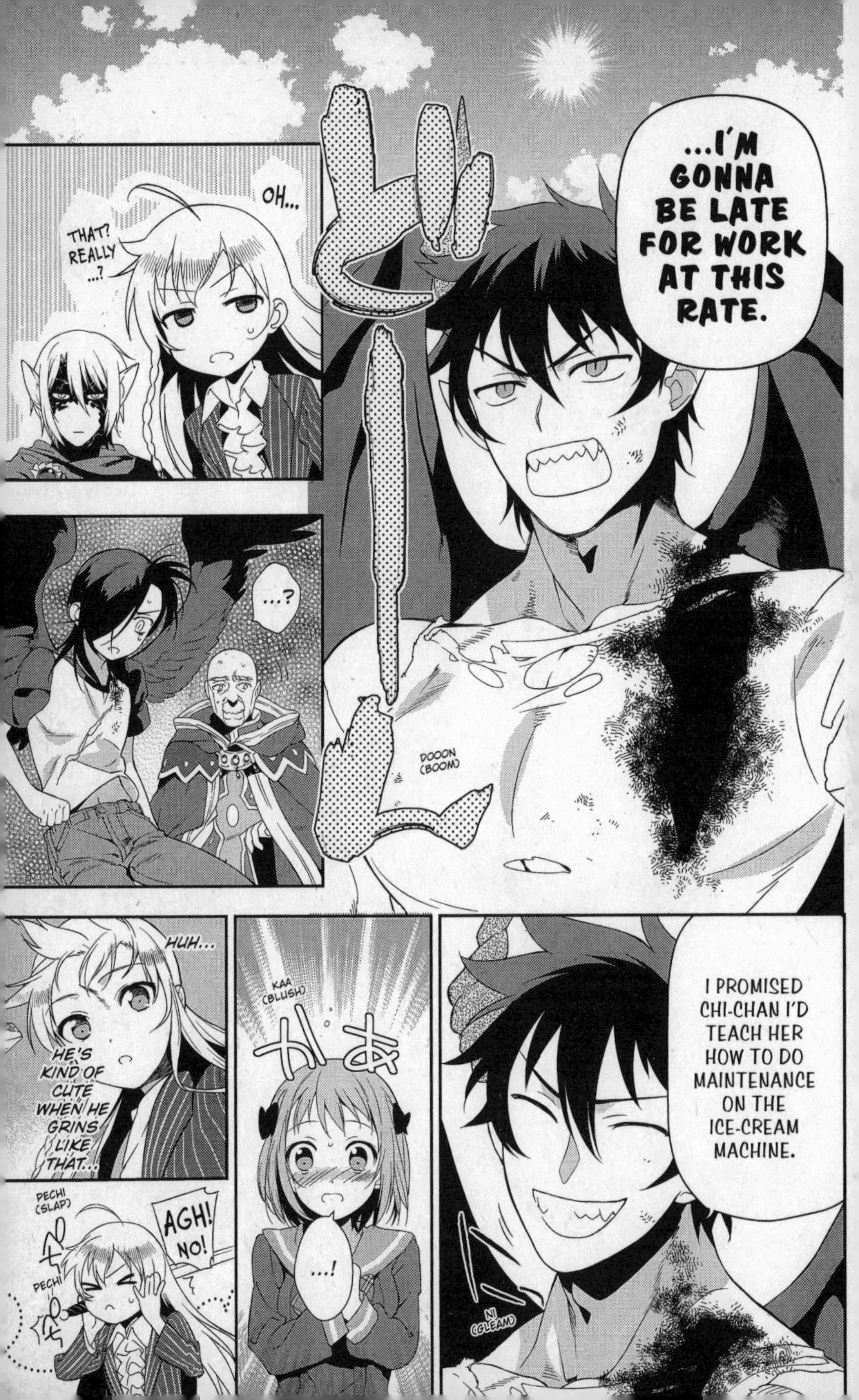
...I'M GONNA BE LATE FOR WORK AT THIS RATE.
DOOON (BOOM)
OH...
THAT? REALLY ...?
...?
I PROMISED CHI-CHAN I'D TEACH HER HOW TO DO MAINTENANCE ON THE ICE-CREAM MACHINE.
NI (GLEAM)
KAA (BLUSH)
...!
HUH...
HE'S KIND OF CUTE WHEN HE GRINS LIKE THAT...
PECHI (SLAP)
AGH! NO!
PECHI

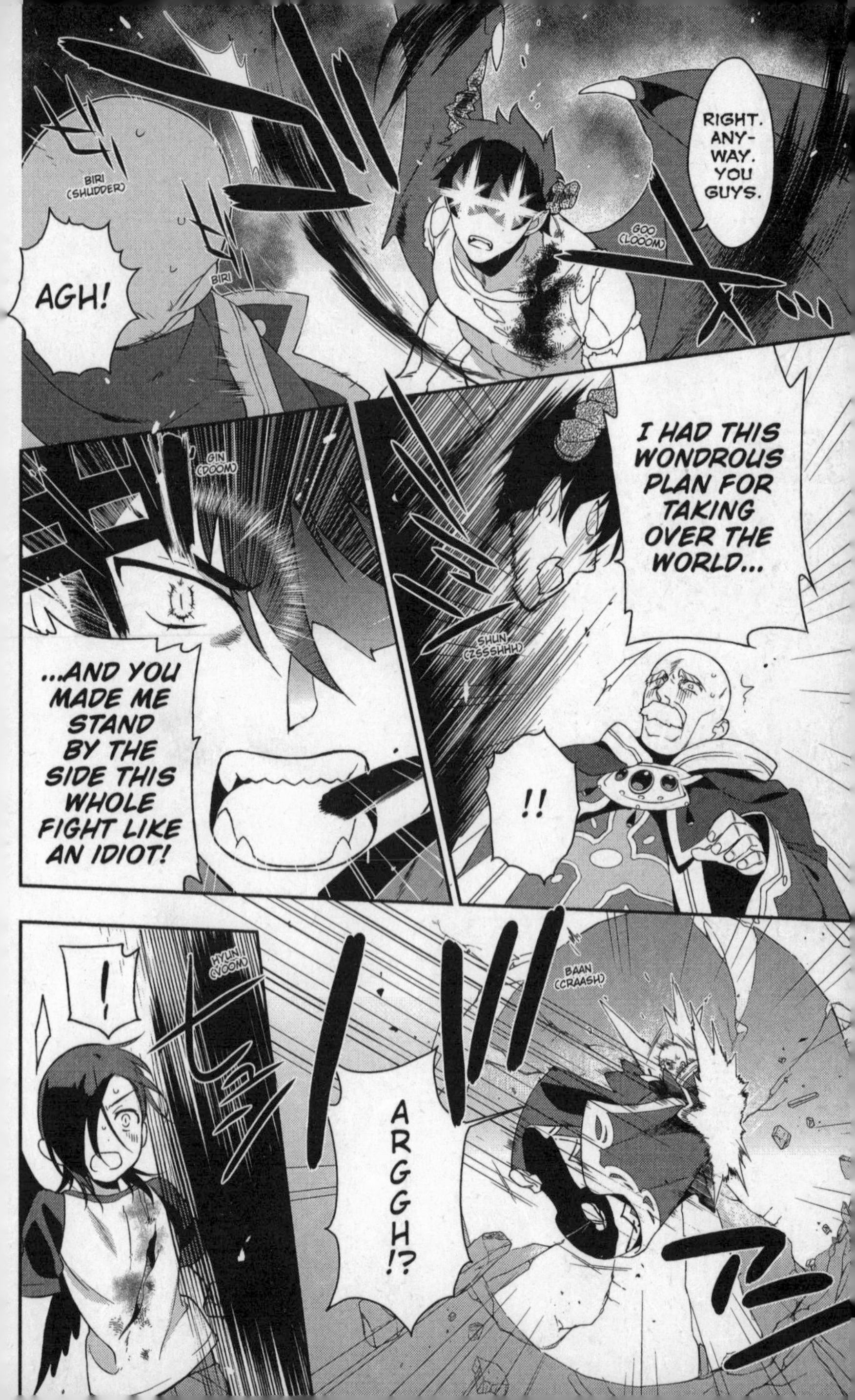
RIGHT. ANY-WAY. YOU GUYS.
GOO (LOOOM)
BIRI (SHUDDER)
AGH!
BIRI
I HAD THIS WONDROUS PLAN FOR TAKING OVER THE WORLD...
SHUN (ZSSSHHH)
!!
GIN (DOOM)
...AND YOU MADE ME STAND BY THE SIDE THIS WHOLE FIGHT LIKE AN IDIOT!
BAAN (CRAASH)
ARGGH!?
HYUN (VOOM)
!

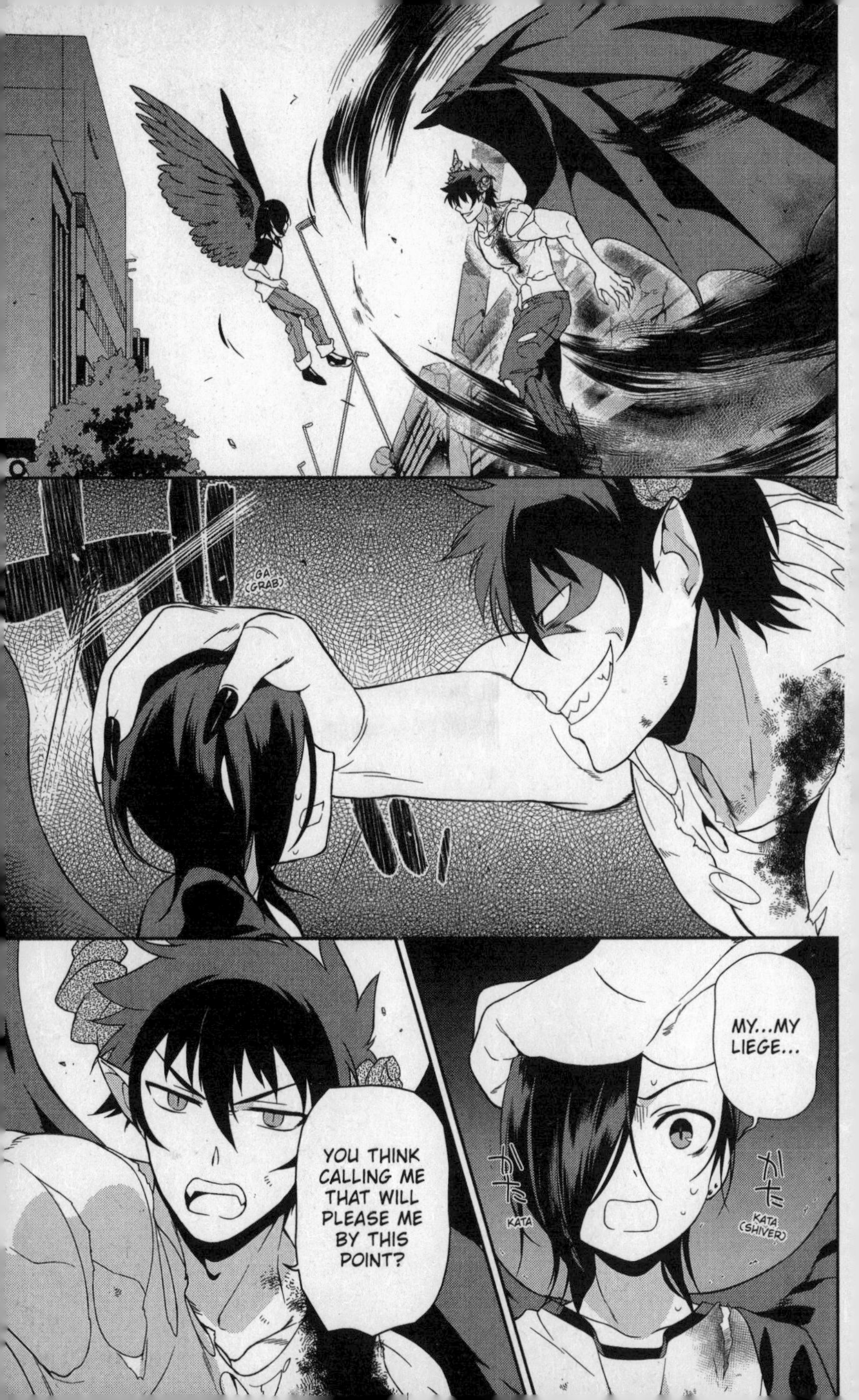
GA (GRAB)
MY...MY LIEGE...
カタ
KATA (SHIVER)
カタ
KATA
YOU THINK CALLING ME THAT WILL PLEASE ME BY THIS POINT?

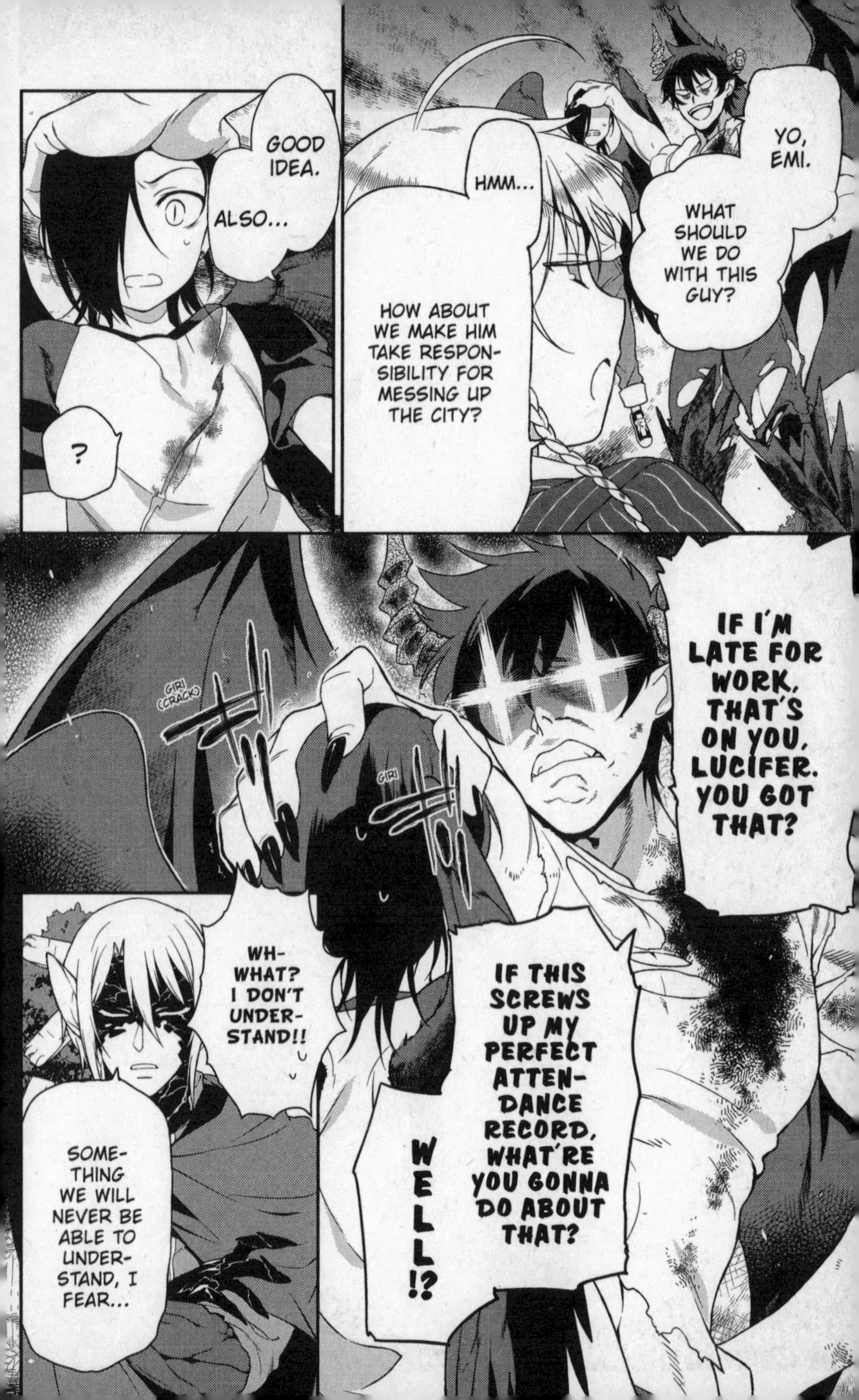
YO, EMI.
WHAT SHOULD WE DO WITH THIS GUY?
HMM...
HOW ABOUT WE MAKE HIM TAKE RESPONSIBILITY FOR MESSING UP THE CITY?
GOOD IDEA.
ALSO...
?
IF I'M LATE FOR WORK, THAT'S ON YOU, LUCIFER. YOU GOT THAT?
GIRI (CRACK)
GIRI
IF THIS SCREWS UP MY PERFECT ATTENDANCE RECORD, WHAT'RE YOU GONNA DO ABOUT THAT?
WELL!?
WH-WHAT? I DON'T UNDERSTAND!!
SOMETHING WE WILL NEVER BE ABLE TO UNDERSTAND, I FEAR...

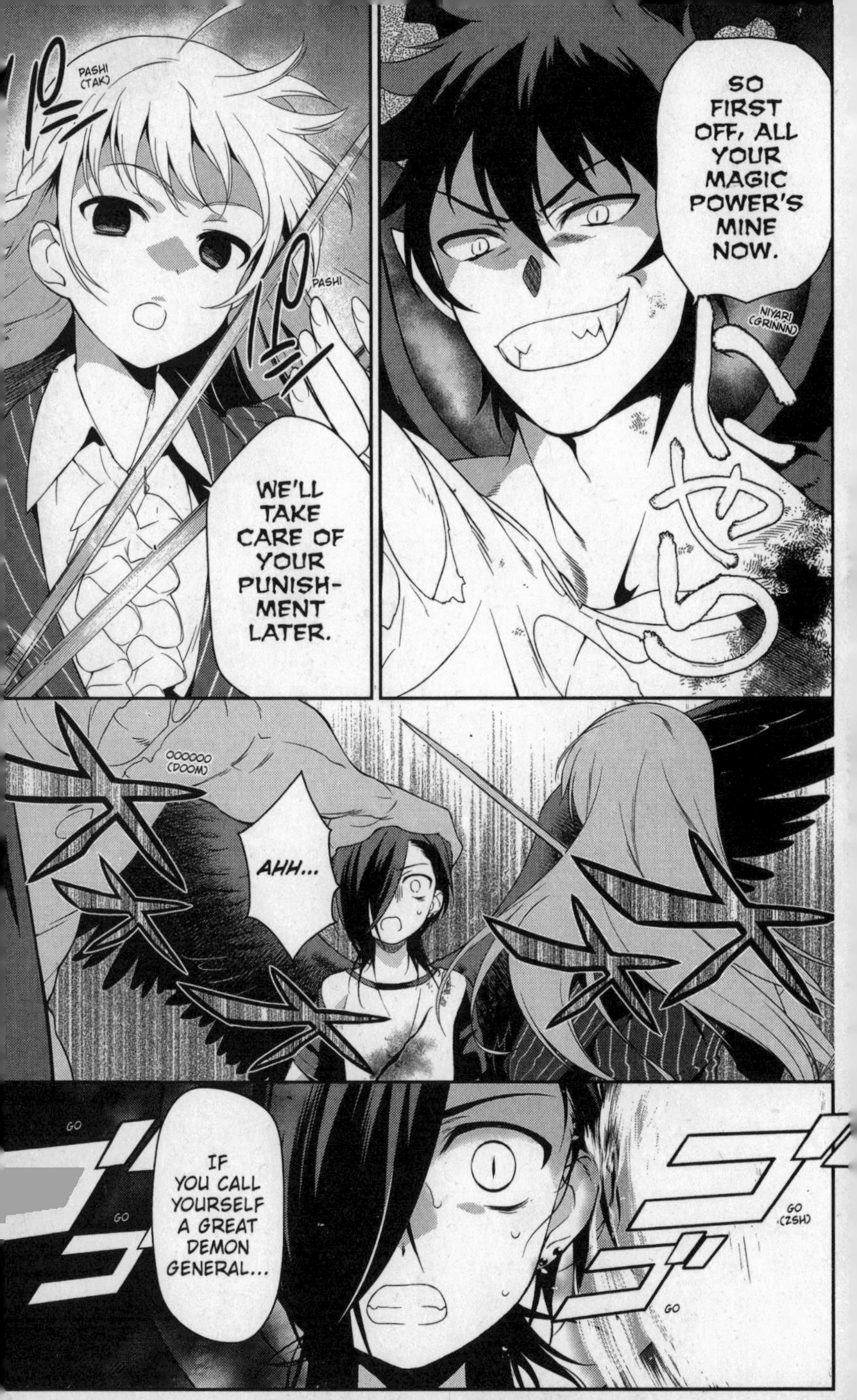
SO FIRST OFF, ALL YOUR MAGIC POWER'S MINE NOW.
NIYARI (GRINNN)
PASHI (TAK)
PASHI
WE'LL TAKE CARE OF YOUR PUNISHMENT LATER.
OOOOOO (DOOM)
AHH...
GO (ZSH)
GO
GO
IF YOU CALL YOURSELF A GREAT DEMON GENERAL...
GO

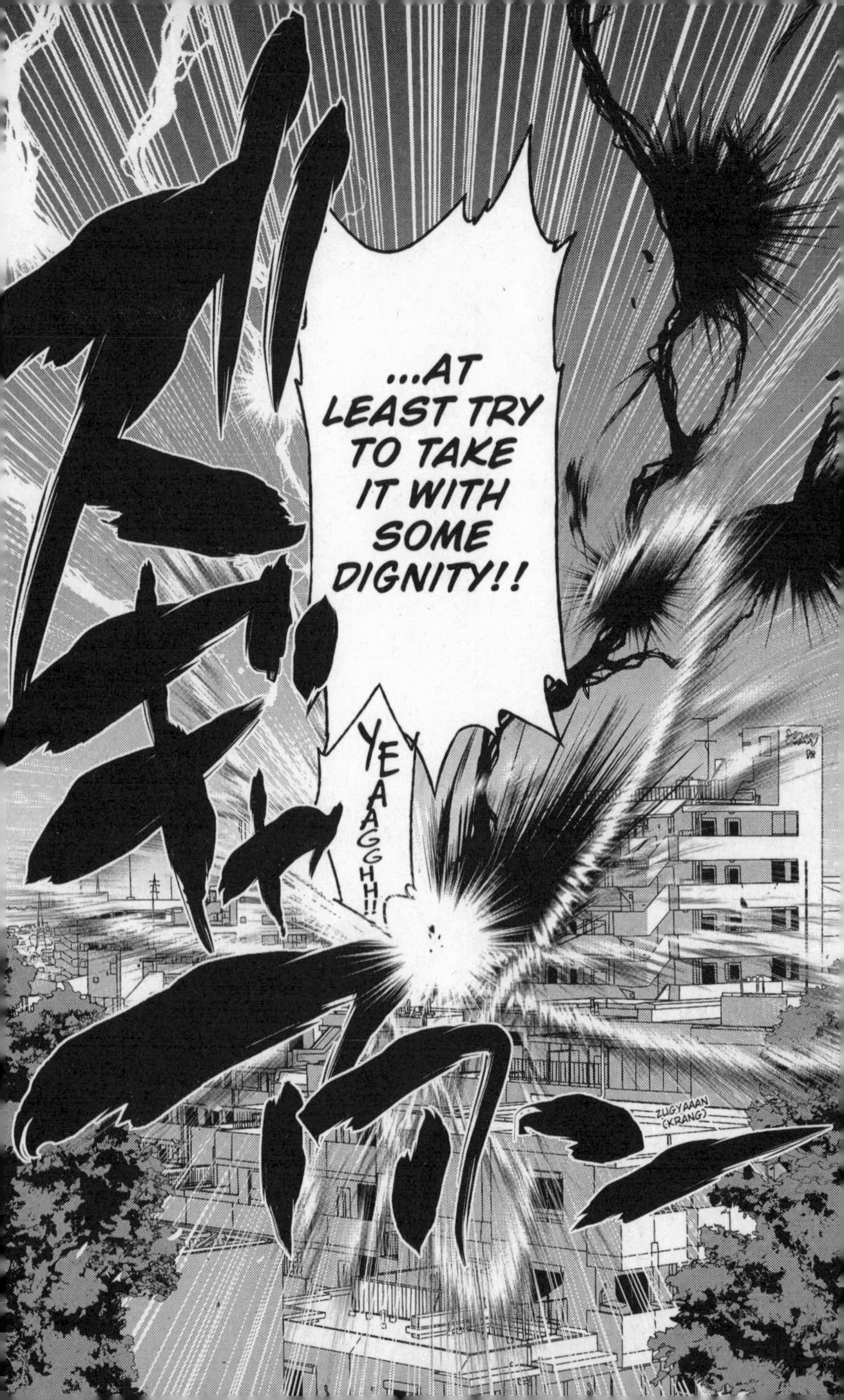
...AT LEAST TRY TO TAKE IT WITH SOME DIGNITY!!
YEAAAGGHH!!
ZUGYAAAN (KRANG)

Lucifer

THE DEVIL IS A PART-TIMER!

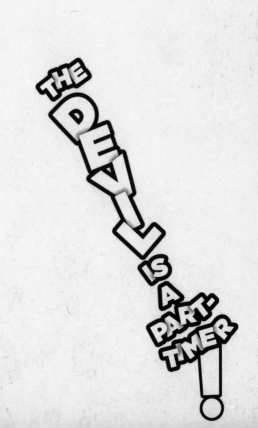

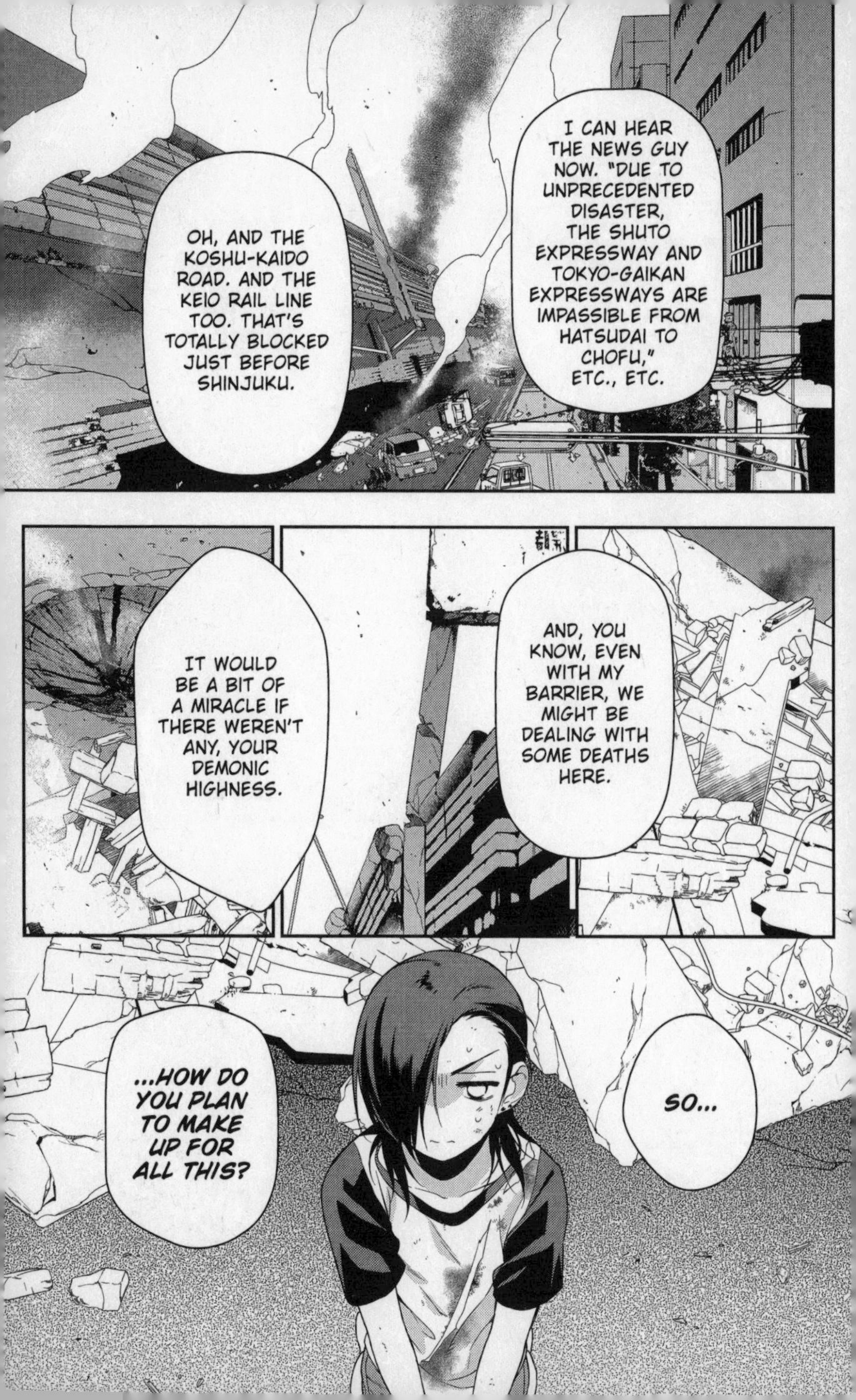
I CAN HEAR THE NEWS GUY NOW. "DUE TO UNPRECEDENTED DISASTER, THE SHUTO EXPRESSWAY AND TOKYO-GAIKAN EXPRESSWAYS ARE IMPASSIBLE FROM HATSUDAI TO CHOFU," ETC., ETC.
OH, AND THE KOSHU-KAIDO ROAD. AND THE KEIO RAIL LINE TOO. THAT'S TOTALLY BLOCKED JUST BEFORE SHINJUKU.
AND, YOU KNOW, EVEN WITH MY BARRIER, WE MIGHT BE DEALING WITH SOME DEATHS HERE.
IT WOULD BE A BIT OF A MIRACLE IF THERE WEREN'T ANY, YOUR DEMONIC HIGHNESS.
SO...
...HOW DO YOU PLAN TO MAKE UP FOR ALL THIS?

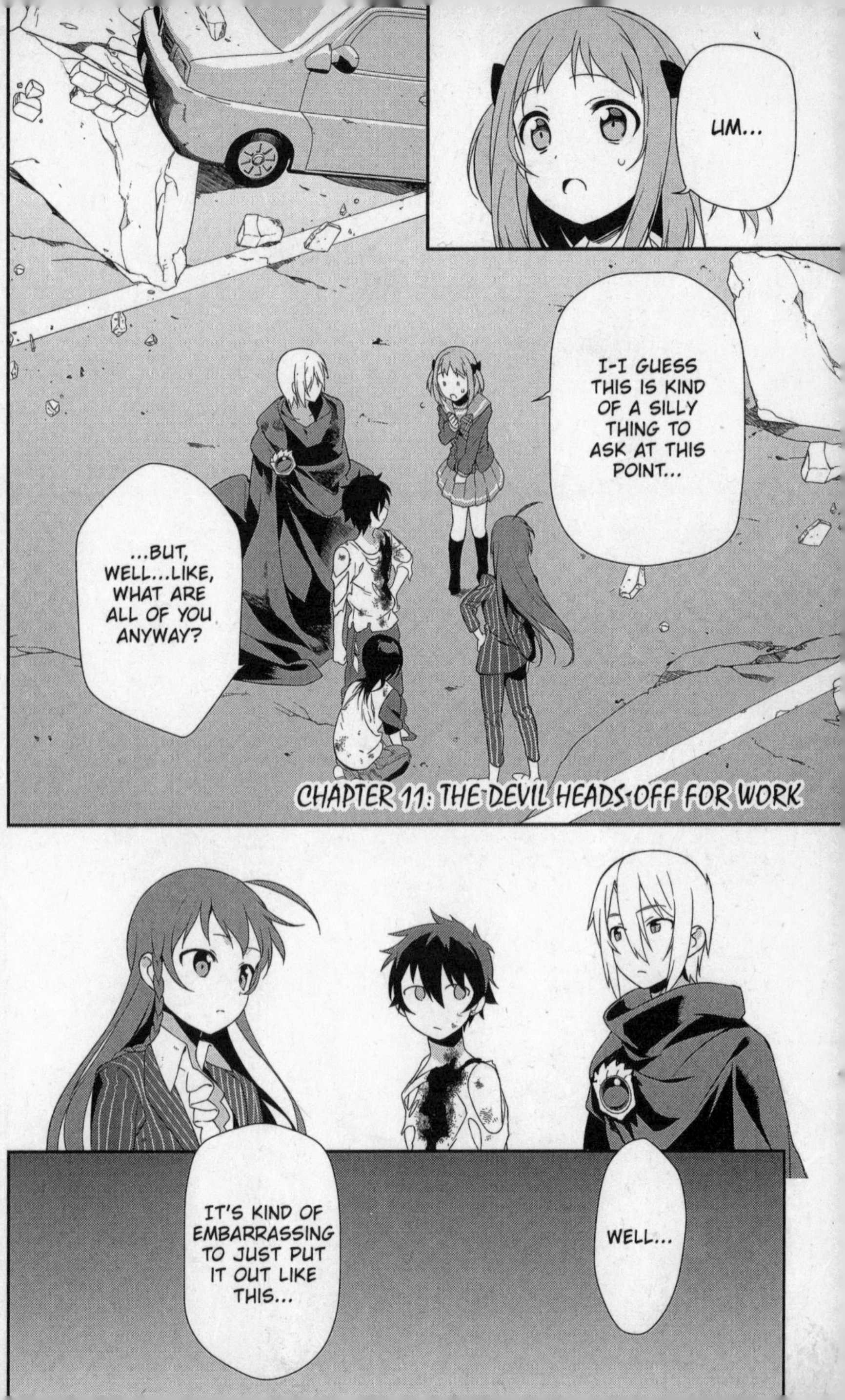
UM...
I-I GUESS THIS IS KIND OF A SILLY THING TO ASK AT THIS POINT...
...BUT, WELL...LIKE, WHAT ARE ALL OF YOU ANYWAY?
CHAPTER 11: THE DEVIL HEADS OFF FOR WORK
WELL...
IT'S KIND OF EMBARRASSING TO JUST PUT IT OUT LIKE THIS...

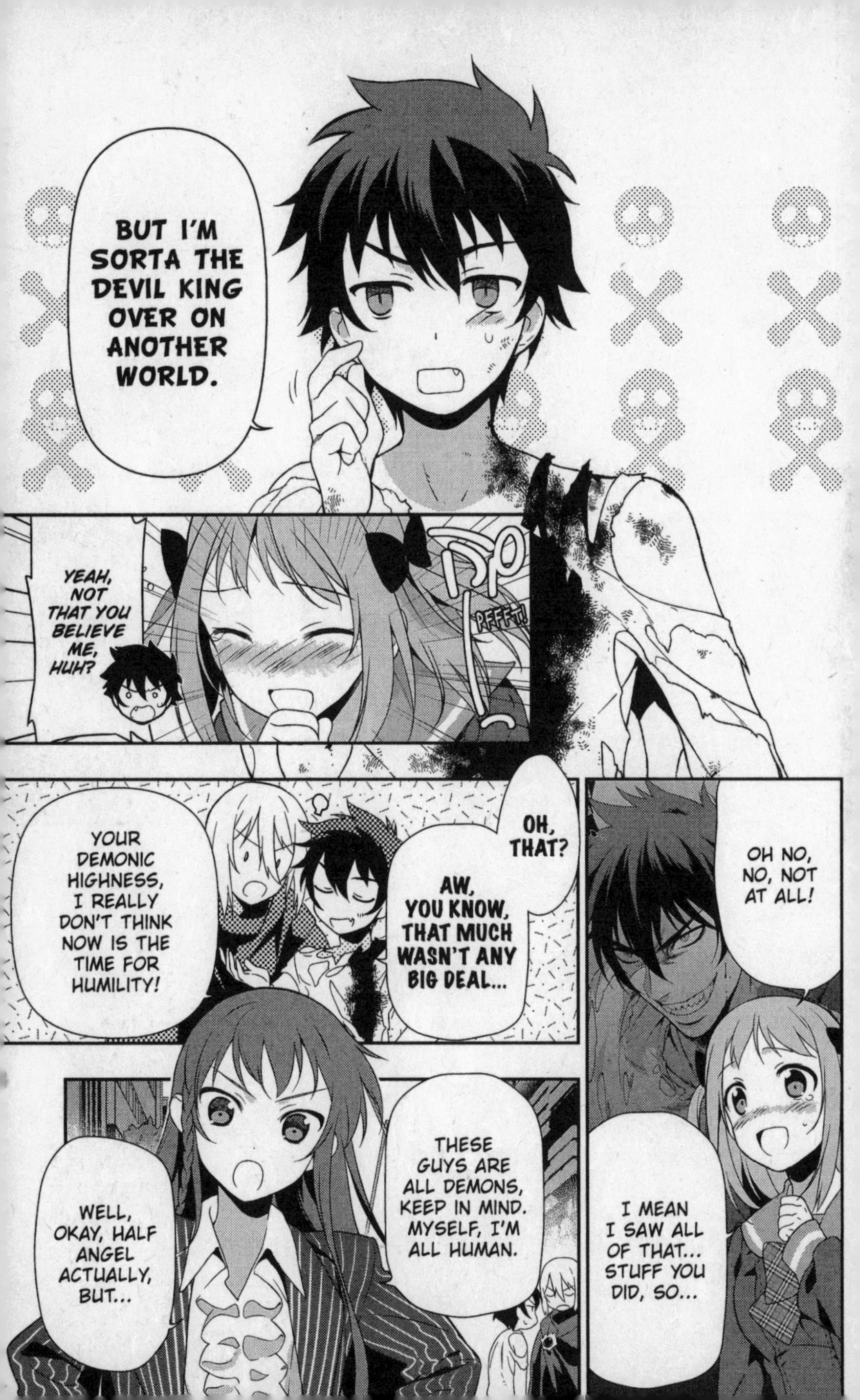
BUT I'M SORTA THE DEVIL KING OVER ON ANOTHER WORLD.
PFFFT!
YEAH, NOT THAT YOU BELIEVE ME, HUH?
OH NO, NO, NOT AT ALL!
I MEAN I SAW ALL OF THAT... STUFF YOU DID, SO...
OH, THAT?
AW, YOU KNOW, THAT MUCH WASN'T ANY BIG DEAL...
YOUR DEMONIC HIGHNESS, I REALLY DON'T THINK NOW IS THE TIME FOR HUMILITY!
THESE GUYS ARE ALL DEMONS, KEEP IN MIND. MYSELF, I'M ALL HUMAN.
WELL, OKAY, HALF ANGEL ACTUALLY, BUT...

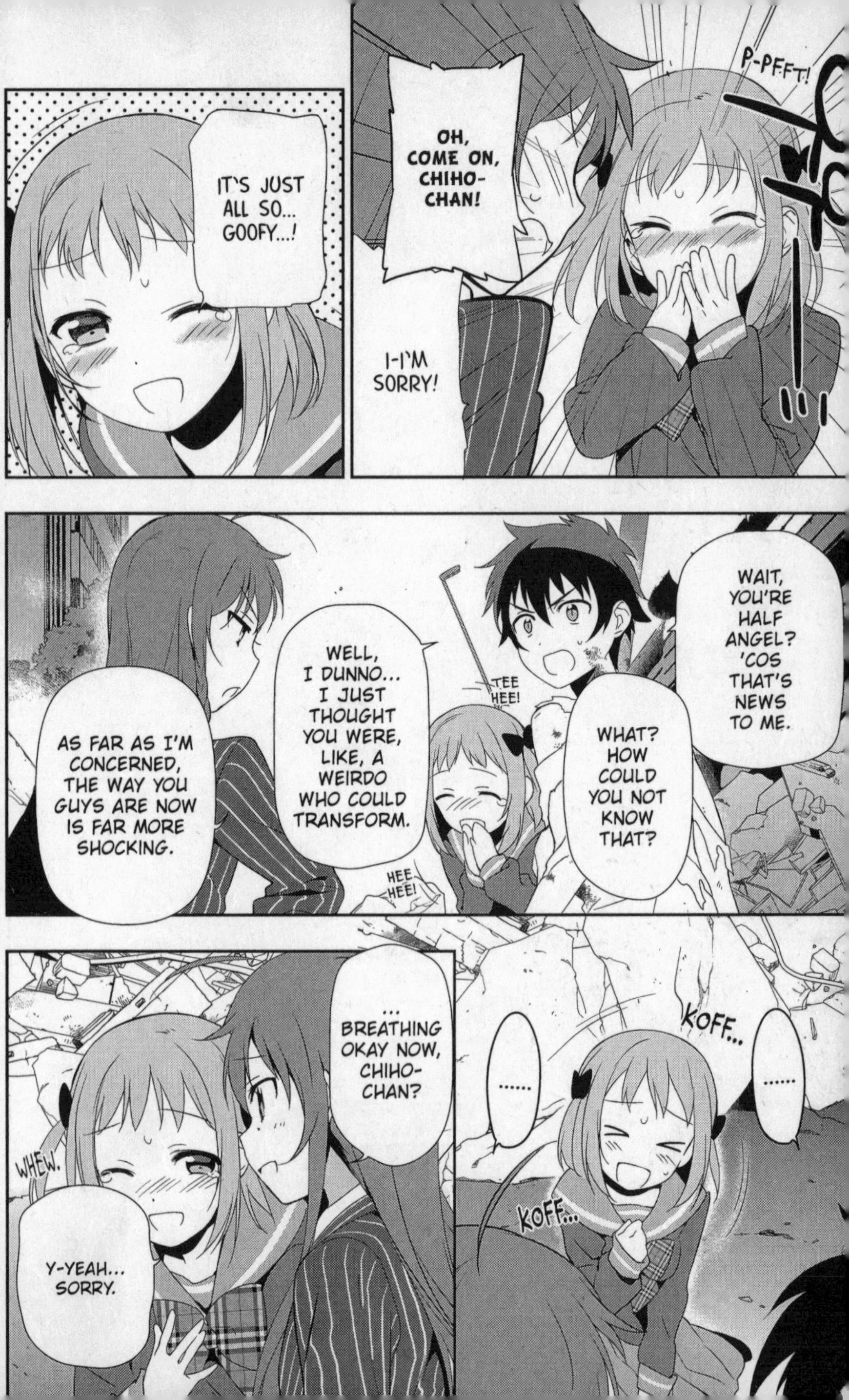
P-PFFT!
OH, COME ON, CHIHO-CHAN!
I-I'M SORRY!
IT'S JUST ALL SO... GOOFY...!
WAIT, YOU'RE HALF ANGEL? 'COS THAT'S NEWS TO ME.
WHAT? HOW COULD YOU NOT KNOW THAT?
TEE HEE!
WELL, I DUNNO... I JUST THOUGHT YOU WERE, LIKE, A WEIRDO WHO COULD TRANSFORM.
HEE HEE!
AS FAR AS I'M CONCERNED, THE WAY YOU GUYS ARE NOW IS FAR MORE SHOCKING.
......
KOFF...
......
KOFF...
... BREATHING OKAY NOW, CHIHO-CHAN?
WHEW.
Y-YEAH... SORRY.

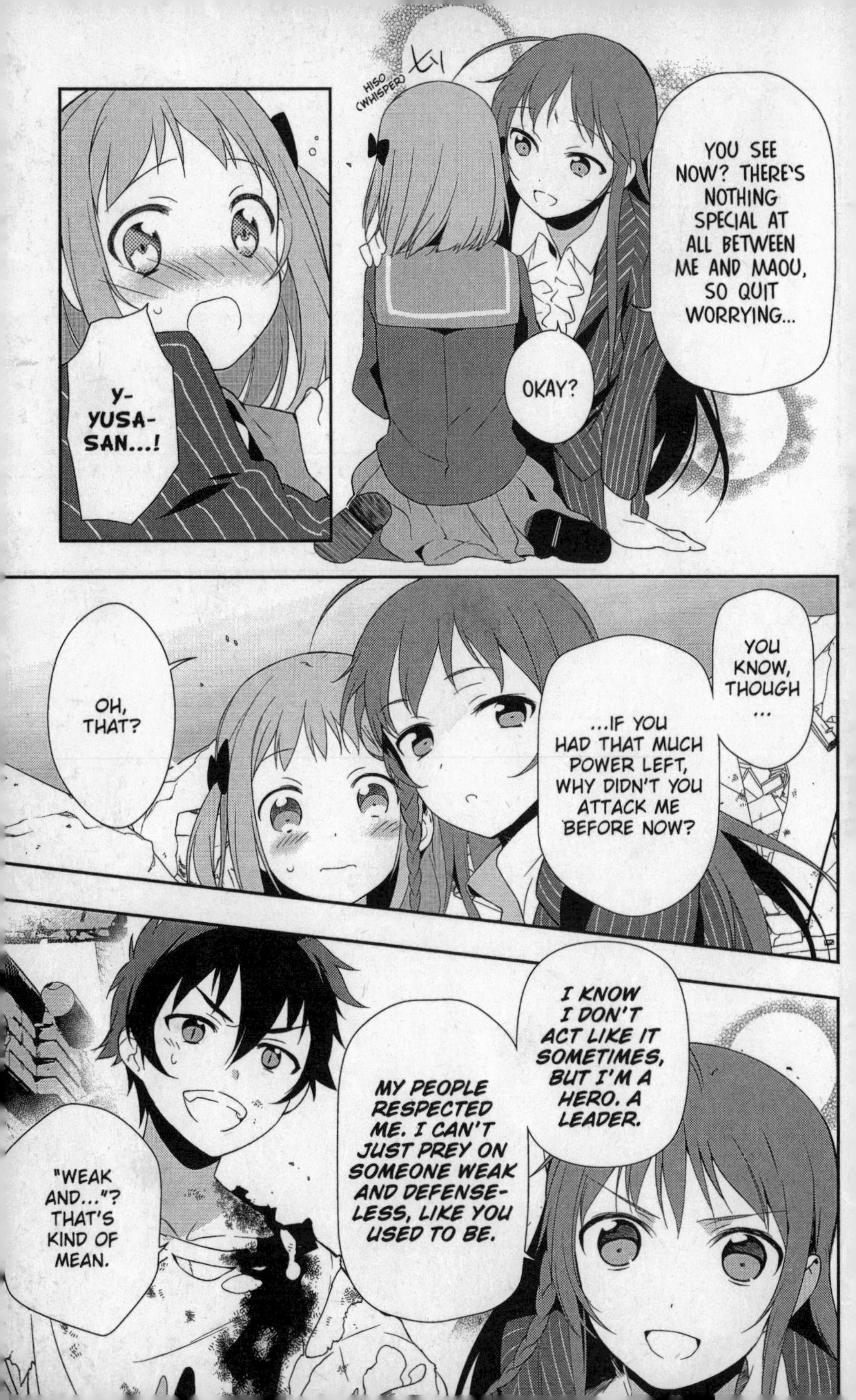
ヒソ
HISO (WHISPER)
YOU SEE NOW? THERE'S NOTHING SPECIAL AT ALL BETWEEN ME AND MAOU, SO QUIT WORRYING...
OKAY?
Y-YUSA-SAN...!
YOU KNOW, THOUGH ...
...IF YOU HAD THAT MUCH POWER LEFT, WHY DIDN'T YOU ATTACK ME BEFORE NOW?
OH, THAT?
I KNOW I DON'T ACT LIKE IT SOMETIMES, BUT I'M A HERO. A LEADER.
MY PEOPLE RESPECTED ME. I CAN'T JUST PREY ON SOMEONE WEAK AND DEFENSE-LESS, LIKE YOU USED TO BE.
"WEAK AND..."? THAT'S KIND OF MEAN.

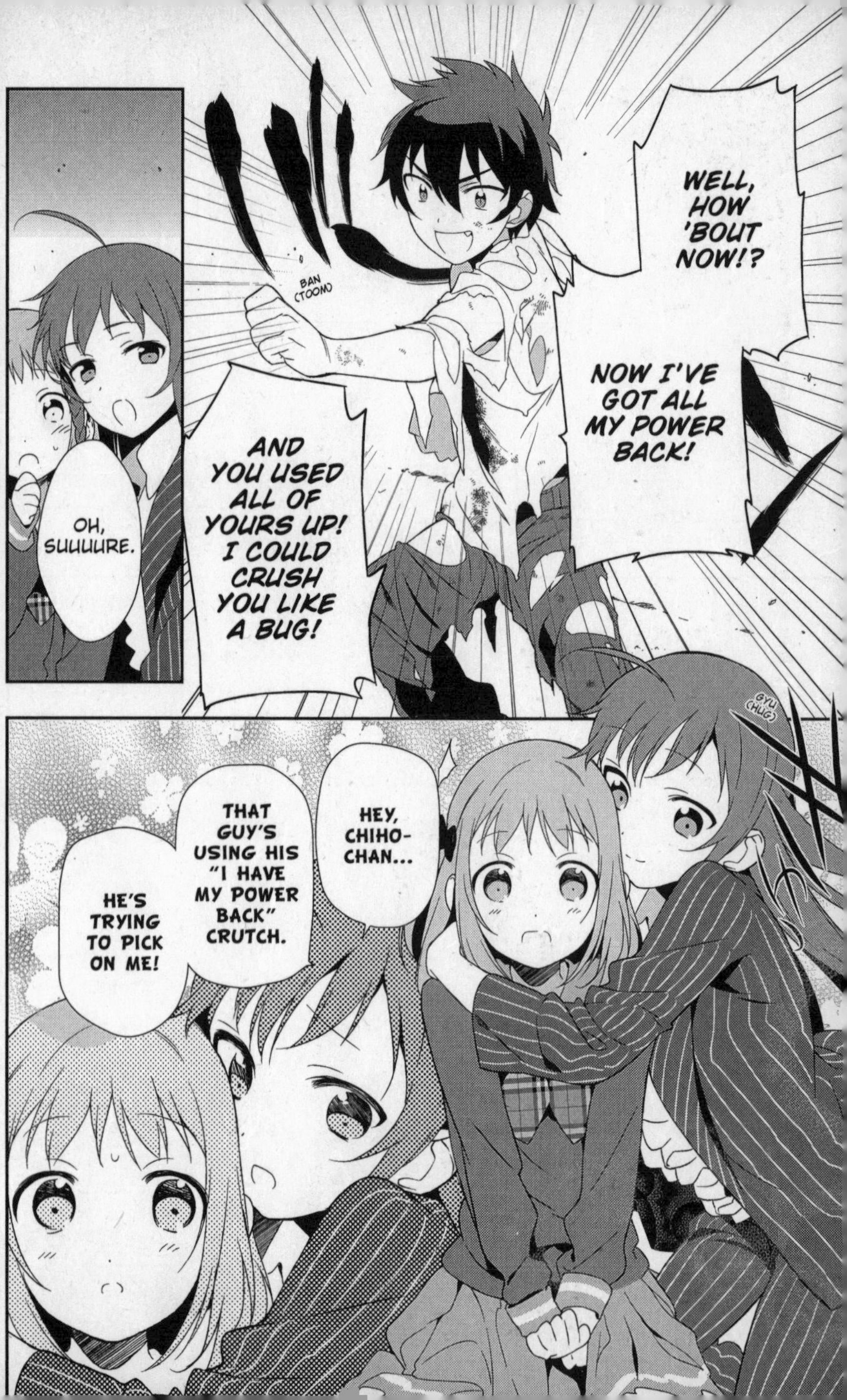
WELL, HOW 'BOUT NOW!?
NOW I'VE GOT ALL MY POWER BACK!
BAN (TOOM)
AND YOU USED ALL OF YOURS UP! I COULD CRUSH YOU LIKE A BUG!
OH, SUUUURE.
GYU (HUG)
HEY, CHIHO-CHAN...
THAT GUY'S USING HIS "I HAVE MY POWER BACK" CRUTCH.
HE'S TRYING TO PICK ON ME!

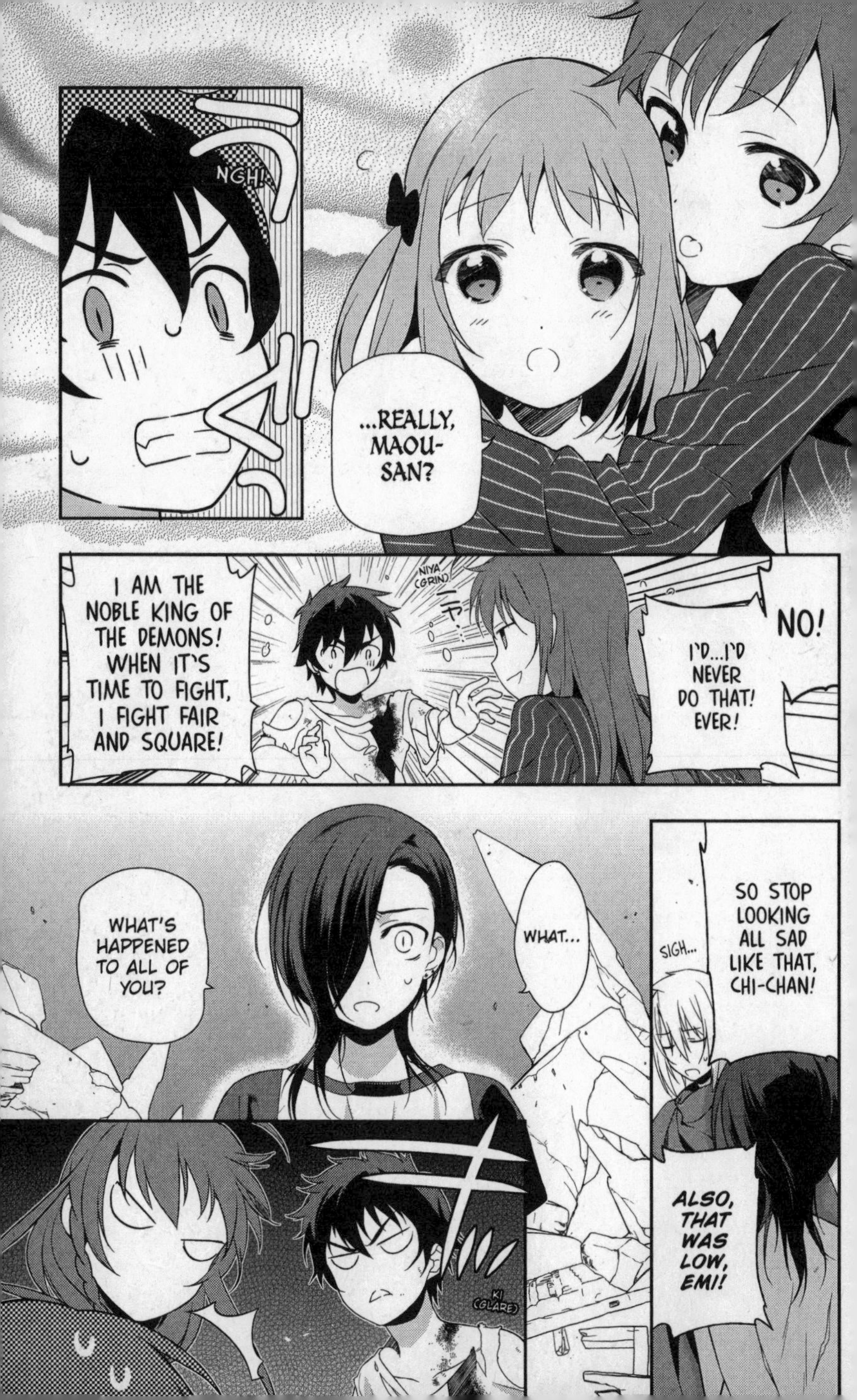
...REALLY, MAOU-SAN?
NGH!
NO!
I'D...I'D NEVER DO THAT! EVER!
NIYA (GRIN)
I AM THE NOBLE KING OF THE DEMONS! WHEN IT'S TIME TO FIGHT, I FIGHT FAIR AND SQUARE!
SO STOP LOOKING ALL SAD LIKE THAT, CHI-CHAN!
SIGH...
ALSO, THAT WAS LOW, EMI!
WHAT...
WHAT'S HAPPENED TO ALL OF YOU?
KI (GLARE)

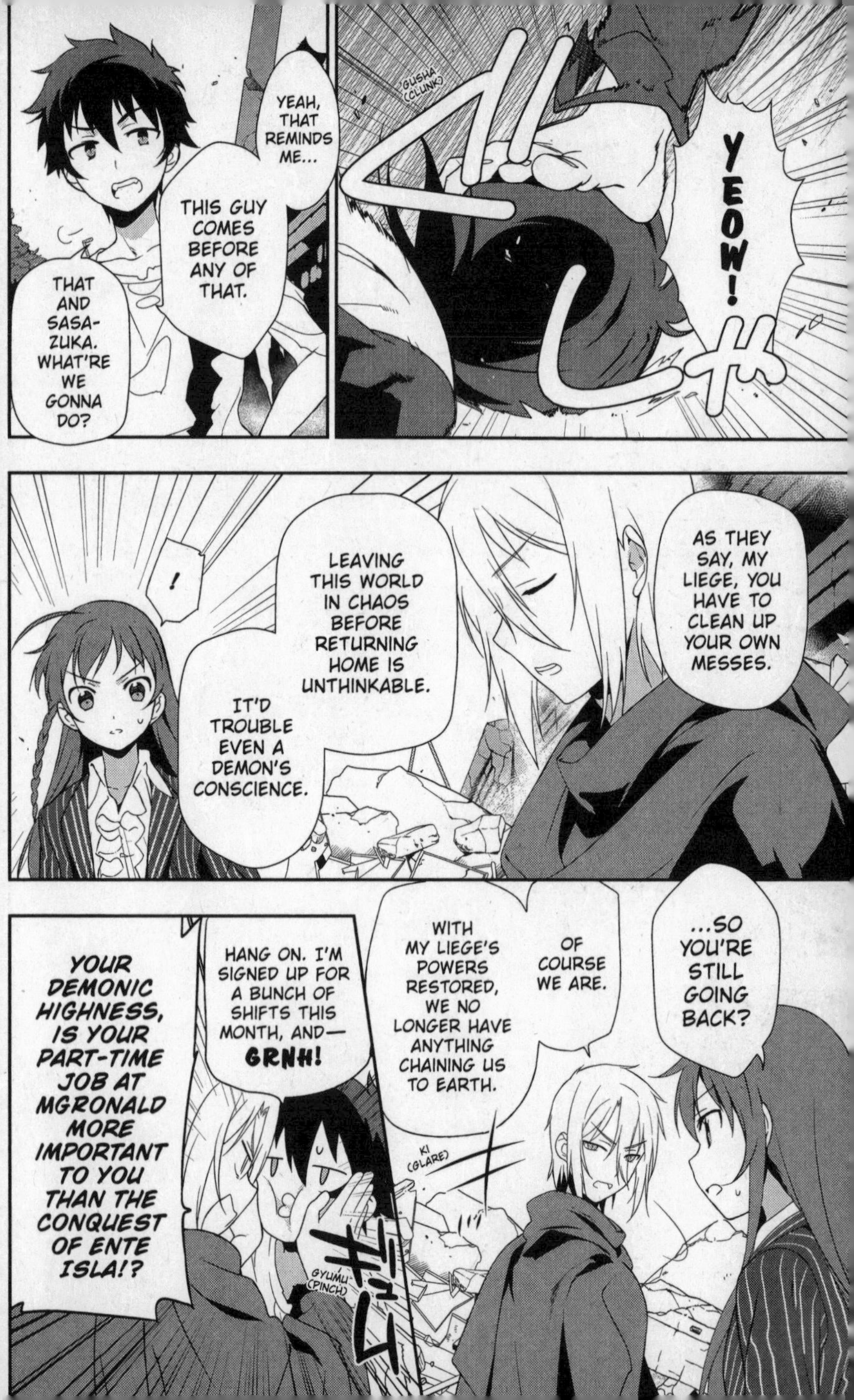
GUSHA (CLUNK)
YEOW!
YEAH, THAT REMINDS ME...
THIS GUY COMES BEFORE ANY OF THAT.
THAT AND SASAZUKA. WHAT'RE WE GONNA DO?
AS THEY SAY, MY LIEGE, YOU HAVE TO CLEAN UP YOUR OWN MESSES.
LEAVING THIS WORLD IN CHAOS BEFORE RETURNING HOME IS UNTHINKABLE.
IT'D TROUBLE EVEN A DEMON'S CONSCIENCE.
!
...SO YOU'RE STILL GOING BACK?
OF COURSE WE ARE.
WITH MY LIEGE'S POWERS RESTORED, WE NO LONGER HAVE ANYTHING CHAINING US TO EARTH.
KI (GLARE)
HANG ON. I'M SIGNED UP FOR A BUNCH OF SHIFTS THIS MONTH, AND— GRNH!
GYUMU (PINCH)
YOUR DEMONIC HIGHNESS, IS YOUR PART-TIME JOB AT MGRONALD MORE IMPORTANT TO YOU THAN THE CONQUEST OF ENTE ISLA!?

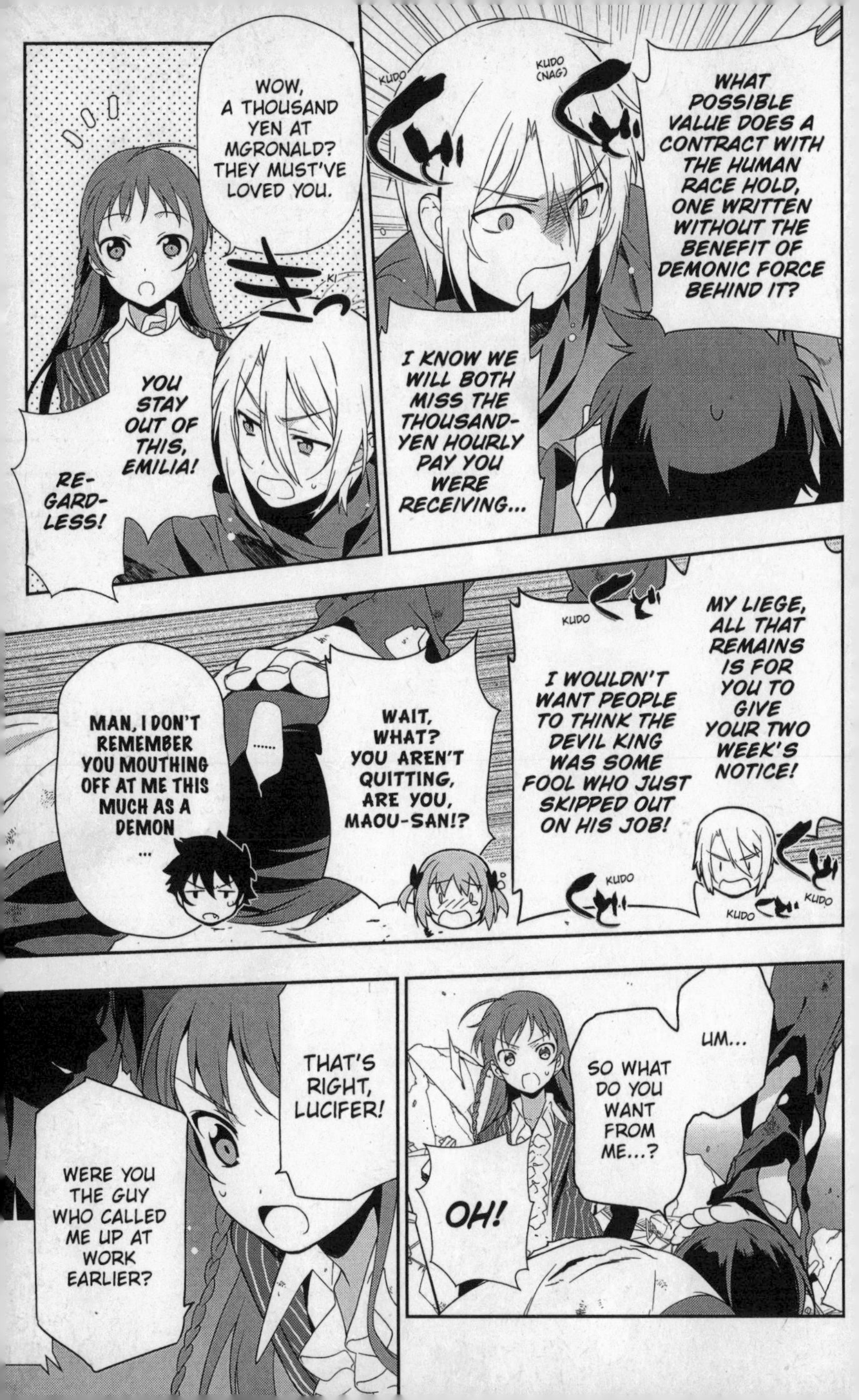
KUDO
KUDO (NAG)
WHAT POSSIBLE VALUE DOES A CONTRACT WITH THE HUMAN RACE HOLD, ONE WRITTEN WITHOUT THE BENEFIT OF DEMONIC FORCE BEHIND IT?
I KNOW WE WILL BOTH MISS THE THOUSAND-YEN HOURLY PAY YOU WERE RECEIVING...
WOW, A THOUSAND YEN AT MGRONALD? THEY MUST'VE LOVED YOU.
KI
YOU STAY OUT OF THIS, EMILIA!
RE-GARD-LESS!
MY LIEGE, ALL THAT REMAINS IS FOR YOU TO GIVE YOUR TWO WEEK'S NOTICE!
KUDO
I WOULDN'T WANT PEOPLE TO THINK THE DEVIL KING WAS SOME FOOL WHO JUST SKIPPED OUT ON HIS JOB!
KUDO
KUDO
KUDO
WAIT, WHAT? YOU AREN'T QUITTING, ARE YOU, MAOU-SAN!?
......
MAN, I DON'T REMEMBER YOU MOUTHING OFF AT ME THIS MUCH AS A DEMON ...
UM...
SO WHAT DO YOU WANT FROM ME...?
OH!
THAT'S RIGHT, LUCIFER!
WERE YOU THE GUY WHO CALLED ME UP AT WORK EARLIER?

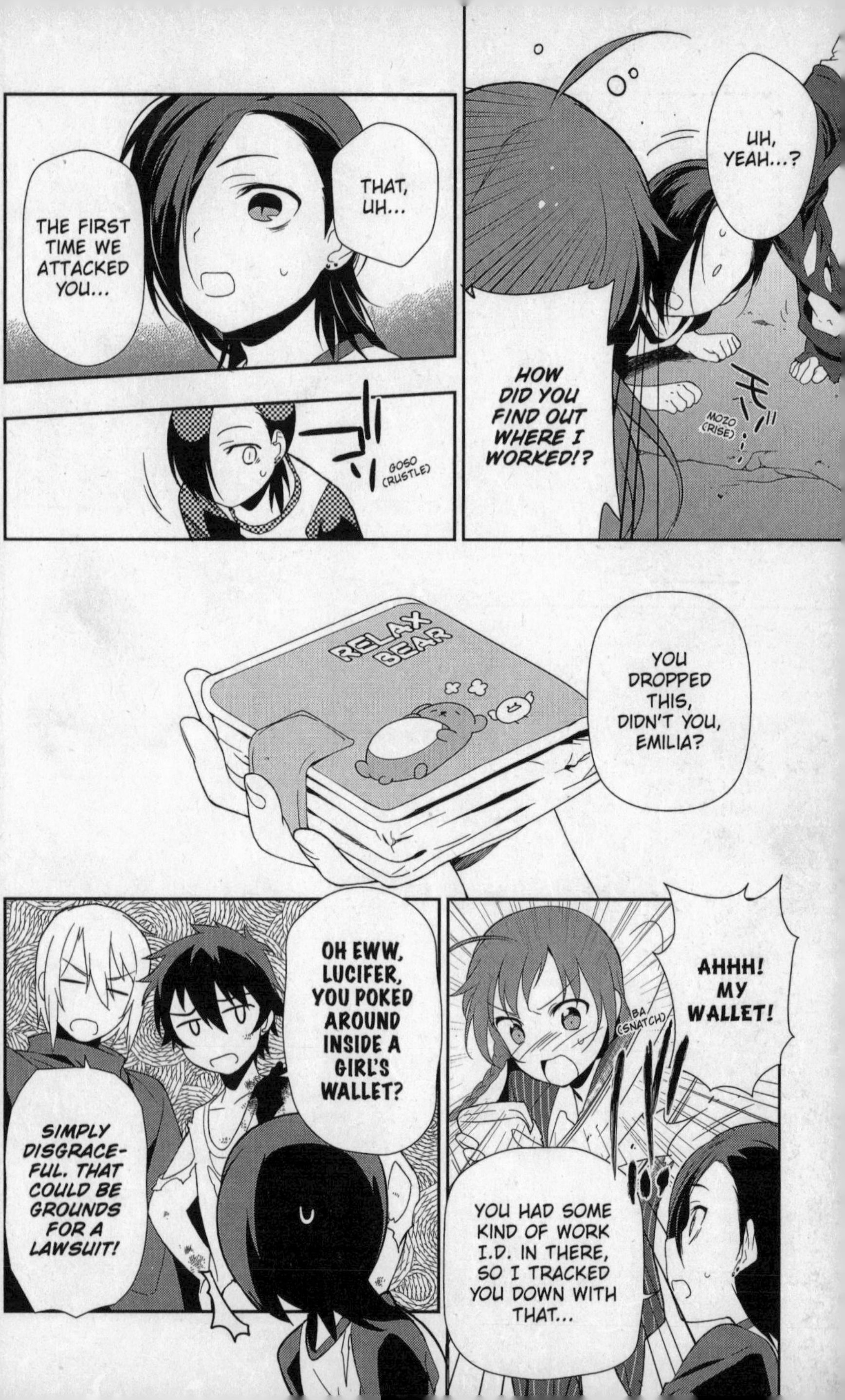
UH, YEAH...?
HOW DID YOU FIND OUT WHERE I WORKED!?
MOZO (RISE)
THAT, UH...
THE FIRST TIME WE ATTACKED YOU...
GOSO (RUSTLE)
RELAX BEAR
YOU DROPPED THIS, DIDN'T YOU, EMILIA?
AHHH! MY WALLET!
BA (SNATCH)
YOU HAD SOME KIND OF WORK I.D. IN THERE, SO I TRACKED YOU DOWN WITH THAT...
OH EWW, LUCIFER, YOU POKED AROUND INSIDE A GIRL'S WALLET?
SIMPLY DISGRACEFUL. THAT COULD BE GROUNDS FOR A LAWSUIT!

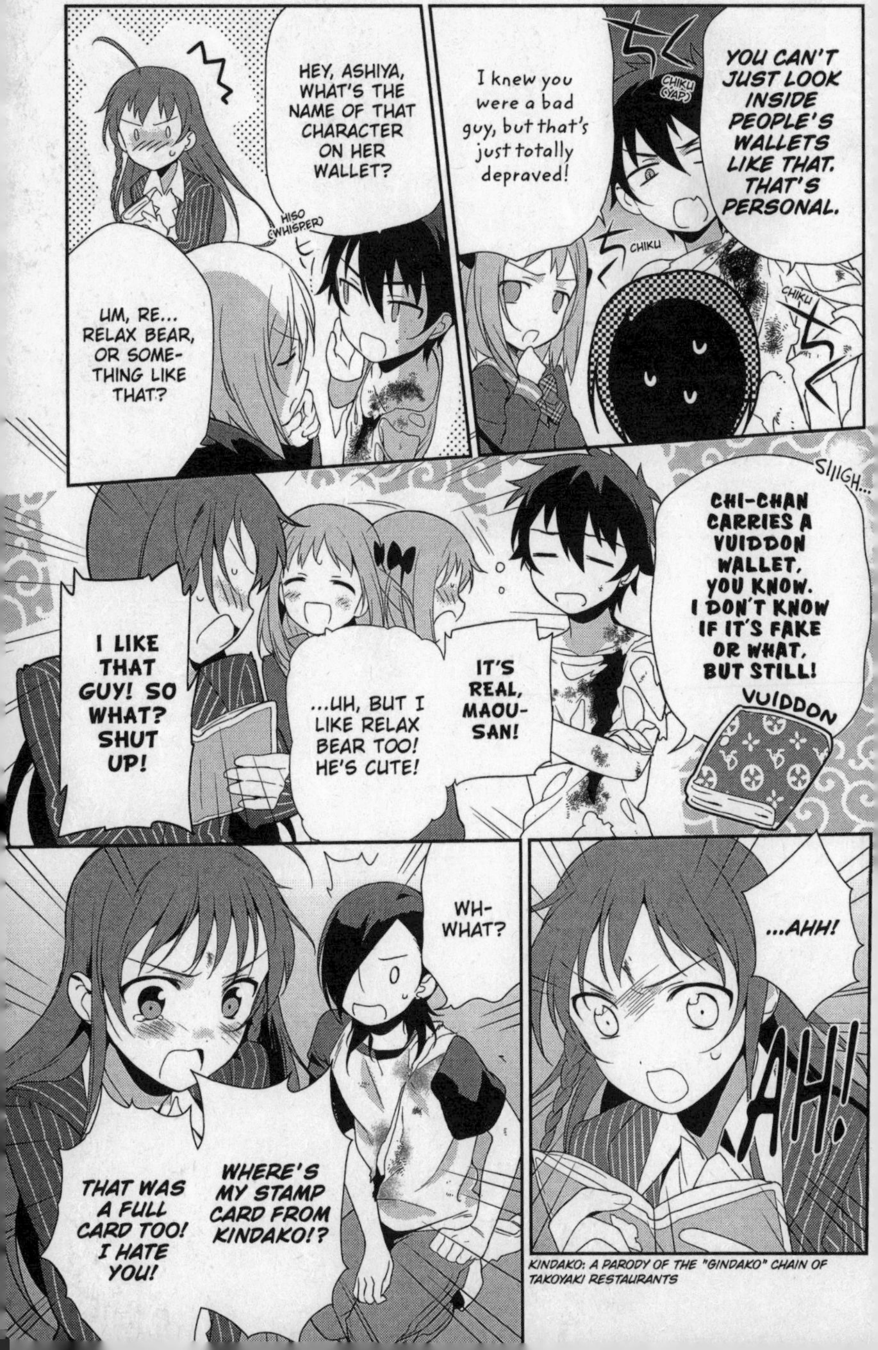
YOU CAN'T JUST LOOK INSIDE PEOPLE'S WALLETS LIKE THAT. THAT'S PERSONAL.
CHIKU (YAP)
I knew you were a bad guy, but that's just totally depraved!
CHIKU
CHIKU
HEY, ASHIYA, WHAT'S THE NAME OF THAT CHARACTER ON HER WALLET?
HISO (WHISPER)
UM, RE... RELAX BEAR, OR SOME-THING LIKE THAT?
SIIIGH...
CHI-CHAN CARRIES A VUIDDON WALLET, YOU KNOW. I DON'T KNOW IF IT'S FAKE OR WHAT, BUT STILL!
VUIDDON
IT'S REAL, MAOU-SAN!
...UH, BUT I LIKE RELAX BEAR TOO! HE'S CUTE!
I LIKE THAT GUY! SO WHAT? SHUT UP!
...AHH!
AH!
WH-WHAT?
WHERE'S MY STAMP CARD FROM KINDAKO!?
THAT WAS A FULL CARD TOO! I HATE YOU!
KINDAKO: A PARODY OF THE "GINDAKO" CHAIN OF TAKOYAKI RESTAURANTS

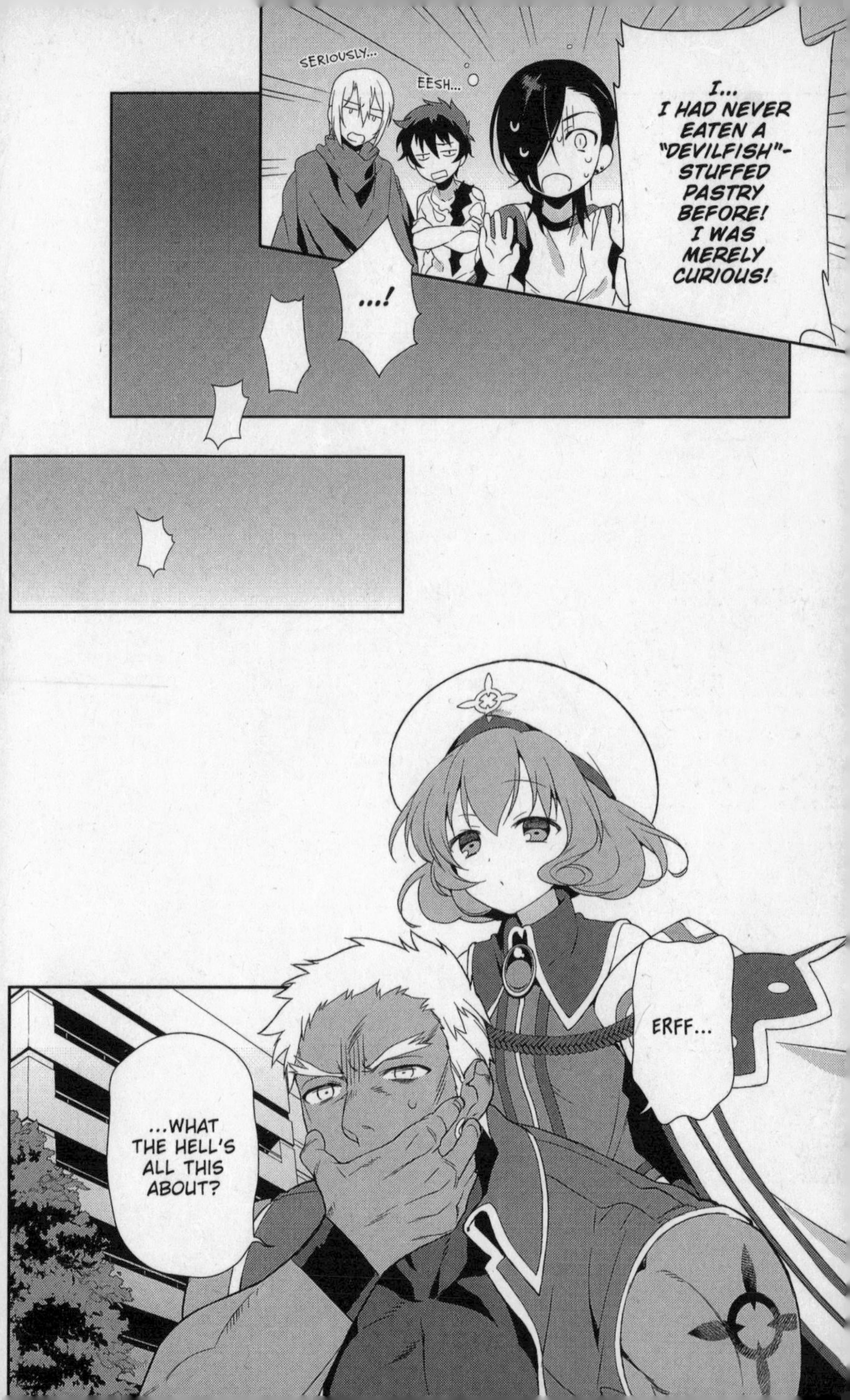
I... I HAD NEVER EATEN A "DEVILFISH"-STUFFED PASTRY BEFORE! I WAS MERELY CURIOUS!
EESH...
SERIOUSLY...
...!
ERFF...
...WHAT THE HELL'S ALL THIS ABOUT?

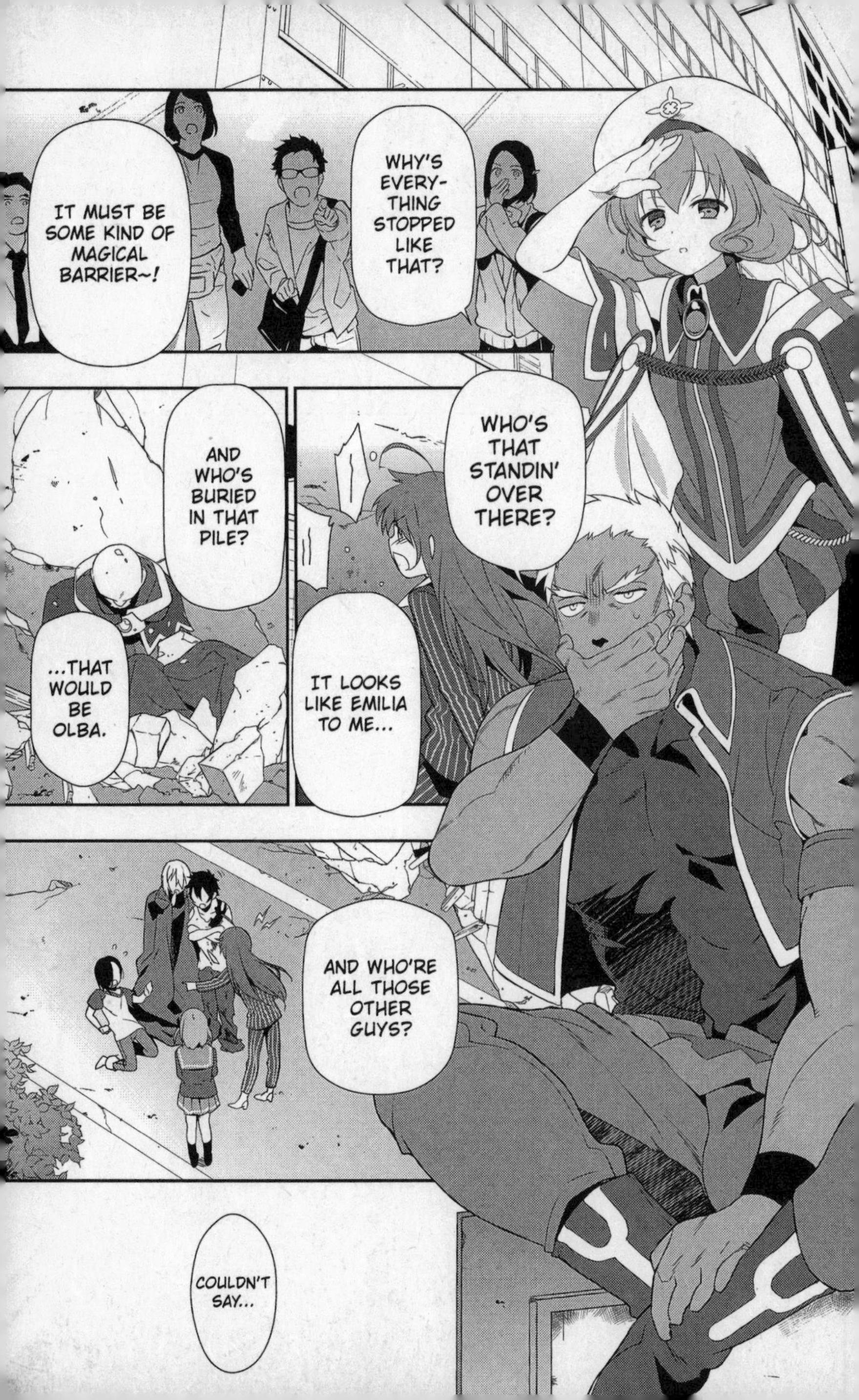
WHY'S EVERY-THING STOPPED LIKE THAT?
IT MUST BE SOME KIND OF MAGICAL BARRIER~!
WHO'S THAT STANDIN' OVER THERE?
IT LOOKS LIKE EMILIA TO ME...
AND WHO'S BURIED IN THAT PILE?
...THAT WOULD BE OLBA.
AND WHO'RE ALL THOSE OTHER GUYS?
COULDN'T SAY...

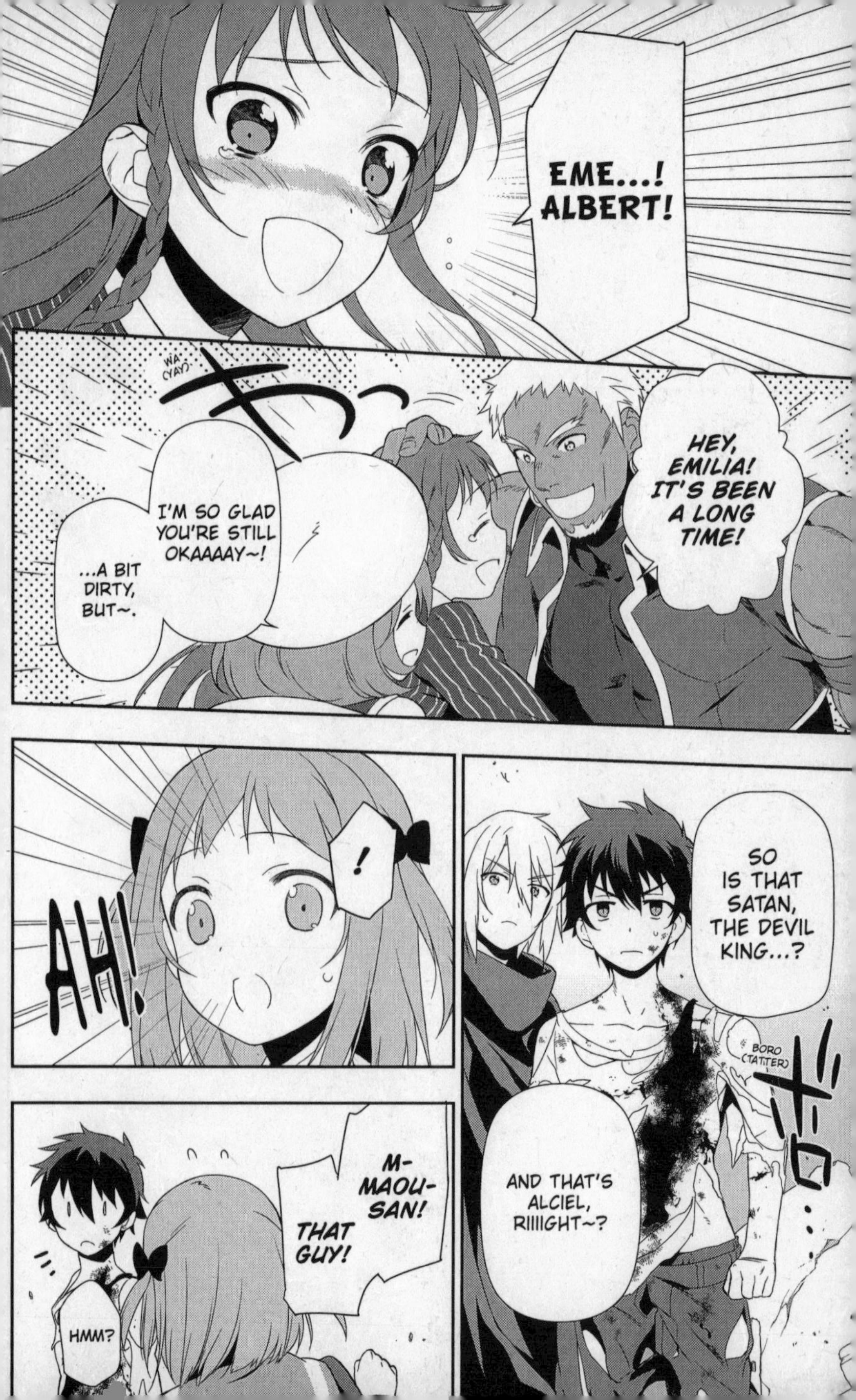
EME...! ALBERT!
HEY, EMILIA! IT'S BEEN A LONG TIME!
WA (YAY)
I'M SO GLAD YOU'RE STILL OKAAAAY~!
...A BIT DIRTY, BUT~.
SO IS THAT SATAN, THE DEVIL KING...?
BORO (TATTER)
AND THAT'S ALCIEL, RIIIIGHT~?
AH!
!
M-MAOU-SAN!
THAT GUY!
HMM?

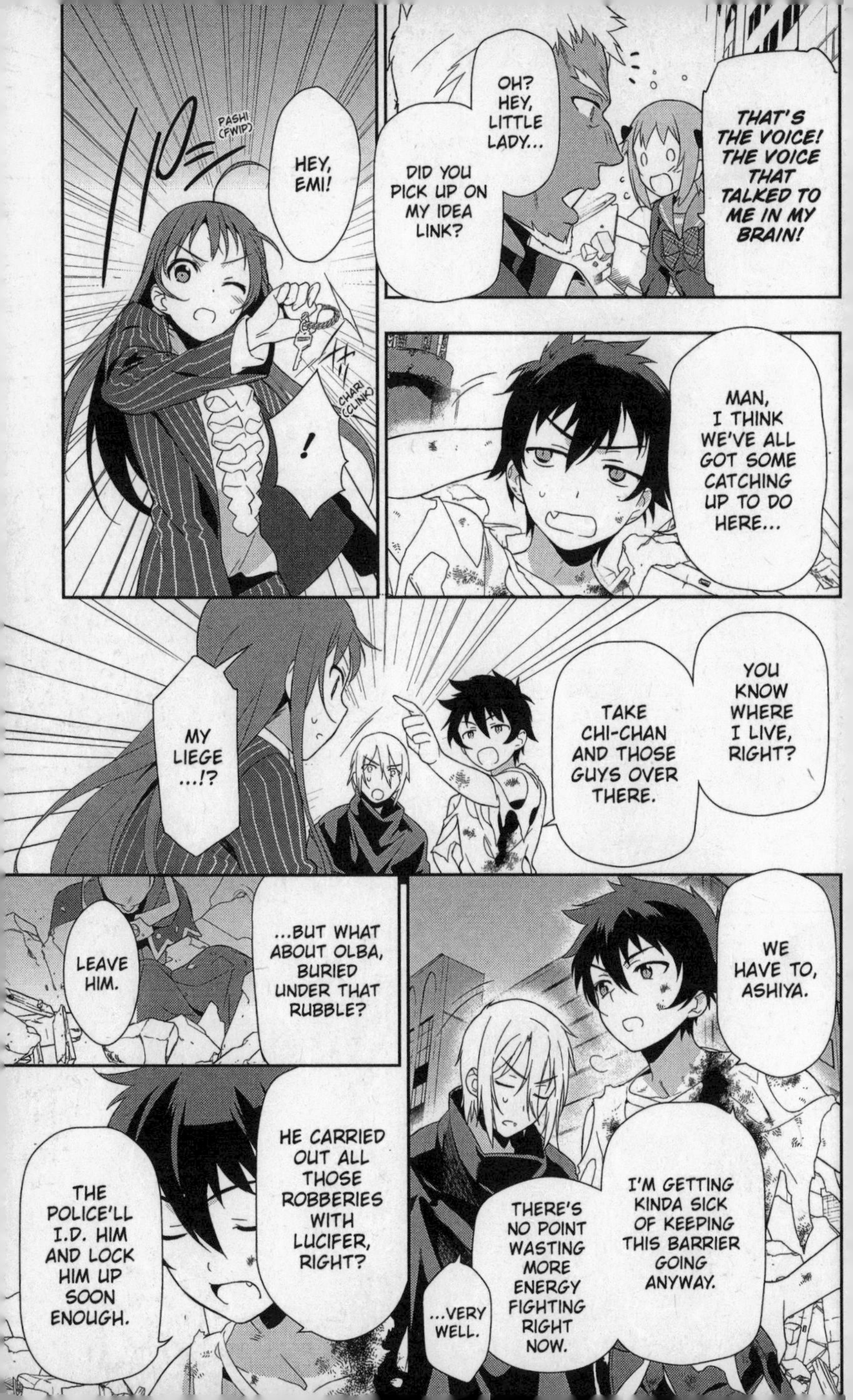
THAT'S THE VOICE! THE VOICE THAT TALKED TO ME IN MY BRAIN!
OH? HEY, LITTLE LADY...
DID YOU PICK UP ON MY IDEA LINK?
MAN, I THINK WE'VE ALL GOT SOME CATCHING UP TO DO HERE...
PASHI (FWIP)
HEY, EMI!
CHARI (CLINK)
!
YOU KNOW WHERE I LIVE, RIGHT?
TAKE CHI-CHAN AND THOSE GUYS OVER THERE.
MY LIEGE ...!?
WE HAVE TO, ASHIYA.
I'M GETTING KINDA SICK OF KEEPING THIS BARRIER GOING ANYWAY.
THERE'S NO POINT WASTING MORE ENERGY FIGHTING RIGHT NOW.
...VERY WELL.
...BUT WHAT ABOUT OLBA, BURIED UNDER THAT RUBBLE?
LEAVE HIM.
HE CARRIED OUT ALL THOSE ROBBERIES WITH LUCIFER, RIGHT?
THE POLICE'LL I.D. HIM AND LOCK HIM UP SOON ENOUGH.

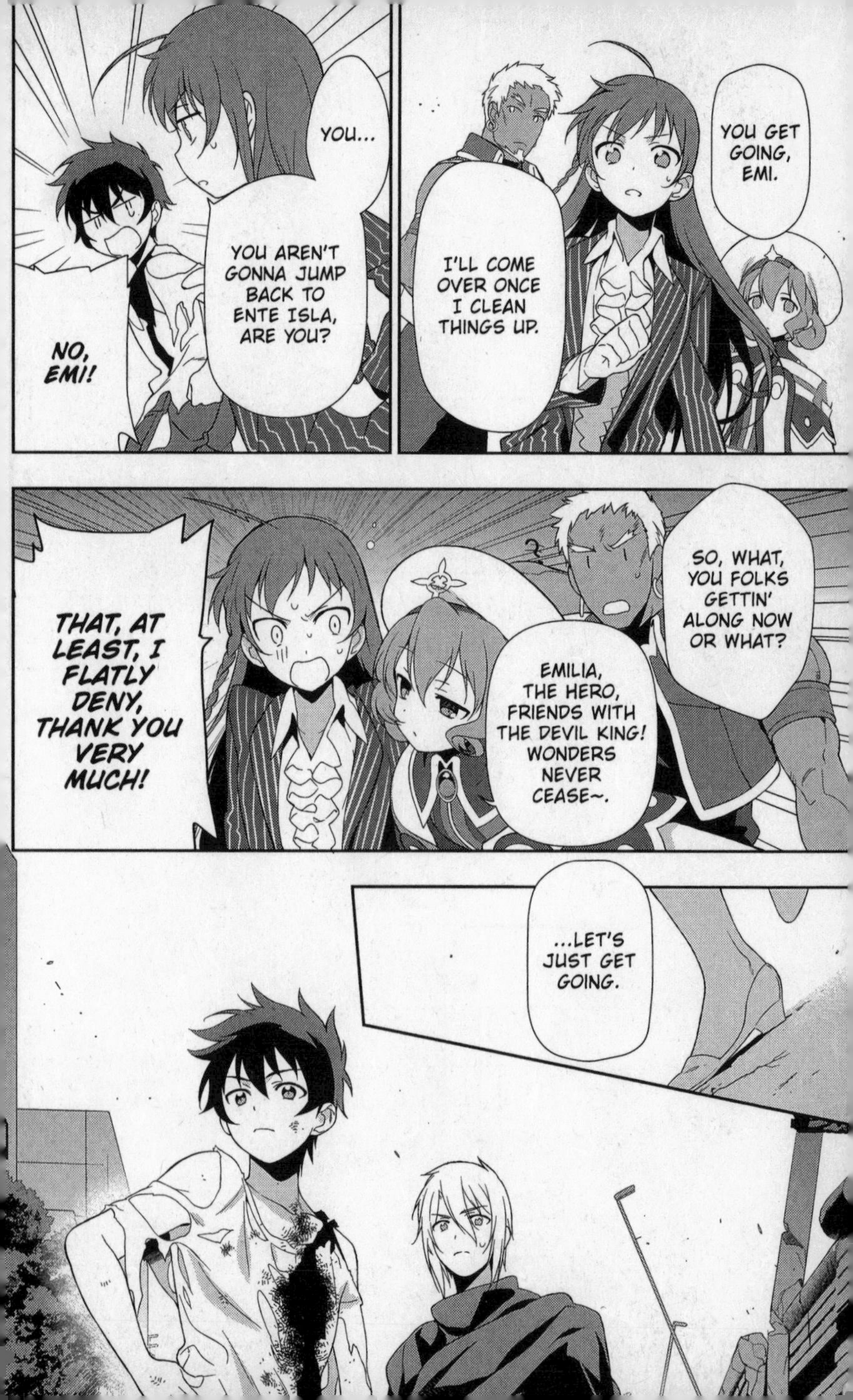
YOU GET GOING, EMI.
I'LL COME OVER ONCE I CLEAN THINGS UP.
YOU...
YOU AREN'T GONNA JUMP BACK TO ENTE ISLA, ARE YOU?
NO, EMI!
SO, WHAT, YOU FOLKS GETTIN' ALONG NOW OR WHAT?
EMILIA, THE HERO, FRIENDS WITH THE DEVIL KING! WONDERS NEVER CEASE~.
THAT, AT LEAST, I FLATLY DENY, THANK YOU VERY MUCH!
...LET'S JUST GET GOING.

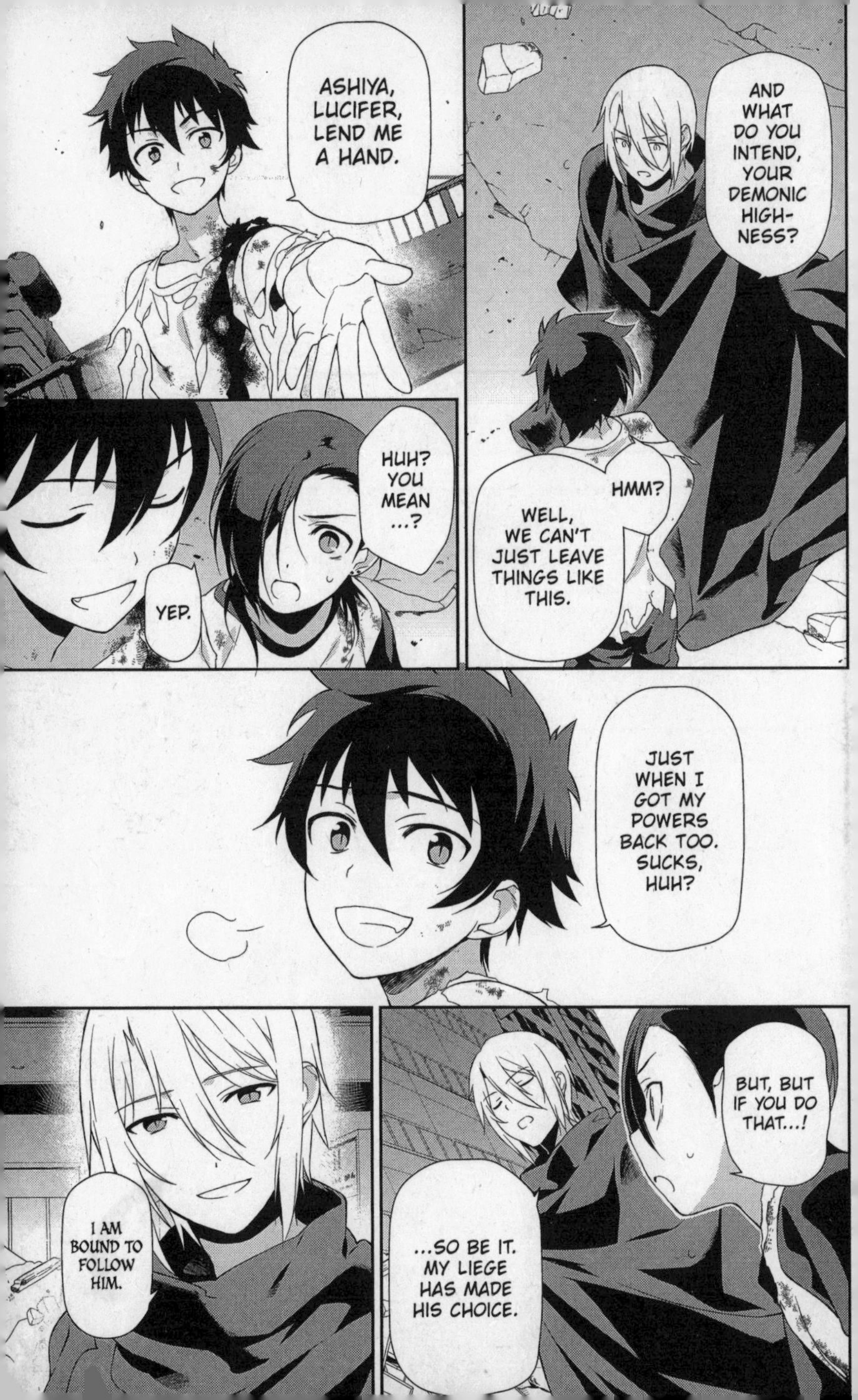
AND WHAT DO YOU INTEND, YOUR DEMONIC HIGH-NESS?
HMM?
WELL, WE CAN'T JUST LEAVE THINGS LIKE THIS.
ASHIYA, LUCIFER, LEND ME A HAND.
HUH? YOU MEAN ...?
YEP.
JUST WHEN I GOT MY POWERS BACK TOO. SUCKS, HUH?
BUT, BUT IF YOU DO THAT...!
...SO BE IT. MY LIEGE HAS MADE HIS CHOICE.
I AM BOUND TO FOLLOW HIM.

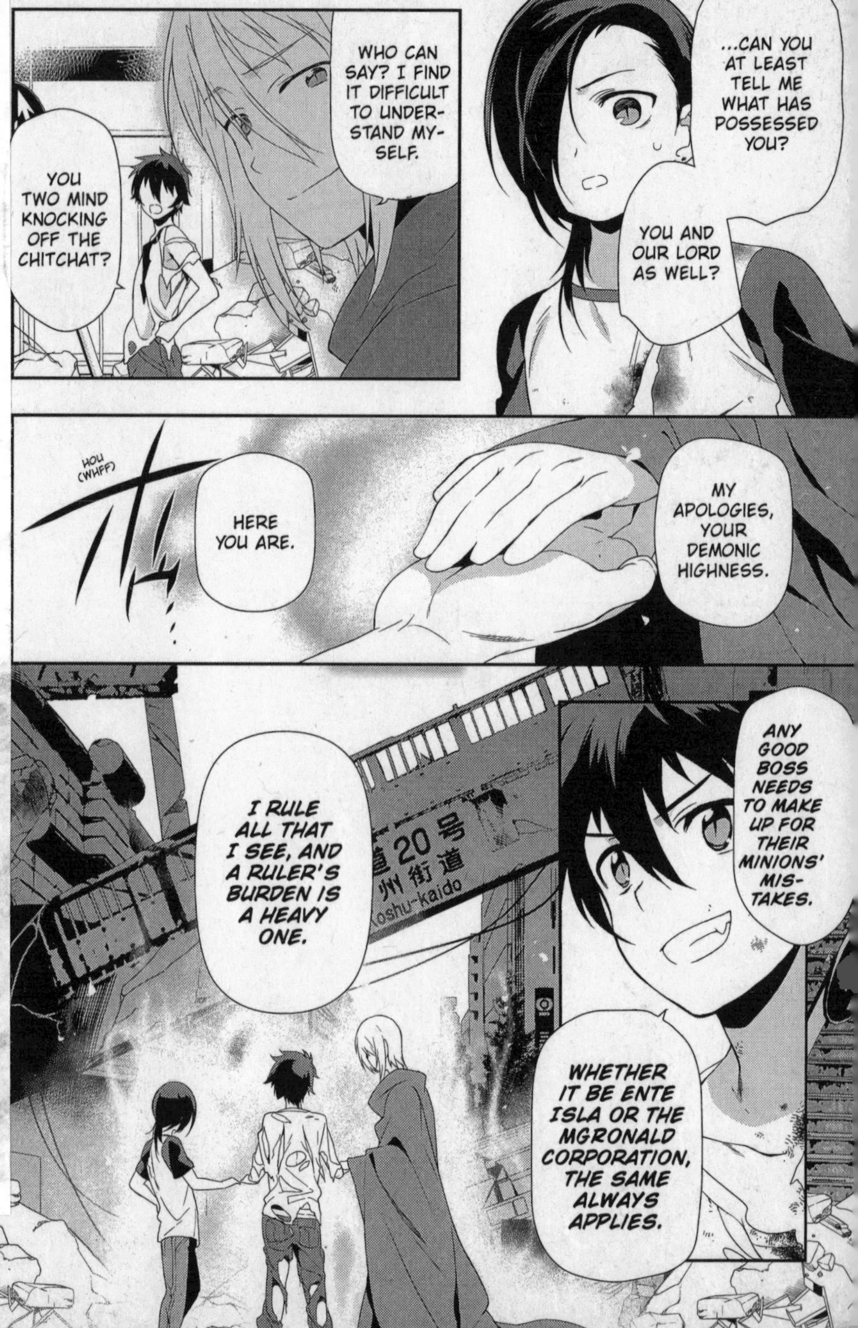
...CAN YOU AT LEAST TELL ME WHAT HAS POSSESSED YOU?
YOU AND OUR LORD AS WELL?
WHO CAN SAY? I FIND IT DIFFICULT TO UNDER-STAND MY-SELF.
YOU TWO MIND KNOCKING OFF THE CHITCHAT?
MY APOLOGIES, YOUR DEMONIC HIGHNESS.
HERE YOU ARE.
HOU (WHFF)
ANY GOOD BOSS NEEDS TO MAKE UP FOR THEIR MINIONS' MIS-TAKES.
WHETHER IT BE ENTE ISLA OR THE MGRONALD CORPORATION, THE SAME ALWAYS APPLIES.
I RULE ALL THAT I SEE, AND A RULER'S BURDEN IS A HEAVY ONE.
Koshu-kaido

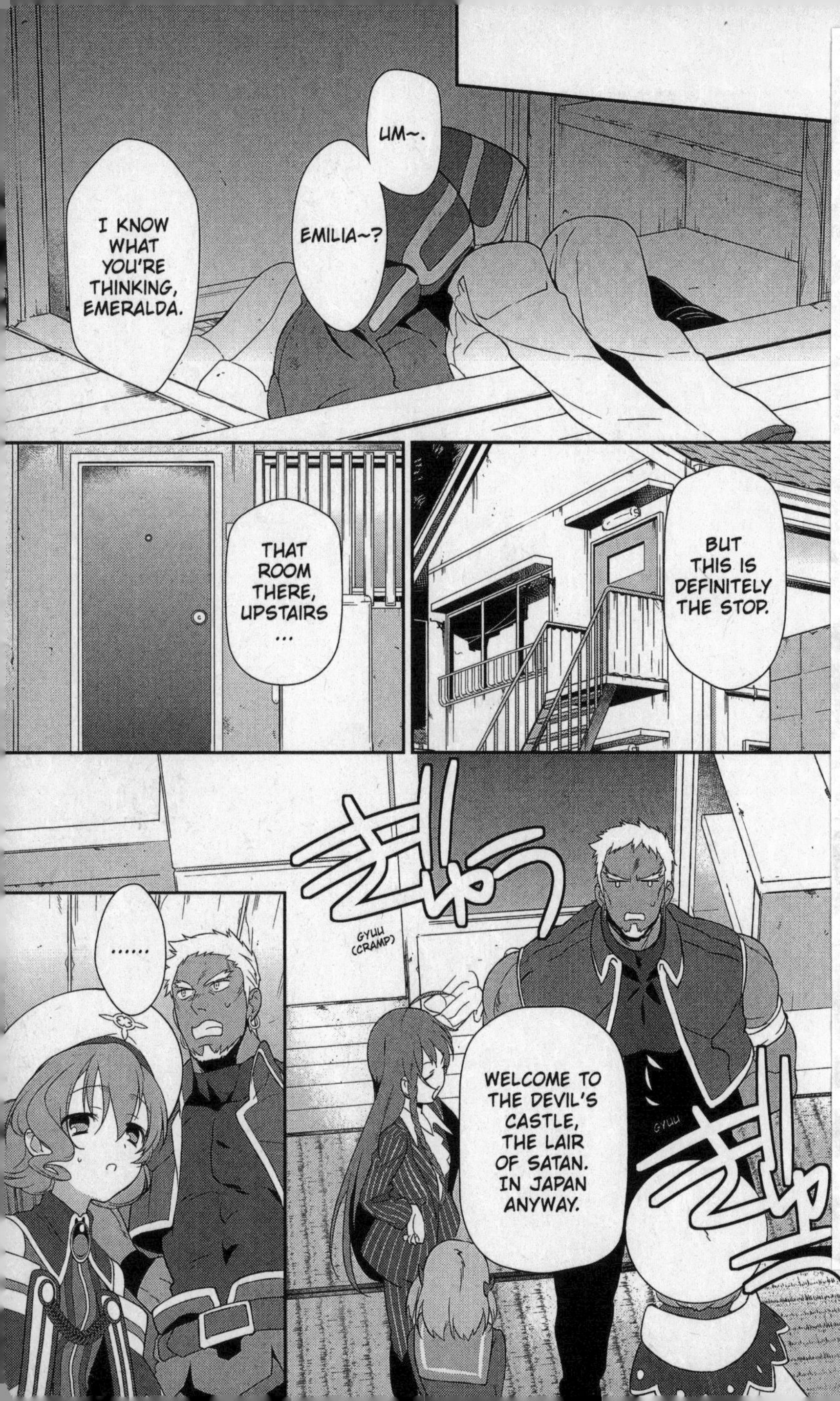

UM~.
EMILIA~?
I KNOW WHAT YOU'RE THINKING, EMERALDA.
BUT THIS IS DEFINITELY THE STOP.
THAT ROOM THERE, UPSTAIRS ...
GYUU (CRAMP)
WELCOME TO THE DEVIL'S CASTLE, THE LAIR OF SATAN. IN JAPAN ANYWAY.
GYUU
......

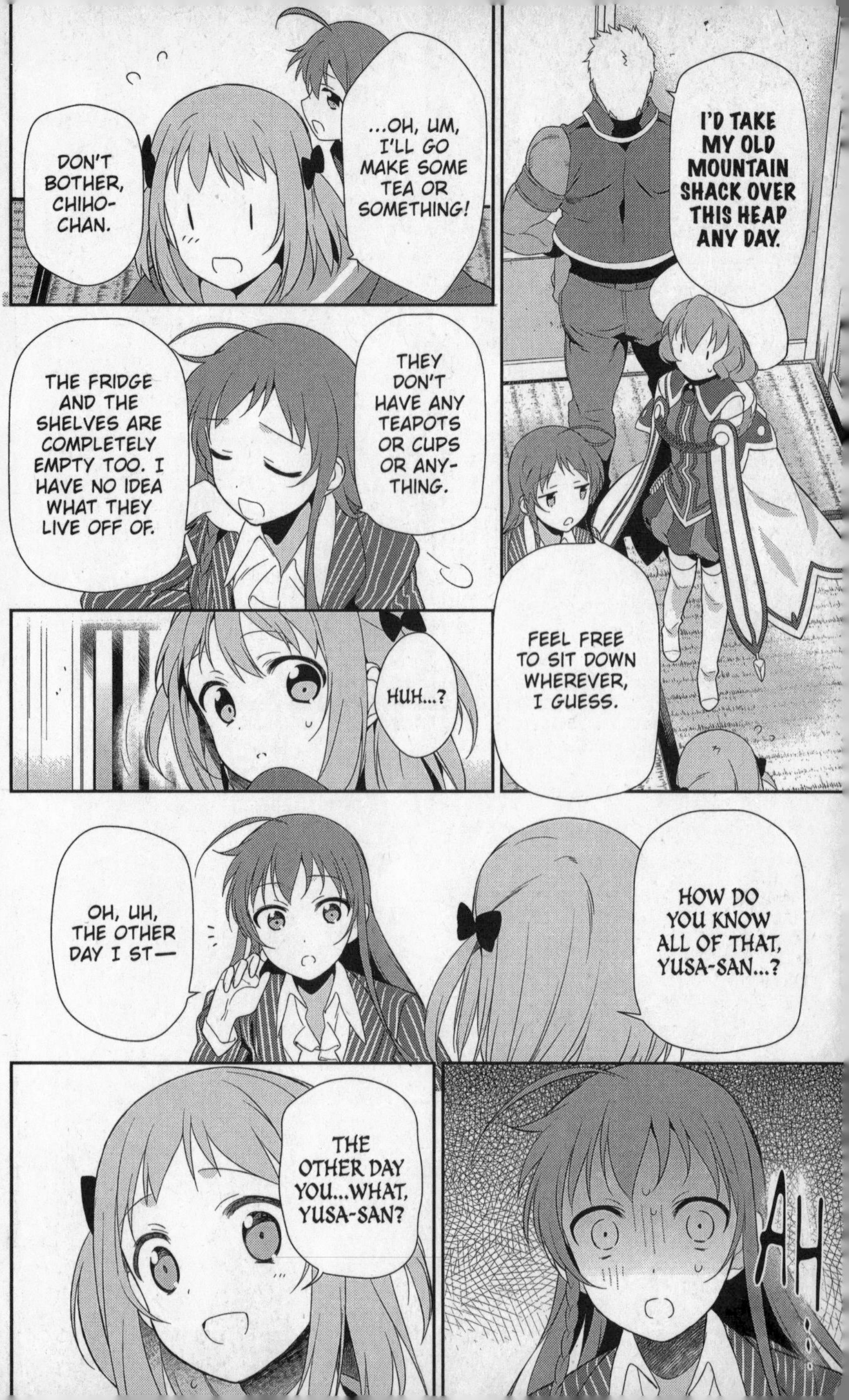
I'D TAKE MY OLD MOUNTAIN SHACK OVER THIS HEAP ANY DAY.
FEEL FREE TO SIT DOWN WHEREVER, I GUESS.
...OH, UM, I'LL GO MAKE SOME TEA OR SOMETHING!
DON'T BOTHER, CHIHO-CHAN.
THEY DON'T HAVE ANY TEAPOTS OR CUPS OR ANY-THING.
THE FRIDGE AND THE SHELVES ARE COMPLETELY EMPTY TOO. I HAVE NO IDEA WHAT THEY LIVE OFF OF.
HUH...?
HOW DO YOU KNOW ALL OF THAT, YUSA-SAN...?
OH, UH, THE OTHER DAY I ST—
AH...
THE OTHER DAY YOU...WHAT, YUSA-SAN?

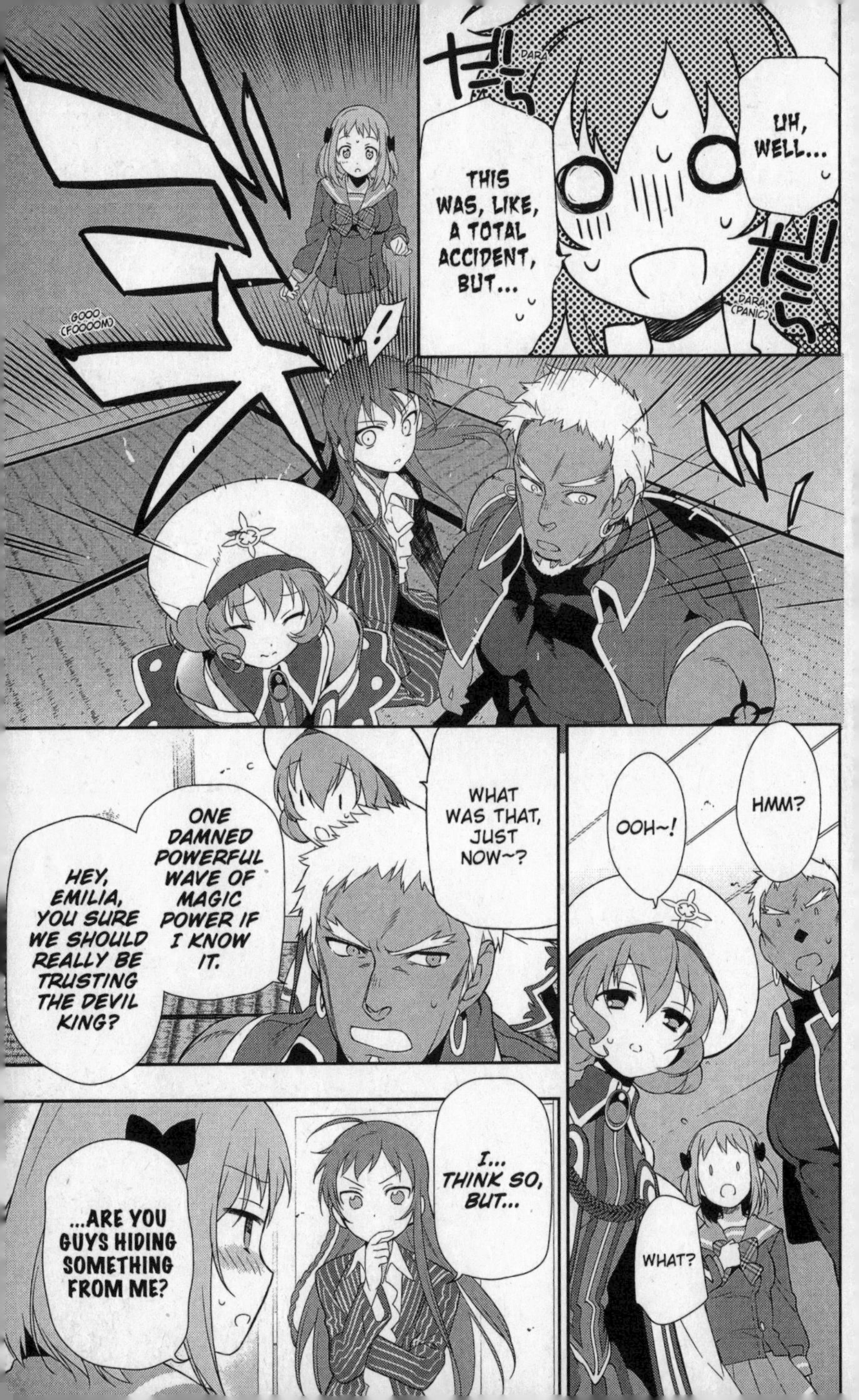
UH, WELL...
DARA
THIS WAS, LIKE, A TOTAL ACCIDENT, BUT...
DARA (PANIC)
GOOO (FOOOOM)
!
HMM?
OOH~!
WHAT?
WHAT WAS THAT, JUST NOW~?
ONE DAMNED POWERFUL WAVE OF MAGIC POWER IF I KNOW IT.
HEY, EMILIA, YOU SURE WE SHOULD REALLY BE TRUSTING THE DEVIL KING?
I... THINK SO, BUT...
...ARE YOU GUYS HIDING SOMETHING FROM ME?

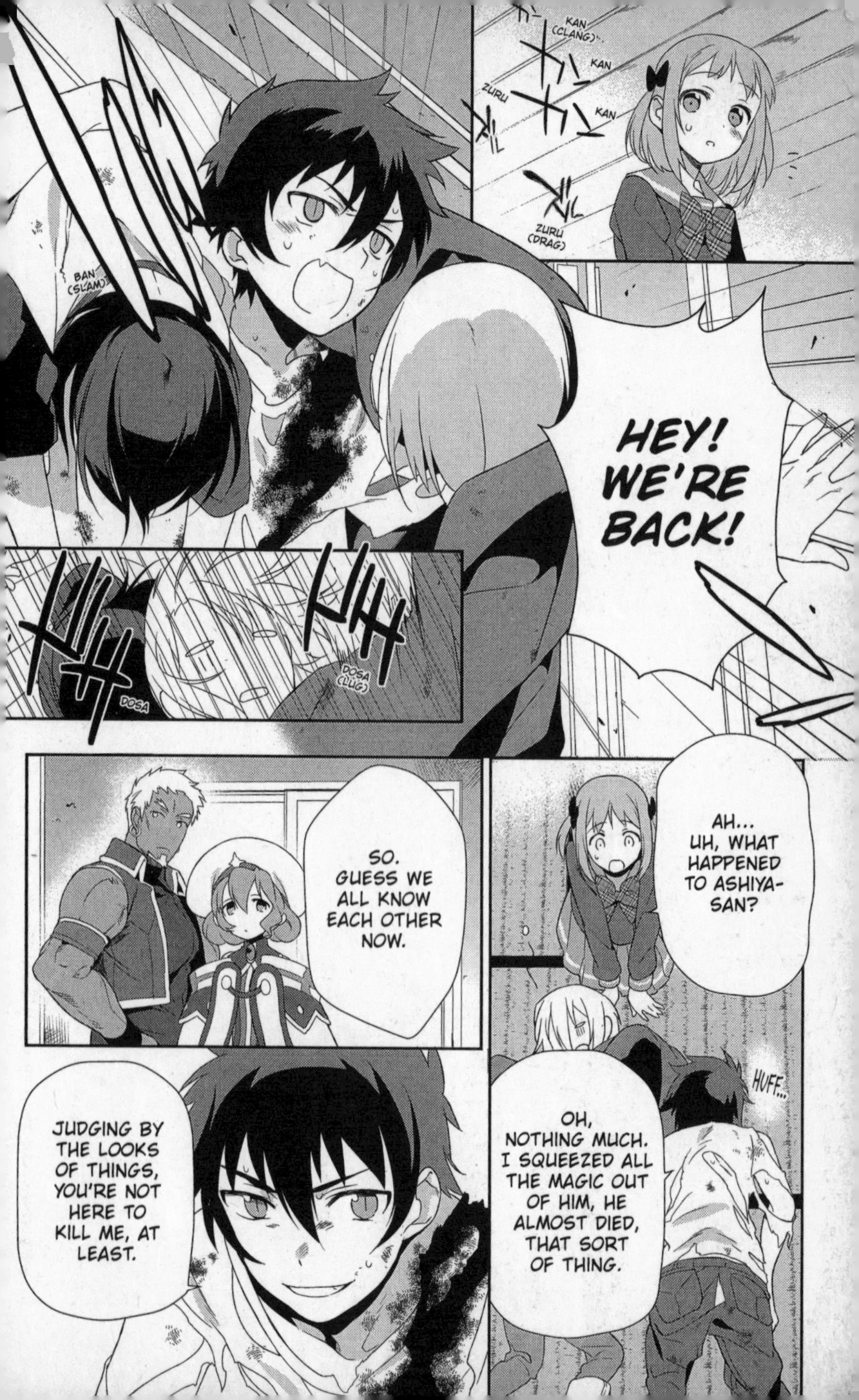
KAN (CLANG)
KAN
KAN
ZURU
ZURU (DRAG)
HEY! WE'RE BACK!
BAN (SLAM)
DOSA (LUG)
DOSA
AH... UH, WHAT HAPPENED TO ASHIYA-SAN?
SO. GUESS WE ALL KNOW EACH OTHER NOW.
HUFF...
OH, NOTHING MUCH. I SQUEEZED ALL THE MAGIC OUT OF HIM, HE ALMOST DIED, THAT SORT OF THING.
JUDGING BY THE LOOKS OF THINGS, YOU'RE NOT HERE TO KILL ME, AT LEAST.

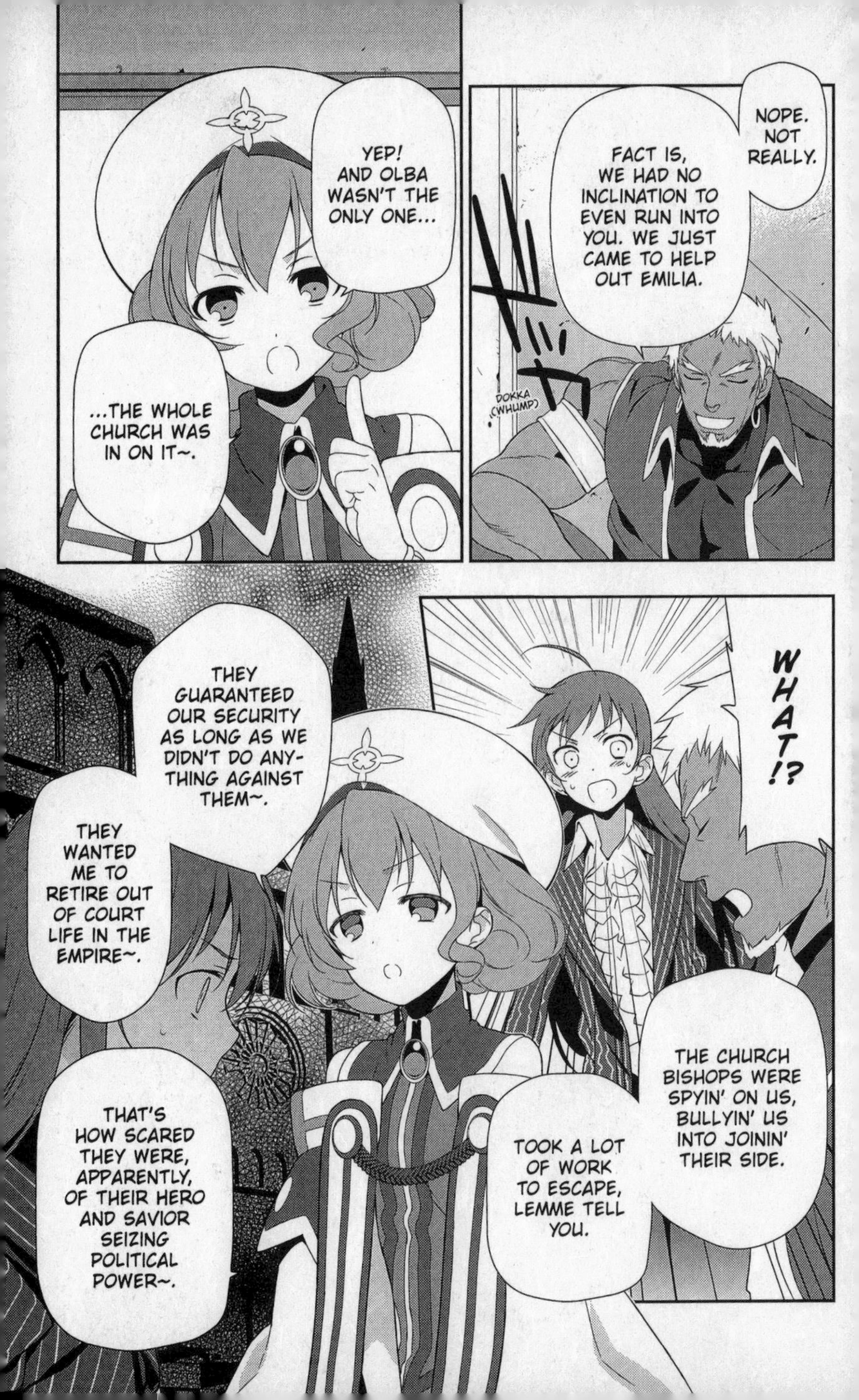
NOPE. NOT REALLY.
FACT IS, WE HAD NO INCLINATION TO EVEN RUN INTO YOU. WE JUST CAME TO HELP OUT EMILIA.
DOKKA (WHUMP)
YEP! AND OLBA WASN'T THE ONLY ONE...
...THE WHOLE CHURCH WAS IN ON IT~.
WHAT!?
THEY GUARANTEED OUR SECURITY AS LONG AS WE DIDN'T DO ANY-THING AGAINST THEM~.
THEY WANTED ME TO RETIRE OUT OF COURT LIFE IN THE EMPIRE~.
THE CHURCH BISHOPS WERE SPYIN' ON US, BULLYIN' US INTO JOININ' THEIR SIDE.
TOOK A LOT OF WORK TO ESCAPE, LEMME TELL YOU.
THAT'S HOW SCARED THEY WERE, APPARENTLY, OF THEIR HERO AND SAVIOR SEIZING POLITICAL POWER~.

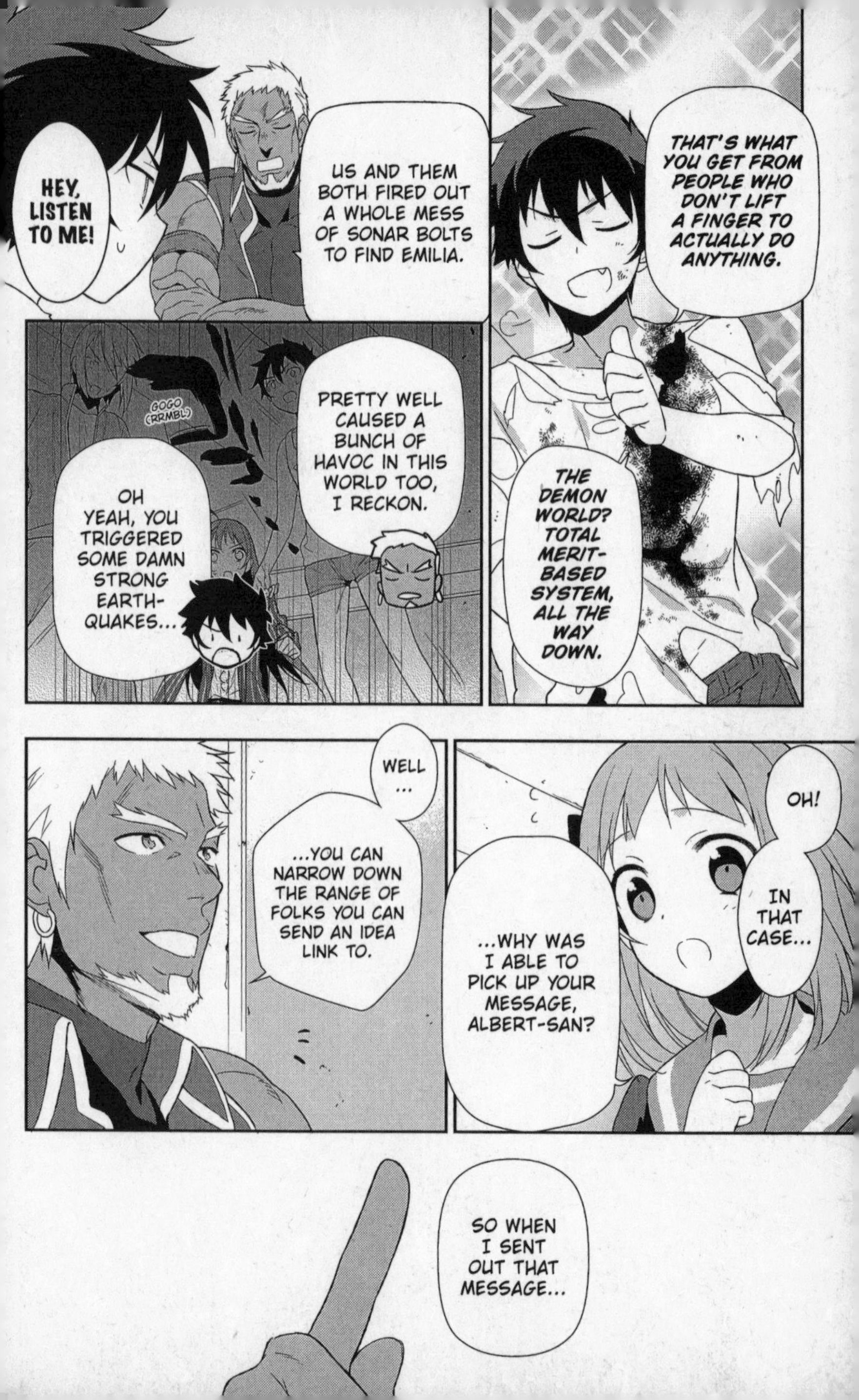
THAT'S WHAT YOU GET FROM PEOPLE WHO DON'T LIFT A FINGER TO ACTUALLY DO ANYTHING.
THE DEMON WORLD? TOTAL MERIT-BASED SYSTEM, ALL THE WAY DOWN.
US AND THEM BOTH FIRED OUT A WHOLE MESS OF SONAR BOLTS TO FIND EMILIA.
HEY, LISTEN TO ME!
PRETTY WELL CAUSED A BUNCH OF HAVOC IN THIS WORLD TOO, I RECKON.
GOGO (RRMBL)
OH YEAH, YOU TRIGGERED SOME DAMN STRONG EARTH-QUAKES...
OH!
IN THAT CASE...
...WHY WAS I ABLE TO PICK UP YOUR MESSAGE, ALBERT-SAN?
WELL...
...YOU CAN NARROW DOWN THE RANGE OF FOLKS YOU CAN SEND AN IDEA LINK TO.
SO WHEN I SENT OUT THAT MESSAGE...

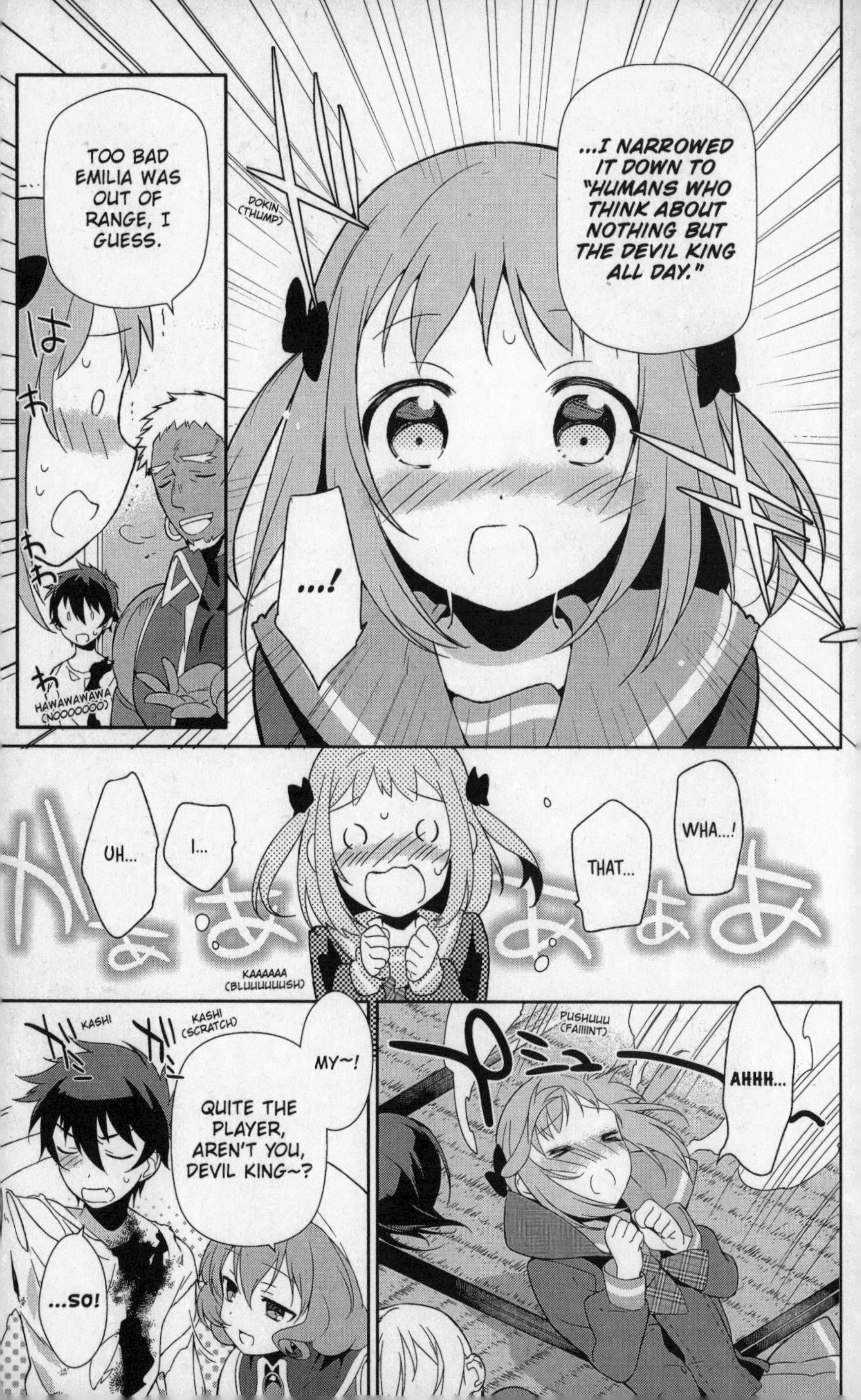
...I NARROWED IT DOWN TO "HUMANS WHO THINK ABOUT NOTHING BUT THE DEVIL KING ALL DAY."
DOKIN (THUMP)
...!
TOO BAD EMILIA WAS OUT OF RANGE, I GUESS.
HAWAWAWAWA (NOOOOOOOO)
WHA...!
THAT...
I...
UH...
KAAAAAA (BLUUUUUUSH)
PUSHUUU (FAIIIINT)
AHHH...
KASHI (SCRATCH)
KASHI
MY~!
QUITE THE PLAYER, AREN'T YOU, DEVIL KING~?
...SO!

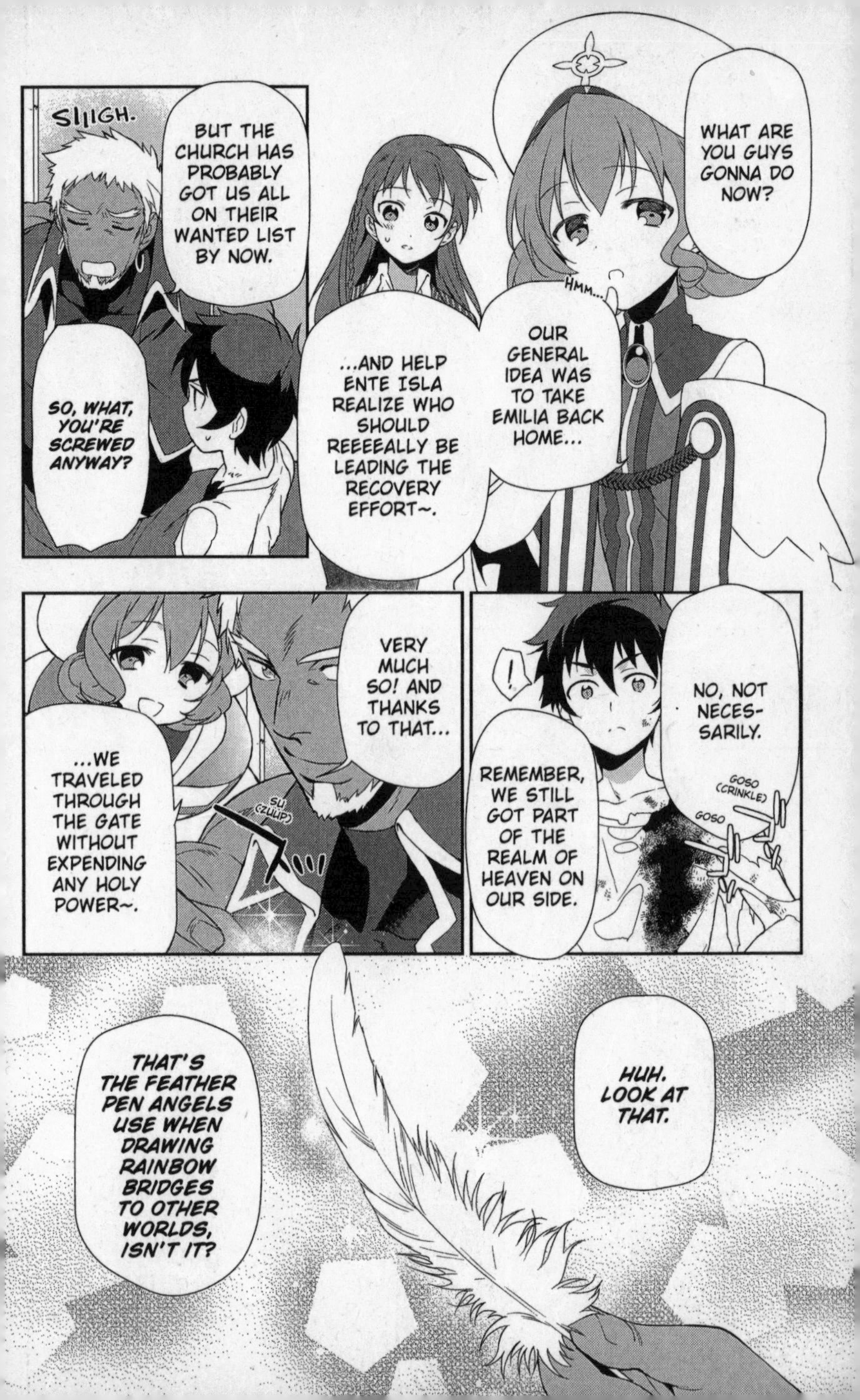
WHAT ARE YOU GUYS GONNA DO NOW?
HMM...
OUR GENERAL IDEA WAS TO TAKE EMILIA BACK HOME...
...AND HELP ENTE ISLA REALIZE WHO SHOULD REEEEALLY BE LEADING THE RECOVERY EFFORT~.
SIIIGH.
BUT THE CHURCH HAS PROBABLY GOT US ALL ON THEIR WANTED LIST BY NOW.
SO, WHAT, YOU'RE SCREWED ANYWAY?
!
NO, NOT NECES-SARILY.
GOSO (CRINKLE)
GOSO
REMEMBER, WE STILL GOT PART OF THE REALM OF HEAVEN ON OUR SIDE.
VERY MUCH SO! AND THANKS TO THAT...
SU (ZUUP)
...WE TRAVELED THROUGH THE GATE WITHOUT EXPENDING ANY HOLY POWER~.
HUH. LOOK AT THAT.
THAT'S THE FEATHER PEN ANGELS USE WHEN DRAWING RAINBOW BRIDGES TO OTHER WORLDS, ISN'T IT?

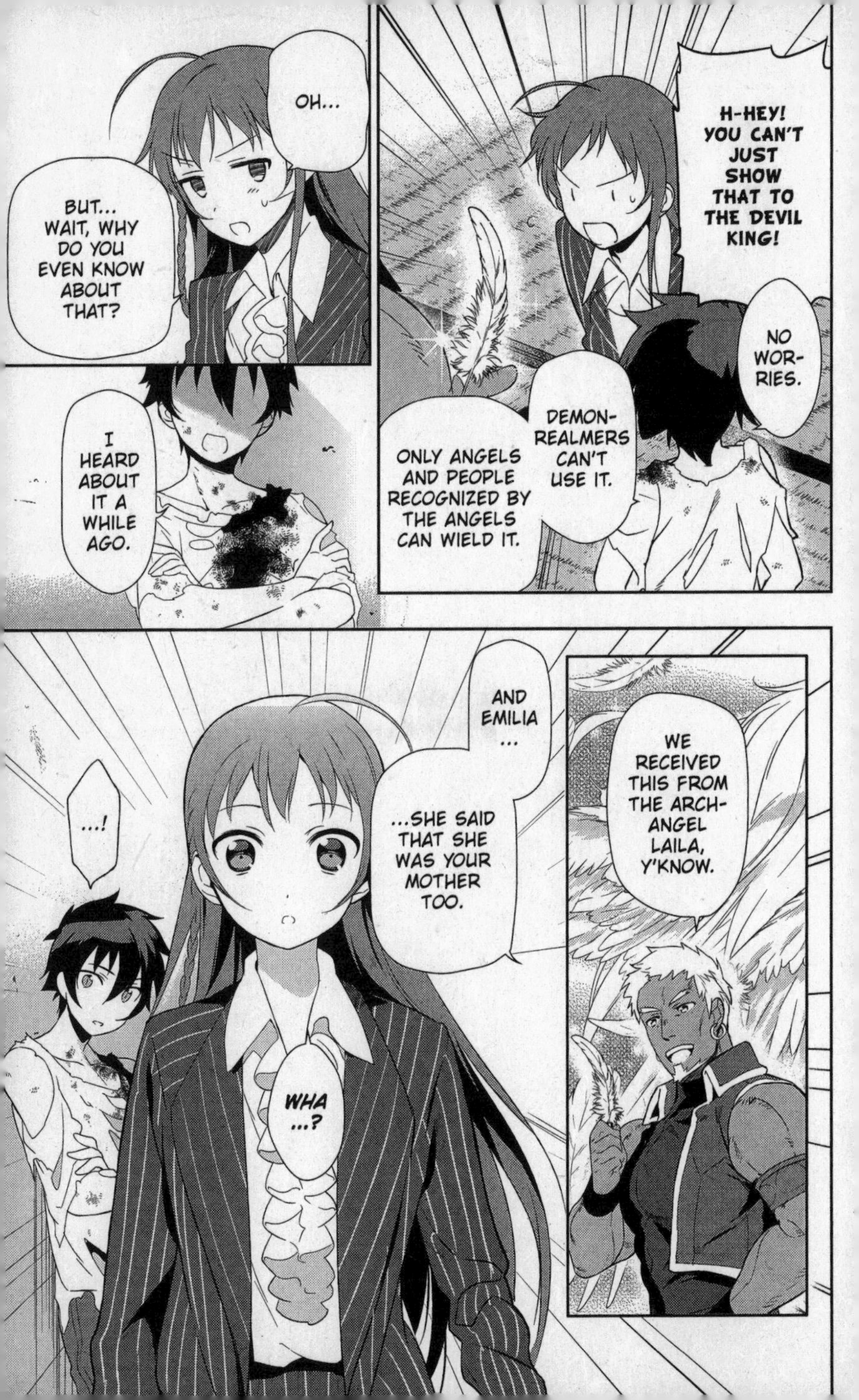
H-HEY! YOU CAN'T JUST SHOW THAT TO THE DEVIL KING!
NO WOR-RIES.
DEMON-REALMERS CAN'T USE IT.
ONLY ANGELS AND PEOPLE RECOGNIZED BY THE ANGELS CAN WIELD IT.
OH...
BUT... WAIT, WHY DO YOU EVEN KNOW ABOUT THAT?
I HEARD ABOUT IT A WHILE AGO.
WE RECEIVED THIS FROM THE ARCH-ANGEL LAILA, Y'KNOW.
AND EMILIA ...
...SHE SAID THAT SHE WAS YOUR MOTHER TOO.
...!
WHA ...?

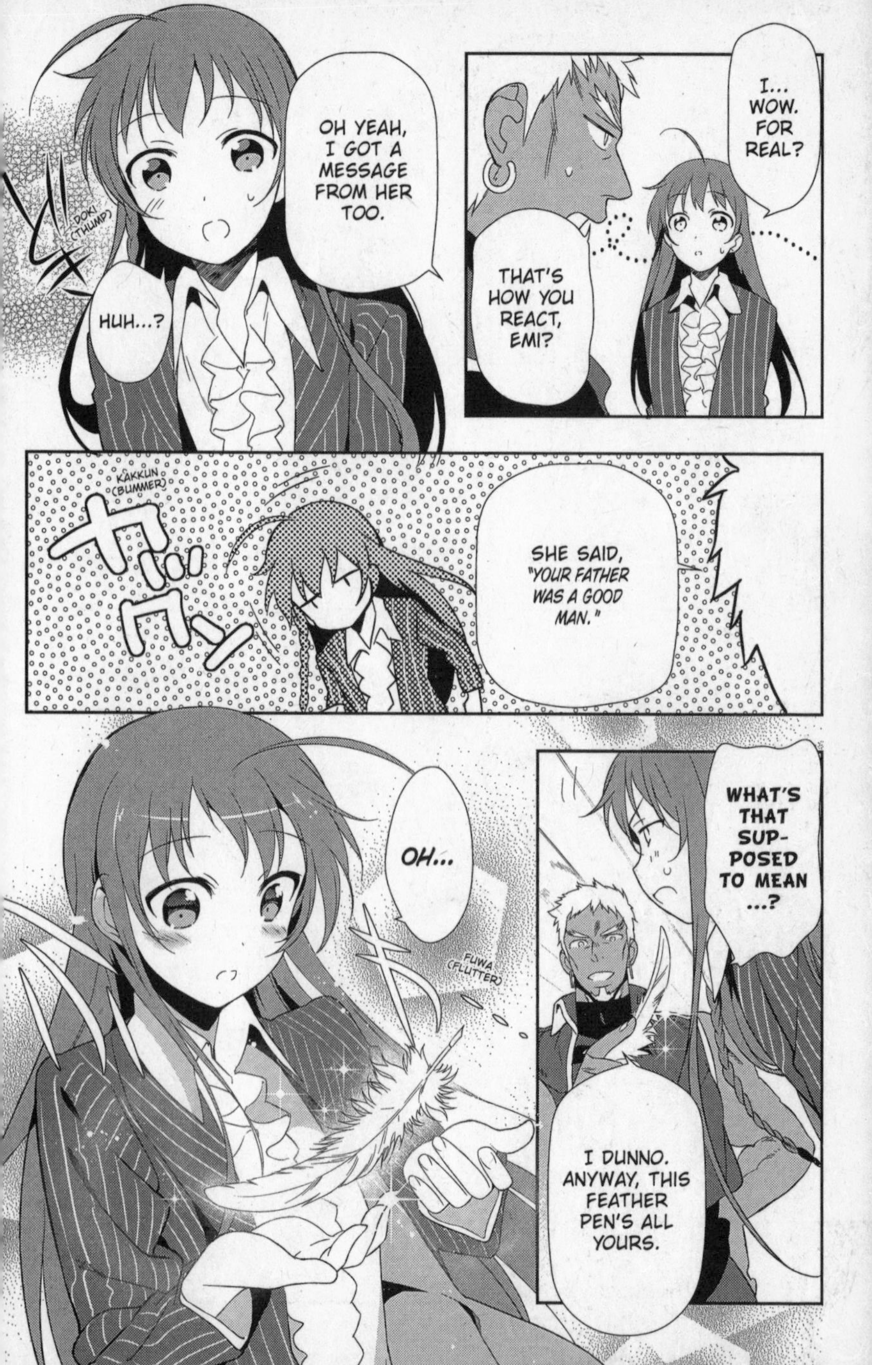
I... WOW. FOR REAL?
THAT'S HOW YOU REACT, EMI?
OH YEAH, I GOT A MESSAGE FROM HER TOO.
DOKI (THUMP)
HUH...?
SHE SAID, "YOUR FATHER WAS A GOOD MAN."
KAKKUN (BUMMER)
WHAT'S THAT SUP-POSED TO MEAN ...?
I DUNNO. ANYWAY, THIS FEATHER PEN'S ALL YOURS.
OH...
FUWA (FLUTTER)

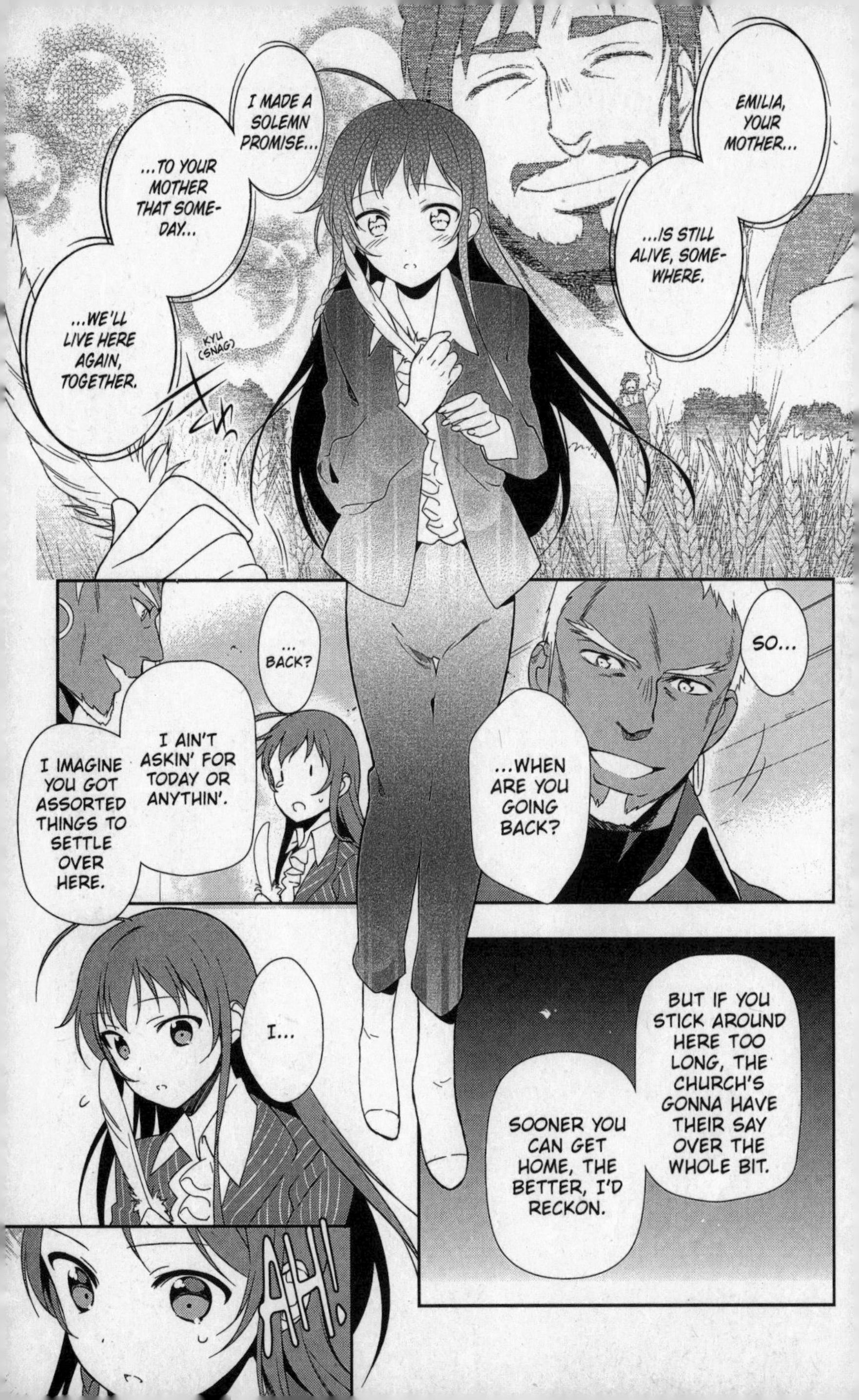
EMILIA, YOUR MOTHER...
...IS STILL ALIVE, SOME-WHERE.
I MADE A SOLEMN PROMISE...
...TO YOUR MOTHER THAT SOME-DAY...
...WE'LL LIVE HERE AGAIN, TOGETHER.
KYU (SNAG)
SO...
...WHEN ARE YOU GOING BACK?
...BACK?
I AIN'T ASKIN' FOR TODAY OR ANYTHIN'.
I IMAGINE YOU GOT ASSORTED THINGS TO SETTLE OVER HERE.
BUT IF YOU STICK AROUND HERE TOO LONG, THE CHURCH'S GONNA HAVE THEIR SAY OVER THE WHOLE BIT.
SOONER YOU CAN GET HOME, THE BETTER, I'D RECKON.
I...
AH!

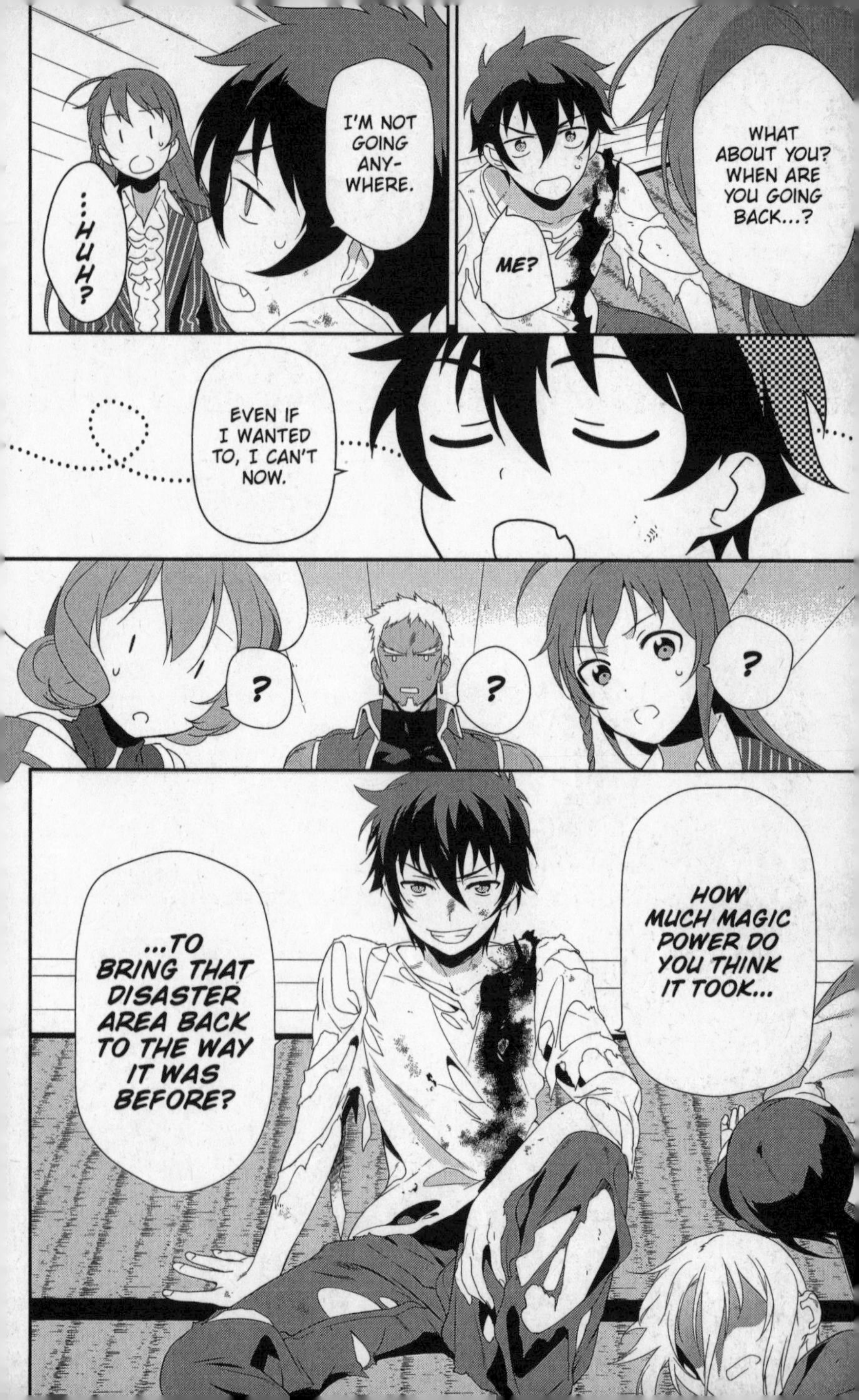
WHAT ABOUT YOU? WHEN ARE YOU GOING BACK...?
ME?
I'M NOT GOING ANY-WHERE.
...HUH?
EVEN IF I WANTED TO, I CAN'T NOW.
?
?
?
HOW MUCH MAGIC POWER DO YOU THINK IT TOOK...
...TO BRING THAT DISASTER AREA BACK TO THE WAY IT WAS BEFORE?

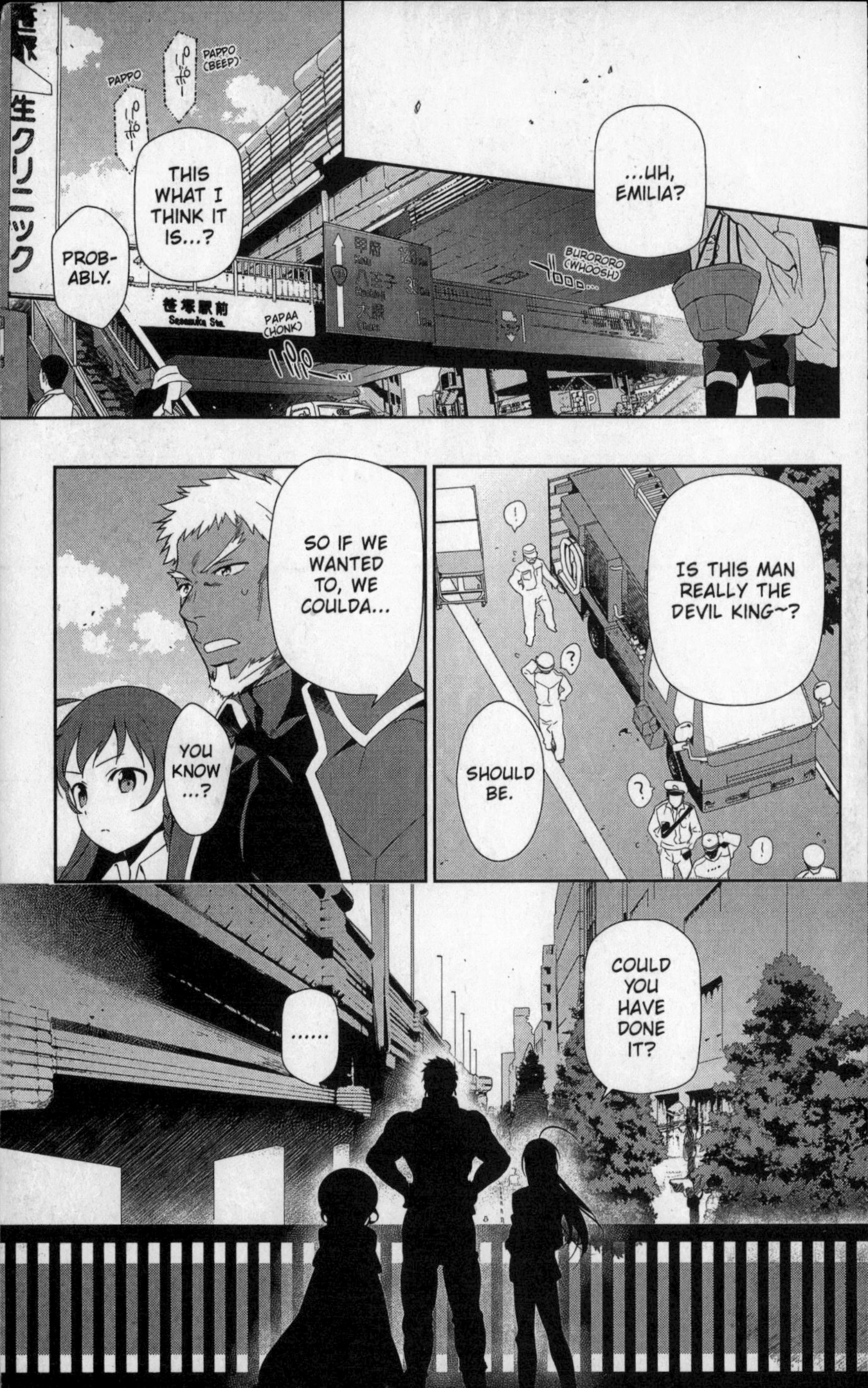
...UH, EMILIA?
BURORORO (WHOOSH)
PAPAA (HONK)
THIS WHAT I THINK IT IS...?
PROBABLY.
PAPPO (BEEP)
PAPPO
Sasazuka Sta.
IS THIS MAN REALLY THE DEVIL KING~?
SHOULD BE.
SO IF WE WANTED TO, WE COULDA...
YOU KNOW ...?
COULD YOU HAVE DONE IT?
......

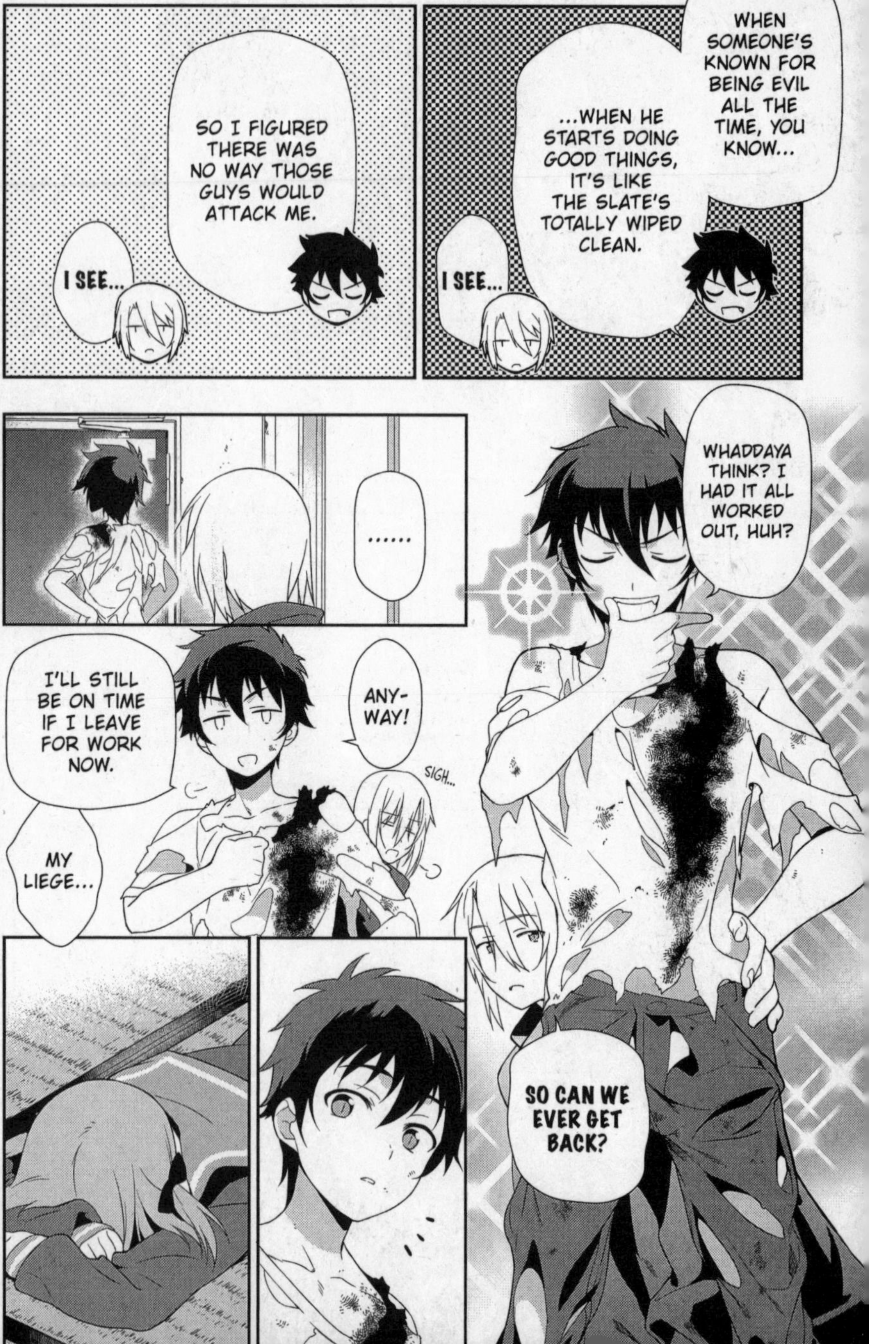
WHEN SOMEONE'S KNOWN FOR BEING EVIL ALL THE TIME, YOU KNOW...
...WHEN HE STARTS DOING GOOD THINGS, IT'S LIKE THE SLATE'S TOTALLY WIPED CLEAN.
I SEE...
SO I FIGURED THERE WAS NO WAY THOSE GUYS WOULD ATTACK ME.
I SEE...
WHADDAYA THINK? I HAD IT ALL WORKED OUT, HUH?
......
ANY-WAY!
I'LL STILL BE ON TIME IF I LEAVE FOR WORK NOW.
SIGH...
MY LIEGE...
SO CAN WE EVER GET BACK?

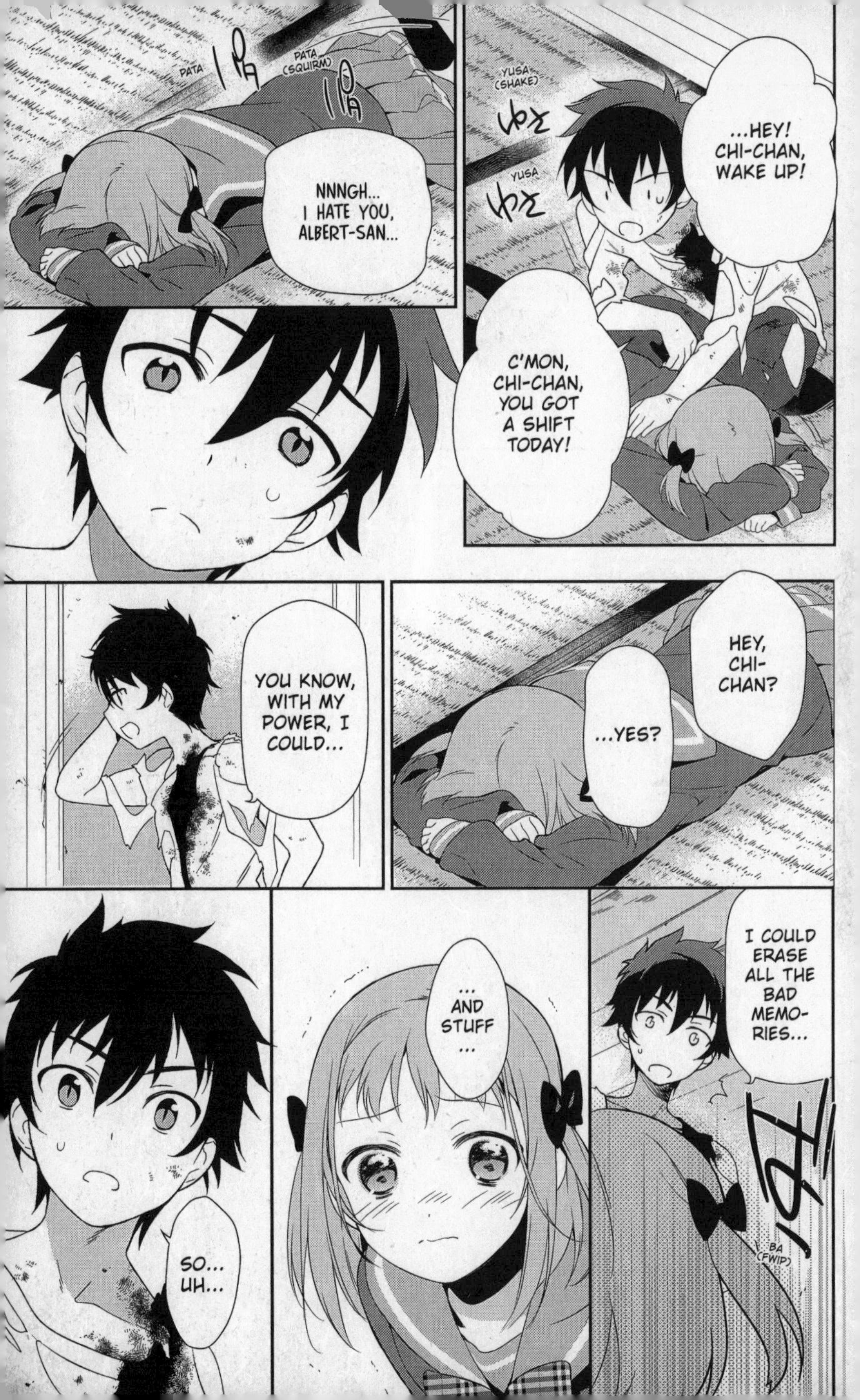

...HEY! CHI-CHAN, WAKE UP!
YUSA (SHAKE)
YUSA
C'MON, CHI-CHAN, YOU GOT A SHIFT TODAY!
PATA (SQUIRM)
PATA
NNNGH... I HATE YOU, ALBERT-SAN...
HEY, CHI-CHAN?
...YES?
YOU KNOW, WITH MY POWER, I COULD...
I COULD ERASE ALL THE BAD MEMO-RIES...
BA (FWIP)
... AND STUFF ...
SO... UH...

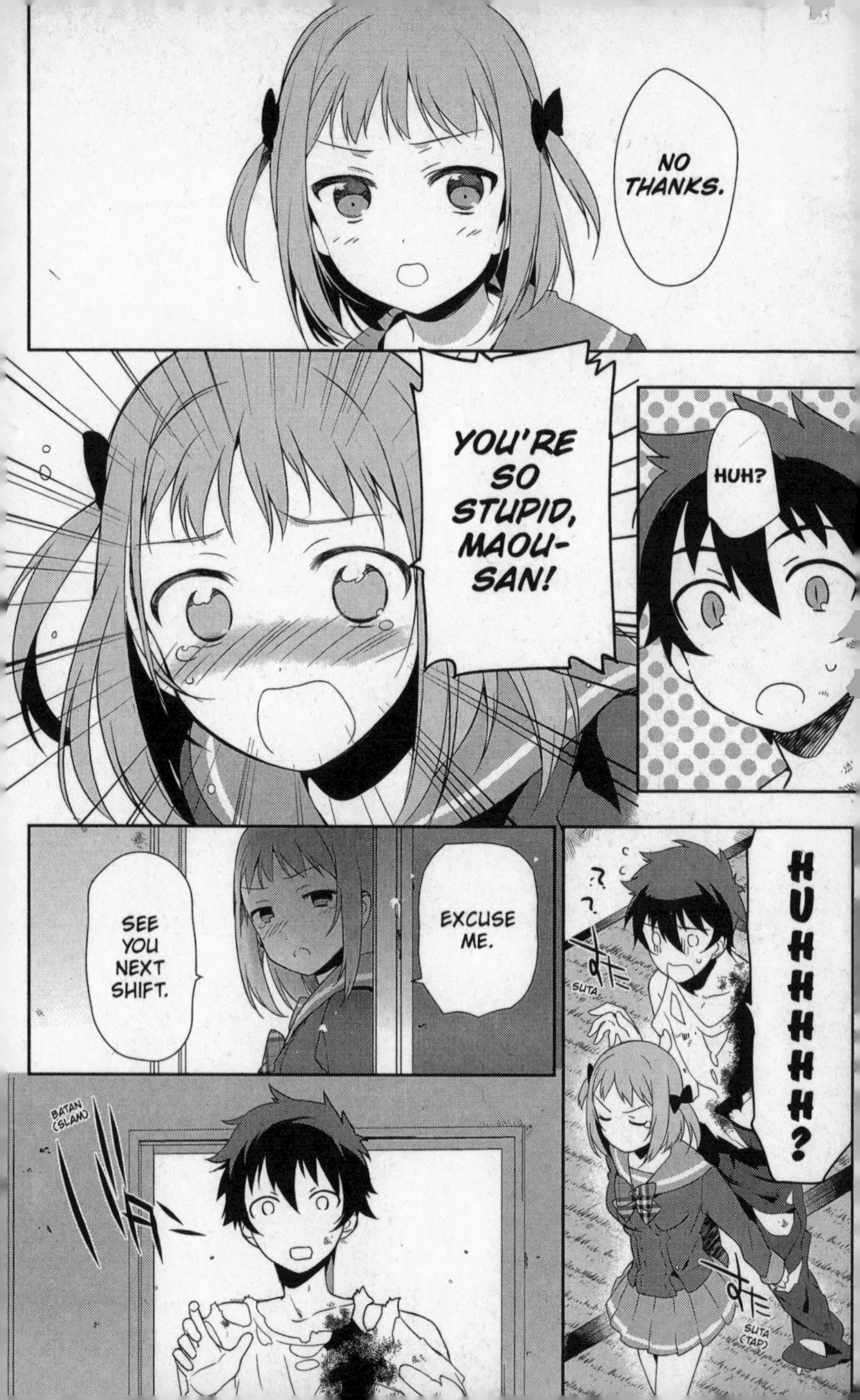
NO THANKS.
HUH?
YOU'RE SO STUPID, MAOU-SAN!
HUHHHHH?
SUTA
SUTA (TAP)
EXCUSE ME.
SEE YOU NEXT SHIFT.
BATAN (SLAM)

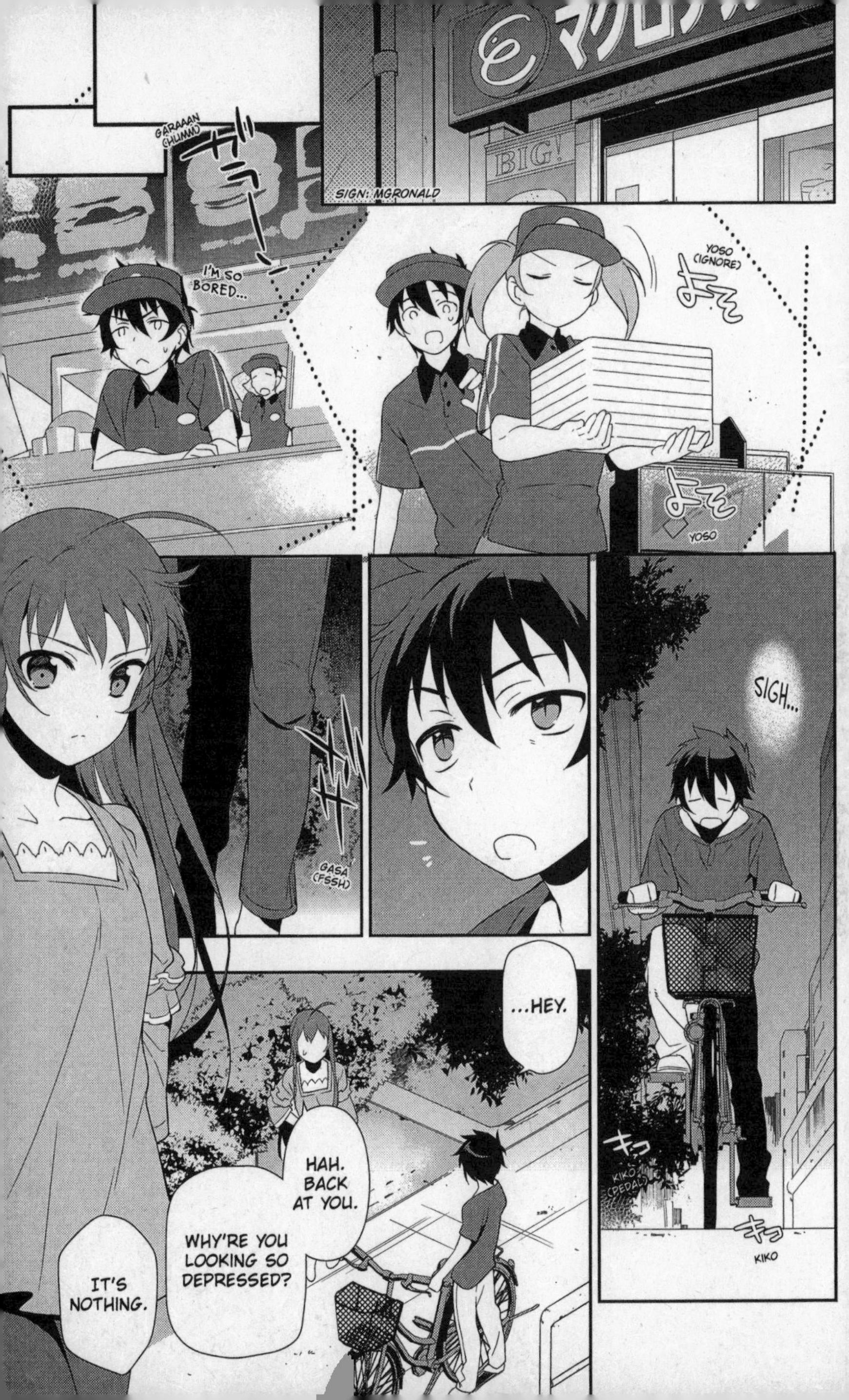
SIGN: MGRONALD
GARAAAN (HUMM)
I'M SO BORED...
YOSO (IGNORE)
YOSO
SIGH...
KIKO (PEDAL)
KIKO
GASA (FSSH)
...HEY.
HAH. BACK AT YOU.
WHY'RE YOU LOOKING SO DEPRESSED?
IT'S NOTHING.

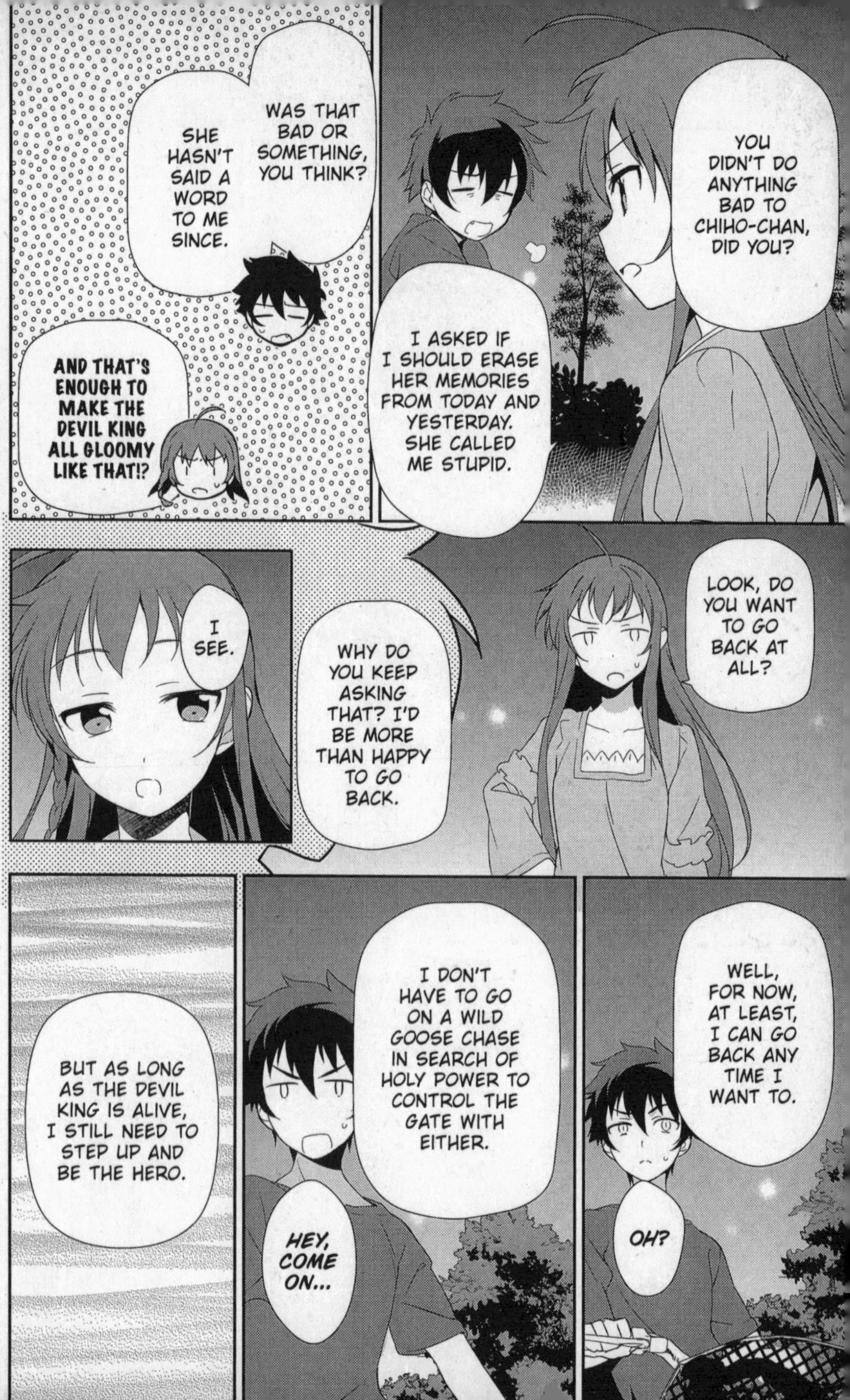
YOU DIDN'T DO ANYTHING BAD TO CHIHO-CHAN, DID YOU?
I ASKED IF I SHOULD ERASE HER MEMORIES FROM TODAY AND YESTERDAY. SHE CALLED ME STUPID.
WAS THAT BAD OR SOMETHING, YOU THINK?
SHE HASN'T SAID A WORD TO ME SINCE.
AND THAT'S ENOUGH TO MAKE THE DEVIL KING ALL GLOOMY LIKE THAT!?
LOOK, DO YOU WANT TO GO BACK AT ALL?
WHY DO YOU KEEP ASKING THAT? I'D BE MORE THAN HAPPY TO GO BACK.
I SEE.
WELL, FOR NOW, AT LEAST, I CAN GO BACK ANY TIME I WANT TO.
OH?
I DON'T HAVE TO GO ON A WILD GOOSE CHASE IN SEARCH OF HOLY POWER TO CONTROL THE GATE WITH EITHER.
HEY, COME ON...
BUT AS LONG AS THE DEVIL KING IS ALIVE, I STILL NEED TO STEP UP AND BE THE HERO.

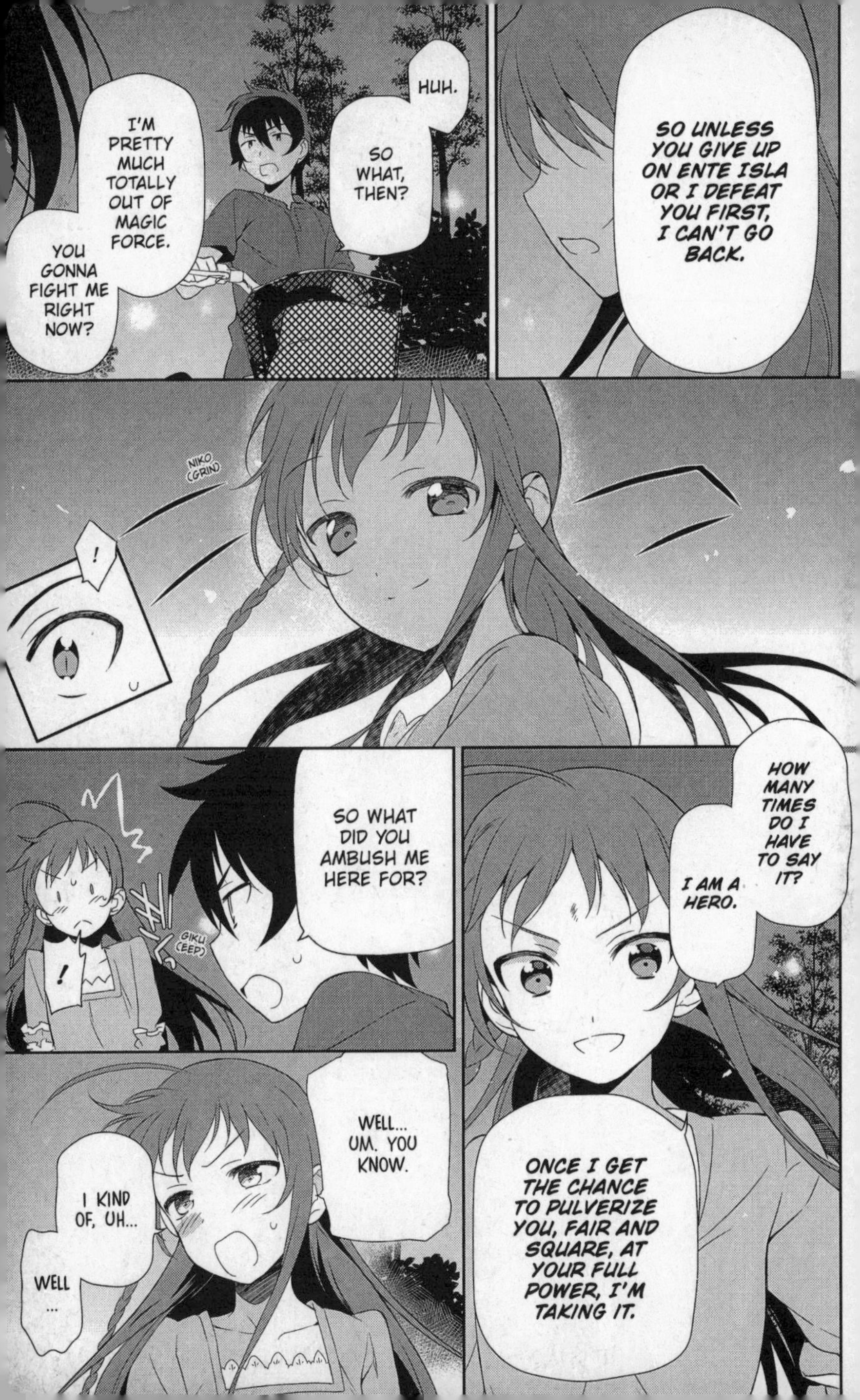
SO UNLESS YOU GIVE UP ON ENTE ISLA OR I DEFEAT YOU FIRST, I CAN'T GO BACK.
HUH.
SO WHAT, THEN?
I'M PRETTY MUCH TOTALLY OUT OF MAGIC FORCE.
YOU GONNA FIGHT ME RIGHT NOW?
NIKO (GRIN)
!
HOW MANY TIMES DO I HAVE TO SAY IT?
I AM A HERO.
ONCE I GET THE CHANCE TO PULVERIZE YOU, FAIR AND SQUARE, AT YOUR FULL POWER, I'M TAKING IT.
SO WHAT DID YOU AMBUSH ME HERE FOR?
GIKU (EEP)
!
WELL... UM. YOU KNOW.
I KIND OF, UH...
WELL ...

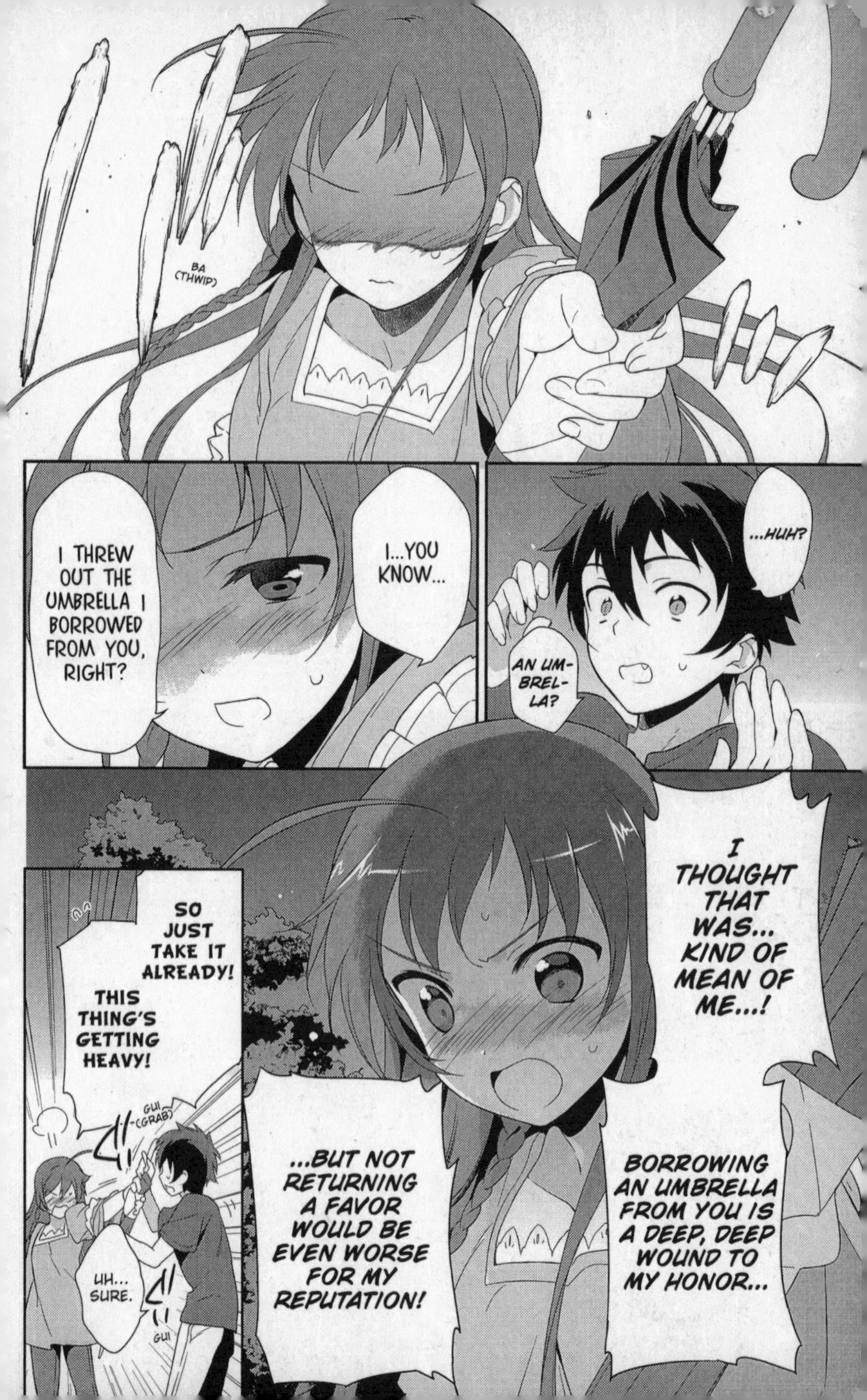
BA (THWIP)
...HUH?
AN UM-BREL-LA?
I...YOU KNOW...
I THREW OUT THE UMBRELLA I BORROWED FROM YOU, RIGHT?
I THOUGHT THAT WAS... KIND OF MEAN OF ME...!
BORROWING AN UMBRELLA FROM YOU IS A DEEP, DEEP WOUND TO MY HONOR...
...BUT NOT RETURNING A FAVOR WOULD BE EVEN WORSE FOR MY REPUTATION!
SO JUST TAKE IT ALREADY!
THIS THING'S GETTING HEAVY!
GUI (GRAB)
UH... SURE.
GUI

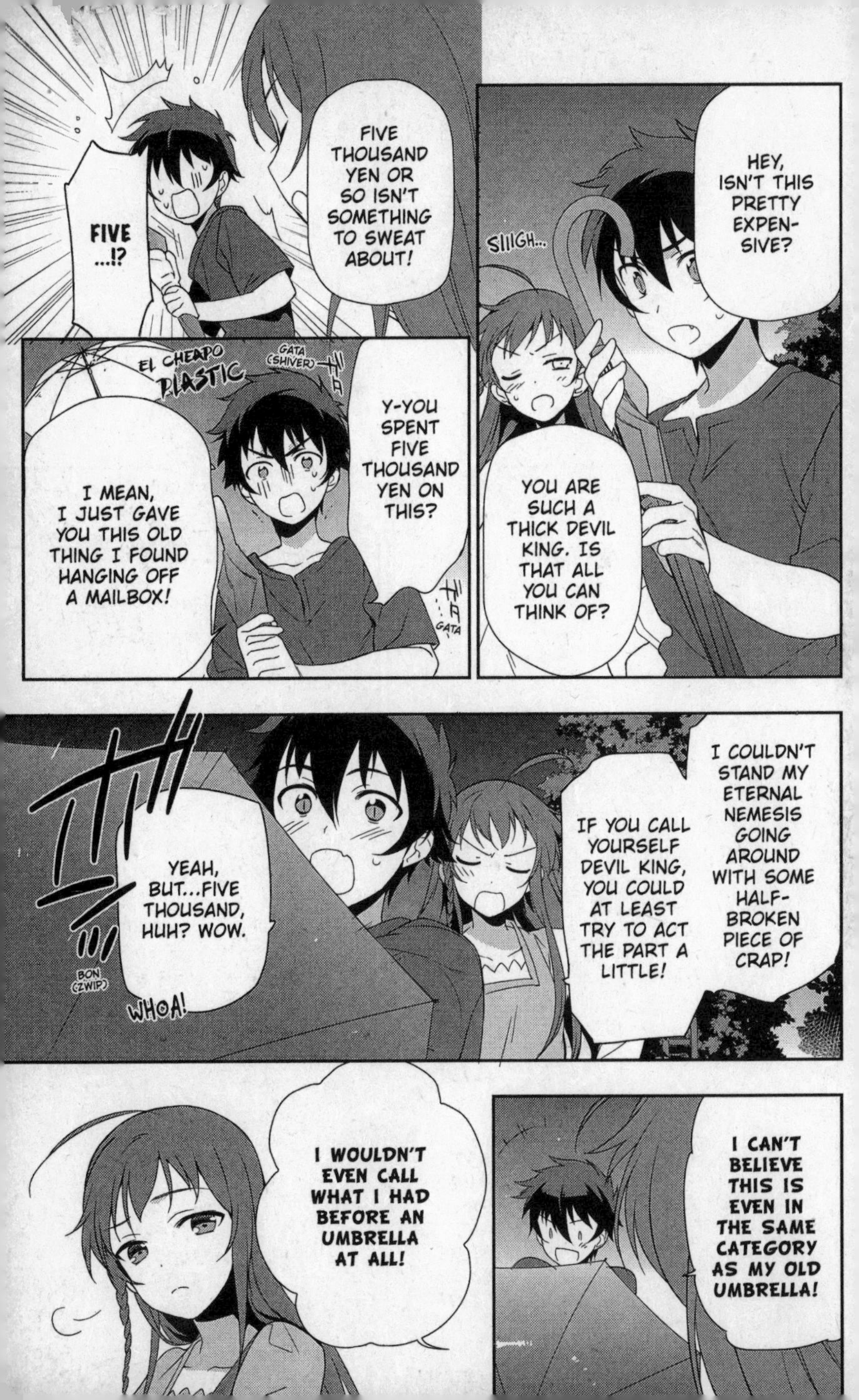
HEY, ISN'T THIS PRETTY EXPENSIVE?
SIIGH...
YOU ARE SUCH A THICK DEVIL KING. IS THAT ALL YOU CAN THINK OF?
FIVE THOUSAND YEN OR SO ISN'T SOMETHING TO SWEAT ABOUT!
FIVE ...!?
Y-YOU SPENT FIVE THOUSAND YEN ON THIS?
GATA (SHIVER)
EL CHEAPO PLASTIC
I MEAN, I JUST GAVE YOU THIS OLD THING I FOUND HANGING OFF A MAILBOX!
GATA
I COULDN'T STAND MY ETERNAL NEMESIS GOING AROUND WITH SOME HALF-BROKEN PIECE OF CRAP!
IF YOU CALL YOURSELF DEVIL KING, YOU COULD AT LEAST TRY TO ACT THE PART A LITTLE!
YEAH, BUT...FIVE THOUSAND, HUH? WOW.
BON (ZWIP)
WHOA!
I CAN'T BELIEVE THIS IS EVEN IN THE SAME CATEGORY AS MY OLD UMBRELLA!
I WOULDN'T EVEN CALL WHAT I HAD BEFORE AN UMBRELLA AT ALL!

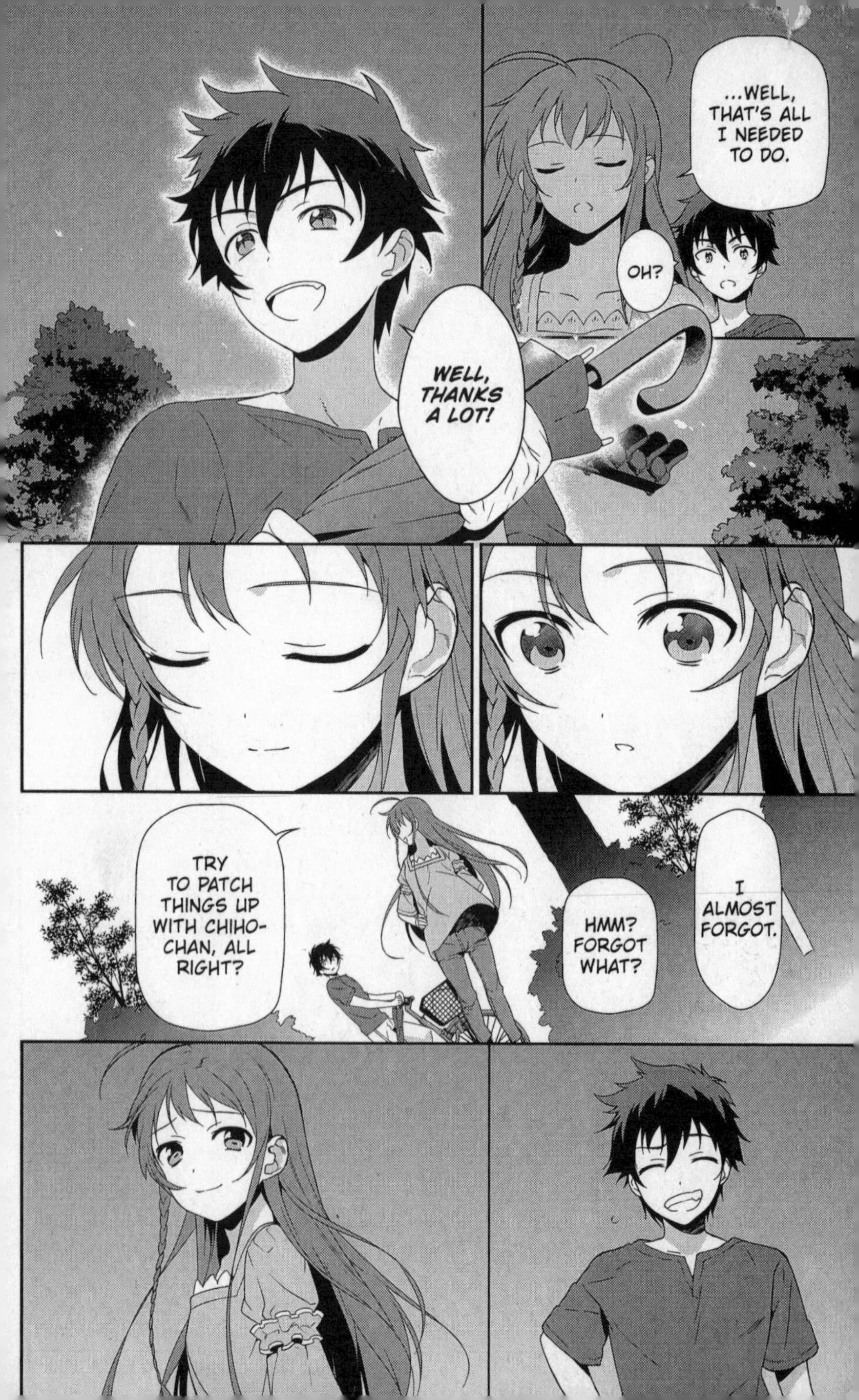
...WELL, THAT'S ALL I NEEDED TO DO.
OH?
WELL, THANKS A LOT!
I ALMOST FORGOT.
HMM? FORGOT WHAT?
TRY TO PATCH THINGS UP WITH CHIHO-CHAN, ALL RIGHT?

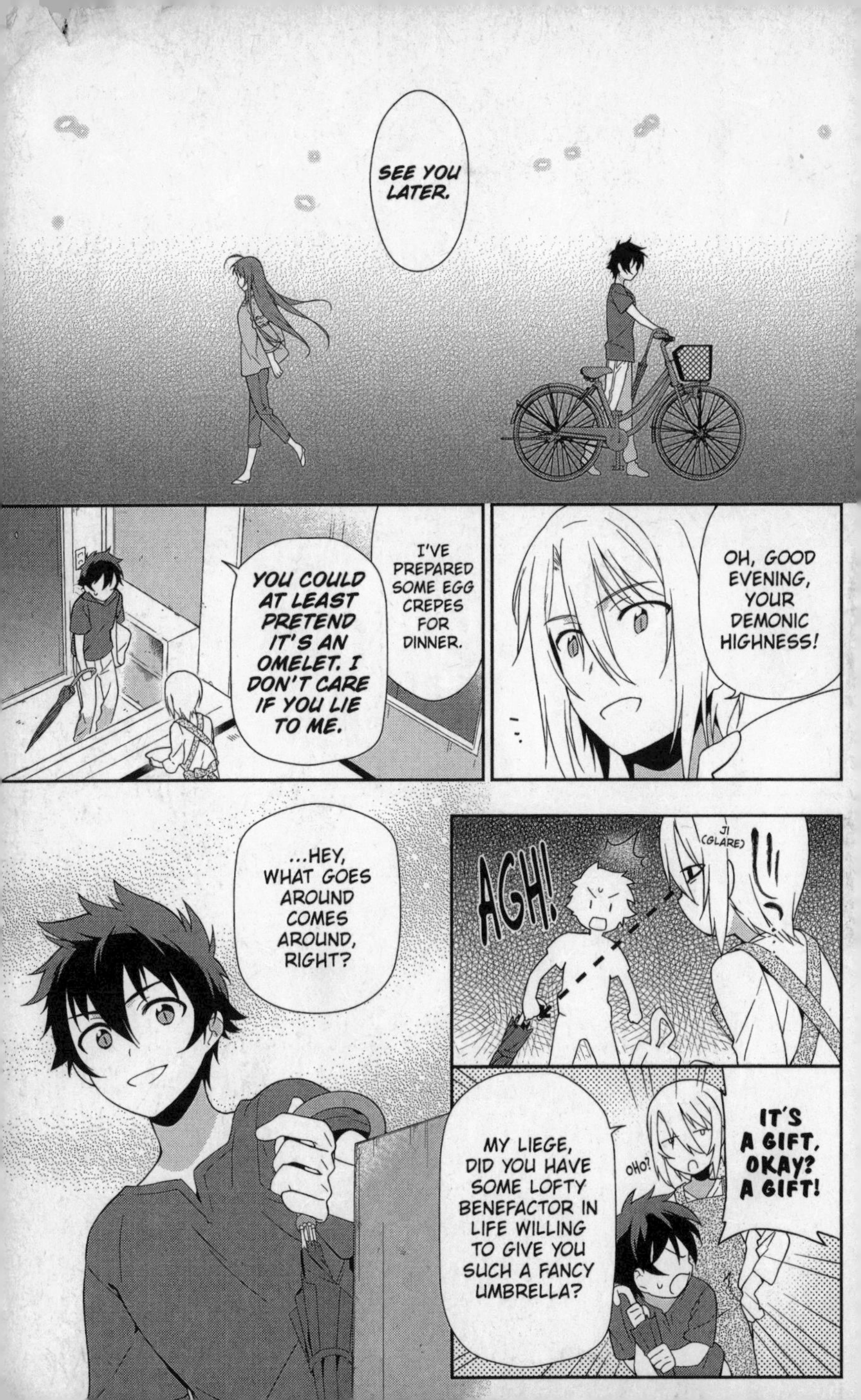
SEE YOU LATER.
OH, GOOD EVENING, YOUR DEMONIC HIGHNESS!
I'VE PREPARED SOME EGG CREPES FOR DINNER.
YOU COULD AT LEAST PRETEND IT'S AN OMELET. I DON'T CARE IF YOU LIE TO ME.
JI (GLARE)
AGH!
MY LIEGE, DID YOU HAVE SOME LOFTY BENEFACTOR IN LIFE WILLING TO GIVE YOU SUCH A FANCY UMBRELLA?
OHO?
IT'S A GIFT, OKAY? A GIFT!
...HEY, WHAT GOES AROUND COMES AROUND, RIGHT?

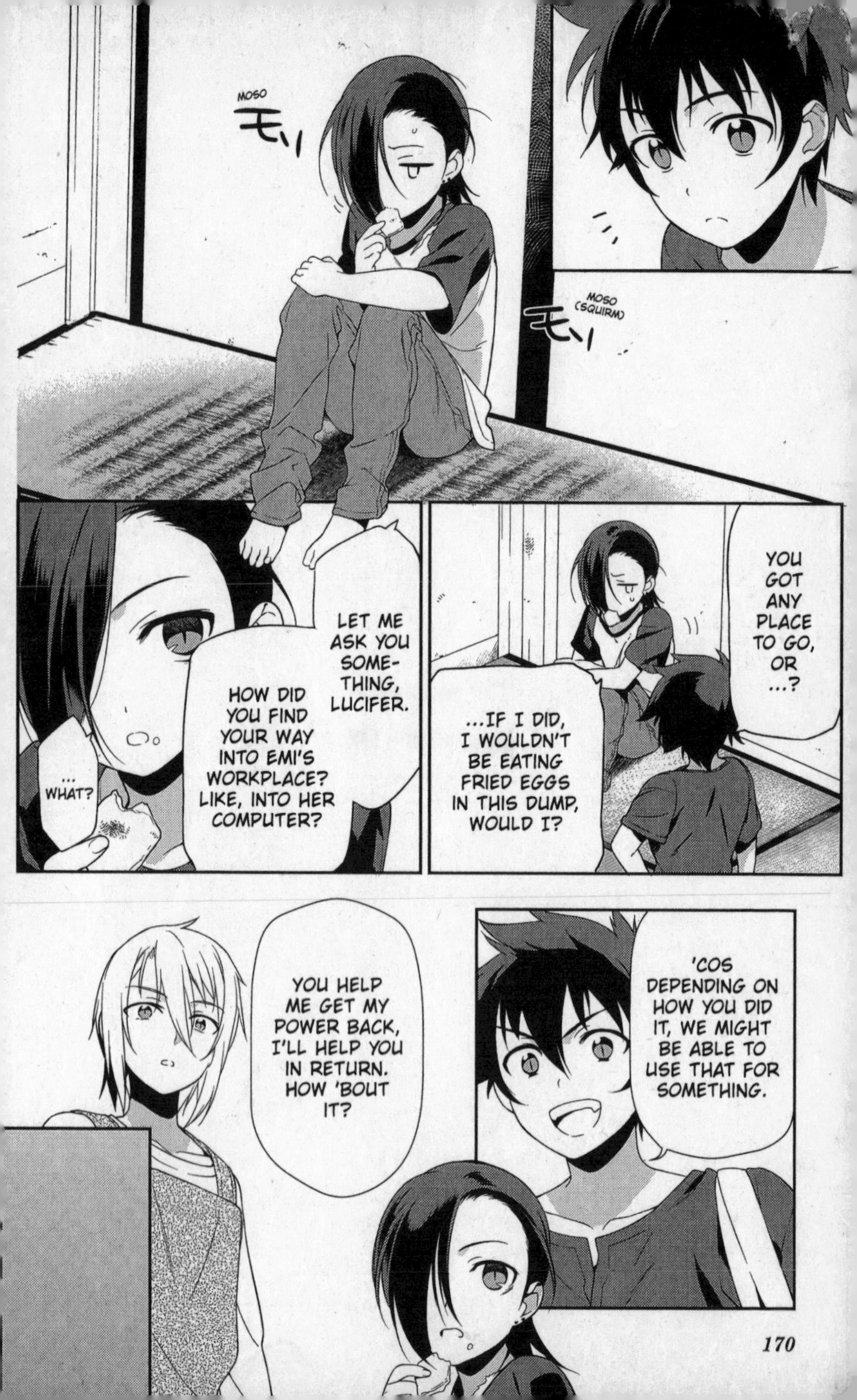
MOSO (SQUIRM)
MOSO
YOU GOT ANY PLACE TO GO, OR ...?
...IF I DID, I WOULDN'T BE EATING FRIED EGGS IN THIS DUMP, WOULD I?
LET ME ASK YOU SOMETHING, LUCIFER.
HOW DID YOU FIND YOUR WAY INTO EMI'S WORKPLACE? LIKE, INTO HER COMPUTER?
... WHAT?
'COS DEPENDING ON HOW YOU DID IT, WE MIGHT BE ABLE TO USE THAT FOR SOMETHING.
YOU HELP ME GET MY POWER BACK, I'LL HELP YOU IN RETURN. HOW 'BOUT IT?

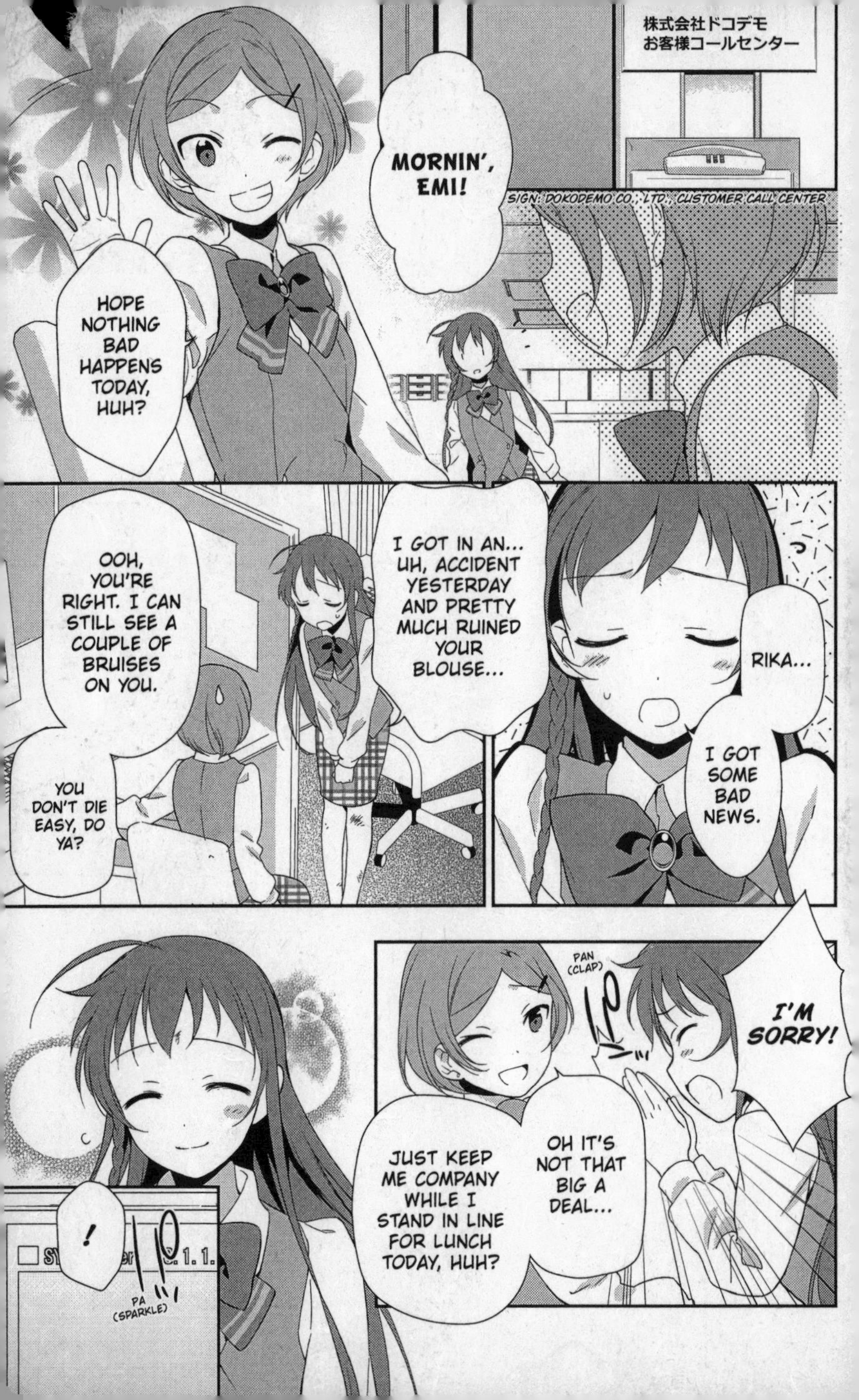
株式会社ドコデモ
お客様コールセンター
SIGN: DOKODEMO CO., LTD., CUSTOMER CALL CENTER
MORNIN', EMI!
HOPE NOTHING BAD HAPPENS TODAY, HUH?
RIKA...
I GOT SOME BAD NEWS.
I GOT IN AN... UH, ACCIDENT YESTERDAY AND PRETTY MUCH RUINED YOUR BLOUSE...
OOH, YOU'RE RIGHT. I CAN STILL SEE A COUPLE OF BRUISES ON YOU.
YOU DON'T DIE EASY, DO YA?
I'M SORRY!
PAN (CLAP)
OH IT'S NOT THAT BIG A DEAL...
JUST KEEP ME COMPANY WHILE I STAND IN LINE FOR LUNCH TODAY, HUH?
!
PA (SPARKLE)

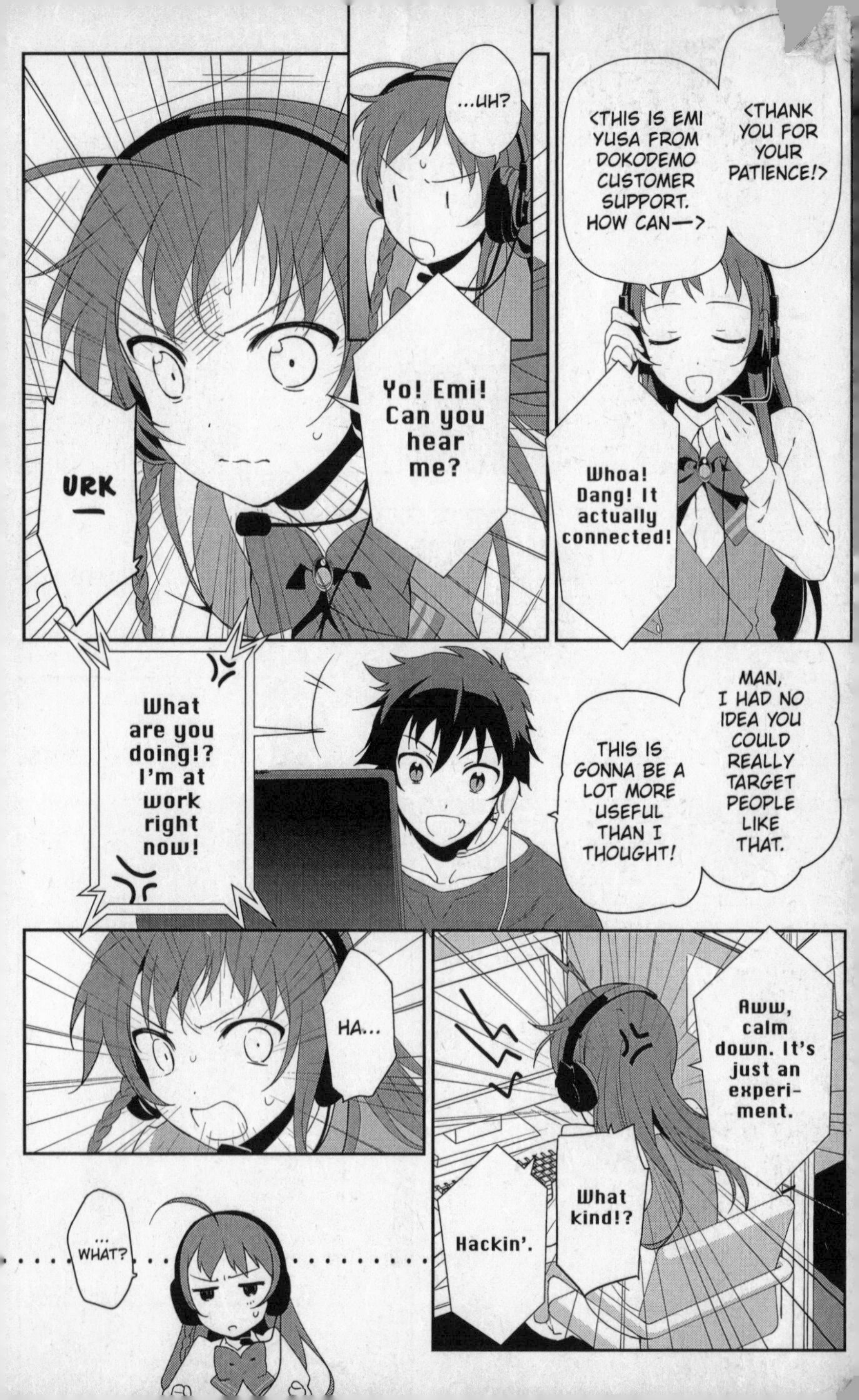
<THANK YOU FOR YOUR PATIENCE!>
<THIS IS EMI YUSA FROM DOKODEMO CUSTOMER SUPPORT. HOW CAN—>
Whoa! Dang! It actually connected!
...UH?
Yo! Emi! Can you hear me?
URK—
MAN, I HAD NO IDEA YOU COULD REALLY TARGET PEOPLE LIKE THAT.
THIS IS GONNA BE A LOT MORE USEFUL THAN I THOUGHT!
What are you doing!? I'm at work right now!
Aww, calm down. It's just an experi-ment.
What kind!?
Hackin'.
HA...
...WHAT?

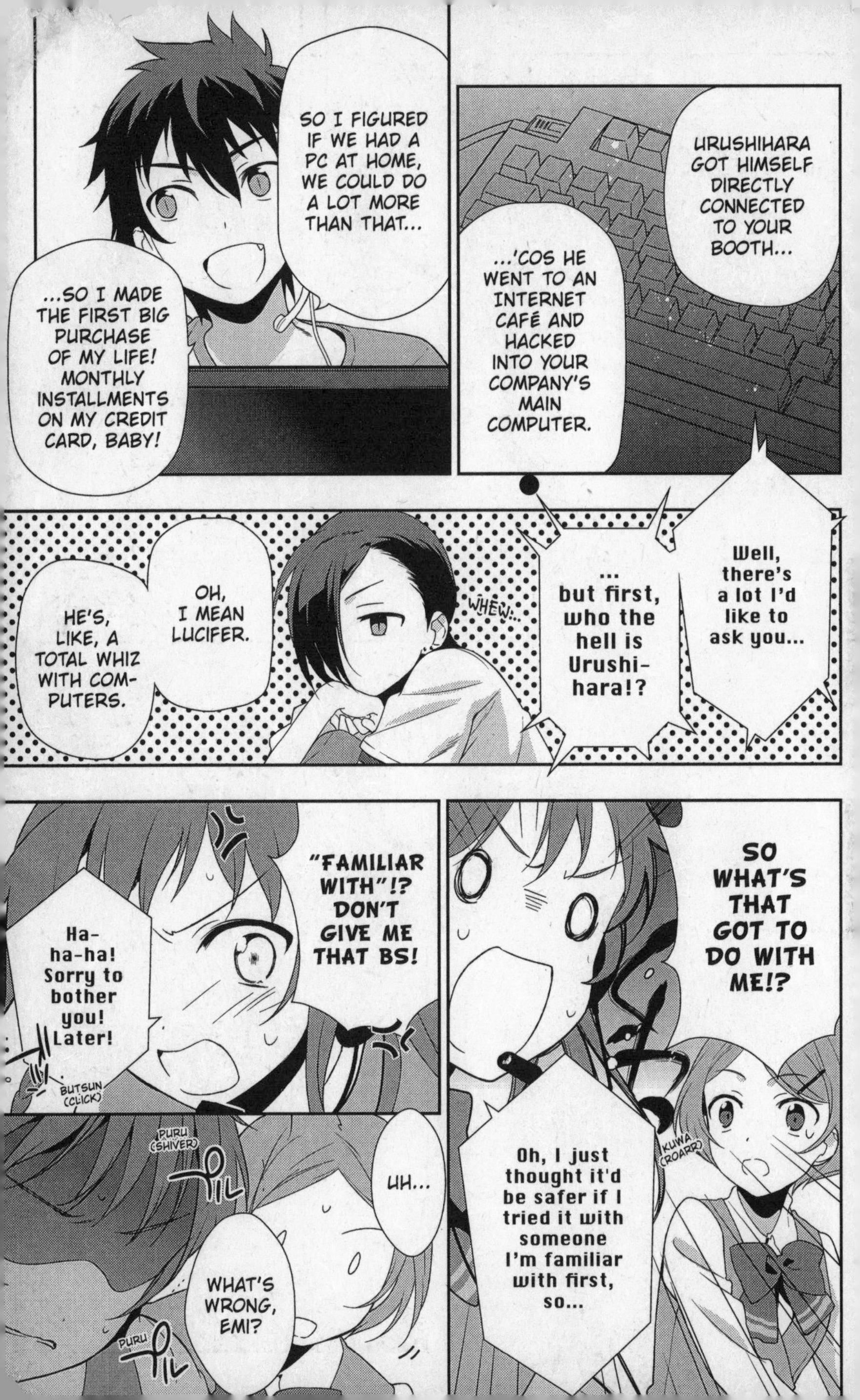
URUSHIHARA GOT HIMSELF DIRECTLY CONNECTED TO YOUR BOOTH...
...'COS HE WENT TO AN INTERNET CAFÉ AND HACKED INTO YOUR COMPANY'S MAIN COMPUTER.
SO I FIGURED IF WE HAD A PC AT HOME, WE COULD DO A LOT MORE THAN THAT...
...SO I MADE THE FIRST BIG PURCHASE OF MY LIFE! MONTHLY INSTALLMENTS ON MY CREDIT CARD, BABY!
Well, there's a lot I'd like to ask you...
... but first, who the hell is Urushi-hara!?
WHEW...
OH, I MEAN LUCIFER.
HE'S, LIKE, A TOTAL WHIZ WITH COM-PUTERS.
SO WHAT'S THAT GOT TO DO WITH ME!?
KUWA (ROARR)
Oh, I just thought it'd be safer if I tried it with someone I'm familiar with first, so...
"FAMILIAR WITH"!? DON'T GIVE ME THAT BS!
Ha-ha-ha! Sorry to bother you! Later!
BUTSUN (CLICK)
UH...
PURU (SHIVER)
WHAT'S WRONG, EMI?
PURU

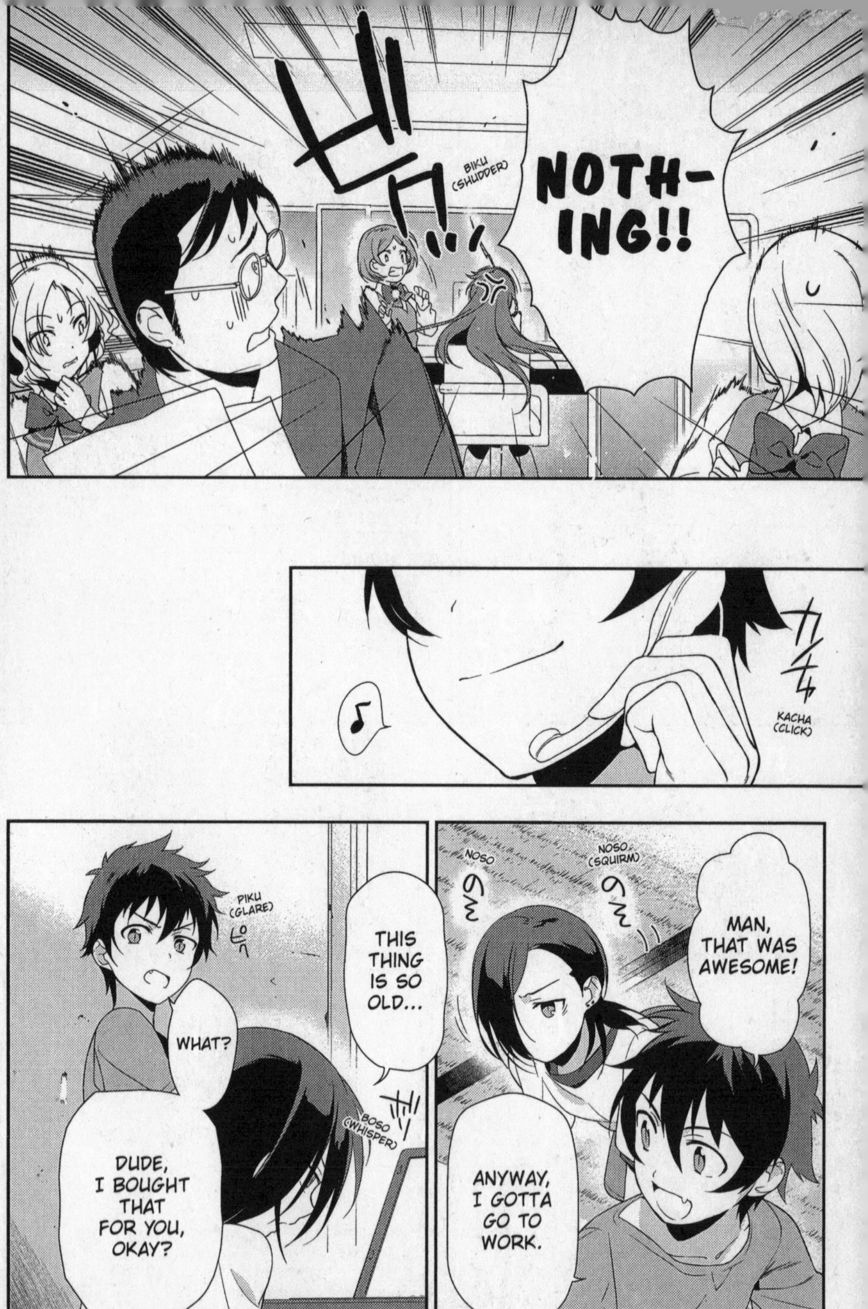
NOTH-ING!!
BIKU (SHUDDER)
KACHA (CLICK)
MAN, THAT WAS AWESOME!
NOSO (SQUIRM)
NOSO
ANYWAY, I GOTTA GO TO WORK.
THIS THING IS SO OLD...
BOSO (WHISPER)
PIKU (GLARE)
WHAT?
DUDE, I BOUGHT THAT FOR YOU, OKAY?

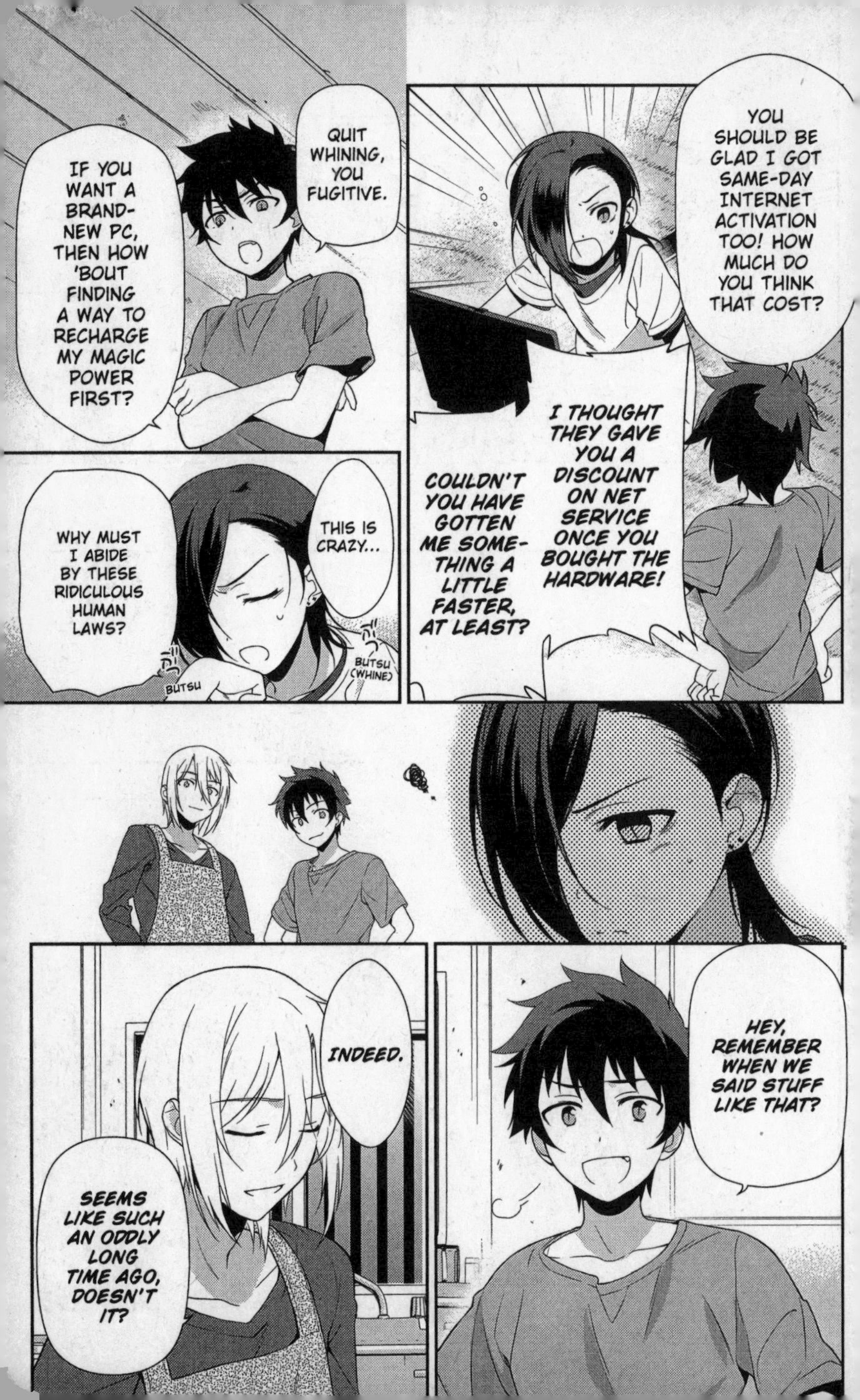

YOU SHOULD BE GLAD I GOT SAME-DAY INTERNET ACTIVATION TOO! HOW MUCH DO YOU THINK THAT COST?
I THOUGHT THEY GAVE YOU A DISCOUNT ON NET SERVICE ONCE YOU BOUGHT THE HARDWARE!
COULDN'T YOU HAVE GOTTEN ME SOME-THING A LITTLE FASTER, AT LEAST?
QUIT WHINING, YOU FUGITIVE.
IF YOU WANT A BRAND-NEW PC, THEN HOW 'BOUT FINDING A WAY TO RECHARGE MY MAGIC POWER FIRST?
THIS IS CRAZY...
WHY MUST I ABIDE BY THESE RIDICULOUS HUMAN LAWS?
BUTSU (WHINE)
BUTSU
HEY, REMEMBER WHEN WE SAID STUFF LIKE THAT?
INDEED.
SEEMS LIKE SUCH AN ODDLY LONG TIME AGO, DOESN'T IT?

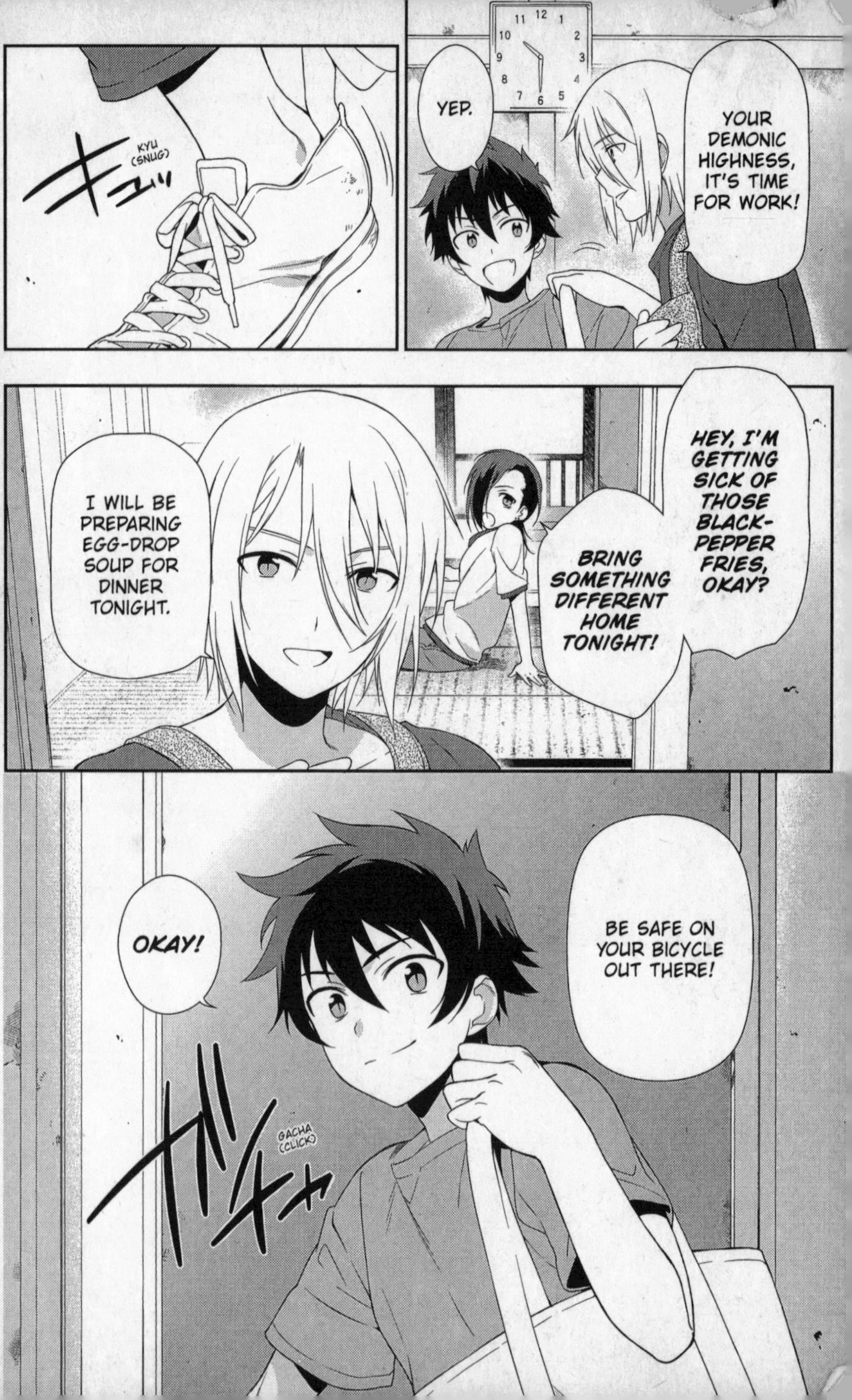
YOUR DEMONIC HIGHNESS, IT'S TIME FOR WORK!
YEP.
KYU (SNUG)
HEY, I'M GETTING SICK OF THOSE BLACK-PEPPER FRIES, OKAY?
BRING SOMETHING DIFFERENT HOME TONIGHT!
I WILL BE PREPARING EGG-DROP SOUP FOR DINNER TONIGHT.
BE SAFE ON YOUR BICYCLE OUT THERE!
OKAY!
GACHA (CLICK)

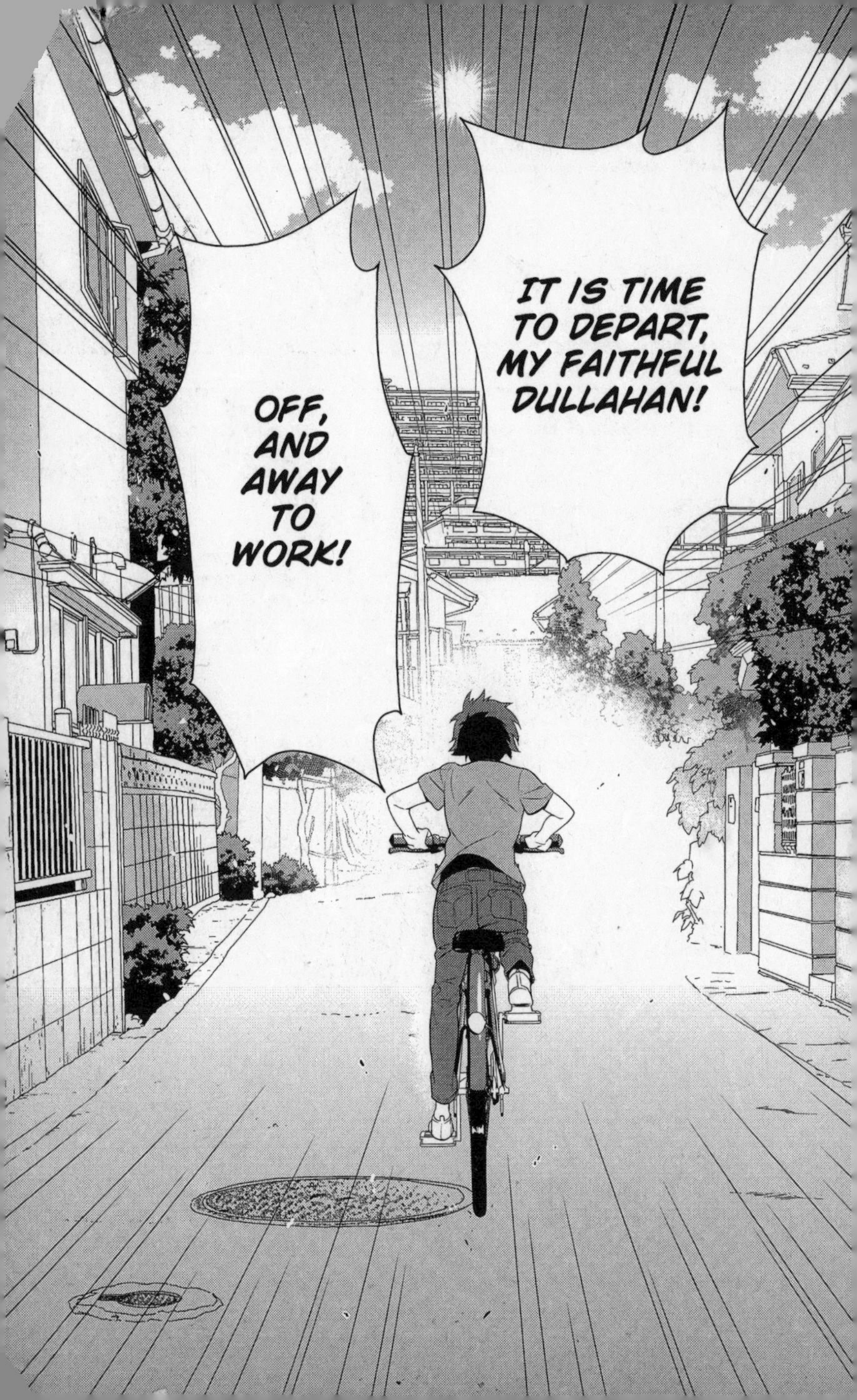
IT IS TIME TO DEPART, MY FAITHFUL DULLAHAN!
OFF, AND AWAY TO WORK!

THE DEVIL IS A PART-TIMER! ②

ART: AKIO HIIRAGI
ORIGINAL STORY: SATOSHI WAGAHARA
CHARACTER DESIGN: 029 (ONIKU)

Translation: Kevin Gifford

Lettering: Lys Blakeslee

HATARAKU MAOUSAMA! Vol. 2
© SATOSHI WAGAHARA / AKIO HIIRAGI 2012
All rights reserved.
Edited by ASCII MEDIA WORKS
First published in Japan in 2012 by KADOKAWA CORPORATION, Tokyo.
English translation rights arranged with KADOKAWA CORPORATION, Tokyo, through Tuttle-Mori Agency, Inc., Tokyo.

Yen Press
Hachette Book Group
1290 Avenue of the Americas
New York, NY 10104

www.HachetteBookGroup.com
www.YenPress.com

Yen Press is an imprint of Hachette Book Group, Inc. The Yen Press name and logo are trademarks of Hachette Book Group, Inc.

The publisher is not responsible for websites (or their content) that are not owned by the publisher.

First Yen Press Edition: July 2015

ISBN: 978-0-316-38507-7

10 9 8 7 6 5 4 3 2 1

BVG

Printed in the United States of America